Ultimate Realities

A Volume in the Comparative Religious Ideas Project

Edited by

ROBERT CUMMINGS NEVILLE

Foreword by

TU WEIMING

STATE UNIVERSITY OF NEW YORK PRESS

Published by
State University of New York Press, Albany

© 2001 State University of New York

For information, address State University of New York Press,
90 State Street, Suite 700, Albany, NY 12207

Production by Marilyn P. Semerad
Marketing by Dana E. Yanulavich

Library of Congress Cataloging-in-Publication Data

Ultimate realities / edited by Robert Cummings Neville; foreword by Tu
Weiming.
    p. cm. — (The comparative religious ideas project)
    Includes bibliographical references and index.
    ISBN 0-7914-4775-8 (alk.paper)—ISBN 0-7914-4776-6 (pbk.: alk paper)
    1. Religion—Philosophy. 2. Reality I. Neville, Robert C. II. Series.
    BL51.U63 2000
    291.2—dc21   00-020269

10 9 8 7 6 5 4 3 2 1

Ultimate Realities

The Comparative Religious Ideas Project

Robert Cummings Neville, Director

To

William Eastman, Publisher

Who, as Director of the State University of New York Press, fostered the extraordinary variety and depth of studies of world religions, and the careers of young scholars working with novel approaches, that have made possible such ambitious comparative inquiries as this one.

Contents

~

Foreword
TU WEIMING   xi

Preface
ROBERT CUMMINGS NEVILLE   xv

Acknowledgments   xxvii

Introduction
ROBERT CUMMINGS NEVILLE and WESLEY J. WILDMAN   I

1 *Ultimate Reality: Chinese Religion*
LIVIA KOHN with JAMES MILLER   9
1.1 General Considerations   9
1.2 The Order of the Cosmos   17
1.3 The Actualization of Cosmic Order in Human Experience   21
1.4 Myths, Metaphors, and Symbols   26
1.5 Conclusion   31

2 *Ultimate Realities: Judaism: God as a Many-sided Ultimate Reality in Traditional Judaism*
ANTHONY J. SALDARINI   37
2.1 Definitions of Ultimate   38
2.2 Paths to Ultimacy   40
2.3 Biblical and Talmudic Views of God   42
2.4 Torah as the Mediating Ultimate Reality in Rabbinic Literature   45
2.5 Early Rabbinic Mysticism   46
2.6 Maimonides and the Philosophical Quest for God   49
2.7 Medieval Mysticism   51

2.8 Enlightenment Philosophy and the Jewish Tradition   53
2.9 Modern Orthodoxy   55
2.10 Language and Method in Speaking of Ultimacy   56

3 *Ultimate Reality in Ancient Christianity:*
    Christ and Redemption
PAULA FREDRIKSEN   61
3.1 Introduction   61
3.2 Paul, the Gentiles, and the God of Israel   62
3.3 Christ as Blood Sacrifice in Later New Testament Writings   68
3.4 Ultimate Realities   70

4 *Ultimate Reality: Islam*
S. NOMANUL HAQ   75
4.1 Categories of Ultimacy   75
4.2 Revelationary Data   78
4.3 Divine Names and Epithets   80
4.4 Traditionalism and the Theological Rationalism of *Kalām*   82
4.5 The Theological Problem of Attributes   84
4.6 *Tashbīh* and *Tanzīh* as Questions of Ultimate Reality   87
4.7 *al-Ḥaqīqa* in Sufism   88
4.8 The Synthesis of Ghazālī   90

5 *Vedānta Deśika's Īśvarapariccheda ("Definition of the*
    Lord") and the Hindu Argument about Ultimate Reality
FRANCIS X. CLOONEY, S.J., with HUGH NICHOLSON   95
5.1 Introduction: Vedānta Deśika and His *Īśvarapariccheda*
    ("Definition of the Lord")   96
5.2 Deśika's Fourteen Points Regarding the Lord (Īśvara)
    as Ultimate Reality   99
5.3 Three Examples of the Argument   105
5.4 Extending the Conversation   110

6 *Cooking the Last Fruit of Nihilism:*
    Buddhist Approaches to Ultimate Reality
MALCOLM DAVID ECKEL with JOHN J. THATAMANIL   125
6.1 The Myth of Reference   126
6.2 Hypothesis and Confirmation   128
6.3 What Kind of Reality Is Ultimate?   129
6.4 The Problem of the Absolute   130

7 Comparative Conclusions about Ultimate Realities
ROBERT CUMMINGS NEVILLE and WESLEY J. WILDMAN   151
7.1 Defining the Vague Category   151
7.2 Specifying the Category   156
7.3 Comparing within the Category   164
7.4 Relating to the Ultimate   178

8 On Comparing Religious Ideas
ROBERT CUMMINGS NEVILLE and WESLEY J. WILDMAN   187
8.1 Comparison of Religious Ideas as a Cognitive Enterprise   187
8.2 The General Principle of Comparative Categories   191
8.3 The Logical Structure of Comparative Categories   196
8.4 Vagueness and Specificity: The Making of Comparison   198
8.5 Vulnerability and Phenomenological Testing   202
8.6 The Historical Provenance and Discursive Form of
     Comparative Categories   206

9 How Our Approach to Comparison Relates to Others
WESLEY J. WILDMAN and ROBERT CUMMINGS NEVILLE   211
9.1 Comparison as Impossible   212
9.2 Comparison as Something Other than an Explicit
     Cognitive Process   215
9.3 Comparison Based on Categories Justified by Existing
     Theories of Religion   218
9.4 Comparison Based on Categories Justified from
     Similarities in Data   222
9.5 Comparison Based on a Dialectic of Data and Categories   224
9.6 The Significance of Comparison Conducted as Dialectic
     Between Categories and Data   225
9.7 Learning from the Past   230

10 The Idea of Categories in Historical Comparative
   Perspective
JOHN H. BERTHRONG   237
10.1 Introduction   237
10.2 Categories as Intellectual Constructs   239
10.3 Fast Forward to the Modern World   251

Appendix A:
On the Process of the Project During the Second Year
WESLEY J. WILDMAN   261

Appendix B:
Suggestions for Further Reading   275

Contributors   339

Index of Names   341

Index of Subjects   345

Foreword

Tu Weiming

⌒

Ultimate Reality is often perceived as an elusive cognitive "category" requiring a sophisticated conceptual approach. We are never certain that we have arrived at a true understanding of it. It is also said to evoke an experienced presence in our childlike mind, so immediate and intimate that no symbolic representation is needed to apprehend its transformative power. The interplay between its ineffable cognitive status and its experiential certainty has generated some of the most inspiring philosophical meditations and penetrating poetic insights in human history.

In this volume, six specialists and four generalists invite us to take part in a joint venture to explore "ultimate realities," both as articulations of highly selective forms of received wisdom and as a collaborative effort to think comparatively about religious ideas. The exercise is profoundly meaningful for our understanding of human religiousness and our appreciation of what several great spiritual traditions have offered us as the foundations of their faiths. In our pluralistic academic world, with its hermeneutics of suspicion, we know for sure that there are no definitive answers to the question of "ultimate reality." The designation of this volume as *Ultimate Realities* suggests that there are several attempts to address it.

The six experts discuss "ultimate reality" from their respective traditions: Chinese religion, Judaism, ancient Christianity, Islam, Hinduism, and Buddhism. No one provides us with a ready-made answer. Each offers an evolving perspective based on textual analysis, historical investigation, and personal knowledge. No claims are made of either revelatory guidance or sacred authority. What these specialists propose is a series of necessarily idiosyncratic strategies to provide accounts of painfully obtained scholarly interpretations. However, underlying the complex array of learned conceptual approaches to the issue, all six world religions share a tacit understanding that we are endowed with the ability to experience a sense of ultimate reality as a defining characteristic of who we are, not simply an abstract universality unconnected with the ordinary way of living our daily life.

As students of religion, the reasons to participate in such a joint venture are threefold. First, it is a pioneering attempt, guided by a coherent vision, to study a seminal religious idea cross-culturally. Second, it is meant to be an open inquiry, with a self-correcting methodological reflexivity. And, third, it addresses a core concern of human religiousness in a pluralistic spirit.

The coherent vision guiding this joint venture grew out of a conviction that major religions' articulations of "ultimate reality" are not incommensurable linguistic universes so contextualized in their particular world views that comparison is nonsensical and that translation is impossible. Rather, while acknowledging conflict of interpretation in intracultural as well as intercultural sense, the possibility of a sustained conversation to share insights indicates, at a minimum, the potential global significance of local knowledge. Indeed, the willingness to share stories is more than an expression of tolerance. It recognizes the necessity of coexistence and the desirability of mutual reference.

The six experts, challenged by a compelling *Problematik,* address issues that significantly push their expertise toward a comparative mode of questioning. At the same time, the four generalists, informed by the complexity of the ever-changing landscape, allow their "vague" concepts enough maneuverability for fruitful ambiguities. This is an unprecedented effort to revisit a great religious idea as a comparative enterprise.

It is rare for an academic work to include a critical self-analysis as an integral part of its conclusion. Since "ultimate realities," as the middle part of a three-volume study, provides the transition from "human condition" to "religious truth," attention is paid to methodology. This methodological reflexivity gives the book a particular texture, transforming it from a series of close narratives to an open inquiry. The tentativeness and fluidity of the project are not defects to be glossed over but salient features vulnerable to correction. The second part of the book (chapters 7–10) is not postmortem reflections but justification for the joint venture. The discussion on categories, neither Aristotelian nor Kantian, recommends a way to generate explanatory models from a variety of "thick descriptions" and avoid the trap of relativism. This daunting task is necessarily and admittedly incomplete. Other "experts," with varying degrees of sensitivity to and receptivity of the proposed method, may tell their stories very differently. The openness of the inquiry is deliberate; it is also inviting.

An obvious strength of the book is its implicit rejection of an inclusivist, let alone exclusivist, perspective and its honest effort to transcend a hegemonic discourse. From a liberationist point of view, we can easily critique the "explicit cognitive process" with emphasis on "world religions" as a form of male-oriented elitism. A careful reading, however, suggests that the project, as an open inquiry, encourages an accommodating trajectory. Surely, the incorporation of a feminist or an indigenous dimension requires a methodological choice that is not clearly evident in its present form. The pluralistic approach it embodies is not at all incompatible with a new and broadened agenda. Indeed, the title "Ultimate Realities," rather than "Ultimate Reality," is more congenial to alternative visions and multiple interpretations.

When I first initiated the "Dialogue of Civilizations" at the East-West Center in Honolulu in 1990, I realized the art of listening, indeed "deep listening," was vital to our project. When the voices of multiple spiritual traditions and faith communities are heard by our spirit as well as our hearts, minds, and ears, they are more than enriching messages. They are transformative acts. We begin to learn not just tolerance, the need for co-existence, but dialogical relationship and mutual appreciation. If the danger of the clash of civilizations is real, dialogue becomes imperative. I recommend the collaborative spirit embodied in this joint venture with a view toward 2001, the year the United Nations has designated to be the year of Dialogue Among Civilizations.

Preface

Robert Cummings Neville

❦

The Comparative Religious Ideas Project, based at Boston University, ran from the fall of 1995 through the spring of 1999, meeting as a seminar for twenty-five days in total. Its results are published in three volumes: *The Human Condition, Ultimate Realities*, and *Religious Truth*. The conclusion of the project was a conference in May, 1999, at which the participants in the project were joined by a number of distinguished scholars of world religions, including Anne Birdwhistell, Jose Cabezon, Julia Ching, Jordan Pearlson, Arvind Sharma, Jonathan Z. Smith, Max Stackhouse, Tu Weiming, and Lee Yearley, who had not been involved in the project save Stackhouse and Tu as mentioned below. The conference reflected on drafts of the volumes and produced helpful insights into what we had done and not done with the special virtue of external but experienced perspectives. Although the three volumes were drafted sequentially, they are published together and thus benefit from a retrospective overview in the form of this preface, which appears in each volume.

Two purposes motivate the project: to develop and test a theory concerning the comparison of religious ideas, and to make some important comparisons about religious ideas of the human condition, ultimate realities, and religious truth. These two aims are intimately connected: the theory cannot be tested without putting it to work making comparisons, and comparisons are not to be trusted without a justified second-order reflection on the nature of comparison.

In the study of religion in Western cultures today, the making of comparisons among religions on topics such as ours is not novel or surprising. Despite the fact that scholars are worried about the imperialism of interpretive categories, comparisons are standard fare in undergraduate religion courses—how else can people learn about religions new to them? Moreover, ignorance of the world's major religions is simply unacceptable today in any discipline within religious studies, even in confessional theologies, if only for the sake of keeping imperialist prejudices in check. The larger worlds of politics, economics, and cultural communications are deeply shaped by conceptions of how religions relate comparatively to one another, often conceptions that are unnecessarily ignorant and parochial. So what we propose here is to offer some better comparisons on very important religious topics, better for having been refined through the comparative methods of the theory.

The careful presentation of an elaborate theory of comparison for religious ideas, by contrast, is extremely surprising in religious studies today and a significant contribution if successful. Precisely because of raised consciousness about the imperialism of earlier comparisons and theories of comparison, theoretical approaches to religion and especially to comparison are highly suspect. Theory as such is unpopular. Our most unusual purpose, then, is to present a theory of comparison and make it work. This purpose itself has brought some serious qualifications and limitations to the project as will be indicated shortly.

The design of the project has been to assemble a working group of persons in the greater Boston area consisting of both tradition-specialists in different religious traditions and generalists of several types, along with graduate students, and then to set to work discussing the three large topics of religious ideas comparatively in structured ways, one each year, with a fourth year for editorial polishing of the three volumes mentioned.

The project's working group was selected to set in tension two contrary tendencies in thinking about the comparison of religious ideas. One is the tendency to see each religion, perhaps even each text within a religion's intellectual tradition, to be unique and special—and to be in danger of misconstrual when subjected to comparisons. For this purpose we recruited six specialists in different religions with a strong commitment to historical specificity: Francis X. Clooney, S.J., expert in Hinduism; Malcolm David Eckel, expert in Buddhism; Paula Fredriksen, expert in Christianity; S. Nomanul Haq, expert in Islam; Livia Kohn, expert in Chinese religion; and Anthony J. Saldarini, expert in Judaism. The list of contributors page in each volume gives the particulars of their affiliations. Of course, each of these scholars specializes in only some strands of his or her tradition and in only some periods, usually the ancient or medieval. Moreover, to emphasize the difference between scholarly comparative purpose and the worthy though different purpose of interfaith dialogue, these scholars were selected because their tradition of expertise is different from the tradition with which they primarily identify, with only one exception (Haq).

Each of these scholars was helped by a graduate assistant, sometimes to the extent of co-authorship of their papers; working with the scholars as listed above were Hugh Nicholson (with Clooney), John Thatamanil (with Eckel), Tina Shepardson the first year and Christopher Allen the next two (with Fredriksen), Celeste Sullivan (with Haq), James Miller (with Kohn), and Joseph Kanofsky (with Saldarini). The purpose of including the graduate students as full partners in the working group was not only to facilitate the research and writing but also to develop ways of teaching collaborative research in religious studies at the doctoral level. Whereas the natural sciences sponsor collaborative projects in which experts from very different fields come together on a common problem, the custom in religious studies, especially its humanistic side as involved in textual research, has been to gather like-minded and similarly trained scholars. Inspired by the sciences, our project explicitly seeks diversity.

The other tendency we sought for the working group was integration, synthesis, and generalization, a drive to raise new questions for each of the traditions that we bring into comparative perspective. Four of us represented this move, each in different ways: Peter Berger, a sociologist; John H. Berthrong, an historian of religions; Wesley J. Wildman, an historical and constructive theologian and philosopher; and myself, a philosopher, theologian, and theorist about comparison. In the first year of our study, we thought of this second group as the "comparativists" and the first group as "specialists." Quickly it became clear, however, that the specialists compared in their own ways and that the generalists had specialized religious perspectives behind their integrative work. We are pleased to find now that all of us engage in comparison, each in ways reflecting our beginning tendencies but even more what we have learned from one another in the collaboration. Moreover, as the group became conscious of itself as having an integrated identity, with habits of language and thought developed through time invested together, we came to think of our project in terms of the comparisons to which we all contribute rather than merely the comparisons each of us makes as influenced by the others. This process is by no means complete, but it is discernible and in fact described in each of the volumes in Wildman's appendices, "On the Process of the Project." In the original formulation of the project we were clear that the ways the group worked together would have to develop over time. What we had not anticipated in the original formulation of the project is the importance of the reporter, Wildman, who produced the seminar minutes and who called us continually to assess what we had accomplished, how stable our comparative hypotheses are on the one hand and how tentative on the other.

In addition to the working group the project had a board of senior advisors who reviewed the initial design and met with the working group at the end of the first year and in the concluding conference. These include Julia Ching, Jordan Pearlson, Max Stackhouse, and Tu Weiming. The outside advisors helped to bring our shared work into new and critical perspectives.

The thought was that, though both specialists and generalists are comparativists in one sense or other, the specialists would prevent too-easy generalized comparisons while the generalists would keep the specialists in comparative conversation with one another. There have been some discouraging times when we realized just how hard it is to learn to think together without dropping to a lowest common denominator, or giving in to pressures for consensus, or quickly agreeing to disagree without pushing the arguments as far as possible. The labor of joining these two kinds of approach is apparent in the progress through the three volumes. In *The Human Condition* the specialists discuss what their separate texts or traditions say about the topic, and the generalists' "conclusion" maps these and other points onto a comparative grid. In *Religious Truth*, the last volume, the comparisons take place within the specialists' chapters and the generalists' "conclusions" are indeed summaries and then reflections on important topics that emerged from the comparisons. The middle volume, *Ultimate Realities*, is truly transitional with the grid gone but the conclusions heavily formed up by the generalists. After much discussion, and with the encouragement of the outside experts at the concluding conference, it was decided to leave the form of the progressive collaboration as it was in fact, and indeed to gloss it more explicitly in appendices to each volume. These volumes thus reflect the learning process of the working group.

⌐

Why study the human condition, ultimate realities, and religious truth instead of other topics? Although each is explained and its importance outlined in the respective volumes, in a sense the selection is arbitrary. Our initial grant proposals put forward six topics of which these are only three. Salvation, food and diet, ritual, religious journeys, religious cosmologies, religious communities, illness and health, goodness and evil, the nature of religious practices such as meditation, the roles of women, social stratification, religious violence, religious beliefs as social constructions—these and many more major topics were suggested at various points and could just as well have been chosen. Most of these receive some discussion in one or more of the volumes, but each could have been treated as a major category.

In another sense the choice of topics is not arbitrary because these three lend themselves very well to investigation while laboring to develop effective collaborative strategies and to test our theory of comparison. The great religious traditions each have a literature about these topics, variously construed. These topics also have been under discussion in the Western academy for over two centuries, and there is a growing body of literature here, too. Therefore we could limit our work to examining texts, and doing so within academic traditions of interpreting these or like texts. We know, of course, that there are many non-textual expressions of ideas, but we simplified our work so as not to have to deal with them here.

To the question whether these topics and the categories that spell them out are *justified*, the answer is more complex. They certainly are justified in that they have a trajectory of scholarly analysis into which we have stepped with three volumes of further reflection that go a long way toward refining them. But have we shown that reality is such that the human condition, ultimate realities, and religious truth identify very important elements? In *Ultimate Realities*, chapter 7.1, and again in chapter 8.6, Wildman and I say that at least four tasks are required for justifying our kind of categories. First is to identify relevant plausible possibilities for comparison; second is to explore the logical or conceptual structures of the categories and to justify this conceptual or philosophical work; third is to provide a genetic analysis of the religious symbols compared and to relate this to the comparing categories, including within the genetic analysis accounts of historical, social, psychological, neurophysiological, and environmental evolution; and fourth is appropriate analysis of the circumstances that accompany the key shifts in symbolic representation during the history of the religious ideas. The Comparative Religious Ideas Project focused almost entirely on the first step in justification; nearly all of our debates were about the plausibility and relative importance of these categories. *Ultimate Realities* introduces a theory of contingency in chapter 8, and *Religious Truth* presents a theory of religious truth in chapter 8, both of which begin to address the approach to justification through logical and philosophical analysis; but these do not go far enough to justify our categories. The third and fourth steps are almost entirely absent except for an occasional genetic account of the history of ideas. The entire field of religious studies is decades away from a thorough justification of any categories in this rich sense. From time to time we have drawn close enough to see what real justification of our categories would mean, and have drawn back before the enormity of the project. Our contribution here is rather simple and fragmentary.

Why did we choose these six "traditions," and how do we study them? The religious traditions studied and compared in this project are, in alphabetical order, Buddhism, Chinese religion, Christianity, Hinduism, Islam, and Judaism. The obvious anomaly in this list is Chinese religion, because we might expect a distinction between Daoism and Confucianism, and maybe Chinese Buddhism. After all, contemporary scholars divide their expertise, intellectual styles, and professional loyalties into Daoist, Confucian, and Chinese Buddhist studies respectively. In our group, Livia Kohn is a specialist in Daoism and John Berthrong in Confucianism, so the temptation to distinguish Chinese religion into subtraditions is genuine. On the other hand, both Kohn and Berthrong take a stronger interest in Chinese Buddhism than David Eckel, our Buddhist specialist whose language expertise is in Indian and Tibetan tongues, suggesting that Chinese Buddhism is at least as Chinese as it is Buddhist. Moreover, Confucianism and Daoism share an ancient Chinese cosmology that is also vital to Chinese folk religions and an important influence on Chinese Buddhism. Thus, it seemed to us that the major literate traditions within Chinese religion should be considered together.

For the sake of comparison of the religions' ideas about our topics it is highly advantageous to be able to analyze some particular texts in detail. Yet these texts are meaningful as representative of the religions only when we also have in place some more general characterizations of the religions. And then of course the texts represent the religion of which they are a part in only one way, and other texts might develop the religion in quite different directions: Augustine, some of whose texts we discuss, interprets the Christian view of the human condition differently from Origen, for instance, or Mary Baker Eddy. So our strategy is as follows.

For the general characterizations of the religious traditions we go to their core texts and motifs. These are ancient scriptures and classics, events illustrated in them such as the Exodus and the Confucian revolt against disorder, or thought patterns such as yin-yang complementarity and the search for underlying unity. Religious traditions form around and take their initial identity from these core texts and motifs in such a way that all subsequent developments in each tradition have to come to terms with them. Religious traditions, as we know, are extremely diverse internally, often in contradictory, sometimes warring, ways. Yet all the kinds of Hinduism accept the importance, if not authority, of the Vedas, which are their core texts. Buddhism, a religion originating in the same South Asian environment, does not. Rather, its core texts and motifs have to do with the sermons and other teachings of the Buddha, early tales of his life, and the understanding of authority in terms of the Buddha, Dharma, and Saṅgha. Both Daoism and Confucianism base themselves on the ancient Chinese yin-yang cosmology and the classic texts of the Spring and Autumn and the Warring States periods; the *Yijing* is as Confucian as Daoist, and plays crucial roles in both throughout their histories. Sunni and Shi'ite Muslims war with one another but still define themselves as Islamic based on the core text of the Qur'ān. Orthodox, Roman Catholic, Protestant, and Radical Reformation Christians, as well as the Independent Christian Churches of Africa, identify themselves through the ways they interpret the Christian Bible, however different those ways are. Orthodox, Conservative, Reform, and Reconstructionist Jews take very different stances toward the Torah and the rest of the Hebrew Bible, but they are all forms of Judaism because that is their core text, especially in virtue of its motif of the Exodus and formation of the people of Israel.

Our strategy is to consider the six religious traditions on the one hand in terms of their core texts and motifs, and on the other hand in terms of some one or few texts that can be analyzed in detail for comparative purposes, especially in terms of how they relate to the core texts and motifs. Thus we avoid the pitfalls of attempting to describe the "essence" of a religious tradition and can still make general characterizations based on the core texts and motifs and the diverse ways they have been interpreted.[1] We also honor the nervousness of our specialists about making comparisons without specific texts to work on and their careful circumscription of the comparisons to the content of those texts.

There are two further advantages to this strategy of specific texts plus core classic texts and motifs. The first is that it invites other scholars to treat yet other texts as different representatives of religious ideas within a religion, and to make comparisons among different authors. The limitation of the texts we actually discuss here is an example of the fragmentariness of our enterprise, in the face of which our model invites supplementation. The second is that it makes our arguments vulnerable to correction by inviting criticism of our representations of the core texts and motifs, of our interpretations of how the specific texts relate to them, and of our comparisons.

It should be clearer now why we have chosen to examine six religions that have long intellectual traditions. Each has a rich mine of core texts and motifs and long, complicated histories of diverse interpretations of them. By contrast, we do not have core texts for Native American religions that have been supplemented by long traditions of diverse interpretation, although we do have core motifs for those religions that, with advancing scholarly interpretation, might soon make those religions candidates for our kind of comparison of religious ideas. Within the limits of the six traditions represented, therefore, the religious ideas we want

to compare can be understood in terms of their histories and their polyse-
mous qualities.

The experts in our group are all specialists in the ancient or medieval
periods of their traditions, first millennium CE developments at the latest.
We have depended on the specialists to emphasize historical and textual
details. The generalists, by contrast, tend to have more philosophical
interests and a higher tolerance for generalizations. Thus a healthy tension is induced in our work between the historian's concern for ancient
identifications of the religions and the philosophically or sociologically
minded generalist's concern for what about them is really important to
compare in our late-modern historical situation.

⏤

The heart of our conception of the comparative enterprise is that it is an
ongoing process, always proceeding from comparative assumptions, formulating comparisons as hypotheses, making the hypotheses vulnerable
to correction and modification until they seem steady and properly qualified, and then presenting them for further correction while accepting
them as the new comparative assumptions. This pragmatic approach to
inquiry structured the design of the project, the actual course of our discussions, and the editorial composition of our books.

Closely related to this pragmatic emphasis on process and vulnerability is a particular conception of how a comparison is made, namely, by
means of a vague category such as the human condition that is variously
specified by different conceptions of the human condition. The different
specifications are translated into the language of the vague category,
with three resulting moments or elements: the vague category as such,
the multitude of different specifications, and the restatement of the
vague category as now enriched with specifications. Comparison and its
problems are closely allied with translation and its problems. These issues of process and theory in comparison are discussed somewhat infor-
mally in *The Human Condition*, chapter 1, which is all the methodology
a reader needs to get into the specific comparative chapters of that book
or of *Ultimate Realities* or *Religious Truth*. But for those interested in a
more explicit elaboration and defense of this approach, see *Ultimate
Realities*, chapter 8, "On Comparing Religious Ideas," chapter 9,
"How Our Approach to Comparison Relates to Others," and chapter
10, "The Idea of Categories in Historical Comparative Perspective." For
how these methodological considerations relate to a theory of religion,
see *Religious Truth*, chapter 9, "On the Nature of Religion: Lessons We
Have Learned."

The structure of the three volumes of The Comparative Religious Ideas Project is the following. Each is written to be read by itself, providing an extended multidisciplinary and comparative essay on its topic, the human condition, ultimate realities, or religious truth, and situated with a self-conscious methodology. Each has an introduction to the topic that also explains the specific structure of the book. Each book has six chapters by the specialists, with each of these chapters giving part of one tradition's perspective on the topic, followed by one or more chapters of conclusions and essays on topics related to comparison or the topics studied. Each volume has an appendix describing the process of the project and one or more annotated lists of suggestions for further reading.

❧

Authorship is a complicated matter for a collaborative project. Nothing in any of the volumes is unaffected by the collaborative discussions of the working group and usually it is not possible to cite the origins of the ideas and influences. Nevertheless, each chapter is the primary if not sole responsibility of some one author. The six specialists had different working relationships with their graduate research assistants, and in several cases the assistants contributed texts to the chapters as secondary authors. These are indicated in the tables of contents with the formula "X with Y," where X is the primary specialist author and Y the contributing research assistant. The collaboration between Wildman and myself grew dramatically throughout the project. I was the first author of the methodological and summary chapters. He believes himself not to have made sufficient contribution to the second summary chapter in *The Human Condition* to be listed as a secondary author, although I myself know the influence of his ideas. He is a strong secondary author in all the others, and indeed those written later show his hand nearly as much as mine. The two chapters of which he is primary author and I secondary, *Ultimate Realities*, chapter 9, and *Religious Truth*, chapter 9, are strongly his own and are oriented to relating our project to larger ongoing comparative work. Because of this full collaboration, we list outselves as joint authors in *Ultimate Realities* and *Religious Truth*, despite the fact Wildman or I wrote the first draft. We have made no attempt to disguise the differences in temperament, approach, or conviction among our authors.

❧

Important limitations of this project need to be discussed because they derive from the choices made about the project design itself. (These are in addition to limitations that come from our incompetence or plain foolishness, which we are not prepared to admit.)

Limiting our sources to literate traditions among the "world religions" means that we have cut ourselves off from the ideas of other traditions on our topics of the human condition, ultimate realities, and religious truth. We are limited to the Axial Age religions, for instance, and some scholars are now saying that the study of religion needs to move beyond the dominance of those religions and properly seek wisdom from Native People, traditional religions, or New Age religions. This is particularly important in light of ecological concerns, for instance. Although we are not attempting to compare contemporary religious ideas, particularly, our focus makes us vulnerable to the charge that the non-literate traditions may have been far more important for our topics than we indicate. We admit that this might turn out to be the case.

Limiting our sources to six literate world religions means also that we cut ourselves off from the methods and kinds of understanding that come from disciplines that deal with mainly non-literate religion, for instance, anthropology and other social sciences, ritual studies, art-and-religion, studies of popular religion, folk culture, and the rest. We focus on the old-fashioned approaches of textual studies, literary analysis, historical research, philosophy, and methodology itself. This was a deliberate choice on our part in order to work out effective collaboration. If collaboration has seemed difficult and occasionally baffling to us, think what it would have been if it had to include the vast array of other approaches to religious studies. That we do not include them does not mean that we reject them nor deprecate their importance. Rather, it means that our approach to the religious ideas of the traditions we cover is fragmentary. Moreover, it means that our analyses and conclusions are vulnerable to being greatly qualified or overthrown when those other approaches are finally brought into collaborative connection. The strength of our approach in this matter, however, is precisely here: we are clear about the limits of what our literary methods can do, and it will be a great advance when our comparisons are corrected by what arises from outside those limits.

Limiting our discussion of the relations among different religions' ideas on our topics to *comparison* does not do justice to the problem of *translation*. The extensive literature on translation, and the history of European translations of religious texts in the nineteenth century, come at many of our problems from another angle. By no means is translation identical with comparison, but there are many analogies and overlapping concerns. One difference is that, at least according to our theory of comparison, a vague comparative category has a moment of quasi-neutrality relative to the specific things compared, and can be assessed in that regard, whereas translation does not employ a third language to mediate between the two being related. Translation indeed exhibits what Jonathan Z. Smith calls "magic" when a speaker of two languages "just knows" how to say in one language what the other says and how that sometimes cannot be said. In our theory, as developed in *Ultimate Realities*, chapter 8, translation is a proper part of comparison but set within a larger process of checks.

The limitation of our project to comparing "basic ideas" such as the human condition, ultimate reality, and religious truth, makes it very difficult sensitively to register many of the points made by the "hermeneutics of suspicion." Most writers of our religious texts have been men and reflect the male point of view. Feminists have rightly argued that a text-based approach such as ours thus is cut off from what the women around the men were thinking, and the women's thinking might have been very important for shaping the religious realities. Feminists also have rightly pointed out that our approach reinforces the general patriarchal assumption that what is important in religion is the men's opinions, expressed in texts, and that this reinforcement is worse the more effective our approach is. Other liberation perspectives, speaking on behalf of marginalized voices and religious movements, rightly can criticize our choice to deal only with the "central" world religions. Our answer to these forms of the hermeneutics of suspicion is two-fold.

First, we plead for mercy in light of the difficulty of the task of comparison. We need to begin with the most elementary and direct expositions and comparisons that we can in order to get started. Unless we can bring some greater self-consciousness and a self-correcting procedure to comparison, comparative judgments will remain at the level of anecdote and prejudice.

The second answer follows from the first. The only way to make progress in comparison, from the standpoint of the hermeneutics of suspicion, is to have steady and well-formulated hypotheses to criticize. Does the hermeneutics of suspicion overturn these comparisons? Supplement them by comparisons on behalf of women and the marginalized? Reconstruct the intellectual causal boundaries? To respond Yes to any of these questions and to justify the affirmative answer would be to make solid and important progress. Our comparisons are aimed to be in a form vulnerable to precisely these corrections. (The forms of the hermeneutics of suspicion that consist in scientific reductionism and anti-colonial theory are spoken to throughout the texts of all volumes.)

One of the subtlest limitations of this project was pointed out at the concluding conference by Jose Cabezon. The very structure of the project, with a director, co-directors, senior scholars, and graduate students,

with authorship shared as primary and secondary, reflects what he called
a hierarchical Cartesian approach. He meant not only the obvious hierarchical organization but also the supposition of the importance of clarity, order, and classification. A Buddhist would not have done it this way.
Others in the project earlier had pointed out what they called the Confucian orientation of the project itself as well as in the expressions of conclusions; I am a Boston Confucian and this complaint was made in good
humor, but much to the point of Cabezon's remark. Cabezon focused on
what he took to be our attempt to reduce comparison to filling in a comparative grid. He believes our procedure claims that a comparative hypothesis works by fitting things into their Cartesian places.

To this I admit first that the project is indeed organized hierarchically,
that I do not know how else to get grants from funding agencies who
want someone to be responsible, and that as a Confucian I believe it is the
responsibility of those with age and power to foster those down the line,
step by step. Moreover, it should be reported that a fairly constant refrain through the four years of the project was that I should be more di-
rective and not let the seminar flow under the guidance of its format
alone. Though perhaps embarrassed to admit it, most of the participants
believed the academic process could benefit from a Confucian Daddy.

But Cabezon was right that all this nudges the process toward order
and definiteness. In defense of this arrangement, we believe this is the way
to make progress. If our hypotheses have a definiteness that is false to reality, that can be pointed out. An hypothesis without definiteness cannot
be criticized. If the very process itself cooks its conclusions, then that can
be pointed by showing another possible process. This was a recurrent
theme of our discussions from the first year, when it was proposed that
we relate narratives rather than compare in our way, or that we suspend
definiteness in favor of indirection. But we could never quite organize the
alternatives. This means that our procedure is vulnerable, and possibly
misguided, but that someone else needs to say just how this is so and to
do better. For us, at least most of us, our procedure has advanced comparison and we offer these volumes for use and criticism.

Note

1. See M. David Eckel's argument in "The Ghost at the Table," *Journal of the American Academy of Religion* 63 (1995): 1085–1110, to the effect that it is possible to talk about what is essential in the sense of *necessary* to a religious tradition without presupposing an *essence*.

Acknowledgments

∾

The Cross-Cultural Comparative Religious Ideas Project has been supported by generous grants from the National Endowment for the Humanities and the Henry Luce Foundation, Inc., as well as cost sharing on the part of Boston University. We are deeply grateful to these sponsors without which the Project would have been impossible.

We are also grateful to Dr. Susan Only, who was the Project Administrator for the four years of its duration and who superintended finances and arrangements with great skill. We thank Ms. Shirley Budden, Financial Officer of the Boston University School of Theology, and the Boston University Office of Sponsored Programs, especially Ms. Phyllis Cohen, for their careful work on behalf of the Project. At various times, Christopher Allen, Raymond Bouchard, Mark Grear Mann, and James E. Miller performed valuable editorial services in the preparation of our publications, and they deserve great thanks.

Several people outside the Project read some or all of drafts of the three volumes that report its findings, and we thank them all for very helpful advice that has guided revisions. They include Anne Birdwhistell, Jose Cabezon, Julia Ching, Jordan Pearlson, Arvind Sharma, Jonathan Z. Smith, Max Stackhouse, Tu Weiming, and Lee Yearley. Ching, Pearlson, Stackhouse, and Tu were senior advisors to the Project from the beginning.

Our colleagues at the State University of New York Press have been extraordinary in bringing our publications to light, beginning with our acquisitions editor, Ms. Nancy Ellegate. We also thank our production editor, Ms. Marilyn Semerad, and the marketing manager, Dana E. Yanulavich. We dedicate these volumes to William Eastman, whose daring in the publication of religious studies made projects such as this possible.

Introduction

*Robert Cummings Neville
and Wesley J. Wildman*

⤳

"Ultimate Realities" is perhaps the most obvious topic to Westerners for comparing religious ideas. It is the topic of God, or gods, or why some religions such as Buddhism do not have gods, or rather have so many that they are not associated with ultimate reality. Sophisticates such as we in the Comparative Religious Ideas Project realized quickly that defining religion in terms of God expresses a monotheistic bias. If religion is first approached anthropocentrically, in terms of salvation, enlightenment, and release from suffering, ultimacy need not be construed ontologically but perhaps only in terms of what is most sought. Indeed, perhaps what is ontologically ultimate is too far away to be religiously interesting to people dealing with their own existence. These complications are explored at length in this volume.

We began our project discussion of ultimate realities by changing to that phrase from "ultimate reality," which was in the initial design of the project. That initial category of ultimate reality in the singular came from the assumption in Christianity that God is the object of ultimate religious concern and that it is important to compare various ideas of God and what alternatives there might be to conceptions of God—an assumption congenial to a number of religious perspectives besides most forms of Christianity. The category of ultimate reality is obviously fruitful for comparison. Clooney here (chapter 5) examines a discussion of God (Nārāyaṇa) as the creator of the world on which all else depends. Saldarini (2) discusses the God of Israel as the creator of the world and goal of human existence, and Fredriksen (3.1) says the first Christians assumed the Jewish view of God as the ultimate reality and are interesting rather for what they say about Jesus. Haq (4) treats God as the ultimate reality in Islam and raises both epistemological and metaphysical questions about it. Kohn (1.1–2) discusses ultimate reality in Chinese religion explicitly in relation to theistic conceptions of God, as well as in other ways; Eckel (6.3, note 22) cites Tu Weiming as likening the Confucian notion of Heaven to God. Eckel himself (6) affirms the ontological status of ultimate reality as being a central point of debate within Buddhism and points out (6.4) that for the Mādhyamikas, from the standpoint of conventional truth, "ultimate reality can be equated with the Buddha." So, the initial plausibility of the category of an ontological ultimate reality is borne out in what our specialist colleagues take to be important for their traditions, and the diverse ways of speaking about ultimate reality construed ontologically can be traced with great interest.

Nevertheless, in saying that God or ultimate reality (so as not to prejudice the ontological ultimate theistically) is important for religions it was claimed that this is because ontological ultimate reality is the object of ultimate religious concern. "Ultimate concern" is Tillich's phrase for the form of human orientation to what is ontologically ultimate. A very different focus on ultimacy arises if the topic is what is most important in human life, or in its religious dimension. If we examine ultimacy as a human project, we might even get a handle on what the religious dimension of life is, though that is not our topic here. The study of anthropological ultimate realities allows us not only to examine how people in some religions relate ultimately to what is ontologically ultimate, but also to how ultimacy functions in religions such as some forms of Buddhism where it is ultimately important to realize that there is no ontological ultimate, or at least nothing ontological to refer to ultimately. So our second ultimate reality is the orientation and drive of the religious path, the project of sagehood and perfection (1.1.3), the quest for God (2.2, 2.5–7), the mediator between God and humans (3.2–4), the mystic path (4.7), and the bodhisattva's path toward liberation (6.4).

Ultimate realities, in the plural, refers to ontological ultimate reality (which may itself be plural) on the one hand and anthropological ultimate reality (which also may itself be plural) on the other. But concretely they constitute one topic, not two or more. We found again and again that we could not talk about one without talking about the other. There is only one vague category in play here—ultimate realities. Kohn (1.1.1) cites Eckel in describing the category as "the order of the cosmos itself and the actualization or realization of that cosmic order in human experience." The subcategories by which this is spelled out, for instance, creation of the world from something or nothing, whether there are finally two truths about the ultimate or only one, whether religious perfection separates one from the ordinary or returns one to it, and so forth, all take their meaning from the roles they play within that larger vague category.

We try hard in this volume not to assume that we know what the ultimate realities are and then cite which aspect this or that text or tradition reveals. That is made easier by the fact that we (the entire group) are in severe disagreement among ourselves on that question as well as on the question about whether we can know much about ultimate realities anyway. Nonetheless, there is a difficulty in principle with our efforts to be fair, and this difficulty needs to be mentioned here.

What we have learned from this is that religious ideas cannot be compared except with a heuristic theory of what religion is, what is important, and what ought to be looked at. Of course, we are not speaking of a fixed, dogmatically held theory of religion, which would be worse than useless, but of a flexible interpretation of religion just specific enough to yield tentative and revisable criteria for detecting what is important in religion and so for suggesting what we curious comparativists should invest our time in studying. In the present state of the discourse, however, there is no general agreement on a "theory of religion," certainly not among us. This topic is reviewed in detail in the volume, *Religious Truth*, chapter 9.

We not only have a method for comparing religious ideas, explained in detail in chapter 7, we are constantly evaluating it. Testing the method is just as important for us as sharpening, changing, or inventing tools is for the sculptor. An important phase of testing the method is self-evaluation of our project. Our first year's topic, the human condition, was exciting at the time the project focused on it and extraordinarily frustrating subsequently in drawing and writing up conclusions. This was because, in developing our collaborative habits of learning from one another, we concentrated on the first two moments of comparison, that is, the elaboration of the vague categories—wild and fun philosophy—and the specification of them with examples from the various traditions—many "golly-gee-whiz" experiences for each of us. For many of the specialists, this was a crash-course seminar in various forms of unfamiliar philosophy and theology, while for the generalists it was a crash-course in history of religions. Most of the specialists, too, were beginners in at least some of the other traditions, though no one, it turned out, was expert only in one. What the seminar failed to do was to integrate the specifications in the language of the comparative categories so as to lay out important comparisons. That fell to Neville after the fact. The concluding chapters of the volume reporting that year's discussion, *The Human Condition,* feel external to the preceding evidentiary chapters and the comparisons drawn there reflect Neville's own take on what the specialists had said and not said. In retrospect, it seems that our group could not have short-circuited this slow process of coming to substantial comparisons, and it is worthwhile pointing out what is good about that fact.

First, we learned that uncommon erudition is required for comparative conversation that none of us had coming from our own disciplines. Partly the erudition is simply finding out a lot about what the others know so that no one has to talk down to be understood. This point has consequences for graduate education in religious studies: special disciplines ought to be supplemented with knowledge from other disciplines so that a public for comparative thought is possible. Another part of the erudition we had to acquire consists in creating a language and set of intellectual habits through the history of our own discussions. This is not a private language but a somewhat new discourse. The discourse holds within it the embarrassment of ideas that turned out to be silly, comparisons that were premature, cautions that proved excessive, and a good nose for what smells promising. Especially, we found ways to relate things that would not have occurred to us before the seminar. Although doubtless a function of excited *hubris* as well as seasoned experience, most of us now look upon many of the other comparative conversations in which we have participated as a bit innocent.

Second, we discovered during the first year how true it is that comparative categories cannot be imposed from the top but need to be formulated and reformulated in terms of what is discovered in the specifics. We began like most scholars today with an acute consciousness of the fact that comparison has been dominated by conceptions of religion from the West. Our project topics, the human condition, ultimate realities, and religious truth, are clearly *at least* Western categories. One of our questions about them was how exclusively Western they are: can they be applied in the comparison with non-Western religious traditions? Indeed, the categories are all found in Christian thought and we were worried, especially in light of the history of comparative ventures, that this in itself might bias the understanding of Judaism and Islam. So in just about every seminar we asked whether the text or tradition under discussion would call for the reformulation of the comparative category, and if so, how. The upshot was to make the comparative categories increasingly vague, so as to be specifiable by an ever more surprisingly diverse group of religious commitments. In their vagueness, the categories became increasingly more precise about what they could include as specifications and what not.

Third, and related to the second point, we came to appreciate the force of the claim that religions and texts need to speak in their own voices, their own rhetorics, their own intellectual and practical styles, and we saw that this must be registered in the specification of the categories. After marveling at the genuine diversity of expressions, we took great pains to talk about how our presuppositions about the human condition, and again this year ultimate realities, might bias our interpretations of the texts and traditional positions. We found it important to be able to appreciate and enjoy the differences before we tried to understand how they relate to one another. In particular, we aimed to make sure that we looked at the specifications from several angles to guard against bias and simplified treatment. These angles were their intrinsic expressions, their theoretical implications, the ways the world looks from their standpoint, and their practical implications. We called these "phenomenological sites of analysis."

Yet at the end of the first year we were rather stuck at the virtues mentioned so far and were unable to spell out stable comparisons as a group. The result was that Neville constructed a grid from the categories that had emerged during the first year's work as most useful for parsing the human condition, and then filled in what each tradition or text had to say about the position on the grid, adding comparisons with each new tradition. In each case he looked at the specification from the standpoints of the four phenomenological sites. These conclusions at least give the appearance of being wonderfully systematic.

These comparisons were based on categories that bubbled up from our first year's conversations, they were presented systematically and from several points of view (the phenomenological sites), and they were reflective of what Neville takes to be stable comparative hypotheses worth further investigation; that is all good. Nevertheless, they remain externally related to the preceding arguments. The specialists' chapters made few explicit comparisons. Moreover, their discussions were not coordinated regarding the levels of specificity and vagueness, with the result that Neville often had to change the focus of what was cited from the specialists' chapters, making their claims either more specific or more general, so as to render them relevant to one another in the same respects. Thus, his conclusions not only asked questions of the traditions and texts they themselves did not ask—and answered "for them"—he asked and answered new questions of the specialists' representations of their material. The result was that Neville's views sit alongside the separate views of the others, as if the concluding comparative hypotheses were the result of another specialty and not of the collaborative work. To be sure, his views on the comparative topic were formed largely through the group's work in the seminar. But they still are more external than we had hoped because the goal of the project is to build a concrete collaborative understanding of the topics as parsed by our traditions and texts.

The externality of the conclusions to our project at that stage is not a bad thing, as frustrating as the writing and group discussions of the first volume's conclusions were. In fact, it marks the distinction between the degree to which the specialists were comfortable in talking about their subjects in conjunction with others, and the degree to which the generalists understood comparison to be something over and above a listing of various things the different texts and traditions have to say about the human condition. It now seems to have been an unavoidable and helpful stage in our growing corporate consciousness.

Our purpose in this volume is, by contrast with the first volume, to take all three steps in comparison as a group. Most of all, this involves attempting that last step, the concrete interpretation of the category of ultimate realities and its subcategories in terms of what we have learned through exploring its specifications. Furthermore, unlike in *The Human Condition,* here we derive our explicit comparisons from the specialists' concrete re-representations of ultimate realities. The form of chapter 7 in this volume is thus not a grid of comparisons but an essay.

Some obvious limitations need to be called to mind for the record. First, we have by no means made an exhaustive study of how even the six traditions we examine treat ultimate realities. Our scattered specifications are almost like random spot-checks in a field so vast that it is hard to be sure that we have a fair sample. In many respects our specifications are accidental, reflecting the current interests and predilections of our specialist authors. We have made an effort in the specialist chapters however, to provide both a general representation of the tradition at hand as well as an analysis of a particular text, locating that text in its peculiar place in the tradition. Moreover, this volume reflects a far greater comprehension than was evident in *The Human Condition* of how and why the specialists choose the texts or authors they do. Because our specifications are not exhaustive, or even very many, it is difficult to say much in general about how religions treat ultimate realities. But we can say what the material we have studied says about ultimate realities.

Second, that we (Neville and Wildman) employ our own biases and perspectives in constructing a concrete representation of ultimate realities and drawing comparative hypotheses is inevitable. Describing ultimate realities in their own terms but as specified by our texts is a process of translation that requires creative imagination. The translation goes from one language to another (few of the texts we examine use phrases such as "ultimate realities" though our authors in each case discuss how that phrase might apply). But it also goes from specific to vague levels of discourse and back again. Moreover, drawing out the specific comparisons, determining what to relate to what in which precise respect, involves selection. All this requires what Aristotle would have called "hitting upon a third term," or what Jonathan Z. Smith has called a bit of "magic." There are two saving features regarding this limitation, however. One is that our biases and perspectives have now been formed in significant measure by the seminar in all its features. The other is that our conclusions are vulnerable to correction. The version here itself is the product of criticisms of early drafts by the seminar, and we anticipate many shifts and amendments when other scholars put our conclusions in the context of their work.

Third, the classic philosophical dispute between nominalism and realism was present in our discussions, not only of the importance and reality of vague categories, so important for our theory of comparison, but also in another context. How do traditions "say" what they say? Eckel, citing the authority of Wilfred Cantwell Smith, insists that *traditions* as such do not say anything. Only individual authors within traditions, or particular texts, say things about ultimate realities. In deference to this nominalism, we tried, especially in *The Human Condition,* to avoid writing that "Buddhism says x about the human condition whereas Hinduism says y." Rather we would write "Nāgārjuna in the Madhyamaka Buddhist school says x whereas Śaṅkara, in the Advaita Vedāntin, says y." Neville, on the other hand, an unrepentant realist, insists that ideas are general and that it is the society or tradition that says things, through individuals as tokens. Of course particular texts have a singularity, an haecceity, that distinguishes them from one another within the tradition, and important texts modify the tradition. Yet the discourse is that of the community, the tradition; the individual authors are important to the degree that they express or modify the tradition. Perhaps no single author says fully what the tradition itself is saying with its complex and interpersonal, usually intergenerational, play of assertive signs. For the realist, "Nāgārjuna says x" is a metonymous abbreviation for "Madhyamaka Buddhism (as shaped by Nāgārjuna) says x." Of course there is truth on both sides, and also error. The balance lies somewhere between the view that there are a great number of religious authors distributed by loyalties through six traditions and the view that the traditions with their assorted means of influence speak through their writers. And the associated limitation is that we allow more messiness around what or who has ideas in this volume than we allowed in *The Human Condition.*

The specialist chapters here (1–6) are ordered with the following rationale. The first is Kohn's because it is most explicit about the internal diversity in the notion of ultimate realities, and because it is one of two that does not interpret the ontological side of ultimate reality theistically. We want to prevent theism from preempting the discussion of ultimate realities. Then by contrast we move to Saldarini's paradigmatically theistic study of Judaism, and thence to Fredriksen who, as already mentioned, says the first Christians simply assumed the Jewish theism of their time and concentrates instead on the ultimacy of Jesus. Islam follows historically of the Abrahamic faiths, as represented in Haq's chapter. Clooney's discussion of Vedānta Deśika comes next as an even more scholastic theological discussion of theistic attributes than Haq's treatment of the attributes of Allah. The specialists' chapters conclude with Eckel's return to the breadth of the question of ultimate realities characteristic of Kohn's chapter, and his careful methodological reflection on the whole of our discussion. Our chapter of comparative conclusions about ultimate realities follows the specialists' chapters, and the final three chapters deal with methodological considerations. Chapter 8, in particular, lays out the philosophical method of comparison with the distinctions between vague and specific categories.

1

Ultimate Reality

Chinese Religion

Livia Kohn
with James Miller

∾

1.1 General Considerations

1.1.1 *Categories and Modes of Analysis*

The discussion of ultimate reality, it seems, moves between two poles. As David Eckel describes them, they are "the order of the cosmos itself and the actualization or realization of that cosmic order in human experience," the abstract definition of what is the underlying principle or order in a given worldview and the real experience of that principle in the personal life of a believer. These two poles, however, are not exclusive or absolute but in their interaction raise the issue of the relation between the order of the cosmos and its actualization.[1] Believing Steven Katz, there is no experience without some conceptual framework, and thus the order of the cosmos is directly responsible for its actualization. Vice versa, ultimate reality even in its most abstract description as "order of the cosmos" is only a reality if and when it is—or at least at some point has been—experienced by human beings. This, of course, revives the old debate on the nature of mystical experience, the many problems of immediacy, pure experience, referent, background beliefs, physical preparation, and so on.

In addition, it also opens the question of the relationship of ultimate reality to the human condition. Where the latter is the state of predicament experienced by the majority of human beings and thus can be described as the ordinary way of being, the former is a special and highly inspiring experience or way of life, a sense of overarching order, of inherent meaning in all-that-is. Ultimate reality as an experience is therefore an extraordinary state, a state so extraordinary that it is described as ultimate by the person in it. It is then conceptualized in religious ideas, speculative thought, and mystical philosophies and formulated by certain extraordinary people—mystics, prophets, philosophers, saints, or other religious virtuosi—who grow out of but are not, or no longer, subject to the human predicament.

These religious virtuosi of various ages and cultures then speak about ultimate reality in a variety of modes that can be generally classified as either philosophical, practical, or mythical. Philosophically, thinkers and theologians provide abstract systems of thought, interpretations of subtle concepts, and theories of logic and cognition; practically, mystics and inspired masters outline distinct stages and give instructions on specific techniques (fastings, purifications, meditations) that will allow others to have similar experiences of ultimacy; mythically, prophets, saints, and visionaries describe the splendor and the names of the deity, the way in which the world was created, and the splendor of the heavenly halls.

All three modes of discourse have been applied widely in the field, with most traditions engaging in philosophical and theological analysis of their basic doctrines, and the major comparative schemes of this nature. Practical discourse has found its most common expression in discussions of mysticism, with Evelyn Underhill's division of the *via purgativa, contemplativa,* and *unitiva* being frequently invoked and serving as a general framework for comparison. The mythical, too, has been widely applied, scholars having set up comparative patterns and typologies of myths, be they origin stories or tales of the hero with a thousand faces.[2] There is no point in making a value judgment between these modes but it might be possible to distinguish certain aspects of ultimate reality that are approached better or more commonly through one rather than the other. It may, for example, appear reasonable to assume that philosophical discourse is applied most often in discussing the order of the cosmos in an abstract mode, while practical discourse emerges more frequently when speaking about its actualizations, with the mythical mode bridging the two by giving general descriptions of how the cosmos works in its images, metaphors, and symbols but also outlining a way to its actualization in its various narratives.

1.1.2 *"Ultimate Reality" in Chinese Religion*

Ultimate reality being most generally the promise of order and a way to resolve the predicament of the human condition and the human condition in China being defined as the attempt to attain harmony and transcendence, one can sweepingly state that ultimate reality in China is harmony and transcendence and their actualization in human life. This, of course, is parallel to the Buddhist relationship between the first and third noble truths, the Jewish match between the constant attempt to obey God's law and its full realization, and so on.

Within that framework, however, simple and sweeping statements become impossible very quickly. While the Chinese have a rather high level of agreement on what the human predicament consists of, they also have a veritable smorgasbord of looking at, and outlining ways of, overcoming it, so that practically every and any idea or practice used in religions the world over—be it rules of purity, mystical visions, names and images of god, or theories of cognition—can be found somewhere or somehow in China.

This situation is complicated by the fact that the Chinese have no proper term for "ultimate reality"—unlike "human condition," which is easily translated by three descriptive words: *ren zai shi* or "human being(s) in world." Confronted with this, a Chinese would immediately answer that in all the world, among all creatures, humans are the most numinous, that they form a triad with heaven and earth, that their life is basically good, and that they constitute an important part of a larger and intrinsically harmonious cosmos. Being conscious, they moreover have the power to either support or upset this intrinsic harmony, jeopardizing it through their desires and egoistic delusions of an independent self.

With ultimate reality, now, we face a completely different situation. Aside from the general term "Dao," which can mean anything from the road one walks on through the way one speaks to the ineffable power at the root of creation, there is no clear word or phrase that conveys to a Chinese exactly what we mean by ultimate reality. One would therefore try to do a word-for-word rendition, beginning with "ultimate" and moving on to "real" or "reality." Individually taken, these two words provide no difficulty. "Ultimate" is *ji,* the dictionary definition of which is "the utmost point," "extreme," "to reach the end of," "utmost," and therefore "ultimate." The word, written with the radical "tree," originally indicates the ridgepole of a house, the central and uppermost beam in a construction, a place from where one can go no further. "Reality," on the other hand, is *shi,* for which the dictionary gives "solid," "substantial," "hard," "authentic," and "real." Its original meaning is "kernel," "nut," the pit of a piece of fruit.

Now, not only is there no established combination of these two words—*jishi*—in the language, but if one put them together like this, they would constitute a contradiction in terms: the highest point or ridgepole *plus* the deepest, hardest core or inner kernel, the uppermost spot in a construction *and* the innermost center of a natural object. Or, on a more abstract level, the ultimate point of a development or endeavor combined with the hard-core facts of solid reality. A Chinese confronted with such a combination would determine it absurd, senseless, and ask what one were trying to get at: the ultimate or reality. If it's ultimate, he would say, it's not real; and if it's real, it's not ultimate. Or, to quote a medieval scripture, "If it's the Dao, you cannot see it; if you can see it, it's not the Dao."[3]

Not quite ready to give up, we would then take the interview one step further and replace "ultimate" with "true" or "perfect" (*zhen*).[4] "True reality," "perfect reality," now that is something to which he can relate. However, as we are not really interested in his idea of what is really real in his life but want to know about his ideas of ultimate reality, we would phrase the question in the subjunctive: "If reality was true/perfect, what would it be like?" And there we come to another full stop, face yet another dead-end. Not only would it be close to impossible to phrase the question in Chinese (or in Japanese, for that matter), but counterfactuals, as linguists have shown, are simply not dealt with. "What?" our Chinese would ask, and we would repeat the question, maybe rephrasing it a bit. Another "what" would follow, and after a few more tries, when the question has finally sunk in far enough, the clear and obvious answer would be: "But reality is not perfect!" In other words, whatever is not, is not, and there is no sense at all wasting time even trying to think about it.[5] The obvious objection at this point is that there are, of course, utopian visions of the perfect state, ideals of personal virtue (sincerity), and notions of the mystical dissolution of self in the Dao or immortality in Chinese culture. However, they fall short of our abstract concept of ultimate reality on two points: they are not generally applicable but limited to individual persons or specific groups, presenting a multiplicity of situationally determined "ultimate realities" and making it necessary to redefine the notion in terms of highly specific personal or communal goals (and their related theories of world origin and development); and they are not ultimate in the sense of being unchangeable: what may be the highest personal goal of someone in his twenties may be not at all desirable to the same person thirty years later; what may look to be the ideal state to a newly founded religious community may be completely different from their vision after a century of organization.

We are therefore compelled to agree with A. C. Graham who states categorically that Western scholars or thinkers when looking at ancient Daoist texts tend to ask the wrong question. The question should not be the Western "What is the truth?" but the Chinese "Where is the Way?" As Julia Hardy adds: "Too many interpreters probe the text trying to decode mysterious statements, which they believe reveal the nature of some ultimate reality, when in fact the *Daode jing* is about values and a philosophy of life."[6] A similar point regarding the futility of a search for ultimate reality is also made by Alan Chan in his discussion of Wang Bi's interpretation of the *Daode jing*. Here the creation is examined for its origins and a chain of beings unfolded, each of which again depends on another for its existence. This, however, cannot go on indefinitely, forcing the thinker to the conclusion that "the idea of a first being or substance seems self-defeating," the only proper resolution being the conclusion that at the root of all, the ultimate beyond existent being, is *wu*, "what being is not."[7]

In other words, there is no ultimate reality as reality or original substance at the root of the cosmos and its order. Instead, whatever is at the root is by definition what is not, it is what is not real or manifest in the world. Nevertheless this what-is-not can be made real in the personal experience of human beings and thus attained in a number of ways or methods—the question of which is the central point of the Chinese approach to the ultimate and the reason why there is such a multiplicity of views and methods in their religious life.

The multiplicity and situationally determined nature of ultimate realities in Chinese culture in turn leads back to the relation of ultimacy to experience. Reality, if it is to be real at all, has to be part of experience, so that the ideal reality envisioned by the various Chinese groups and/or individuals has its basis in certain personal experiences. In other words, for anyone to imagine a certain state as ideal or perfect, he or she must have had a glimpse of that state in real life, a moment of pure bliss, of perfect righteousness, a vision of the divine.

In religious studies, we think of these experiences as moments of conversion; in psychology, they are described by Abraham Maslow as "peak experiences."[8] They are experiences so different from ordinary life, so perfect and yet so real, that whoever has them thinks of them as ultimate reality. But unlike other religions, the Chinese acknowledge that, beyond the most vague description of such experiences as a sense of harmony or transcendence, they are utterly personal and subjective. Reality in itself is never and can never be seen in the exact same mode by two different people or by the same person at two different moments—a circumstance made chillingly clear in the movie *Rashomon*. Ultimate reality, understood as something fundamentally real yet unchanging and the highest or end point of life, thus again comes out as a complete contradiction in terms.

To rephrase the argument again in yet other words, while one can safely say that the overall goal and ideal of life on earth in China is the establishment and continuation of harmony and transcendence, whatever these terms mean to specific people or groups at any given point in time varies considerably. And they are never ultimate in the sense that one can go no further. Times change and so will the forms harmony and transcendence take. Asking a Chinese about "ultimate reality," we end up discussing his personal peak experiences, the moments when he thus has felt perfect in some way. Taking ultimate reality to China, we lose it in favor of a feeling of perfection, be it personal or communal, culturally unusual or part of an established tradition, yet commonly coupled with a tremendous sense of subjectivity and a great tolerance for whatever others may find perfect. Ultimate reality in China thereby becomes a vaguely sensed but unreal ultimate that is turned into reality by way of any number of different ways of religious experience. From "ultimate reality" as one abstract concept we therefore move to "ultimate-turned-reality" as an experiential process.[9]

1.1.3 Sages and the Perfected

Experience being central, the initial point of inquiry into the nature of this "ultimate-turned-reality" in China should be the people who have undergone the necessary experiences and reached the perfection promised. There are, in the classical literature, two types of such beings who have successfully attained ultimacy, the sage and the perfected, *shengren* and *zhenren*. To look at the latter term first, it is rendered either "realized one," "true man/person," or "perfected," the last among which is particularly handy because it allows for the translation of *zhen* as "perfection" as and when it is used to describe the abstract quality or state of such a being.

Prominent in philosophical Daoism, the true man or person resides either on earth or on a wondrous, far-off mountain, being described as completely free from ordinary thoughts, feelings, and physical needs. The true man, Zhuangzi says, "sleeps without dreaming and wakes without worrying, eats without savoring, and breathes from deep inside. . . . He knows nothing of loving life, knows nothing of hating death. He emerges [into life] without delight and goes back without a fuss" (chap. 6). The "spirit man" on Mount Gushe, moreover, has "skin like ice or snow" and is "gentle and shy like a young girl. He doesn't eat the five grains, but sucks the wind, drinks the dew, climbs up on the clouds and mist, rides a flying dragon, and wanders beyond the four seas" (chap. 1).[10]

In religious Daoism, the perfected is an immortal who, like Zhuangzi's resident of Mount Gushe, is a being beyond ordinary physicality and sensory experience, lives on pure essences, breathes cosmic energy, and is free from the limitations of time and space: existing forever, he can go into the past and future; part of cosmic energy, he can move freely in all directions, appear and disappear at will. Immortals are denizens of the heavenly spheres who reside at the root of all existence and have power over the workings of the universe. On occasion they appear on earth, where they are magicians and wonderworkers, healers and bringers of good fortune. They change as swiftly as the wind and can never be compelled, only appearing at a true believer's door out of their own free will.

A classical example for a group of such beings are the eight old men who, according to the *Shenxian zhuan* (*Biographies of Spirit Immortals*) of the fourth century, visit the court of Liu An, a Han noble with profound Daoist inclinations. When the gatekeeper conveys to them his master's reluctance to acknowledge them because they are so old and thus obviously do not have the power to preserve life, they simply say: "Oh, if the prince dislikes us old—well, then we shall become young!" and in an instant all "turn into youths of fourteen or fifteen." They then go on to describe their various arts, which include the power to control wind and rain, collapse mountains and let rivers run dry, appear in several places at once, fly through the air, enter fire and water unharmed, as well as the prevention of disasters and the transmutation of gold from mud (chap. 4).[11]

The Confucian sage, too, is a being beyond the ordinary, although he would not engage in such rather frivolous magical feats. On the other hand, he has the power of a highly tuned intuition that allows him to sense the changes and tendencies of heaven and earth and match his actions and thoughts accordingly. The word for sage, *sheng*, itself is indicative of this trait, as it consists of the characters for "ear," "mouth," and "king," indicating that a sage is one who has control over and is the master of his senses.

Indeed, there is one rather apocryphal story in the *Liezi*, according to which two officials of neighboring states discuss the relative merits of their respective sages. Confucius, from Lu, is said to be "able to discard his mind and use his body," while Gengsangzi, from Chen, is claimed to have the power "to see with his ears and hear with his eyes." The official of Lu, most astonished at such a feat, invites the sage in person. The latter arrives and immediately unveils the story as a canard: "The rumor is false," he says, "I can see and hear without using eyes and ears. I cannot exchange their function" (chap. 4).[12] Still, the point of the story is clear—the power of a true sage lies in his ability to perceive intuitively, without relying on the senses, which serve more to filter and interpret data than clarify them. As Gengsangzi says in the *Liezi:* "Whenever the minutest existing thing or the faintest sound affects me . . . I do not know whether I perceive it with the seven orifices in my head and my four limbs, or know it through my heart and belly and internal organs. It is simply spontaneous knowledge, and that is all."[13]

Whereas the perfected is thus beyond all feeling and ordinary perception, even has powers over the physical world, the sage is in a state of acute nonsensory cognition that allows him to match his every move to the rhythm of the universe. What both ideal types have in common is the attainment of the nonreal ultimate by overcoming the limits of the physical body and the sensory realm. Their "perfection," in other words, lies in the fact that they can be in the world without being subject to, and having to rely on, their physical and sensory apparatus. This goes hand in hand with the notion that their true realm is not the world but lies either in the golden age of antiquity, the far-off isles of the blessed, or the pure heavens of the Dao. Although fundamentally removed and typologically different from ordinary people, they yet appear in the world to give guidance, work wonders, or set up models of goodness, thus helping humanity along. They represent an ideal to strive for, a form of godliness and holiness that can be reached by long-term efforts of transforming body and mind toward a level of ultimacy beyond the senses.

The sages and perfected are understood to consist of a spirit essence that is subtler than the material from which the common world is made. To establish contact with them or even enter their world, the human being has to overcome his or her sensory nature, purify himself to a higher level of being, replace sensual impressions with spontaneous intuition, enter a deep trance, or leave his physical form behind and travel ecstatically to the heavens of the immortals. The wondrous beings he meets there are perfect and spiritual, ultimate in the sense that they are completely different from humans, no longer subject to the hardships of mundane life, to hunger, thirst, sickness, old age, death, losing what one loves, encountering what one hates—in other words, all those things Buddhists define as "suffering" in the first noble truth and that make up the basic situation of human existence.[14]

Ultimacy in the Chinese context can thus be defined as a state of being that is beyond the sensual sphere, that cannot be experienced or described with the help of ordinary perception, and that is far removed from the common world yet can be accessed if one is willing to make the right efforts. Ultimacy actualized in human life, moreover, always involves the controlling and overcoming of sensory experience, the transformation of the physical creature into a spiritual and perfected being, be it temporarily in trances and ecstatic journeys or permanently through the attainment of perfect intuition in sagehood or celestial status in immortality. In all the three modes of discourse, then, we find attempts at describing and outlining this mode of nonsensory existence: philosophically, for example, in the "Dao that cannot be told" and is "invisible, inaudible, and intangible"; practically in instructions given to aspiring immortals on how to change their bodies, emotions, and conscious minds to the level of pure spirituality; and mythically in stories about the clear spheres of heaven, the paradises, and the wondrous activities of immortals.

1.2 The Order of the Cosmos

1.2.1 *The Dao of the* Daode jing

> There is a being, in chaos yet complete that preceded heaven and earth.
> Silent it is, and solitary; standing alone, it never changes.
> It moves around, yet never ends. Consider it the mother of all-under-heaven.
> I do not know its name. To call it something, I speak of Dao. Naming its strength, I call it great.
> Great—that means it departs. Depart—that means it is far away. Far away—that means it will return.
> Therefore the Dao is great, heaven is great, earth is great, the king, too, is great. (chap. 25)

The cosmic hierarchy that is the context for human society is constituted ultimately by Dao. Beyond Dao there is no principle, no power, no thing that is in any way normative (*fa*) for human society—Dao is continuously self-constituting (*ziran*). For this reason Dao is not to be considered a "thing" (although the conventions of metaphysical imagination may require that it be denominated), and it is best to consider Dao in its basic meaning, which is path or way.

"Way" should in fact be construed both prescriptively and descriptively. Dao is from one perspective the path traced by cosmic evolution and from another perspective the structuring power of that evolution. Dao is simultaneously actual and normative in the myriad affairs of the cosmos, and it is in the cosmic interstices between actuality and normativity, between what is now becoming and what is the horizon of Sky's or Heaven's commanding (*tianming*) that the potential for human being (*de*) is located. It is on one level entirely appropriate to "name" Dao, despite the famous caveat at the beginning of the *Daode jing*. This tradition of naming later equated Laozi with the personification of Dao, and went on to name the cosmic powers, the gods of the celestial realms. This naming mirrors the activity of Dao itself, calling things into being, and endowing them with life, thereby underscoring the powerful position of human beings within the cosmic order: we ourselves have the power to *dao*. When we attempt to "*dao* Dao," however, we fall into dangerous paradox, for the human act of *dao* is itself a product of Dao. Here language fails because it attempts to denominate its ground.[15]

To approach ultimate reality, therefore, we could, as in the Western tradition, engage in a dialectic of *via positiva* and *via negativa* whereby we name the name, "God is like a rock" and then throw the name away "but not like any rock." This is not the Chinese approach. What we must do to approach Dao is not to speak or to be silent (the reversal of speech), unless we first listen, for Dao itself is speaking.[16] The symbolic affirmation of Dao is therefore always tempered by the recognition that Dao is subtle and mysterious, something difficult to perceive unless we tune up our faculties of perception. Certainly Dao is great (*da*: the character shows a big man with arms outstretched), the mother of all that is, the fount of cosmic power that is its own generating, the root recursion that is "ultimate of nonbeing—and also great ultimate" (*wuji er taiji*).

But Dao is not obvious: "Great—that means it departs. Depart—that means it is far away. Far away—that means it will return" (chap. 25). This is because Dao is nothing apart from that which is manifest in the cosmos—which is everything. It is not as though there could ever have been Dao-thing "before" the existence of the universe, for Dao is vacuous and abysmal (chap. 4). Here it is important to see what is meant by Dao "models itself after its own spontaneity." Dao is not the ultimate one thing from which all being depends, as though without all beings Dao would still be ultimate or self-subsistent. Rather it is only from a certain perspective that Dao has the quality of ultimacy, and that perspective is of a human being considering the subtle spontaneity of cosmic movement of which he forms a part. Dao is not really "infinite" or "transcendent" but rather infinitesimal, the faintest, most imperceptible of breaths, the darkest shade of light, the smallest possible contrast that, in its infinite fractal-like recursions, multiplies to constitute the shocking wealth of cosmic power. This is the ultimate mystery of Dao: that subtle void and intangible formlessness should be the root of all becoming.

1.2.2 *Forms of Virtue (De)*

The overwhelming picture of cosmic unity that Dao traces does not, however, lend itself easily to a social utopia of organic primordial eco-harmony. The Daoist cosmos is resolutely hierarchical, and the great heroes of Chinese civilization were those who were able to wield sufficient technological power over nature to control the periodic flooding along the Yangzi River basin. The human being, and most especially the king as priestly representative, is in a unique cosmic position of being able to a large degree to manage his own immediate environment. The successful king is said to be possessed of great charismatic power (*de*) endowed (*de*) from Sky/Heaven, a power that has been compared to ancient Roman *virtus* and to Polynesian *mana* in that it combines human potency with cosmic strength and the power of magical compulsion. The implication of this older, cosmological understanding of De is that De is a particular manifestation of Dao. It is the instant of transformation of Dao, when cosmic potential is realized, when the horizon of destiny momentarily discloses itself and in which the present state of affairs is restructured. The one who is able to negotiate this constant transformation in the cosmos becomes translucent to it and thus manifests in his person the actuality of power.

The insight of the *Daode jing* is that only by becoming small, low, weak, imperceptible, quiet, desireless, and empty we can ever get close to the heart of this truth of cosmic reality. The process of ultimate transformation, therefore, begins in attention—making ourselves so small that we are able once and for all to grasp the staggering spontaneity of all around us. Thus, the first line of the second half of the *Daode jing* (which is the first line of the whole classic in the Mawangdui edition) states "[The person who possesses] superior De does not [practice] De and this is how he possesses De" (chap. 38). Simply stated, very little cosmic power can be stored up in oneself and so the one who succeeds in manifesting great power in reality is drawing on the latent power of his environment by becoming ever more attuned to his cosmic location, his Sky-destined concrete embeddedness.[17]

This paradigm is most clearly applied in the text to rulers, military leaders, and administrators (i.e., those who already have positions of power), despite the obvious "spiritual" interpretation to which it has lent itself, particularly under the influence of Buddhism. Chapter 59 of the *Daode jing* is clear that the ruler who is able to draw on unlimited reserves of De will be able to transcend the bounds of normal kingly existence. Now the two chief boundaries that apply to warlords are the size of their dominion and how long they can hold onto it. Thus, the warlord of superior De (i.e., of little self-De) is able to extend both of these because his De is grounded beyond himself, not grounded in himself. In such a case "no-one knows his limit, he can possess the state. Possessing the Mother of the state, he can last a long time" (chap. 59).

To theorize from this military advice, we should say that the possibility extended by being translucent to cosmic potential is quite simply that limits do not apply. The horizon of destiny that structures our actuality can be comprehended and transgressed. There is, in a particular but real sense, no ultimate reality, no end point, no terrifying apocalypse that the sage is unable to negotiate. Daoism in all its religious and philosophical forms has in one way or another been constant in its attempt to chip away at the boundaries of existence like the slow and steady erosion of a rock by water.

The concept of De, however, is most frequently taken in its ethical sense of virtuous behavior. But even in the most morally oriented of early Confucian texts, the *Mengzi,* this virtuous behavior is still chiefly associated with royal power. The text opens with the famous dialogue with King Hui of Liang who is interested in profit. Mencius's subtle advice is that the method of profit promotes discord and competition and will lead certainly to the usurping of the throne, whereas the way of moral virtue and timeliness in respect of the seasons will lead to harmony and eventually to the growth of the kingdom. Although De is operating here on an axiological rather than a cosmological dimension, the paradigm is essentially the same: the chief in the hierarchy must in some sense become minimal for the organism to be harmonious. Being harmonious entails growth. Growth of the organism ultimately entails the growth of its chief. The goal is achieved by setting out in the opposite direction.

This is significant not merely because it works, but because it parallels the natural rhythm of cosmic harmony, in which the primordial cosmic exhalation of Qi is preceded by an corresponding inhalation, a pregnant vacuity, an ultimate of non-being.

1.2.3 *The Great Ultimate in Neo-Confucianism*

Questioning boundaries and negotiating horizons is a profound aspect of Chinese thought, captured diagrammatically in the yin/yang symbol and expounded philosophically in Zhou Dunyi's *Taiji tushuo* (Explanation of the Diagram of the Great Ultimate), whose opening line is conventionally translated as "The Ultimate of Nonbeing and also the Great Ultimate."[18] In the *Daode jing* we see that Wuji is not a reified concept (nonbeing) but means something like inexhaustible or limitless. Only under the influence of Buddhism, for instance, in the texts of Numinous Treasure, does it acquire the notion of some "primordial substance" (*benti*).[19]

In this "substance" language we may understand Taiji as the highest limit, the top ridgepole of the cosmos, the foundation of all metaphysical inquiry. And yet for Zhou, this great ultimate is not itself ultimate, for it is grounded in nonbeing. It is clear that the *Taiji tu* presents a cosmic hierarchy, and yet although it is called a "Diagram of the Great Ultimate," even the Great Ultimate is preceded by something: unlimited, indeterminate nonbeing. His is a hierarchy that reaches beyond the foundations of hierarchy: "Ultimate nonbeing and also great ultimate" (*wuji er taiji*) should be understood as reciprocal, but not complementary. Complementarity would indicate a root cosmic dualism, but in Zhou's resolutely processive cosmological scheme there is a certain priority accorded to *wuji* just because it is first.[20] Hence: "from nonbeing is created great ultimate" (*zi wuji er wei taiji*).[21]

This root asymmetry is mirrored socially: there are no equal relationships in the ultimate Confucian society, but precisely because of this there is a reciprocal, organic harmony.[22] Moreover, the emperor in practicing nonaction (*wuwei*) stands at the summit of his society just as Wuji is the inexhaustible nothing from which the Great Ultimate and the myriad things take their origin, and just as the apex of a pyramid is precisely the point where it ceases to be. Despite the fact that in Zhou's ethical scheme he is not concerned with the king but with the sage, the principle remains the same: being tranquil and without desires is fundamental to becoming a spiritual being because this mirrors the operation of nature itself.[23]

Nature, then, is composed of cycles of hierarchy (yin and yang and the five phases), and these cycles produce the harmony of all that is. This great ultimate, the structuring cosmic power of Dao, the principle that directs all being is itself rooted in vacuity. This is the ultimate insight of the *Taiji tu* and in its various forms and differentiations stands as a core motif of political, religious, and spiritual life in China.

1.3 The Actualization of Cosmic Order in Human Experience

The actualization of cosmic order in human experience is a gradual process of controlling, overcoming, and eventually completely dispensing with one's physical and sensory being.[24] Specifically described in religious Daoist texts by Sima Chengzhen, eighth-century patriarch of Highest Clarity, it is a long sequence of transformations that create changes on all levels of life—body, emotions, and conscious thinking—with the aim to dissolve the limited individual into the larger flow of the cosmos. The body, then, is purified from a personal entity used for sensual gratification to a vehicle of perfection that is in complete oneness with the cosmos. Emotions and feelings become powerless and meaningless, being replaced by a new mode of cognition that sees and feels intuitively and finds itself increasingly distant from the waves of emotions or "passions and desires." The conscious mind, finally, is first controlled rigorously to limit the establishment and use of tense personal categories. From a detached observer's perspective, the practitioner sees how "foolish imaginings" arise, then controls them, and eventually succeeds in stopping them altogether. As a result, the understanding of the self as an individual with a set personality is lost in favor of a wider sense of oneness with the universe, the Dao.

1.3.1 Transforming the Body into Pure Energy

In concrete terms this means that an aspiring practitioner begins by curing acute diseases of his or her body and takes good care to spot latent ones, properly understanding the nature of the human physical makeup, centered as it is around the five inner organs, which store the five main energies of the five phases. Next, he attains harmony of all physical actions: no longer eating normal food, he substitutes a more balanced diet to achieve a higher degree of subtlety in alignment with the cosmos. As the eighth-century *Tianyinzi* (Writings of the Master of Heavenly Seclusion) describes it:

> Any human being is endowed with the energy of the five phases and lives on things which also consist of them. From the time when he or she takes shape in the womb, the human being breathes in and out and circulates blood and essence. How could it be possible to stop eating and attain long life . . . ?
>
> Don't eat anything not well cooked! Don't eat strongly flavored food! Don't eat anything rotten or conserved! These are our basic abstentions. Massage your skin with your hands so that it becomes moist and hot. This will drive out all cold energy. The body will radiate with a glow! (sect. 4)

Beyond that, medicinal drugs are used to replace the five grains and also anything hot and spicy. Normal nourishment, so the theory, causes people to decay and die, whereas drugs distilled from pure plants and possibly minerals will help them to live. Although the first reaction to the ingestion of such medicines is a weakening of the body as it is cleansed and emptied of harmful and superfluous matter, it soon gets used to the purer nourishment and proceeds speedily on its way of purification.

Then one enters the more meditative practices, beginning with gymnastics and breathing. Physical and respiratory exercises, frequently imitating the movements and habits of animals, relax the body and shake off old tensions, provide new flexibility and greater suppleness. Gymnastics are used especially to harmonize the different energies of the body, to stimulate the digestion and the blood circulation. Another eighth-century work, the *Fuqi jingyi lun* (On the Essential Meaning of the Absorption of Qi), in this context refers to the third-century physician Hua Tuo and says:

The body needs a certain amount of movement. This movement serves to properly balance right and left and helps to redistribute and assimilate the energies extracted from grain. In addition, it also causes the blood to circulate properly and prevents the origination of diseases. The human body is like a door hinge that never comes to rest. This is why Daoists practice gymnastics. They imitate the movements of the bear which hangs itself head-down from a tree, of the owl which keeps turning its head in different ways. They stretch and bend the waist, and move all the joints and muscles of their bodies in order to evade aging.[25]

The physical transformation culminates in the absorption of Qi, which increasingly becomes the main source of nourishment. Absorption of Qi is practiced by visualizing the five different colored energies of the five directions as they enter the body from heaven through the nose and from earth through the mouth. These energies are then stored in the five intestines and circulated throughout the body. They eventually will make the practitioner independent of outer air and the normal act of breathing, causing the adept's physical constitution to be reorganized from an individual to a cosmic level and the very flesh and bones of the body to be no longer of personal solidity but only cosmic energy.

1.3.2 Going Beyond all Passions and Emotions

Once the body has been transformed into a flow of pure Qi, passions and desires have to be controlled. To do so, adepts begin with a concentration exercise, focusing their attention on the lower cinnabar field in the abdomen until they are fully concentrated and gain the ability to fixate the mind on whatever object they wish for any length of time. Perfect tranquillity of the will and the intention is realized, the highest of the five phases of the mind attained:

> The mind is turned entirely toward purity and tranquillity. Whether involved in affairs or at leisure, there is no agitation at all. From an efficiently controlled mind, firmness and solidity of concentration develop. (*Cunshen lianqi ming* 2a)[26]

This stability of mind is then used for a critical examination of their psychological constitution. Adepts are led to understand that their conscious mind is originally made up from spirit (*shen*), which works through the human mind and governs life perfectly, but due to delusion is wasted on sensual amusements and the uncontrolled exertions of eyes, ears, mouth, nose, body, and mind. This is the underlying reason for passions and desires.

Spirit is neither black nor white, neither red nor yellow, neither big nor small, neither short nor long, neither crooked nor straight, neither soft nor hard, neither thick nor thin, neither round nor square. It goes on changing and transforming without measure, merges with yin and yang, greatly encompasses heaven and earth, subtly enters the tiniest blade of grass. Controlled it is straightforward, let loose it goes mad. Purity and tranquility make it live, defilements and nervousness cause it to perish. When shining it can illuminate the eight ends of the universe. When dark-ened it will go wrong even in one single direction. You need only keep it empty and still, then life and the Dao will spontaneously be permanent. (*Neiguan jing* 2b)[27]

To control the senses and be liberated from their dictates it is first of all necessary to realize the impermanent nature of the personal body (*shen*). This, rather than the body of flesh and bones, is the body that one identifies with on a more psychological level, one's personality or selfness. Adepts have to understand that this is nothing permanent, but forms part of the continuous natural transformations of Qi or cosmic energy.

The personal body is unstable: there is no true master of body and mind, nor do we have any conscious control over its changes. On the other hand, people tend to artificially create an illusion of such a master. This constructed identity is "the reason why I have terrible vexations. If I didn't have a personal body, what vexations would I have?" This famous quotation from chapter 13 of the *Daode jing* is used frequently in Tang dynasty materials. As Li Rong of the seventh century says in his commentary:

As soon as there is a personal identity, the hundred worries compete to arise and the five desires [of the senses] hurry to make their claims.

The understanding that all sensual impressions are fleeting and that all personal identity is an illusion makes absolute control over the emotions possible.

1.3.3 *Making the Conscious Mind One with Pure Spirit*

Only when the negative aspects of any sort of identity and one's captivity in the clutches of the senses have been fully realized, can attention be turned to the heavenly qualities inherent in oneself. One's self (i.e., one's physical yet cosmic body and one's sensual yet unemotional and well-controlled mind) should now be seen as the storehouse of inner nature, as the habitation of the spirit(s), as the vehicle and the host of the Dao. The spirit shines forth from the body like the light from the lamp.

The presence of the spirit light in the self can be compared with the light in a basin lamp. Light arises from fire, fire arises from burning. Burning in turn arises because of the oil, and the oil needs the wick and the basin lamp proper. Once those four [fire, burning, oil, and lamp] are gone, how could there be any light?

The same pattern holds true in that spirit radiates through human action. But spirit is only present when it resides in the mind. The mind exists only within the body, and the body is only complete through the Dao. Thus we speak of the spirit light. (*Neiquan jing* 5b)

Thus, practitioners increasingly identify with the Dao that governs and inhabits the body and thereby loosen attachments to their limited physical and personal selves. They begin to develop a new and wider identity as part of the universe at large and come to see themselves as beings of spirit who are merely housed in this fragile physical framework that will be subject to all the transformations the spirit transcends. All ordinary fear of death is thereby dissolved.

Someone who is horrified by death, for example, should therefore think of his body as the lodge of the spirit. Thus as the body becomes old and sick, as energy and strength decline day by day, it will just be like a house with rotting walls. Once it becomes uninhabitable, it is best to abandon it soon and look for another place to stay. The death of the personal body and the departure of the spirit are a mere change of residence. (*Zuowanglun*, sect. 5)[28]

The resulting personality is entirely unbound by physical limitations, by emotional values, and arguments of reason. Any conscious ego identity that was there before is lost, yet it is hard to determine at what point exactly the individual ends and the Dao begins.

1.3.4 "Ultimate" Realization

Continuing the training, eventually adepts reach full attainment of the Dao in two major phases, which both occur far beyond the point at which ordinary personality is lost. First there is something called "oblivion," a trance-like state of complete immersion in the Dao to the exclusion of all else. This state is characterized by unconsciousness and immobility: "The body is like rotten wood, the mind is like dead ashes. There are no more impulses, there is no more search: one has reached perfect serenity."[29]

In a second phase, adepts are refined to increasingly higher levels of purity. Coming out of ecstatic immersion and the complete cessation of all physical, sensual, and mental functions, they go off and transcend all in ecstatic pervasion. This state is described as a gradual increase in movement, openness, joy, light, even ecstasy, until the successful adept takes up a position next to the Jade Emperor of the Great Dao.

> Going beyond all beings in one's body, one whirls out of normal relations and comes to reside next to the Jade Emperor of the Great Dao in the numinous realm. Here the wise and sagely gather, at the farthest shore and in perfect truth. In creative change, in numinous pervasion, all beings are reached. Only one who has attained this level of cultivation has truly reached the source of the Dao. Here the myriad paths come to an end. This is called the final ultimate. (*Cunshen lianqi ming* 3a)

1.4 Myths, Metaphors, and Symbols

The state of nonsensory existence and the transition to it are also the subject of numerous stories in the Daoist tradition. Myths describe how the universe originated from a primordial level of being that cannot be expressed in common words or experienced with normal means, and immortals' tales express in metaphors and symbols the extraordinary state to be attained and its massive contrast to normal life. Among the most significant in this context, taken from texts of the early Middle Ages, are origin myths, descriptions of the lands of the immortals, accounts of texts or examinations that aspirants have to undergo, and forms of ascension into the higher spheres.

1.4.1 Creation

To begin with, creation in medieval Daoism is not a smooth transition from the nameless and invisible Dao to a formed and physical world but the active involvement of a creator god. As the *Shengmu bei* (Inscription for the Holy Mother), a stele inscription in honor of Laozi's mother, dated to 153 CE, says:

> Laozi, the Dao
> Born prior to the shapeless,
> Grown before Grand Beginning,
> Living in the prime of Grand Immaculate,
> Floating freely through the Six Voids,
> He passes in and out of darkness and confusion,
> Contemplating chaos as yet undifferentiated,
> And viewing the clear and turbid in union.

Here Laozi is the Dao and as such rests at the origin of all—described as the Grand Beginning and the Grand Immaculate, characterized as void, dark, confused, undifferentiated, chaotic, and in primal union. But un-like the Dao, he is not completely immersed in this undifferentiated cos-mic soup, but "contemplates" and "views" it. From this original separa-tion of the deity from the primordial universe, his role as active creator then emerges. Thus he is, as the second-century *Laozi bianhua jing* (Scripture of Laozi's Transformations) has it:

> The utmost essence of spontaneous nature,
> The true root of the Dao,
> The father and mother of the teaching,
> The foundation of heaven and earth,
> The starting point of all life.
> He is the ruler of the gods and spirits,
> The first ancestor of yin and yang,
> The soul of the myriad beings.[30]

This creator deity participates in the nonsensory, utterly unified, and even chaotic nature of the primordial universe, yet at the same time also exerts control over it. With this dual nature he represents the bridge between the unformed cosmos and the existing world and thus stands ex-emplary for the ideal of the ultimate perfected who has transformed his physical and sensory being into a state of primordiality and rests at the root of the cosmos—not in its utter chaos, however, but in its pure realm of heavenly spontaneity. The ultimate of human existence, realized both at the prime of the universe and in transcendence of ordinary life, is thus made mythically visible in the figure of the creator god who is at the same time one with the Dao and a separate figure with independent powers.

1.4.2 Celestial Abodes

Immortals in the heavens reside in special paradises, of which the isles of Penglai and the sacred mountain of Kunlun are the most famous. Both are described as steeply rising mountains, surrounded by dangerous wa-ters impossible to cross except in spirit and covered with the most won-drous glittering palaces. As the *Shizhou ji* (Record of the Ten Conti-nents) has it,

> There are halls of luminescent green jade, mansions of carnelian flores-cence, purple, halycon, and cinnabar mansions, phosphorescent clouds, a candle sun, and vermilion clouds of ninefold radiance.[31]

Typically covered by rich foliage and bringing forth sweet springs, won-drous plants (divine mushrooms, herbs of no-death, soul-returning trees), and strange beasts (wind-born, fire-radiating, and those making piercing sounds), these paradises of the immortals are images for an existence beyond all physical constraints and in an unchanging and ever pleasant environment. Consisting of non-decaying substances and bringing forth magical plants and creatures, they represent a way of being that is permanent but not human, ultimate but not real.

The immortals, moreover, who reside in them do not engage in work or labor of any kind but enjoy banquets and feasts, music, song, and dance in a relaxed atmosphere. Dressed in formal garb made from luminous cloud essences, preciously gleaming radiances, flying brocade, and multicolored mists, they climb in cloudy chariots to meet in large banquet halls, marvelously equipped:

> Flying dragons and poisonous beasts stand guard at the numinous portals. Huge scaly dragons, thousands of feet long, spread their claws as wide as the entire garden. Flowing radiance shines brightly in the eight directions, brilliantly illuminating the entire realm of Jade Clarity. Banners and canopies hang from the walls; flags flow as incense is wafting everywhere. (*Santian zhengfa jing* 3b)

Here they listen to the music made by softly floating jade maidens, watch the dances expertly executed by dragons and phoenixes. Sweet wine flows down on them from rosy clouds, they eat fruit as brilliant and glittering as gems and diamonds. Stringing the celestial zither, they engage in song and rhyme—a never-ending life of ease and pleasure. A wish-fulfilling fantasy, the description of these paradises of the immortals uses sensory images and evokes ordinary human feelings and desires to convey an image of a life that is utterly different, of an experience completely beyond the senses. The mythical description of the heavens, as much as the figure of the creating deity, thus again serves to bridge the gap between the physically real and the transcendent ultimate.

1.4.3 *Examinations*

While the goal of the immortals is described in myths of glittering palaces and happy banquets, their path, the enormous distance they have to cover from their old way of being, is expressed most poignantly with the motif of the examination. Typically, immortals' stories describe examinations either before the master accepts the disciple or when the disciple is about ready to ascend to the higher spheres. In many cases, the freedom from common emotions as documented by the utter absence of fear is tested along with an unquestioning trust in, and total surrender to, the master and the Dao. Often it is also the sense of individual body identity that is put to the test. In all cases, personality has to be transcended completely before successful ascension can be attempted.

A good example in medieval literature is the case of the Gourd Master, Hugong. He accepted Fei Changfang as his disciple but subjected him to three tests before he set about teaching him: first, Fei had to enter into the midst of a pack of tigers; then he had to lie down in an open chamber with a ten-ton boulder over his heart, suspended by nothing more than a rotten piece of rope, on which a swarm of snakes was gnawing happily; and third, he had to prove his complete independence of personal identity and sensual desires by eating a pile of rotten food, foul with the worms of decay.[32] All these, of which Hugong only passes the first two, disqualifying for ascension but allowing him to attain the powers of an exorcist and faith-healer on earth, are typical ways of examining the qualities of a candidate. Beyond that, often also detachment from physical desires is specially tested through the appearance of a beautiful woman near the practicing immortal. Never batting an eyelid, successful candidates withstand all attempts at seduction.

For a later example, there is Lü Dongbin of the Eight Immortals. According to Song and Yuan reports on his life, he is tested not only for physical detachment, but also for social uninvolvement. Coming home one time, he finds his entire family dead but does not show any grief in direct contrast to convention and family feeling. As he matter-of-factly sets about the funeral arrangements, they all come back to life. Another time, he wishes to sell some of his possessions and accepts a ridiculous price without resentment, showing his renunciation of material wealth. Then again, around New Year's, he meets a beggar who demands all the presents he had assembled for his family. He hands everything over without hesitation, disregarding the social problems that will arise when he faces his family empty-handed.[33] These various incidents show the complete dissolution of personal and social identity as the key to the serious pursuit of transcendence, reflecting again, as in Hugong's story described earlier, the central aspect of the ultimate being as his/her overcoming of all normal values and personal feelings in favor of a nonsensory existence and cosmic identity.

1.4.4 Ascension

The highlight of the immortal's career is ascension, which can mythically be described as the opposite of creation in that it is the transition back to the primordial or heavenly state. Like creation, it is a very strong symbol of the ultimate state, showing most explicitly the contest of ordinary and immortal life and perception. Whether a given immortal observes his or her own funeral, whether a high Daoist master exhibits his "transformation" to his disciples, or whether the person just vanishes—in all cases the break with normality is complete, the transcendence of all individuality and social integration is demonstrated.

To give some examples, there is first of all the very famous ascension of the Yellow Emperor as described in the *Shiji* (Record of the Historian; chap. 28). According to this, he was received into the heavenly host by a divine dragon, which he mounted joined by seventy of his followers. While people were still trying to cling to the dragon's beard and whiskers, the imperial entourage was taken off into the empyrean, the Yellow Emperor losing his slipper in the process, which was then buried with all due ceremony.[34] Another famous case is the above-mentioned Liu An, who after receiving an alchemical elixir from the eight old men, ascended on a cloud into heaven in broad daylight. But not alone. Again the *Shenxian zhuan*:

> When Liu An and the eight old men took their departure from this earth, the vessel containing the dregs of the elixir was left lying in the courtyard. The contents were finished up by the dogs and chickens of the establishment, with the result that they too sailed up to heaven. Thus cocks were heard crowing in the sky, and the barking of dogs resounded amidst the clouds. (chap. 4)[35]

A case from the Tang dynasty, moreover, is described as an eyewitness account. According to this, a young Daoist aspirant by the name of Qu Baiting, commonly called Lad Qu, ascended to heaven in broad daylight in a public occurrence in the fifth month of the year 773. He was at that time eighteen years of age and apprenticed to the fifteenth patriarch of the Highest Clarity. The event took place in the courtyard of Peach Blossom Monastery in full view of both monastic and lay onlookers: while holding on to a chestnut tree, Qu's physical form dissolved completely and he vanished into thin air.[36]

In addition, many famous Daoist masters show their translation, a form of "deliverance from the corpse" in a ritual way. Sima Chengzhen, for example, as reported in the *Xuxian zhuan* (Supplementary Immortals' Biographies) announced his impending departure to his disciples. On the date specified a pink cloud surrounded him and he was promoted to full immortal to the sound of heavenly music. His disciples duly proceeded to bury his robe and cap. The Flower Maiden, too, had her disciples leave hear coffin unsealed. A few days after her demise her body vanished toward heaven, leaving a big hole in the ceiling, thus documenting the great transformative powers of the body-turned-ultimate.[37]

1.5 Conclusion

Ultimate reality in Chinese religion does not exist as a single abstract concept or deity that could be named and defined and explained in scholarly or other treatises. There is a fundamental refusal of the tradition to let itself be pinned down to one particular way, and it rather proposes numerous different ways that lead to different ultimates than one single method and ideal. Questioned more closely, the tradition sees a basic contradiction between the ideas of ultimate and reality, one never also being the other, "ultimate" meaning in effect nonbeing or nonexisting while "reality" indicates the concrete ways of life and activity in this world. Ultimate reality in the Chinese tradition therefore is transformed into the conception of an unreal, invisible, and intangible ultimate that is turned into a subjective and personal reality through experience, which in turn can be achieved and conceptualized in a number of different ways.

The very term at the beginning of the Daoist tradition, the Dao, already bears this out. Meaning "the Way" and pointing to itself and yet to something beyond itself, it is conceptualized and imagined and applied manifold—from the practical way of heaven and government in Confucianism through the ineffable mother of the universe in ancient Daoism and the personified deity of cosmic order and unfolding in medieval religion to the very concrete designation of "way" or method throughout. A *daoren*, a "man of the way," can thus be anybody who is pursuing some form of spiritual endeavor, and the term has accordingly been used equally for members of the Daoist and Buddhist schools and even more generally in poetry for someone literally "on the way."

As the ways are many, so are the conceptualizations of the ultimate-turned-reality. Still, if one examines them in context, one finds that they all have in common the overcoming of the sensory field and sensual modes of experience in favor of something nonsensory, something intuitive, spontaneous, immediate, an experience that goes beyond feeling and seeing and thinking into a state of no-mind, no-perception, and no-self. If one were therefore to attempt a definition of what would be ultimate in Chinese tradition, it would be the state of being beyond the sensory field, the way of living and perceiving in the invisible and intangible cosmic realm of nonbeing and nonaction. This ultimate then is ultimate because by the standards of ordinary human existence it is not, but at the same time it is also real because it can be made part of one's experience as a living human being, integrated into one's personal reality, albeit not with the means of the senses or conscious thought.

Ineffable and beyond yet attainable in human experience, the ultimate is never static or stable and has no substance. Instead it is a continuous process of existence and becoming that is realized off and on in experiences that go beyond the mundane level of life. As a result, the ultimate is spoken about as a "way," in the active mode of unfolding and developing, whether the form of religious discourse is philosophical, practical, or mythical. The ultimate in Chinese religion is a process of realization and experience, part of the world yet not accessible with worldly means, and thus the opposite of the Western concept of God, which is substantial and static, entirely beyond the world, and accessible only by transcending the world completely.

Notes

1. See Steven T. Katz's introductions in *Mysticism and Philosophical Analysis*, ed. Steven T. Katz (New York: Oxford University Press, 1978); and in *Mysticism and Religious Traditions*, ed. Steven T. Katz (New York: Oxford University Press, 1983).

2. An example for the philosophical approach to ultimate reality is the perennial philosophy (Aldous Huxley, *The Perrenial Philosophy* [New York and London: Harper & Brothers, 1945]). Underhill's division is found in her *Mysticism* (London: Methuen & Co., 1911). The mythical is represented dominantly in the work of Joseph Campbell, *The Hero with a Thousand Faces*, 2nd edition (Princeton: Princeton University Press, 1968).

3. This is taken from a discussion of sacred images and visualization in the Laozi hagiography *Youlong zhuan* (Like unto a Dragon), dated 1086.

4. This term is used not only in ancient and medieval Daoism to designate the "perfected" in heaven or on earth but also appears in Huayan Buddhism as a way of referring to "reality" as part of the definition. See Imre Hamar, "Chengguan's Theory of the Four Dharma-Dhatus" (Paper presented at the 35th International Congress of Asian and North African Studies, Budapest, Hungary, 1997). Here the term has a strong metaphysical overtone that comes closer to our intention of "ultimate reality" yet is still based strongly in experience.

5. Two examples: (1) When I was teaching English in Japan, I once, inspired by an article on a similar practice in California, tried to get my businessmen students to answer the question: If your company gave you a three-months' sabbatical, what would you do? The uniform answer was, "Our company won't give us a three-months' sabbatical." End of discussion. (2) When I was interpreting at the international Zen symposium, Heidegger's question came up: "Why is there something at all [in the universe] and not actually nothing?" The question was translated by many of the participants, who included the great Nishitani himself, but the result was merely a blank stare from the side of the Japanese. The fact is, the world exists. Why it does so, and why there is not actually nothing, is irrelevant.

6. See A. C. Graham, *Disputers of the Tao: Philosophical Argument in Ancient China* (La Salle, Ill.: Open Court, 1989); and Julia Hardy, "Influential Western Interpretations of the *Tao-te-ching*," *Lao-tzu and the Tao-te-ching*, ed. Livia Kohn and Michael LaFargue (Albany: State University of New York Press, 1998), 180.

7. See Alan Chan, "A Tale of Two Commentaries: Ho-shang-kung and Wang Pi on the *Lao-tzu*," *Lao-tzu and the Tao-te-ching*, ed. Livia Kohn and Michael LaFargue (Albany: State University of New York Press, 1998), 106–7.

8. See Abraham H. Maslow, *Toward a Psychology of Being* (New York: Van Nostrand Reinhold, 1964).

9. The same point is already made in Wang Bi, who states that the underlying non-being is true and perfect but has to be made real by being obtained in experience. See Chan, "A Tale of Two Commentaries," op. cit., 108.

10. Passages are cited after the English translation by Burton Watson, *The Complete Works of Chuang-tzu* (New York: Columbia University Press, 1968), 33, 77–78. The need to reduce desires and attain a state of nonaction is also emphasized in the *Daode jing* and its interpretations. See Chan, "A Tale of Two Commentaries," 110.

11. Lionel Giles, *A Gallery of Chinese Immortals* (London: John Murray, 1948), 43–44. See also Kenneth D. DeWoskin, *Doctors, Diviners, and Magicians of Ancient China* (New York: Columbia University Press, 1983).

12. A. C. Graham, *Book of Lieh Tzu* (London: A. Murray, 1960), 77.

13. Ibid., 77–78.

14. The nature of perfection as a state beyond the senses is also acknowledged in Chinese Buddhism. Robert Gimello in a discussion on the subject (July 1997) said that in Huayan Buddhism, perfection, or true actuality, was "the reality of someone whose mind is no longer influenced by distortions of any sort"— one who functions in a state of no-mind and bodhi-enlightenment beyond the sensory field.

15. On the Dao in its unnamable dimension, see also Benjamin Schwartz, *The World of Thought in Ancient China* (Cambridge: Harvard University Press, 1985), 196.

16. Dao itself means "speech" as well as "way."

17. *Daode jing*, chap. 59, refers to this as accumulating De through being frugal.

18. For a translation of this text, see Wing-tsit Chan, *A Source Book of Chinese Philosophy* (Princeton: Princeton University Press, 1963), 463.

19. For a discussion of the history of *wuji*, see Zhang Liwen, *Song-Ming lixue yanjiu* (Beijing: Zhongguo renmin daxue chubanshe, 1985), 199. A philosophical inquiry in connection with Daoist practice is also found in Isabelle Robinet, "The Place and Meaning of the Notion of *Taiji* in Taoist Sources prior to the Ming," *History of Religions* 29 (May 1990), 373–411.

20. The point of debate in the Neo-Confucian tradition was whether *wuji* was actually a something, or, as Zhu Xi argued, the indeterminacy of *taiji* "before" its manifestation. That Zhu Xi's position became the orthodox interpretation is testimony to the powerful drive for unity in the Chinese cosmic vision over against any ultimate dualism.

21. Some early texts have "give birth" (*sheng*) in lieu of "create" (*wei*) and there is debate in the tradition over whether the five charter first line is Zhou's original. See Zhang, *Song Ming lixue Yanjiu*, 124.

22. This is not to deny the vital importance of correlativity in Chinese thought. Correlativity, however, involves the interrelationship of things with their counterparts from a different dimension of reality. Thus, autumn is correlated with metal, not with summer or spring or winter. The internal relation of the seasons (and the phases) is one of cyclical hierarchy, not mutuality or complementarily.

23. Again this was a sore point for those Neo-Confucians uninclined toward Buddhism or Daoism.

24. The following remarks are based on my earlier discussion of the immortality process, as found in Livia Kohn, "Transcending Personality: From Ordinary to Immortal Life," *Taoist Resources* 2.2 (1990): 1–22.

25. For Hua Tuo and his work, see Catherine Despeux, "Gymnastics: The Ancient Tradition," *Taoist Meditation and Longevity Techniques*, ed. Livia Kohn (Ann Arbor: University of Michigan, Center for Chinese Studies Publications, 1989), 242. A detailed examination of the *Fuqi jingyi lun* is found in Ute Engelhardt, *Die klassische Tradition der Qi-Übungen: Eine Darstellung anhand des Tang-zeitlichen Textes Fuqi jingyi lun von Sima Chengzhen* (Wiesbaden: Franz Steiner, 1987).

26. For a translation and discussion of this text, see Livia Kohn, *Seven Steps to the Tao: Sima Chenzhen's Zuowanglun* (St. Augustin/Nettetal: Monumenta Serica Monograph XX, 1987), 121.

27. A full translation and discussion of this text is found in Livia Kohn, "Taoist Insight Meditation: The Tang Practice of Neiguan," *Taoist Meditation and Longevity Techniques*, 207.

28. This translation follows Kohn, *Seven Steps*, 102.

29. This passage is taken from *Zuowang lun*, sect. 6. See Kohn. *Seven Steps*, 104.

30. This text is both reprinted and translated in Anna Seidel, *La divinisation du Lao-tseu dans le taoïsme des Han* (Paris: Ecole Française d'Extrême-Orient, 1969), 65.

31. A complete translation and study of this text are found in Thomas E. Smith, "The Record of the Ten Continents," *Taoist Resources* 2.2 (1990): 111–12.

32. For this story, see Kenneth DeWoskin, *Doctors, Diviners, and Magicians of Ancient China* (New York: Columbia University Press, 1983), 77.

33. A translation of Lü Dongbin's biography is found in Perceval Yetts, "The Eight Immortals," *Journal of the Royal Asiatic Society* (1916): 790–97.

34. For more on the Yellow Emperor in Han myth, see Yü Ying-shih, "Death and Immortality in Han China," *Harvard Journal of Asiatic Studies* 25 (1964): 102.

35. This biography is translated in a collection by Lionel Giles, *A Gallery of Chinese Immortals*, 45.

36. A description and discussion of this event are found in Sunayama Minoru, "Shu Tō tōsenkō: Chuban Tō no shidaifu to Mōzanha dōkyō," *Tōhōshūkyō* 69 (1987): 1–23.

37. On deliverance from the corpse, see Isabelle Robinet, "Metamorphosis and Deliverance from the Corpse in Taoism," *History of Religions* 29 (1979): 373–411. On Sima Chengzhen's departure, see Engelhardt, op. cit., 52. The Flower Maiden and her transformation are discussed in Suzanne Cahill, "Practice Makes Perfect: Paths to Transcendence for Women in Medieval China," *Taoist Resources* 2.2 (1990): 23–42; and Russell Kirkland, "Huang Ling-Wei: A Taoist Priestess in T'ang China," *Journal of Chinese Religions* 19 (1991): 47–73.

2

Ultimate Realities: Judaism

God as a Many-sided Ultimate Reality

in Traditional Judaism

Anthony J. Saldarini

᪐

If we inquire about ultimate reality in Jewish religious literature from the Bible to the present, God clearly functions as what we may call the "ultimate reality." The numerous and diverse understandings of God and the lack of sustained discursive discussions about God in the normative biblical and Talmudic literature undermine the simplicity of this answer concerning ultimate reality. If we question further about "ultimate realities" in Jewish thought, the traditional narratives, laws, prophecies, commentaries, exhortations, and so on link God closely and intimately with creation, Torah (the Bible, law, revelation, the Jewish tradition, etc.), wisdom, Israel (the people and land), divine providence, history, and eschatology (the world to come, judgement, the Messiah, etc.). Each of these aspects of God's activity, experienced or hoped for by humans, has a claim to ultimacy in its own sphere or as a metonymy for God. Although the category "ultimate" is not indigenous to the Jewish tradition, except in the medieval and modern philosophical schools of thought influenced by the Greek, Arabic, and modern philosophy, many aspects of the Jewish tradition correspond functionally to what is commonly discussed as ultimate.

2.1 Definitions of Ultimate

The term "ultimate" has many meanings. It can refer to something that is first or last in a sequence or something that transcends all the members of a list or group. If we speak of temporal sequence, ultimate is the first or last realities, that is, the beings or events that are primordial or form the consummation of time. If we impute causation to that first something, then we speak of it as the origin, originator, or creator of all the other members of the series. In the biblical narratives and Jewish philosophy the creative, primordial ultimate is God who is uncreated, has no cause, and stands in relation to no prior reality. God is also ultimate at the other end of the temporal and causal series, bringing about the final goal of creation. In the apocalyptic and eschatological terms created during the Second Temple period (c. 450 BCE–70 CE) God intervenes in human history to bring justice through judgment, reward, and punishment. God's direct rule (kingdom) over the world is the final stage of creation that brings salvation and harmony to the world and a transformation of human society. In the spatial world of physical reality the ultimate is that which grounds reality, is self-grounding itself, and/or necessarily exists (in the philosophical sense). In the realm of thought the ultimate is comprehensively adequate and thoroughly cogent in reference to whatever is judged to be real. In Jewish thought God as creator knows his creation perfectly, understands all its mysteries, and supervises its operations. The functional equivalent of this orderly creation in Greek thought is "nature," "dharma" in south Asian thought, and "providence" in Western theology. In the late medieval period Jewish philosophy adopts the concept of "nature" as the Hebrew *teva'*. But in biblical thought God's agent bringing order to creation and its maintenance is wisdom, created first as the plan for all the rest of creation as an orderly whole and personified as God's companion. Rabbinic literature transmutes wisdom into Torah, meaning the biblical law and all the Rabbinic teachings associated with it understood as the paradigm and guide for all of life.

"Ultimate" may also refer to a superlative or unique excellence. The narratives, poems, prayers, and mystical writings of the Jewish tradition treat God as perfect, the best, the most powerful or all powerful, the most wise or all wise, and so on. God is infinite (unlimited) in contrast to humans and the world, which are limited in all ways. All these attributes of God depend explicitly or implicitly on a contrast between God and human imperfections and limitations. But the very act of comparison, implicit in a discussion of ultimacy, troubled some Jewish thinkers. They criticized Jewish philosophers for comparing the creator with the created because they feared that the process of thinking God would enclose God within the limited human world of mind or matter. The Talmudic tradition operates more comfortably in the ethical sphere in which God shows mercy to humans. For example, the names and characteristics with which God describes himself in Exodus 34:6–7 are gathered by the tradition (b. Rosh Hashanah 17b) into a list of the thirteen attributes of God:

1. *YHWH* = merciful to one about to sin. YHWH characterizes God as merciful.
2. *YHWH* = merciful to sinner who needs forgiveness
3. *El* = powerful
4. *Rahum* = merciful
5. *Hannun* = gracious
6. *'erech apayyim* = long-suffering or slow to anger
7. *Rav hesed* = abundant in loving kindness
8. *'emet* = truthful, meaning reliable
9. *Notser hesed la'alapayim* = extending loving kindness to thousands (= generations)
10. *Nose' 'awon* = forgiving iniquity, meaning premeditated sins
11. *pesha'* = (forgiving) transgressions, meaning rebellion against God
12. *hatta'ah* = (forgiving) sins, meaning inadvertant sins
13. *lo' yenaqqeh poqed 'awon* = not clearing the guilty (literally, one seeking iniquity). Positively put, God exonerates those who repent.

These thirteen attributes of God pertain to God's sovereignty over human action and God's unflagging support of goodness and justice in contrast to human sinfulness. The sharp contrast between God and humans preserved God's uniqueness and "ultimacy." Statements about God depend upon implicit or explicit comparisons or contrasts between God and humans. The very discussion of God as ultimate seems to arise from human experience of God as ultimate and of themselves as very limited. Knowledge of one's limitations entails a perception, however uncertain, vague, or imperfectly known, of a reality beyond human limits. Conversely, experience of a transcendent reality (an ultimate in some sense) sharpens the human sense of limitation. Biblical laments at loss and death and prayers for divine assistance and salvation in the biblical narratives, Psalms, and prophets as well as the questioning of God's purposes and justice and bafflement at the success of the wicked in Job and Qohelet (Ecclesiastes) all presuppose the reality of something or someone (God) beyond and more powerful than human life and limitations or disappointment at the uncertainty or ineffectiveness of such a reality.

2.2 Paths to Ultimacy

The search for an ultimate or ultimates often entails a search for coherence, unity, and order in the complexity and even chaos of the world. In Greek philosophical terms it may be compared to the problem of the one and the many; in the Bible it expresses itself as the exploration of divine purpose and justice; in more general terms the search for ultimates explores the relationship of the finite to the infinite. In a more modern mode ultimates relate to the desire of human consciousness to transcend its limitations through understanding and freedom and to achieve happiness, purity, transformation, and so on. In the Jewish tradition narratives, poems, laws, mystical writings, and philosophical treatises explored these frontiers of human thought and experience. But how is that "reality" to be characterized, evaluated, and responded to in human thought and life? Do ultimates explain human life or relativize and confuse it? The mystics ask whether human language can articulate intelligible and useful comprehensions of ultimacy before language and human understanding fall silent in mystery or confusion?

The path of inquiry in Jewish thought is convoluted because the foundational biblical and Talmudic tradition does not explicitly address second-order reflective questions nor consistently use abstract terminology, but rather reflects on the concrete realities of life intensely so that the mundane speaks of the divine. Biblical narratives and poems include God as an actor in story and history. Rabbinic collections of laws and biblical interpretations often assume the importance of God as they treat widely diverse topics. God appears episodically in hundreds of stories, sayings, disputes, questions, interpretations, and prayers in Rabbinic literature. Although Rabbinic literature raises cogent questions about God and suggests solutions to individual problems, as did the biblical wisdom literature before it, it does not systematize its thought about God nor discuss God explicitly as ultimate in the world and human affairs. God is everywhere and nowhere in biblical, Second Temple, and Talmudic literature.

Given the diffuse nature of the traditional comments on God, the challenge for an interpreter is to select, arrange, and analyze texts with some fidelity to their original context while confronting modern philosophical questions like ultimacy. The potentialities of traditional sources and their flexible, imaginative approaches to traditional questions, as well as their limitations, have been expressed neatly by Eliott Dorff in a recent book on God.

> I therefore do what the rabbis, in contrast to the Greeks, did—that is, I entertain and pursue any explanation that sheds light on an issue; I expect

that conflicting analyses may each be true and helpful to some degree, discordant though they be; and I prefer to live with inconsistency rather than distort or ignore features of my experience that do not fit into a given theory, however helpful that theory may be in explaining other facets of my experience. Keeping the limitations of human knowledge in mind does not lead me to abandon the effort to know, but it does afford me a healthy sense of epistemological humility and humor; I must let go of the human quest for certainty and adopt instead a mellow, almost playful, posture vis-à-vis earnest human attempts to understand everything.[1]

Dorff refers to the constant retelling and reinterpreting of the biblical stories and statements about God, the Rabbinic working out of theological problems in exemplary narratives, parables, and proverbs and in the endless debates and commentaries spawned by texts and teachers for three thousand years. He privileges the traditional, unsystematic, back-and-forth of Jewish discussion in the study group, school, Talmud, and commentary over the systematic, theoretical philosophical, or theological treatise. Elsewhere in his book he uses systematic, philosophical treatments of God, God-language, questions of belief, the nature of God, and so on, such as those found in the works of Saadia Gaon (882–941/2), Moses Maimonides (1135–1204),[2] and many other medieval and modern philosophers and theologians. But his attitude toward them shows why Maimonides's magnificent systematic presentation of Jewish law in the Mishneh Torah never replaced the diffuse discussions in the Babylonian Talmud and its commentaries as communally normative. (In fact, some authorities banned Maimonides's writings as heretical.) Traditional Rabbinic discourse always keeps the limitation of human knowledge clearly in mind.

The following categories and generalizations pertain to philosophical and mystical approaches to God and ultimate reality in the Jewish tradition. If these are inadequate, then better, more sophisticated replacements will have to encompass the concerns and characteristics of God and reality surfaced in the following texts and traditions. The Jewish sages wrestle with God as the central reality and symbol of their world and yet as not of their world. From a static viewpoint, God transcends the human world, yet is an immanent participant in it and its creator. God is preeminently present to Israel and in revelation, yet God is also absent in the experience of many Jewish thinkers grappling with the uncertainties and tensions of life. In terms of space and time, God is infinite, yet intimately related to the finite realities of the human world. In terms of human knowledge, God is intimately known through the tradition, from the Bible to the Talmud to the liturgy. Yet God is so radically unknowable to humans that they must speak of God in paradox and contradiction. God is, in metaphoric language, both hidden and revealed. Yet God, humans, and the world are also inexorably linked. The world is never conceived of as "pure nature," but as peopled by humans and in relation to God. Humans can be known only in relation to God. To think of humans as existing independently of God might imply that humans could accurately and completely know and define God. God, too, is always known in the divine-human relationship, even as God's independence is strongly asserted. God is creator and source of all human and worldly action and reality and the power par excellence in contrast to human and natural weakness and impermanence. Ironically, God can only be known in relationship to those lesser creations. In one sense God is all and all else is nothing. Yet, though God is separate from all that is not God, God's uniqueness is the origin of all else. God is unique in two senses: there is no "second" to God and no thing truly comparable to God.

In this brief survey of Jewish thought on God and ultimacy we will begin with some of the traditional biblical and Talmudic materials presumed by all later systematic discussions. We will then incorporate some of the views of early Jewish mysticism that sought a more direct knowledge of God than the core tradition and medieval Judaeo-Arabic philosophy that synthesized rigorous use of reason with the stories, aphorisms, prophecies, and prescriptions of the Bible and Talmud. During the Middle Ages Maimonides's philosophical analysis of God stressed God as spirit and transcendent in order to relativize anthropomorphic statements about God and counter traditional views of God as in some sense corporeal. At the same time mystical speculation claimed its share in the tradition by its very name, Kabbalah (which means that which is received, i.e., tradition). A treatise on the unity of God, pseudonymously attributed to Maimonides, tries to combine the philosophical and Kabbalistic (mystical) approaches to God. During the modern period the Hasidic movement, which was a eighteenth-century pietistic response to Talmudic scholasticism, appropriated mystical themes into an enthusiastic way of life. In this century the neo-Kantianism of Hermann Cohen's *Religion of Reason* "thinks" God as ultimate reality in response to the Enlightenment while modern orthodox teachers have tried to adapt the Jewish tradition using more conventional terms.

2.3 Biblical and Talmudic Views of God

Most Jewish thinking about God begins from the myriad of biblical statements by or about God. In the narratives God fulfills a variety of roles, sometimes as a main character and other times in the background. Biblical poetry (e.g., the Psalms, prophetic oracles, and wisdom literature) and the biblical narratives attribute to God a variety of attributes, characteristics, functions, and roles. God the creator remains active as sustainer, protector, guide, and judge who sustains the good and opposes evil. From a modern point of view, the Bible speaks anthropomorphically and metaphorically of God, using simile, analogy, and superlatives. However, a number of texts indicate that in the biblical period and in traditional Jewish literature through the Middle Ages God has a body, different from, but in some ways analogous to a human body. Thus, the core Jewish tradition ascribes to God functions and attributes that cannot be classified as either purely literal or metaphoric (in our terms), but rather must be analyzed on a spectrum of understandings of God's nature and activity.[3]

The Bible stresses the marvelous aspects of God, especially God's power and how it transcends human limits. As Yahweh says to Abraham in response to Sarah's doubts about her ability to conceive after menopause: "Is anything too wonderful for Yahweh?" (Genesis 18:14). The oldest passage in the Bible (c. twelfth century BCE), a hymn celebrating God's destruction of the pursuing Egyptian army at the Reed Sea, affirms with stark simplicity:

> Yahweh is a man of war;
> Yahweh is his name. (Exodus 15:3)

Yahweh, the God of Israel, who has defeated the Egyptian Gods, including the God-Pharaoh, in battle, is simply a strong soldier who has saved Israel from slaughter. However, the dimensions of Yahweh's supreme power are far from simple in the Bible as a whole. The prophet Jeremiah (seventh–sixth century BCE) turns this foundational confidence in God against a sinful Jerusalem and Judea. An oracle decreeing the destruction of Jerusalem and Judea by the Babylonian Empire begins conventionally enough, "See, I am Yahweh, the God of all flesh; is anything too hard for me?" (Jeremiah 32:27). However, rather than give progeny to Abraham or save Israel in battle, the God who controls all people has arranged to use the Babylonian army to destroy Jerusalem in punishment for sin. But, in another twist, that same God promises to restore a chastened Jerusalem and her people (Jeremiah 32:36–44). These few passages, out of a set of hundreds in the Hebrew Bible, establish God at the narrative level as the ruler of the world and as the most powerful participant in human history. Power includes the ability to physically sanction human action, access to knowledge of the universe and human affairs far beyond human capability, and the fostering of just (correct, right, life-giving) goals and courses of action more perfect that the vagaries of human purposes and decisions.

All these attributes and activities of God derive from human language and understanding and all God's actions take place in relationship to humans. God creates a "peopled" world that would be lacking without humans. Thus, though God is the ultimate cause and goal of the universe and in principle unlimited by human history, functionally speaking God is always limited and his actions relativized by human responses from creation to judgment at the end of history. For example, in the story of the flood that destroyed human civilization (Genesis 6–9) God as cosmic ruler of the universe could have destroyed humanity entirely, but chose to save one just man and his family (Noah) and to relinquish the use of world-destroying floods in the future. Human needs for ecological order prevail over God's potential destructive power. Because God exercises his power and wisdom in a human arena, they sometimes appear ambiguous and uncertain. Consequently the Bible continually defends God's excellence and otherness against appearances to the contrary.

The Bible has little to say about "God himself." If God "appears" at all in the narrative, he is disguised in some way or communicates through a voice, dream or seer. The Bible generally avoids direct contact of humans with God because if humans were to "see" God's face, they would die (Exodus 33:20). At the same time the Bible is fascinated with God's appearance. God is frequently described using the traditional Near Eastern storm imagery associated with the chief sky God. He appears to Moses as fire in a bush (Exodus 3:2) and to Moses and Israel in thunder, lightning, and clouds on Mount Sinai (Exodus 19:16–17). Even when humans "see God," the Biblical narrators draw back. For example, after the revelation of the commandments and covenant code on Mount Sinai (Exodus 20–23), Moses and the elders ascended Mount Sinai and "saw the God of Israel" (Exodus 24:9–11). However, the author coyly takes back what he has given, for we get no description of God's face or person or throne, but of the floor of God's throne room: "Under his feet there was something like a pavement of sapphire stone [that is, Near Eastern blue lapus lazuli], like the very heaven for clearness." Presumably the elders bowed in homage with their foreheads to the floor and saw only the floor. Although the next verse remarks that they ate and drank with God and did not die as might be expected, still there is no description of God. Later when Moses is receiving further laws from God on Mount Sinai, he asks to see God's glory (Exodus 33:18–23), a sure recipe for an early death. God responds benevolently and cleverly by conceding to Moses a glimpse of his back only: "When my glory passes by, I will put you in a cleft in the rock and cover you with my hand until I have passed by. Then I will remove my hand and you will see my back; but my face must not be seen" (Exodus 33:22–23). Clearly God has a body in this passage, no matter how different from human bodies.

The prophet Isaiah, who had a vision of God's throne room where he received his prophetic message, did not really fare much better. He saw "Yahweh sitting on a throne high and lofty" (Isaiah 6:1) but can describe only the hem of Yahweh's robe filling the temple (in Jerusalem). The prophet Ezekiel, in his fascinating, bizarre first chapter, describes the four heavenly beasts who draw God's chariot, the wheels of the chariot with eyes on their rims, the dome of heaven, loud sounds, and God's throne. Finally he describes God, using the word "like" ten times in three verses (Ezekiel 1:26–28), as "something that seemed like a human form" surrounded by fire and splendor. "This was the appearance of the likeness of the glory of Yahweh" (Ezekiel 1:28). These verses testify to the deep sense of difference that underlay the biblical and early Jewish perceptions of God. God has a body that is larger, more awesome, more dangerous, more glorified, and more powerful than any human body and lives in the heavens, which far exceed the earth in attractiveness. The links between God and humans strain to the breaking point. God surpasses all limits and criteria and imperfections associated with the human world.

2.4 Torah as the Mediating Ultimate Reality in Rabbinic Literature

The Rabbis unthematically but constantly invoked God as the ultimate foundation of their Torah-based way of life. Torah (literally "instruction") refers first to the Pentateuch, the first five books of the Bible that contain the laws given to Moses on Sinai, according to the narratives in Exodus and Deuteronomy. For the Rabbis who compiled the Mishnah and the two Talmuds (second–sixth centuries CE), Torah refers to all the interpretations and teachings they derived from the Bible and their whole systematic, complex, highly self-referential worldview. Torah that comes from God serves as a practical and concrete ultimate for Rabbinic thought. All that they teach must be derived from Torah and itself constitutes Torah; all knowledge of God comes from Torah and contact with God is mediated by Torah and its rules for life. For example, Deuteronomy 11:22–23 promises that if Israel observes the commandments, it will possess the land that God had promised to Abraham and his descendants. The Rabbis transmuted observing the commandments and loving God into diligent study of Torah since study leads to practice and to knowledge of God (Sifre Deuteronomy 48).[4] But the phrase "to walk in all his [God's] ways" (Deuteronomy 11:22) also turns the commentator's attention to the qualities characteristic of God, especially God's mercy as found in Exodus: "These are the ways of 'Yahweh, God, merciful and gracious'" (Exodus 34:6). This verse is part of an old, and often repeated, poetic passage that introduces the renewal of Israel's covenant with God that was broken when Israel worshipped a golden calf in the wilderness by affirming God's mercy as well as his justice. All the attributes of God listed in this passage have been extracted as thirteen attributes of God and used in the liturgy and Jewish literature. The dual assertion of God's mercy and justice that is central to the verse appears with variations in many biblical passages (Exodus 20:5–7; Numbers 14:18; Nehemiah 9:17; Psalms 86:15, 103:8, 145:8; Jeremiah 32:18; Joel 2:13; Jonah 4:2; Nahum 1:3) and fascinated the Rabbinic commentators. They interpreted the generic name "God" to refer to God's justice and God's proper name, "Yahweh" (often translated as the title LORD) to refer to God's mercy. Both qualities are necessary for the orderly governance of the universe, but in many cases the Rabbis favor mercy. For example, in Sifre Deuteronomy 49 they cite the prophet Joel who describes the "Day of Yahweh" when God (justice) will come to judge the evil nations who have harmed Israel. But the passage is read with a twist by the Rabbis to emphasize God's mercy: "Everyone [from Israel] who calls upon the name of Yahweh will be saved" (Joel 3:32; Hebrew 4:5). The commentator then works out the implications of God's mercy: "But how is it possible for a human to be called by the name of God (*ha-maqom*)? Just as God is called merciful, so you be merciful. The Holy One, blessed be He, is called gracious, so you be gracious, as Scripture says, 'Gracious and merciful is Yahweh'" (Psalm 145:8). The justice of God, which for the wicked is frightening and destructive, is firmly suppressed here in favor of God's mercy and faithfulness to Israel. Thus, God's authority and control of the universe, expressed as his justice, are mediated through the balancing attribute of mercy in the same way that God's ultimacy is always related to the limitations of the human world.

2.5 Early Rabbinic Mysticism

The dominant system of thought in the Rabbinic Talmud is so acutely aware of God's transcendence that it very seldom tries to speak of God as he is in his glory. God appears as a character in parables and stories and God's relationships with humans, his justice, mercy, love, protection, and so on, are constantly invoked. However, most Rabbis see no need for direct contact with God because the Torah (teaching) revealed at

Sinai contains everything necessary for understanding God as well as the divine-human relationship and the world. Final revelation and a perfect understanding of Torah will come only at the end of the world when God intervenes apocalyptically to remove evil and the imperfections of this life. In the meantime study of Torah and prayer are the proper human activities.[5] However, this heavily mediated access to God did not satisfy some Rabbis who turned to mysticism to gain more direct access to and knowledge of God. The early Jewish mystics presumed and drew upon the thought world of the Bible and Talmud but supplemented the toil of studying Torah with prayers, incantations, and mystical interpretations of Scripture designed to bring them into contact with God and gain them a perfect knowledge of Torah. Thus, to the mystics God is both hidden and revealed and they sought to examine the extreme limits of their world and know God more immediately as the ultimate reality and truth.

Rabbinic mystical speculation was centered on three topics: creation (*Ma'ase Bereshit*), the chariot on which God rides in Ezekiel 1 (*Merkabah*), and the heavenly palaces (*Hekhalot*) in which God and the angels dwell in heaven. These three topics constitute the ultimate boundaries of the human world in time (creation), place (the heavenly palaces), and perception (God on his chariot). Studying and speculating on these topics and practicing what was learned about contact with the heavenly world in one sense fulfilled the revelation about God and the constitution of the world contained in the wisdom of Torah but in another sense transcended the proper boundaries of human knowledge and activity, at least in the view of the majority of Rabbis. The goal of the mystic is both a visionary experience of God and participation in the heavenly life of God and his servants (angels). The mystic comes to know God through God's reaction to angelic praise and when he returns to the earthly community, he communicates his experience to his fellow Jews and incorporates the human community in the cosmic liturgy.[6] The fundamental powers of the universe become in some senses available to the community both in the realm of knowledge and also in action. Adjuration of God and his angels with magical formulas and the consequent ability to call upon divine power to affect life as well as the capacity to master the Torah flow from mystical practice. All reality can be comprehended through knowledge of the names of God and his angels and, even more important, the adept can achieve a significant control over the world.[7] The divine names as well as God's own speech in the tradition bridge the gap between God and humans and become themselves the "mystical shape of the deity."[8] This divine immanence and consequent intimacy between man and God highlight, but also threaten to transgress the boundaries between the ordinary and sacred, the finite and infinite.

The tension between immanence and transcendence in the mystic apprehension of God pervades Jewish mystical literature. Biblical references
to God's shape (*temunah*) and the making of humans in God's image (*tse-
lem*) led to speculation on God's physical shape. The mythical images
that were tightly controlled in Rabbinic and liturgical writings flourished
as mystical symbols in esoteric writings.[9] In many mystical texts God has
a mystical physical form that manifests itself in speech

> "in the tangible shape of a human being seated on the throne of glory, con-
> stituting the supreme primal image in which man was created; aurally, at
> least in principle, it is manifested as God's name, broken into its compo-
> nent elements, whose structure anticipates that of all being. According to
> this doctrine, God's shape is conceived of, not as a concept or idea, but as
> names. This interlocking of tactile and linguistic anthropomorphism" per-
> vades the Shiur Komah [see below].[10]

The mystical literature privileges language as the tool God used for creation (Genesis 1), a source of power, and a means of communication: the
"names of God, which are the hidden life of the entire Creation, are not
only audible, but also visible as letters of fire." It is the "primal name of
God that constitutes the form of everything."[11] However, the medieval
and modern preferences for a spiritual God should not obscure the stub-
born insistence that God has a heavenly body. Modern commentators
usually tag statements about God's body as metaphor or anthropomorphism. However, the Bible, Talmud, mystical literature, and traditional
interpreters all retained the ancient view of the heavenly world and its inhabitants as physical. Not only God, but the newly created first human
(*'adam,* in its generic meaning) was a primordial creature who had an
enormous body spanning the universe.[12] In the *Shi'ur Qomah* (measure-
ment of stature or of the body) mystical texts, God's appearance and
body are described. This tradition is one of the most physical and, in the
view of some philosophical commentators, "crassly material" of the
mystical approaches to God. Needless to say, Maimonides strongly rejected this old tradition and argued at length for God's spirituality. Many
of the medieval Rabbis rejected Maimonides's total system partly because they perceived it as a departure from the traditional experience of
God in Jewish tradition. But, in a complex twist, the concrete apprehen-
sions of God in mystical literature do not do away with God's transcendence and spirituality so zealously guarded by philosophy in the tradition of Maimonides. Many of the Kabbalists took God's spirituality for
granted before they turned to the mystical shape of a God. Fundamentally, God's self is totally unknowable, infinite (*'ein Sof*). No names,

images, or cognitive statements can directly describe God, only negations. In other traditions, God's body mediates between the heavenly world of divine perfection and the imperfect physical world of human experience. God and humans share bodies. Before he sinned the first human had a body far superior to present human bodies. But now God's dimensions so exceed all human measurements and categories that God transcends humans precisely in his body's dissimilarity to human bodies. Interestingly, these esoteric speculations do not separate the mystics from human life; the mystics integrated their speculations into ethical schemes based on their sophisticated appreciation of the divine-human relationship.

2.6 Maimonides and the Philosophical Quest for God

Maimonides's *Guide of the Perplexed* contains extensive philosophical discussions of the nature of God in the light of Aristotelian philosophy mediated through the Arabs. Maimonides argues that passages such as Exodus 24 and 33, in which Moses "sees" God, really refer to an intellectual knowledge of God when they speak of seeing and visions. [13] For Maimonides Aristotle's *theoria,* theoretical knowledge, is the highest human activity. It transcends metaphors and anthropomorphisms and is the only kind of knowledge able to give reliable knowledge of God. [14] Furthermore, true knowledge of God can come only through the *via negativa,* that is, through denial of any human knowledge as adequate to God. [15] The multiple attributes of God tend to mislead believers into a kind of idolatrous apprehension of God and they do not pertain to God's essence, which is one. [16] Maimonides preserves not only the oneness of God but God's essential unity and simplicity and God's immateriality against more literal interpreters of Scripture who, in his view, naively took biblical anthropomorphisms to imply a kind of divine corporeality.

Some later writers combined philosophical and mystical trends in Jewish thought. For example, the "Nine Chapters on the Unity of God" (*Tishah Perakim Miyuchad*) is a brief treatise wrongly attributed to Maimonides in the tradition. [17] It is a highly derivative work that draws philosophical arguments from Maimonides, borrows mystical interpretations from the "Book of Creation" (*Sefer Yetzirah*), and abbreviates many expositions from the Kabbalistic book, the "Orchard of Nuts" (*Ginnat Ęgoz* [cf. Song of Songs 6:11]) by Joseph Gikatila (1248–1300). It contains aspects of Judeo-Arabic philosophy that it tries to reconcile to Kabbalistic thought and it omits Kabbalistic expositions from the Ginnat Egoz that are totally alien to philosophy. Both traditions are used for the same goal: knowledge of and acceptance of the unity of God. On the whole it gives a brief glimpse into common medieval (c. 1300) Jewish approaches to God as the ultimate reality and into the struggle between mysticism and philosophy.

The influence of mysticism and piety on philosophical approaches to God can be seen in the first line of chapter 1 when it is contrasted with the passage in Maimonides's *Mishneh Torah* on which is modeled. (Chapters 1–4 in the treatise draw heavily from Maimonides's *Mishneh Torah*.)

Nine Chapters on the Unity of God	Maimonides's *Fundamental Principles of Torah* 1:1
The beginning of faith and the beginning of trust is that there exists a First Being who preceded every existence. It is he that confers existence on all things that exist since they did not exist and it is he who carries them all.	The fundamental principle of all principles and the pillar of all sciences is to realize that there is a First Being who brought every existing thing into being. All existing things, whether celestial, terrestrial, or in between, exist only through his true existence.

Maimonides, as a rigorous philosopher, speaks of science, understanding, and a first being that causes all other being. The author of the *Nine Chapters* has moved the discussion into theology, invoking faith and trust as the way to know a personal First Being who confers existence. He requires a knowledge of God and of the nature of reality which is attained by rigorous philosophical, scientific study as a later passage in chapter one shows (1:3), but that philosophical, scientific knowledge must be complemented with the mystical knowledge of God's name.

Nine Chapters on the Unity of God	Maimonides's *Fundamental Principles of Torah*
1:3. A person should have knowledge of everything in creation individually and examine each vis-à-vis each other. By such critical examination they will form a composite that will establish for him the existence of a single Being from whom all other beings hang; and he carries them and there is no other beside him. And if a person examines the carriers and the carried, he will understand their purpose.	1:4. All these things about which we spoke become clear to a person who comprehends and examines the verity of his great name, may he be praised, and that is the name referred to as "his exclusive name" whose letters are yod, he, vav, he [the Tetragrammaton]. This is the name that demonstrates and testifies to his truth and he has no other name that testifies about him, for all (other names) are appellations that describe his activities.

Maimonides expounds the meaning of the Tetragrammaton, God's proper name, like any other name used for God in the philosophically oriented *Guide of the Perplexed* (1.63). Contrary to Maimonides, the author of the *Nine Chapters* treats the Tetragrammaton briefly here (1:3–4) and then devotes part of chapter 7 and the whole of chapter 8 to it. For him and the mystical circles in Judaism, God's proper name, YHWH, was filled with deep meaning concerning God's uniqueness and nature and was the subject of endless speculation. Exploration of God's name must complement the scientific, philosophical study of created reality and the creator in the *Nine Chapters;* in a complementary way, mysticism cannot proceed without rational learning because "faith is not established save after cognition."[18]

In the *Nine Chapters,* detailed knowledge of physical reality shows that God is one and separate from all other existences, which are composite. "When a person understands the manner in which the Exalted One is separated from all other existences, he will be able to profess the Unity of God to the exclusion of all other existences" (1:8). A person "must understand that this Unity is not related to numbers but he is One because he is single in relation to all other existences, because the Almighty cannot be classified within the concept of numbers" (1:10). God's unity is thus a uniqueness beyond comparison to other existences. One can understand God only "by distancing from him all things that attempt to measure him, on order to call him truly one" (1.14). The goal of this study of God is to understand that "He has no one that carries (= causes) him and has no one that maintains him" (1:9). As a result, "according to this essential principle, a person must search and examine the existence of all creation beside Him in a scientific manner. And when he understands their existence, and their essence becomes clear to him, and he perceives the matter correctly, only then will he seat the Creator in his fixed place, i.e., on his heavenly throne)" (2:10). The rest of the *Nine Chapters* goes into great detail concerning the composite nature of the world and God's immutability, even though God rewards, punishes, and is the subject of prayers. The final three chapters (7–9) explore the meaning of the most important of God's names and attributes. The author struggles to reconcile the spiritual, transcendent God of philosophy and creation with the personal God of the Bible and Talmudic tradition who is addressed in prayers and known through the mystical meanings of his names.

2.7 Medieval Mysticism

The medieval mystical tradition began with "The Book of Creation" (*Sefer Yetzirah*, seventh–tenth century) that sought to address those questions of ultimate reality that the mainstream legal tradition downplayed. The creation of the universe, the problem of evil, and the relation of the Divine to the human were explored using ten *sefirot* (originally "numbers," later divine emanations) and the letters of the Hebrew alphabet. The Kabbalah (literally, "tradition"), a complex series of medieval mystical movements, began around the twelfth century in Southern France. To explain the world and its creation Kabbalistic mystics frequently introduced new terms such as the "light without end" (*'or 'ein sof*), "contraction" (*tzimtzum*), "emanations" (*sefirot*), and "vessels" (*keilim*). These terms acquired more or less constant usages in mystical discourse, while still varying in context and meaning. They became shorthand or working terms for the unknowable God, especially as manifest in the world. For example, the "light without end" is the most common metaphor with which Kabbalah speaks of the Divine. It has always existed, but is distinguished from God. Joseph Albo (fifteenth century, himself a rationalist who is largely rejected by the tradition) writes that (1) the existence of light cannot be denied, (2) light is incorporeal, (3) light causes the faculty of sight and the visible colors to pass from potentiality to actuality, (4) light delights the soul, (5) one who has never seen a luminous body cannot conceive of colors or the delightfulness of light, and (6) even one who has seen luminous objects cannot look at an intense light too long, for if he does so his sight becomes weak and he cannot thereafter see what is normally visible.[19] *Tzimtzum* refers to the process of divine contraction that allowed the world to be created. Before the world existed, according to Kabbalistic cosmogony, the "light without end" was present everywhere. Since the world could not occupy the same space with the "light without end," God had to, so to speak, withdraw or contract into God's self in order to create space in which the world was then created. But this space was not left vacant of God's presence since the divine radiance descends through emanations known as *sefirot*, usually catalogued into ten types.[20] These emanations do not divide or multiply God. They are inseparable from God as is the flame from the coal and of themselves have no form or substance.

The perfection and serene reality of the divine existence and powers may seem at first an escape from human life. However, the mystics and Rabbis connected these speculations about God and the origin of the world to the realities of human existence. The problem of evil and human activity are parts of the Kabbalistic model known as the shattering of the vessels (*shevirat ha-keilim*). After God withdrew and created the space in which the world would come to be, God intended to allow the emanations to illuminate and form the world in very controlled, sharply defined measures, called vessels (*keilim*). The emanations were to fill the vessels and provide just the right measure of Godly illumination to create a world in accordance with the divine plan. However, by divine accident, the emanations proved too overpowering to be contained in the vessels, which shattered. This shattering of the vessels resulted in a world of imbalances among severity and love, intelligence and wisdom, and all the other possible permutations of emanations. Thus, one can obscure the other in different situations, so what we perceive as evil is actually an imbalance or concealment of emanations. The human task, from the Kabbalist's point of view, is repair of the vessels (*tikkun ha-keilim*). By performing acts of goodness as defined by Torah (*mitzvot*, commandments), humans actually participate in rectifying the manufacturer's error in the world by restoring the vessels to their completion. Once whole, the vessels would be able to contain the divine emanations in proper balance, restoring divine balance and harmony to the world.

As esoteric as this cosmology sounds, it has found its way into the eighteenth-century Haśidic movement and continues until the present. Mystical explorations of the limits of the knowable have almost always been linked with a Torah-observant life according to the Talmudic tradition. Fidelity to Torah demands acceptance of the traditional language about God; mystical speculation stresses the experience of God and the tradition (in tension with scholastic understanding). Although the probing of God, God's creative acts, and the nature of the world with its human inhabitants are in great tension with the canonical texts (the Bible and the Talmud), the conventional barriers between the human and divine, finite and infinite, immanent and transcendent are relativized enough that communication and interchange take place across the boundaries. Intimacy with God becomes possible in a variety of degrees along a spectrum. For many Jewish groups, the fruits of this exploration outweigh the dangers and difficulties.

2.8 Enlightenment Philosophy and the Jewish Tradition

Hermann Cohen stands out as a well-established Jewish philosopher who sought to combine traditional Jewish literature with neo-Kantian thought. Kantian philosophy stands closer to Platonism than much medieval Jewish philosophy, which stands in the Aristotelian tradition. As a professor at Marburg, Cohen was deeply influential on Jewish and Christian theologians, including Rudolf Bultmann. His *Religion of Reason out of the Sources of Judaism* was published posthumously in 1919.[21] The first chapter on God's uniqueness explores various expressions of God's oneness, unity, and singleness that together give meaning to monotheism. As might be expected, Cohen seeks to penetrate and overcome history and myth in order to clarify the ideal relationship between the essence of monotheism and the world (37). He seeks to establish true relationships among ideas and to explain the world in all its complexity at the level of human thought. For example, God's oneness or unity eliminates polytheism theologically and compositeness philosophically (35). On the other hand, the negative expression of monotheism tends to turn into pantheism by identifying God and the world (40). But the essence of pure monotheism is God's uniqueness, which changes God's entire relationship with the world (35).

> [Uniqueness] gathers under its protection the concepts of being and God, but now the strict *identity* of both concepts sets in. . . . Only God has being. Only God is being. And there is no unity that would be an identity between God and world, no unity between world and being. The world is appearance. This thought already flashes its light into the future: only God is being. There is only *one* kind of being, only one unique being: God is this unique being. God is the Unique One. (41)
>
> Throughout the development of religion unity was realized as uniqueness, and this significance of the unity of God as uniqueness brought about the recognition of the uniqueness of God's being, in comparison with which all other being vanishes and becomes nothing. Only God is being. . . .
>
> The difference between Jewish religion and Greek speculation, including pantheism, consists in the designation of this being as One Who Is Being, in the transformation of the neuter into a person. (41)

Clearly Cohen is combining Jewish religion with the Western philosophical tradition concerning being. He had already affirmed that, although religion is not philosophy, "the religion of reason, by virtue of its share in reason, has at least some kinship with philosophy." Reason "begins to stir within religion . . . with its concept of God" (36). And this God brings Cohen's philosophical synthesis to a certain kind of climatic completion, though a religion of reason is not part of his *System of Philosophy* in the strict sense. Using God as a beginning Cohen unites the natural and moral worlds into a vital synthesis and evades the ontological (Christian) tradition (36; 44–45). Because God is unique and incomparable to anything else, God is the justification for the idea that the world and humanity are subject to improvement. Based on the God of reason Cohen constructs the idea of religion, an ideal religion, as such, permanently intelligible and valid and safe from the vagaries of history. From the Jewish tradition Cohen understands God as a personal other and so integrates into his rational system a relationship of the self to God. Biblical revelation understood outside the particularities of its historical context is a process of discovering reason in the broadest sense. As such it is a rational construction that leads humans to recognize that moral reason is what beings them into contact with God, the perfect being who is the generative principle of reason.[22]

The personalization of God in his philosophy of religion involves Cohen in an unceasing struggle against anthropomorphism (41–42). God is not a perceptible existent (44) nor is God actual, for "actuality is a concept relating thought to sensation" (160). In the realm of human, intentional, moral action a person loves and is motivated by, not an anthropomorphic God, but the idea of God, an ideal, holy, loving God (160). "The love of man for God is the love of the moral ideal. Only the ideal can I love, and I can grasp the ideal in no other way than by loving it. The ideal is the archetype of morality" (161). Although Cohen lives in an intellectual universe far different from the medieval Jewish mystics, he shares with them a passion for knowing God as an ultimate reality and a commitment to searching beyond the realities of everyday life for a reality that is ultimate in some sense.

2.9 Modern Orthodoxy

After the enlightenment the adherents of traditional Judaism became known as the "orthodox." They were grounded in the same belief system of God, revelation, and election of the Israelite nation as the medieval Rabbis, but their backgrounds and methods vary enough to give us a sample of the range of modern thought on the issue of God as ultimate reality. Rabbi Samson Raphael Hirsch, the intellectual father of German orthodoxy, published a volume titled "Nineteen Letters on Judaism" in 1836. In the epistle, "God and the World," Hirsch describes a God who is above history, but acts in history: "To our eye God reveals himself only in his works. Through the concept of Israel, and Israel's duty, this Torah thus leads us to the knowledge of God, the world and the missions of mankind and history."[23] Continuous with Mendelssohn's acceptance of the biblical notion of God, which is then reconciled with contemporary philosophical inquiry into ultimate realities, Hirsch holds that "Scripture is the full and absolute embodiment of the religious consciousness, and this is identical with philosophic truth."[24] Both Mendelssohn and Hirsch in their own ways hold that ultimate reality understood through rational investigation is synonymous with religious truth as taught in Torah.

Rabbi Avraham Yitzhak HaKohen Kook was the first Ashkenasic (European) Chief Rabbi of Palestine, an office he held until his death in

1935. In the last four decades of his life, Kook became the leading advocate of Zionism in religious quarters, a decidedly unpopular position in that age of political isolationism among the orthodox Rabbinical leadership. Kook took radical activist stands of dialogue and cooperation with the secular Zionist movement. He advocated this political activism as an ethical imperative to hasten the messianic redemption and, for these stands, was labeled "the devil incarnate" by more than one critic.[25] Kook's embrace of quietistic mysticism at one extreme and political activism on the other shows interesting possibilities for the implications of God's ultimate reality as it acts upon and is acted upon on the human stage of affairs. In what we might call a radically mystical posture, Rabbi Kook is "literal in his denial of the existence of a world or reality that are separate from God."[26]

2.10 Language and Method in Speaking of Ultimacy

The core Jewish tradition has stubbornly insisted on including God in human life as it constructs and communicates life. Narratives, poems, oracular prophetic communications, sayings, debates, legal discussions, parables, and so on all freely refer to God as necessary, mulling over God's ambiguities, rejoicing in God's gifts, and lamenting God's punishments. Although a rich variety of similes, metaphors, and symbols are used of God, they all revolve around God as a person who participates in human society and history and especially in Israel's life. At each step of the way and in almost all expressions of God's reality, power, activity, mercy, justice, and so on, despite the overwhelming use of anthropomorphisms, the tradition quickly and constantly insists that God is not really like humans, that God is greater, more powerful, not subject to human limitations, and in the end beyond complete human comprehension. The hundreds of explicit and implicit statements about God are none of them absolute, but rather dynamically related to one another by contrast and complementarity.

Language that would speak directly and thematically about God arose in the Middle Ages in the Islamic world. Philosophical categories from Aristotle and Plato were received from the Arab philosophers and adapted to Jewish thinking about God. At the same time a number of mystical schools arose and began to speak directly of God in highly symbolic and esoteric language derived from the biblical and Talmudic traditions, but modified greatly to open a new way to God.

The majority of Jews remained anchored in the Talmudic tradition, mediated through its medieval commentators and codifiers. People indirectly knew God through the observance of God's commandments, as a people relates to its king through hard work and good citizenship. Yet communities also knew God in prayer, daily in the synagogue, weekly in their Sabbath observance, and seasonally in the festivals that celebrated God's presence in the world and Israel's history and life, which in turn were structured by God's word and commandments in the Bible. The divine-human world of the Jerusalem Temple, destroyed in 70 CE, lived on in synagogue observances of the biblical festivals and in prayers that memorialized the sacrifices that could not longer be offered. The Rabbis studied biblical laws concerning Temple sacrifices, festivals, purity, and offerings in such minute and loving detail that the world of the Temple lived on in their minds and worldview. The historical catastrophes did not interrupt the Jewish community's relationship with the ultimate source of its life and identity.

In one way or another both philosophers and mystics treat God, the first cause, the heavenly world, complete knowledge of the universe, and so on, as ultimate realities next to which the world as we know it is "nothing" in some sense or at least of much less worth. God and ultimate knowledge of the world in all its presuppositions and implications are hidden and difficult to understand, but knowable nonetheless, under the right circumstances. As a corollary, the immediate world of life experience ultimately makes sense only through knowledge of God.

Persistent philosophical and mystical speculation endanger humans who teeter between frightened awe and enthusiastic intimacy when seeking God through reason or mystical experience. The exploration of the immanence and transcendence of God may be symbolized by the mystical heavenly journey. Nothing is farther away or more foreign to humans that heaven and its divine ruler. But when the mystic journeys to heaven and sees the palaces, angels, heavens, secrets of history, divine attributes, and so on, the change of location and experience renders the transcendent, ultimate realities immanent. The mystic, and, in a less intense sense, the philosopher, gain a certain knowledge of divine transcendence, power and ultimacy that gives a certain control of reality and even of God, through knowledge and participation. While acknowledging that all is in God's hands and next to God everything is nothing, the mystic and thinker participates in and knows God and ultimate reality.

Notes

1. Elliot N. Dorff, *Knowing God: Jewish Journeys to the Unknowable* (Northvale, N.J./London: Jason Aronson, Inc., 1992), 14.

2. Saadia Gaon, *Book of Beliefs and Opinions* (New Haven: Yale, 1948); Moses

Maimonides, *The Guide of the Perplexed*, 2 vols. (Chicago and London: University of Chicago Press, 1963).

3. David H. Aaron, *Biblical Ambiguities: Metaphor, Semantics and Problems in Biblical Interpretation*, chap. 4 (in manuscript, 1997), 61ff.

4. Sifre Deuteronomy is a commentary on parts of the biblical Book of Deuteronomy that cites mostly Rabbis from the first two centuries CE and was compiled, probably, in the third century.

5. Peter Schäfer, *The Hidden and Manifest God: Some Major Themes in Early Jewish Mysticism* (Albany: State University of New York Press, 1992), 161–62.

6. Ibid., 164–65.

7. Ibid., 148–50, 165.

8. Gershom Scholem, "Shi'ur Komah: The Mystical Shape of the Godhead," *On the Mystical Shape of the Godhead: Basic Concepts in the Kabbalah* (New York: Schocken, 1991), 17.

9. Ibid.

10. Ibid., 28. For the Shi'ur Komah, see immediately below.

11. Ibid.

12. The few hints about God's appearance and cosmic reality in the Bible were exploited by later mystical writings. Like the biblical text, rabbinic writings and mystical works thought of God as having a body. See David H. Aaron, "Shedding Light on God's Body in Rabbinic Midrashim: Reflections on the Theory of a Luminous Adam," *HTR* 90 (1997): 299–314. Although modern commentators quickly attribute descriptions of God to metaphor and figurative anthropomorphism, ancient views on God range closer to the literal than metaphoric end of the spectrum of human language.

13. Maimonides, op. cit., 1.4; cf. also 1.21.

14. Ibid., 3.51.

15. Ibid., 1.51–60.

16. Ibid., 1.52–54; 3.53.

17. Fred Rosner, ed., *The Existence and Unity of God: Three Treatises Attributed to Moses Maimonides* (Northvale and London: Aronson, 1990) gives a translation, introduction, and notes based on the edition by Georges (Judah Arieh) Vajda, "Tishah Perakim Miyuchad Hamiychasim le-Rambam," *Qobetz al Yad*, N.S 5 (1950–51): 103–37; and on his "Le Traite Pseude-Maimonidien: Neuf Chapitres sur l'Unite de Dieu," *Archives d'Histoire Doctrinale et Litteraire du Moyone Age* 28 (1953): 83–98, reprinted in *Melanges Georges Vajda . . . in Memoriam* (Hildesheim: Gerstenberg, 1982), 535–50.

18. *Nine Chapters*, op. cit., 1:7.

19. Joseph Albo, *Ikkarim*, 2:29, cited in J. Immanuel Schochet, *Mystical Concepts in Chassidism* (New York: Kehot, 1979), 21–22.

20. Gershom Scholem, *Kabbalah* (New York: New York Times Book Co., 1974), 100.

21. Herman Cohen, *Religion of Reason Out of the Sources of Judaism*, trans. Simon Kaplan; reprinted (Atlanta: Scholars Press, 1995).

22. Kenneth Seeskin, "Jewish neo-Kantianism: Hermann Cohen," *History of Jewish Philosophy*, ed. Daniel Frank, et al. (London/ New York: Routledge, 1997), 786–98 at 790.

23. Samuel Hirsch, *Nineteen Letters*, trans. Bernard Drachman (New York: Feldheim, 1969), 30.

24. Quote cited in Julius Guttman, *Philosophies of Judaism* (New York: Holt, Reinhart, Winston, 1964), 314.

25. Bezalel Naor, introduction to *Orot* (Northvale, N.J.: Jason Aaronson, Inc., 1993), 11. The attacks on Rabbi Kook are attributed to Rabbis Y. Y. Diskin and Y. H. Sonnenfeld, leaders of the Eda Hachareidis, the ultra-orthodox community of then Turkish-, later British-controlled Palestine.

26. Julius Guttman, *Philosophies of Judaism: The History of Jewish Philosophy from Biblical Times to Franz Rosenzweig*, trans. David W. Silverman (London: Routledge, 1964), 126.

3

Ultimate Reality in
Ancient Christianity

Christ and Redemption

Paula Fredriksen

∽

3.1 Introduction

In Christianity, as in Judaism, God is the ultimate reality—the absolute
foundation of everything that is, and the end toward which all points. To
grasp the conception of God that informed the religious convictions of
those first Christians whose work survives in the New Testament (NT), we
could all stop reading here and move directly over to Saldarini's essay: the
God of (non-Gnostic) Christians was the God of Abraham, Isaac, and
Jacob. Later Trinitarian and Christological theology will articulate strong
variations on this idea of deity, but its basic contours, identifiably biblical,
remain. To focus on their idea of God, then, will not move us very far
along in an investigation of what made these early generations Jews of a
peculiar sort—that is, Christians. To do that, we must attend to Christianity's characteristic, indeed foundational, ultimate reality: Jesus Christ.

I propose to ignore those NT passages so favored by the high philosophical formulations of patristic theologians, such as the Johannine Prologue or Philippians 2:5–11. The Christologies they classically supported—essences, substances, persons, and processions—only obscure

our view of the ways that "Jesus Christ" functioned as an ultimate reality for the first generations of the new movement. I propose, rather, that we attend to the ways that Jesus *appears as, is imagined as, or functions as* a blood sacrifice. I will concentrate on the earliest stratum of the NT evidence, namely, the Pauline epistles, to present a reconstruction of the way that both Paul as a Jew of the late Second Temple period, and Paul's mid–first-century formerly pagan audience would have understood the 'person and work' of Jesus Christ. I will then move from this reconstruction to see how it makes coherent the rich sacrificial imagery that we have in other, slightly later NT writings: the Gospels of Matthew and John, the Epistle to the Hebrews, the Apocalypse of John. We have to stop thinking theologically and instead think sacrificially. Purity, holiness, separation, blood, flesh, eating: these orient us in the first-century understanding of the new reality wrought in Christ.

3.2 Paul, the Gentiles, and the God of Israel

". . . in the priestly service of the gospel of God." (Romans 15:16)

Moderns tend to analyze ancient religions in terms of their ideas. Thus, ancient Judaism was monotheist, 'nationalist', and exclusive; paganism, polytheist and, while local, in principal ecumenical.[1] In terms of religiously motivated practices and behavior, however, Jews and pagans were much more alike than different. What bound them together—indeed what distinguishes all modern Western religion, *grosso modo*, from ancient—was *cult*: the offerings, blood sacrifices, and purity rules universally prescriptive of antiquity's religious etiquette.

Greek males sacrificed, usually within the *oikos*, by pouring out the animal's blood and burning the fat and bones to or for the god(s), parceling out and eating roasted viscera (liver, lungs, hearts, and kidneys), boiling and distributing other meat to a wider circle of worshipers (including, perhaps, women). The point of the act was not the animal's death, but the ritual reorganization of its body, which in turn culticly established lines of kinship and generated for these men a family relationship through the pure blood of sacrifice that women could achieve only through the impure blood of childbirth.[2] As in majority culture, sacrifice in Judaism was a male preserve. Jewish men—primarily priests but, depending on the category of the offering, also non-priests—sacrificed at the temple in Jerusalem.[3] The details of these offerings bulk large in the last four of the five books of the Torah, and they might be brought for many reasons: worship and communion with God, glorification of him, purification, atonement, thanksgiving, commemorative feasting.[4] Again, the blood would be poured out on the altar, the animal's body reorganized and distributed (some to the altar, some to the priest, some to the worshiper; though in the case of a burnt offering the altar's fire consumed the entire animal). For both Jews and Gentiles, those in proximity to the altar had to be in the correct state of purity—an objective ontological category as much if not more than a moral category.[5]

Jewish proximity to holiness was governed by another binary distinction: not only *impure/pure* but also common or *profane/holy* (Heb. *chol/kadosh*). A blemished animal, or a priest with a physical imperfection, was not suited to be brought near or minister at the altar. Such a priest may eat sacred food—that is, he can be pure—but he may not serve because, since blemished, he is common. His presence would profane the altar, not (since purity is not at issue) defile it.[6] Gentiles did not have direct access to the altar for a similar reason: "though not inherently impure, Gentiles are inherently profane,"[7] that is, common, by definition not members of the holy nation set apart by God, Israel. Paul composed the letters we have to his Gentile communities in the mid-first century—that is, well before Titus's destruction of the Jerusalem Temple. This means that Paul's (Pharisaic) religious sensibility was rooted in the ancient and prestigious cultic practices of Israel established by God as a sign of his special favor toward Israel (the *latreia/avodah* of Romans 9:4), practiced in the Temple where his *kavod* (Paul's *doxa*, again 9:4) uniquely dwelled. It is an obvious point, but it bears considering, as does another: when he wrote, the movement for which he served as apostle was itself within Judaism: the God his Gentiles were now to worship was the God of Israel. A third point: Paul's position—that Gentiles do not have to become Jews in order to participate in Israel's salvation—is itself traditional, to be found at least as early as some passages in the classical prophets, and as late as a century or so later in other Jewish apocalyptic texts and (less exotically) in synagogue prayers.[8] Taking all this together, then, we may proceed to our main question: How, in Paul's mind, does Christ as blood sacrifice effect Gentile redemption and, indeed, the redemption of the world?

"The transference of the language of sanctuary and sacrifice to Christian life is central to Paul."[9] But how does this transference work, and what does it tell us about Paul's Christology? He easily uses the forms of *latreuo*, the word for cultic service (cf., *latreia* above) to characterize the piety of the community: "We are the true circumcision who *worship* by the spirit of God" (*hoi pneumati theou latreuontes,* Philippians 3:3). His Gentiles now serve "the living and true God" (1 Thessalonians 1:9); through Christ's sacrifice, they have been swept up into the redemptive drama of Israel, itself in its final stages. Paul presents Christ as a blood sacrifice at a number of points in his letters, but he neither coordinates these usages nor particularly explains them.

3.2.1   1 Corinthians 5:7: Christ as Paschal Sacrifice

"Your boasting is not good. Do you not know that a little leaven leavens the whole lump? Cleanse out the old leaven, that you may be a new lump, as you really are unleavened. *For Christ our* pascha *has been sacrificed.* Let us therefore celebrate the festival, not with the old leaven of malice and evil, but with the unleavened bread of sincerity and truth."

3.2.2   2 Corinthians 5:21: Christ as Sin Sacrifice

"We beseech on behalf of Christ, be reconciled with God. *For our sake he made him* hamartia *who knew no sin,* so that we might become the righteousness of God in him."

3.2.3   Romans 3:24: Christ as Atonement Sacrifice

"Since all have sinned and fall short of the glory of God, they are justified by his grace as a gift, through the redemption which is in *Christ Jesus, whom God put forward as a* hilastērion *through faith by his blood.*"

If, as I suggested above, Paul's sacrifice-language must be understood within the context of Temple and Torah, we must note that his usages here seem impressionistic and certainly unsystematic. The reference to the *pascha* in 1 Corinthians 5:7, for example, upon examination, turns out to be less a Christological image than a very Jewish way of keeping time. The immediate point of this passage is Paul's exhorting the (Gentile) Corinthians in the *ekklesia* to seemly behavior (cf. their boasting, in chap. 4, and misplaced arrogance, v. 2 above). He then moves into a sustained metaphor combining morality and preparations for Pesach. "Leaven" obviously stands in for pride (which "puffs up"). Christ as paschal sacrifice then comes in as a way of warning the Corinthians that it's too late in the day to persist in acts *of porneia.* In the language of Paul's metaphor, it's already 14 Nisan and there's still *chometz* in the house—a thought that would probably panic a trained Pharisee more than this audience. Compared to the analogies between Christ and the paschal lamb drawn in the passion narrative at John 19:36, Paul hardly exploits his Christological possibilities here at all.

Comparison with other NT writings—the operative metaphors in Hebrews or Revelation with Christ as blood sacrifice; or John's offensive
teasing in chapter 6 about eating Christ's flesh, or even in chapter 2 with
Christ's body compared specifically with the Temple—underscores how
foggy Paul's use of blood sacrifice language for Christ really is. Examples
2 and 3 above, for example, lose their clarity once considered in light of
the practicalities of Levitical sacrifice. *Hilastērion* may mean "atonement," but it might also mean "act of reconciliation," Stanley Stowers
has recently noted, having nothing to do with sacrifice. He also observes
that ancient Mediterranean sacrificing cultures, Jewish and Greek, attached no special significance to the death of the animal itself. "The sacrifice was the ritual use—disorganization and reorganization—*of* the
animal's body that took place after the killing." Sacrifice is not about
death, "whereas Paul's reference in Romans 3 is precisely on the significance of Christ's death."[10]

So too with *hamartia* at 2 Corinthians 5:21. The Hebrew *hattat* behind the Septuagint's (LXX) translation would mean a sin offering (cf. 1
Corinthians 15:3: Christ died "for our sins"). But such sacrifices cleanse
the place (and *sancta*), not the person. Blood offerings purge the Temple,
or its altar: they do not cleanse the sinner.[11] The closest analogy to the
way Paul seems to imagine the dynamics of cleansing here is the scapegoat, offered at Yom Kippur, who bears away the sins of the community.
But Paul nowhere avails himself of this image, and besides—a nod to his
eucharistic instruction—you don't eat scapegoats.

Unpacking Paul's language of sanctuary and sacrifice does not get us
very far in terms of his Christology: an image of Christ as a particular
sort of sacrifice never emerges. But given that Christ's ultimate importance for Paul is the way that he integrates Gentiles into the redemptive
drama of Israel, we might get further in our investigation by attending
to the way Paul speaks about these Gentiles. The Thessalonians, for example, having once worshiped idols, now turn and serve "the living and
true God" (1 Thessalonians 1:9). This results in their *hagiasmos,* rendered in the RSV, via the Latin, as "sanctification." Accordingly they
must now abstain from morally polluting acts such as *porneia;* each
should use his wife or his own body *(skeuos)* "in *hagiasmo* and honor,
not in the passion of lust like the Gentiles who do not know God." For
these Gentiles who, through the gospel, do know God have been called
"not for impurity" *(akatharsia,* the moral consequence of fornication
and idolatry) but "in holiness" *(hagiasmos;* 4:4,8). Elsewhere, he addresses such Gentiles simply as "holy," *hagioi* (Romans 1:7, RSV
"saints"; 1 Corinthians 1:2). They have been made holy in Christ (1
Corinthians 1:2).

Paul exhorts his Gentiles to non-Gentile behavior by asking, "Do you not know that you are God's Temple, and God's spirit dwells in you? . . . For God's Temple is *hagios*, and you are" (1 Corinthians 3:16). "Your body is a temple of the holy spirit"—like the one in Jerusalem (6:19; cf. Matthew 23:2). "We are the Temple of the living God," (2 Corinthians 6:16). His Gentiles are also sacrifices (*thusia*) to that God, "holy and acceptable" (Romans 12:1). Through baptism, God's spirit has incorporated them, somehow, into the eschatological, sacrificed, and resurrected body of Christ: false gods, hostile astral powers, and Sin itself no longer have power over them (1 Corinthians 12:12–13, 27; Galatians 3:28, 4:3–9; cf. Romans 6:11). Thanks to Christ, through his death, by the Spirit, in baptism, they have been set apart.

To be "set apart" for God is, of course, the biblical understanding of "made holy." If we understand Paul's language of separation and sanctification in terms of the biblically based binary terms governing proximity to holiness, we can begin to make sense of his vision of Gentile redemption in Christ. For the Gentile's proximity to holiness is what Christ, through his death and resurrection, has accomplished. "In Christ," these Gentiles have eschewed their former morally polluting acts, with respect to which they are now "clean." *But the operative term, the one that signals their eschatological change of status, is hagiasmos*, holiness: they now—through his spirit, miraculously—are set apart for and by God. To hear this (as we do through the Latinized English of our translations) as "sanctification" has us facing off toward a sacramental, ecclesiastical future that Paul did not know would exist. Understood within the context of Paul's religion, however—pharisaically oriented late Second Temple Judaism—the term means simply that, through Christ, in the Spirit, *these Gentiles are no longer common or profane (chol) but holy (kadosh), and thus suitable to be brought close to Holiness.*

Understanding how Paul constructs the ultimate reality of Christ and of Gentile redemption within this Levitical matrix in turn opens up his understanding of his mission, what he felt himself called to, the ultimate (and existential) reality of his apostolate, especially as he prepares to go to Jerusalem: *to einai me leitourgon Christou Iesou eis ta ethne hierourgounta to euangelion tou Theou hina genetai he prophora ton ethnon euprosdektos hagiasmene en pneumati hagio;* "to be a [Temple] servant of Christ Jesus to the nations, sacrificing the Gospel of God, so that the offering of the Gentiles may be acceptable, made holy by the holy spirit" (Romans 15:16).

A caveat about translation. Just as the RSV obscures Paul's Temple language at Romans 9:4, where *doxa* becomes "glory" (Lat. *gloria)* and *latreia* becomes "worship" (Lat. *obsequium),* so here with *leitourgos* as "minister" and *hierourgeo* as "priestly service."[12] Behind Paul's *doxa* stands the Hebrew *kavod,* God's glorious presence that dwells on earth in the Temple in Jerusalem—Paul's named destination in this closing chapter. *Kavod* evokes the *Shekinah.* Similarly, *latreia* in Paul's native context recalls *avodah:* the cult revealed by God through Moses on Sinai to Israel, and preserved before God's presence at his altar in Jerusalem. "Worship" is too bloodless a translation.

If Temple and Torah stand behind Romans 9, so too Romans 15. "Minister" seems fair for the Latin *minister,* but given the inevitable interposition of the Reformation between Paul's day and ours, its ancient meaning specifically of "a priest's attendant" (Lewis and Short), and thus its specific association with the Jerusalem altar, disappear.[13] And while "priestly service" fits *hierourgounta,* the Latin *sanctificans* inevitably conjures sacrament. Paul's "priestly service" means cult: when Paul says *hieros* here, he's thinking *cohen.*

In brief, Paul draws deeply on the wellsprings of his religious tradition—Genesis, Exodus, Leviticus, Numbers, Deuteronomy; the ultimate reality of Torah—to articulate his convictions concerning the newly revealed ultimate reality of the Gentile's redemption in Christ. Hence too the catena of prophetic quotations *(nevi'im,* the next canonical layer after Torah in Tanak) with which Paul closes Romans, praising God for his gracious inclusion of the Gentiles in Israel's worship. The Gentiles' moral and spiritual transformation articulated and evinced the miraculous change in their status vis-à-vis the Temple—thus God—from common to holy.[14] It confirmed Paul's religious convictions *as a Jew* that in the death and resurrection of Jesus, God had begun the final transformation of the world, as he had promised Israel so long ago. "For I tell you that Christ became a servant to the circumcised to show God's truthfulness, in order to confirm the promises given to the patriarchs, and so that the Gentiles might glorify God for his mercy" (15:8–9).

Paul's use of these biblical images can be confusing if we look for some kind of system. He has none. He's improvising, playing stunning variations from the scriptural sheet music. All the images spill, merge, and mix messily with each other. The Gentiles are the offering and they send their offering too. They have been made both pure and holy. They are God's Temple and so may come near it. Christ is some kind of blood sacrifice, but no single biblical paradigm controls the metaphor. His death empowers the Gentiles to break free of the cosmic forces that encourage their moral impurity; the spirit sets them apart, in holiness, for God.

One last observation: familiarity with biblical imagery aside, Paul's language of purity and sacrifice—not the Levitical details, but the principles of purity, sacrifice, and eating—would have intrinsically made sense to his Gentile audience because of their own embeddedness in their own ancient Mediterranean sacrifice culture. And Paul presents the Eucharist—"flesh" and "blood" of the sacrificial meal—as controlled by altar etiquette (1 Corinthians 10:14–21; cf. 11:23–30, on the consequences of participating in the sacrifice and meal when unfit). Finally, Paul's use of meat language for the Eucharist speaks to his effort to upgrade this meatless, bread-centered meal within its pagan context, where such were the meals of females, and meat meals the singular preserve of men and method of binding together the household (*oikos*) in social birth.

3.3 Christ as Blood Sacrifice in Later NT Writings

"Behold the Lamb of God." (John 1:29)

All the other writings in the NT collection are composed after the year 70, thus after the destruction of the Temple. Whether as Christian Jews (Matthew, John, and arguably the authors of Hebrews and Revelation) or Christian Gentiles (again, the author of Hebrews and Revelation),[15] these authors had to make sense of Judaism without a Temple, and thus without cult—the burden, again, of much of God's instruction in four of the five books of Torah. As the chapter on Judaism in this volume reminds us, traditional narratives, laws, prophecies, revelation, history itself are "ultimate realities" alongside—or as acts of—the ultimate Ultimate Reality, God. In these changed circumstances, then, without the Temple, we see how these authors begin to fill the void left by Rome by using Temple language and sacrificial imagery specifically to define and describe Christ, the Reality to whom they and their communities appeal in making their claim to be the sole legitimate interpreters of the revelation to Israel.

Two significant differences between these later writers' use of sacrificial imagery for Christ and Paul's are the dropping away of purity and holiness language, and the way that they regard the (now no-longer standing) Temple. Both points are related. For Matthew and John, Christ's death serves as a metonymy for the Temple's destruction—explicitly in John 2:19–21; narratively in Matthew 24 and at 27:51, when the Temple's curtain tears in two.[16] For the author of Hebrews, the earthly Temple is relativized by the existence of the heavenly, eternal Temple, the one in which Jesus himself perpetually serves both as perfect high priest and as perfect blood sacrifice (Hebrews 9:11–12). For these writers, absent the earthly Temple, God's holiness is no longer localized, so purity and holiness as cultic terms no longer matter: they continue to be used, but only as moral metaphors. The author of Revelation goes yet a step further: Christ is Sacrifice (the Lamb); but when he returns and the heavenly Jerusalem descends, it comes without any Temple, "for its temple is the Lord God Almighty and the Lamb" (Revelation 21:22).

All these authors understand Christ's crucifixion specifically as a blood sacrifice. Matthew's Christ at the last supper presents the bread and wine as his own body and blood, to be eaten. This effects "forgiveness" (26:28 thus, a sin offering; cf. 20:28, a ransom). An implication of Hebrew's image of Christ as high priest and sacrifice might be the Yom Kippur offering of a goat (cf. 9:12); in any case, the author is explicit on the mediating role of priesthood and blood offerings ("For every high priest chosen from among men is appointed to act on behalf of men in relation to God, to offer gifts and sacrifices for sins," 5:1). The author of Revelation consistently presents Christ as "the Lamb," specifically on Mount Zion (14:1); a slain lamb who "by [your] blood did ransom men for God" (6:1, 9); his sacrifice enabled his followers to serve as priests (hence their white robes) before God's throne "and within his Temple" (7:13–15).

If any one thing categorizes the Johannine images for Christ, it is their bewildering variety: Christ appears as God's Word, Lamb, Son, True Vine, Eternal Water, Bread of Life, Bread from Heaven, the Sheepgate, the Light of the world. Nonetheless, John's two clearly developed references to Christ, his body, the Temple, and Passover are foregrounded by their rhetorically important position in his narrative: at the beginning of the mission, on the Temple Mount in Jerusalem (2:13–22); at the end, again in Jerusalem, on the cross (19:14, 31–33). This particular sacrificial image—tied in via 6:47–58 specifically with eating bread/flesh and drinking wine/blood, and with resurrection/lifting up—thus forms a sort of dramatic inclusio bracketing John's story. John knows his LXX. His blackly humorous emphasis on eating Christ's flesh to have eternal life (which makes the narrative audience and even some of the disciples too queasy to stay on, v. 60) recalls the corban Pesach, which commandment is fulfilled explicitly by eating (Exodus 12:7 on its blood, which saves from death; v. 9ff: "They shall eat the flesh . . . and you shall let none of it remain until the morning . . . you shall eat it"; Deuteronomy 16:7, "and you shall boil it and eat it").

It's a good analogy. The person offering does not get to eat the sin sacrifice, and nobody eats the Yom Kippur sacrifice. Everyone must eat the Pesach sacrifice. Perhaps it was John's development of this theme that led him to shift the narrative chronology of the Passion, moving it back one day from Mark's, wherein Jesus dies the night of the Passover meal. Here,

Jesus dies on the day and at the time when, in the Temple courts, the Passover lambs were still being slaughtered. And, in case anybody missed the point, John alone emphasizes that the Romans did not break Jesus' legs (19:32–33), thus preserving his status as a kosher offering (cf., Exodus 12:46, "you shall not break a bone of it"). Exodus might have redeemed from Egypt; but this Passover offering brings eternal life and redemption from the darkness of the lower cosmos.

3.4 Ultimate Realities

True to its Jewish matrix, earliest Christianity focuses on Torah, Temple, offerings, and community as it speaks of the ways that God works redemption in history. Metaphysics will come to dominate the Christian understanding of biblical revelation, and the revelation of Christ, only centuries after the period we have studied here. The fundamental—or ultimate—emphasis early on is social: eating a sacrifice together binds and creates community with others and with God.

At this stratum, then, there is little to be said of intellectual models of apprehending ultimate reality (cf. Eckel's remarks on Buddhism and rational cognition). God as Ultimate Reality will be parsed, in the patristic period, with the same commitment to intellectual elegance and clarity as we find in Vedānta Deśika's *Īśvarapariccheda,* when the texts we have looked at will provide a hermeneutical point of departure for theological speculations. But the earliest Christian communities whether Jewish or Gentile were evidently comfortable with intellectual messiness—something, perhaps, that we should expect of any new religious (and thus social) movement in its radioactive first phase.

In its insistent concreteness, the Chinese sensibility on these issues is perhaps truest to the tone of our authors. And its construction of Reality (*shi*) as "solid, substantial, hard, authentic, real" (see 1.1.2) stands in sharp contrast to the platonizing intellectual tradition—where nonempirical is precisely more "real"—which, blended with biblical narrative, defines Christianity in its classical phase. The experience of Ultimacy in Paul's communities, brought about by the shared sacrifice meal of the Eucharist, produces concrete effects, both spontaneous (the disruptive charismata of glossolalia and prophecy) and ordered (correct moral behavior toward others and in oneself): as Kohn points out, "Reality, if it is to be real at all, has to be part of experience" (1.1.2).

But the early Christian cosmos is much less stable than the Chinese, thanks to its eschatology. The cosmos stands on the brink of a huge transformation, imagined historically: even the astral stoicheia, the elements of the universe, are being affected by Christ's resurrection and will be defeated or transformed at his (imminent) return (Galatians 4). So too will be the bodies of those in the community, their flesh changed from "physical" to "spiritual" in keeping with the new order (1 Corinthians 15, passim). Thus while following the Dao leads to harmonious realization of cosmic order in the self, following "the Way" does not, because the cosmos is damaged, disrupted, subject to futility, and groaning while it awaits transformation (Romans 8). And nothing like the sage's realization of the ultimate occurs, or has time to occur, in paleo-Christianity's social world: the spirit of God, accessed through ritual acts like immersion and eating, is a disruptive, kinetic jolt presaging the Kingdom to come.

Christ as blood sacrifice, ekklesia as sacrifice-created community, sickness and death as the consequence of approaching the sacrifice in the wrong state ("this is why many of you are weak and ill, and some have died" 1 Corinthians 11:30)—all point to the non-abstract, concrete, intrinsically social way that earliest Christians imagined both Christ and salvation. It is this mode of imagining the Ultimate that marks earliest Christianity as the ancient Mediterranean religion it was, and marks off the point from which it will grow from a sect within Judaism into the separate religion and culture—neither Jew nor Greek—that it will later become.

Notes

1. Hence Nock's distinction between 'adherence' and 'conversion'. See Arthur Darby Nock, *Conversion: The Old and the New in Religion from Alexander the Great to Augustine of Hippo* (London: Oxford University Press, 1933).

2. My very condensed characterization rests on Stanley Stowers, "Greeks Who Sacrifice and Those Who Do Not," *The Social World of the First Christians: Essays in Honor of Wayne A. Meeks*, ed. L. Michael White and O. Larry Yarbrough (Minneapolis: Fortress, 1995), 293–333. See also (for Jewish biblical sacrifices as well) Nancy Jay, *Throughout Your Generations Forever: Sacrifice, Religion, and Paternity* (Chicago: University of Chicago Press, 1992).

3. In principle, such sacrifice was restricted to Jerusalem. In fact, we know from Josephus of at least one other temple, built by dissenting Zadokite priests during the turmoil of the early Hasmonean period, in Leontopolis in Egypt; and Philo states that Jews in the diaspora sacrificed the paschal lamb where they were.

4. Most recent complete study: E. P. Sanders, *Judaism: Practice and Belief 63 BCE–66 CE* (Philadelphia: Trinity Press International, 1992), esp. chap. 7.

5. Semen defiles, according to Leviticus and Numbers, not because sexual activity (always understood: between married partners) was sinful, but because semen was specifically one of the polluting genital effluvia. With some pagan cults, the two categories, ontological and moral, evidently were sometimes

mixed: "In many pagan cults, rules of sexual purity governed entry into a temple and sometimes participation in worship. Generally they excluded people who had recently had sex or specifically committed adultery, but the exclusion was usually brief. Before sleeping in Pergamum's great shrine of Asclepius, clients were expected to have abstained from sex for two days; elsewhere, one day, or a quick wash, sufficed. . . . The rules for a public cult in Pergamum demanded a day's interval after sex with one's wife, two days' after sex with someone else's." Robin Lane Fox, *Pagans and Christians* (London: Harmondsworth, 1986), 347.

On moral impurity as a distinct category within Judaism, see Jonathan Klawans, "Gentile Impurity in Ancient Judaism," *Association for Jewish Studies Review* 20.2 (1995): 285–312, esp. 290ff.

6. I rely here esp. on Klawans, ibid. On the blemished priest, e.g., see Lev 21:18.

7. Ibid., 292.

8. For the full argument, see P. Fredriksen, "Judaism, the Circumcision of Gentiles, and Apocalyptic Hope: Another Look at Galatians 1 and 2," *Journal of Theological Studies* 42 (1991): 532–64.

9. William Horbury, "Land, Sanctuary and Worship," *Early Christian Thought in its Jewish Context* (New York: Cambridge University Press, 1996), 207–24, at 219.

10. For Stower's entire argument on construing *hilastērion,* see *A Rereading of Romans* (New Haven: Yale University Press, 1994), 206–13. The quotation is from p. 207, with specific reference to the work of Jacob Milgrom.

11. For a review of the biblical evidence, see Jacob Neusner, *The Idea of Purity in Ancient Judaism* (Leiden: E. J. Brill, 1973). On Levitical impurities, J. Milgrom's *Leviticus 1–16 A New Translation with Introduction and Commentary* (New York: Doubleday, 1991). Mary Douglas, in *Purity and Danger* (London: Routledge and Kegan Paul, 1966), and her more recent "In the Wilderness: The Doctrine of Defilement in the Book of Numbers," *Religion* 26 (1996): 69–89, offers a cultural-anthropological analysis of the ancient Israelite purity system.

12. Lexicographical information from Charlton T. Lewis and Charles Short, *A Latin Dictionary Founded on Andrews' Edition of Freund's Latin Dictionary* (Oxford: Clarendon Press, 1969); Henry George Liddell and Robert Scott, *A Greek-English Lexicon* (Oxford: Clarendon Press; New York: Oxford University Press, 1996); and William F. Arndt and F. Wilbur Gingrich, *A Greek-English lexicon of the New Testament and Other Early Christian Literature: A Translation and Adaptation of the Fourth Revised and Augmented Edition of Walter Bauer's Griechisch-deutsches Wörterbuch zu den Schriften des Neuen Testaments und der übrigen urchristlichen Literatur* (Chicago: University of Chicago Press, 1957).

13. Cf. the LXX's use of *leitourgia* at Num 8:25 for the performance of service in the Tabernacle; cf. 4:32 LXX.

14. This might be one reason to take seriously the accusation related (and disavowed) in Acts 21:28, where Paul is accused of "bringing Greeks into the Temple."

15. I incline to think that both were Jews, because of their deep familiarity with biblical texts, which were not commonly available outside of synagogue communities. This same fact accounts for Paul's unselfconscious usage of biblical texts, tropes, and figures for his Gentiles: they too must have frequented the synagogue (and probably continued to), or they would have had no prayer of understanding him.

16. This is a theme that Matthew picks up from his narrative source, Mark. For the full argument, see Fredriksen, *From Jesus to Christ* (New Haven: Yale University Press, 1988).

4

Ultimate Reality

Islam

S. Nomanul Haq

∽

4.1 Categories of Ultimacy

I shall construct my exposition in the framework of the analytical taxonomy proposed by Livia Kohn and James Miller in their chapter on ultimate reality in Chinese religion.[1] The variety of modes in which "religious virtuosi" in different cultures speak about ultimate reality, they
observe, can be classified under three categories: philosophical, practical, and mythical. To be sure, we have here a set of very useful comparative analytical tools. In the particular case of Islam, the first category,
the philosophical, would essentially subsume all the feverish *Kalām*[2]
discourses and polemical debates on ultimate reality—an issue that
Muslim theologians reduced to the question of the nature of God and
Godhead: God's essence and His attributes. There exists a fairly massive corpus of Islamic theological literature on this problem, and to this
corpus practically all *mutakallimūn* including the *"Ḥujjat al-Islam"*
(Proof of Islam) Abū Ḥāmid al-Ghazālī (d. 1111) have made substantial
contributions.

Under the category of the practical, Kohn and Miller speak of the experiential dimension of ultimacy: mystical exercises and techniques
aimed at experiencing ultimate reality.[3] It should be noted, however, that

interest in the phenomenon of what is called Islamic mysticism, namely Sufism, lies not so much in actual sufi practices; it lies rather in sufi doctrines and sufi metaphysics, in the *theory* of gnostic experience (*ma'rifa*) rather than the means and modes of attaining it. Indeed, sufi speculative thought has generated a powerful set of religious ideas, yielding a massive legacy of rather "innovative"[4] interpretations of revelationary and prophetic data; and all this has frequently clashed with standard traditional approaches and "orthodoxies." It is particularly important to note that an explicit identification of God with ultimate reality—that is, Reality (*Ḥaqīqa*) and with existence-as-such—that is, Being (*Huwa Huwa*)—this identification is the fundamental thrust of many a sufi theosophy, something that has in many cases provoked even the dark suspicion of pantheism.

Finally, the third category identified comprehends the picturesque accounts of ultimate reality that constitute its "mythic" descriptions offered by prophets, saints, and visionaries: more specifically, the fables, anecdotes, metaphors, images, tales, the visions of glory and splendor, in terms of which apostles convey to the masses their message concerning ultimacy. In the case of Islam, this would be revelationary data—namely, the Qur'ān speaking about ultimate reality. Note particularly that this "mythical" category is fundamentally different from the other two: the Qur'ān is an altogether different literary genre; it is functionally different; its scope is (Islamically) universal; and it is elevated to the highest status of the final arbiter of all else.

Before elaboration, let us briefly pause over all this. *Prima facie*, it already seems evident that here the Islamic case stands in sharp contrast to what we learned concerning Buddhism and Chinese religion; and that, not surprisingly, it has both inherent and historical family resemblance with certain rationalizing religious trends in Judaism whose medieval philosophical thinking had come under Islamic influence. Thus it appears that in Islam ultimate reality is conceived not as some dialectic process but, indeed, as something stable, fixed, and objectively "out there"—ultimate reality was the deity itself with all its standard Abrahamic divine attributes, including eternity and transcendence. Nor is ultimate reality the order of the cosmos or its realization in human experience; nor, still, is it "a vaguely sensed but unreal [!] ultimate that is turned into reality."[5]

On the other hand, there do exist certain modes of thought in Islam that render these characterizations somewhat problematic. How does one explain, for example, the Qur'ānic declaration that "Allah is the light of the heavens and the earth" (24: 35), or that "Whithersoever ye turn there is the face of God" (2: 115), or that "God's throne envelopes the heavens and the earth" (2: 255). To be sure, as we shall see, the master theosophist Ibn 'Arabī (d.1240) considered the cosmos to be a succession of manifestations of being, divine manifestations flowing from within an originally undifferentiated God; it was a succession of theophanies (*tajalliyāt*) brought about by a "Compassionate Divine Breath" (*Nafas Raḥmānī*).[6] In the well-known work the *Fuṣūṣ al-Ḥikam* (*Bezels of Wisdom*), Ibn 'Arabī goes so far as to identify the Compassionate Breath with nature itself. The metaphysical implications of all this are far-reaching. If the cosmic order is *substantially* a manifestation of God, as Ibn 'Arabī expressly says, and if God is the ultimate reality, as he would admit, then the cosmic order is *substantially* a manifestation of ultimate reality; and, furthermore, given the premises, to know the world is to know the Lord: this too is stated expressly in the *Fuṣūṣ*.[7] Does Islam thence stand parallel to Buddhism and Chinese religion?

There is still no easy answer to this question, since the Islamic attitude to nature and cosmic order has throughout history remained fundamentally different from the Eastern traditions, and this is a crucial point. Once again: a decisive feature of Islamic thinking—whether philosophical, theological, legal, or mystical—is that it can never afford to compromise its radical monotheism, the principle of *tauḥīd;* that is, in the end, the God-cosmos/Creator-created duality must be maintained at all costs. Thus, even Ibn 'Arabī despite his notorious *waḥdat al-wujūd* (uniqueness of existence/oneness of being/ontological monism) doctrine, would save himself from slipping totally into pantheism even though he stands dangerously at its very threshold. Divine Names (Compassionate, Kind, Living, First, Last, Light of the heavens and earth, etc.) were the divine Essence itself since the attributes they designate are not different from it, says Ibn 'Arabī: yet they were *not* identical with the divine Essence.[8] Then, though cosmic order constituted reality, it was not the ultimate reality: God Himself was the ultimate reality.

But, let us proceed. The word that denotes reality in Islamic discourses is "*ḥaqīqa*," a word that in the strict philological sense means the intelligible nucleus of the thing existing, or the transcendental truth of that which exists. Explicating his ontological meaning of the word (*ḥaqīqat al-shay'*), the philosopher Avicenna (d. 1037) says that "everything has a *ḥaqīqa* through which it is what it is . . . by that, we have not meant to signify concrete (*ithbāti*) existence"[9] and: "The *ḥaqīqa* is the property of being, requisite for each thing."[10] Thus, we learn from Gardet that "*ḥaqīqa* must . . . be understood not as the thing existing, but as the essence of the thing inasmuch as it exists in its absolute intelligibility."[11] Avicenna also provides a logical meaning (*al-ḥaqīqat al-'aqliyya*): *ḥaqīqa* is the truth that "the exact conception of the thing" establishes in

the intelligence.[12] Clearly, then, *ḥaqīqa* denotes something strictly conceptual; for the philosopher it was an analytical category, the word that
designated reality denotes nothing that is ontologically real!

But Avicenna is much too Hellenistic (better: much too Aristotelian)
for the taste of Islamic thinking at large. We note that the word *ḥaqīqa*
does not occur in the Qur'ān, but *ḥaqq* (the "real," the "true"), which
comes from the same root, does, and numerous times (6:62; 31:30;
20:114; 22:6; 22:62; 24:25 actually refer to God as *al-Ḥaqq*). Indeed,
this Qur'ānic word with the definite article—*al-Ḥaqq*—was a divine
Name most frequently denoting God in sufi usage.[13] What is the difference between *ḥaqīqa* and *ḥaqq*? They can be differentiated as the abstract and the concrete—reality and real, Deity and God. This is borne
out by al-Ḥallāj who says: "The *ḥaqīqa* (essential reality) of a thing is *on
this side* of the *ḥaqq* (real)"[14] and, given this, "everything real [*ḥaqq*], affirms Ḥallāj, has its essential reality [*ḥaqīqa*]."[15] We would be perfectly
justified here in translating *al-ḥaqīqa* as "ultimate reality." The sufi al-
Sulamī (d. 1021) practically conflates the two:

> The Names of God? From the point of view of our comprehension they are
> one single (Name); from the point of view of the Real (*al-Ḥaqq* = God),
> they are Reality (*al-Ḥaqīqa*).[16]

This is not very different from Ibn ʿArabī's doctrine, for we are told
that divine Names *are* Reality; but are divine Names identical with the
Real?—in other words, are *al-Ḥaqīqa* and *al-Ḥaqq* substantially identical? Sulamī cannot afford to answer in the affirmative, for that would
amount to pantheism, so he constructs two contexts: that of ours, the
context of the created; and that of God, the context of the Creator. For
us, then, *tauḥīd* is maintained: "The Names of God . . . are one single
(Name)"! It is in this perspective that we should view the position of Ibn
ʿArabī and his followers, namely, that *al-ḥaqīqa* is the ultimate reality of
the real itself in the uniqueness of being of all existence (*waḥdat al-
wujūd*). All this is a far cry from Avicenna.

4.2 Revelationary Data

What does the Qur'ān say about ultimate reality? Does it speak about ultimate reality at all? We know that the word that denotes ultimate reality,
al-ḥaqīqa, does not occur in the Qur'ān. But on several occasions God is
called *al-Ḥaqq*, the Real:

Then they are restored to God their Protector, the Real (al-Ḥaqq). Surely His is the command and He is the swiftest in taking account. (6:62)

High above all is Allah, the King, the Real (al-Ḥaqq). Be not in haste with the Qur'ān before its revelation to thee is completed, but say: O my Lord! advance me in knowledge. (20:114)

This is so because Allah is the Real (al-Ḥaqq): it is He Who gives life to the dead, and it is He who has power over all things. (22:6)

This is so because He is al-Ḥaqq; and those beside Him whom they invoke—they are but vain Falsehood (bāṭil). Verily Allah is He, Most High, Most Great. (22:62)

On that day Allah will pay them back (all) their just dues, and they will realize that Allah is al-Ḥaqq, that makes all things manifest. (24:25)

The tone and context of all these verses make it perfectly clear that here the Qur'ānic aim is moral guidance, not to develop a rational discourse of an ontological kind about al-Ḥaqq and His (Its) nature. God's existence for the Qur'ān is strictly functional: He is the Creator of the universe and of humanity and He is their Sustainer; in particular, He is the giver of guidance, and He judges human beings both individually and collectively, and metes out merciful justice.[17]

On the other hand, there do exist plentiful Qur'ānic grounds for all the standard metaphysical doctrines concerning existence, essence, reality, and ultimate reality that developed in subsequent Islamic tradition. One of the insistent themes of the Qur'ān, for example, is the cosmic order's contingency upon God: everything except Allah is *contingent* upon Allah; and this establishes the absolute centrality of God in the entire system of existence. The cosmic order is, so it appears from the Qur'ān, a fully integrated system in which every created entity—that is, all-other-than-God—takes its assigned place in the larger whole according to its *amr* (divine command); the cosmic order had its own autonomous laws (again: *amr*, pl. *awāmir*), and, indeed, it embodied God's signs (*āya*, pl. *āyāt*; 2:164; 3:190; 6:95–99; 36:37–40; etc.). But then, the cosmos had no warrant for its own existence and it could not explain itself; and, as Ibn Ḥazm (d. 1064) explicates, actions of things are not created by the things themselves: their creation is due to something transcending the things in which they appear.[18] In other words, the cosmic order has *no* rational, moral, or ontological ultimacy:

And who other than He created the heavens and the earth and sent down for you water from the sky, whereby We cause to grow lush orchards—for it is not up to you to cause their trees to grow! Is there, then, a god beside God?. . .

And who other than He made the earth a firm abode [for you], and set rivers traversing through it, and put firm mountains therein and sealed off one sea from another? Is there, then, a god beside God? . . .

And who other than He responds to the distressed one when he calls Him and He relieves him of the distress and who had made you His vicegerent on earth? Is there, then, a god beside God? . . .

And who other than He guides you in the darkness of the land and the sea? And who sends forth winds heralding His mercy [rain]? Is there, then, a god beside God? . . .

And who other than He brings forth His creation and then re-creates it? And who gives you sustenance from the heaven and the earth? Is there, then, a god beside God? . . . (27:60–64)

In the Qur'ānic environment, then, it seems perfectly legitimate to consider God as the ultimate reality. And the case is stronger: for in the Qur'ān God is also called *al-Muḥīṭ*, all-enveloping, all-encompassing, literally infinite, and He *alone* is infinite. "God is that dimension that makes other dimensions possible."[19] Again and again: "Allah alone [is God], there is no God but He—the Alive, the Sustainer. . . . Upon Him is contingent whatever is in the heavens and on the earth. . . . He knows what is before them and what is behind them, while they encompass none of His knowledge. . . . His Throne envelopes the heavens and the earth . . . He is the High, the Great." (2:255) Further: "Everything in the cosmos [literally, on the earth] is vanishing, there remaining only the Face of your Lord, the Possessor of Majesty and Generosity" (55:26–27). In revelationary terms, God was the very meaning of reality.[20]

4.3 Divine Names and Epithets

It should be noted that the Qur'ān does not take into account the nature of God in the abstract; Allah was an overwhelming personality, and to Him belonged "Beautiful Names" (*al-Asmā' al-Ḥusna*; 7:180; 17:110; 20:7; 59:24) whose number the Islamic tradition quickly fixed at ninety-nine. But what are the Qur'ānic epithets describing God? Following Macdonald, we can identify three classes of descriptions. Allah in and by Himself; Allah in relation to the cosmos; and Allah in relation to humankind. Note that not all of these descriptions, in their nominal forms, came to be included in the ninety-nine Names.[21]

A glance at these epithets makes their theological and metaphysical challenges readily obvious. To begin with, as we have noted, the Qur'ān perpetually suggests the utter dependence of everything on God, and the essential non-existence of everything except Him. In fact, the absolute existence of God is spoken about with such compelling intensity that the later pantheistic tendencies of Muslim mystics are amply conditioned and explained.[22] Then, on the one hand, the Qur'ān's description of God is that of a transcendental Being that is the only reality, governing over, but totally separate from, the world; yet, on the other hand, it depicts picturesquely God's intense personality and His direct working in the world—that is, His immanence. Here, the Qur'ān speaks of God's face, eyes, and hands; there, it declares that "Nought is there like Him" (42:9)—how is one, then, to understand the descriptions of Godhead? To be sure, this tension was not felt by early Muslims who remained undisturbed in the simplicity and clarity of their faith in God's Beautiful Names; on the other hand, it is this very tension wherein the future development of Islamic religious tradition is largely prefigured.

The pious simplicity of early Islam had taken God's Names as given, with all their glaring mysteries and dark veils, to be understood not analyzed, to be found not demonstrated. But this attitude gradually transformed into one of rational, or rationalized, enquiry: now dealing with the philosophical and metaphysical complexities of questionings concerning God's qualities or attributes (ṣifa, pl. ṣifāt) denoted by divine Names. It seems that two historical forces played a key role in this transformation. In the first place, as Wolfson and others have observed, this transformation was brought about originally as an opposition to the Christian doctrine of Trinity.[23] Note that the Muslim contact with Christianity was with its Greek and not Latin branch; and note also that it was John of Damascus (d. c. 754) who had served as the connecting link between Church Fathers and early Islam. Already by the eighth century, the Greek Church had developed fairly elaborate Trinitarian doctrines of God, particularly those formulated by John of Damascus—doctrines considered by Muslims in general to stand in stark contradiction to the principle of God's unity (tauḥīd), and universally condemned by them. So we see that during this period the question arose in Islam as to whether the terms that are attributed to God in the Qur'ān—His qualities—stand for real incorporeal beings that exist in God from eternity; the Qur'ānic nominality of these qualities created embarrassing prospects. God had ninety-nine Names, and Muslims under no circumstances could admit ninety-nine persons in Allah; this would be worse than admitting three, constituting shirk equally.

The second key factor ushering in this transformation of a pious acceptance of divine Names into rationalized discourses on God's attributes, a shift from asmā' to ṣifāt, is the influence of Greek philosophy. Thus, carrying out a logical analysis of the principle of tauḥīd, questions of the following kind were raised. The Qur'ān says that God is the "Knower." Now an analysis of the term "Knower" leads necessarily to the inference that, therefore, God must have the attribute "knowledge." But knowledge of what? And here begins the problem: Does God have knowledge of something within Himself or without? If the former, then there is a duality in Himself. If the latter, His knowledge is dependent upon something outside of Himself and is not absolute—therefore, the possessor of this quality is not absolute. And all this means that if the principle of Allah's unity and independence were to be preserved, He could only be described through the *via negativa*.[24] Some Hellenized philosophers of Islam (*falāsifa*) pushed this analysis to its logical terminus, gradually reducing the nature of Godhead to a bare unidentifiable something.

With regard to the problem of divine attributes, one can identify four tendencies in the Islamic religious tradition: (1) The tendency to shun rational questionings concerning the nature of Allah, and to accept His Qur'ānic attributes the way tradition has accepted it—a tendency often referred to as traditionalism (*naql*). (2) The tendency to deny altogether the reality of all of Allah's attributes, and thereby to separate Him in a thoroughgoing manner from the cosmic order, stripping the conception of Godhead of the faintest hint of anthropomorphism, and removing from God all qualities of impermanence (the doctrine of *tanzīh*)—that is, holding God as strictly transcendental. This is the characteristic tendency of the Mu'tazilite *mutakallimūn*. (3) Then, we find the countertendency, to contemplate on God's immanence, and on His ever-encompassing presence in the larger cosmic order; and to experience the manifestations of divine attributes in the outer world and in the inner depths of one's being: that is, a tendency to merge the cosmos in God, until it could be declared expressly that Allah is All, He is the Ultimate Reality of all existents; that, indeed, He is the only Reality. Bordering perilously on pantheism, this tendency has already been observed by us above, something that constitutes the hallmark of much theosophical sufism. (4) A mediating tendency, largely represented by al-Ghazālī. Until this day, all four of these tendencies one way or another continue to exist in the Islamic world; and among these, the Ghazalian synthesis still reigns supreme.

4.4 Traditionalism and the Theological Rationalism of *Kalām*

The aim of the traditionalists, called *Ahl al-Ḥadīth*, was moral not rational: they were more concerned with keeping intact the faith of the community than with metaphysical explanations; their concern lay in the moral process of establishing a society according to God's commands, and not so much in the logical analyses of a Hellenistic kind that were characteristic of *falāsifa*. So the *Ahl al-Ḥadīth* were willing to sacrifice rational understanding for the sake of preserving the integrity (*islām*)[25] of their total commitment to the Qur'ān. Their message is: If over the centuries a doctrine has been accepted by the Muslim community at large (*ijmā'*), it ought to be accepted as such. If the presumption of the truth of a proposition has been transmitted from generation to generation (*naql*), having been derived from the Qur'ān, and the Sunna of the Prophet, and has been generally agreed upon (*ijmā'*), it must be taken as it stands, without rational enquiry.[26]

The Qur'ān speaks of God's Hands, His Eyes, His Face; it says, for example, that "Allah has firmly settled Himself on the Throne" (20: 5): All this must be believed as such. We must not inquire what God's hands or eyes look *like,* neither are we to *compare* these with human hands or eyes; we must not ask *how* God sits on His Throne, or what the nature of His Throne is, nor, indeed, are we supposed to compare Allah's sitting with the sitting of a human being—we must simply stay by the recorded word. The famous living formula of the traditionalists is *bilā kayf wa lā tashbīh*, "without enquiring how, and without making comparisons." It is in the traditionalist hands that there developed in Islam the doctrine of *mukhālafa*, "difference" (everything in Allah is different from the similarly named thing in human beings or in the world), later on called *tanzīh*, "removal" (removing Allah from any danger of confusion or association with the cosmic order, including, of course, human beings).

This *bilā kayf wa lā tashbīh* creed gave rise to two kinds of approaches. One, which was adopted by the general body of Muslims, was not to push the *mukhālafa* process so far as to render any discovery of the nature of Allah utterly out of the question. Thus, it was considered still possible to form a conception of God; He was different, yet thinkable; the Qur'ānic Names and phrases describing God gave a thought of Him that was not essentially wrong, even though this thought was neither complete nor fully accurate. But there is a second approach: an approach that took the *mukhālafa* doctrine ruthlessly to its logical end. According to this second approach, we cannot from the Qur'ānic descriptions of God form any conception of His true nature—the discovery of the true nature of God is an impossibility; it must always remain a mystery. When the Qur'ān says that God is the "Knower," this does not mean that He has the human quality of knowledge, or anything that is similar. God has "knowledge unlike any other knowledge." He has given Himself the Name "Knower," and what that Name means we cannot know and must not inquire. Thus, there was no language to talk about God! It is this ruthless logic of *tanzīh* that became the touchstone of the Muʿtazilite rationalism, leading it to an explicit denial of the reality of divine attributes.

We have here two standard terms that are to be found occurring throughout Islamic religious literature—*tashbīh* and *tanzīh*. The first literally means "likening something to something else," or "declaring something similar to something else"; or "to compare something to something else"—that is, "to consider something commensurable with something else." For example, when the Qur'ān speaks of God's Hands, and we form a conception of these Hands similar to that of human hands, then this is an instance of *tashbīh*. The other term, *tanzīh*, in its literal sense means "ridding something of something else," "free something of something else," "removing something from something else," or "to declare something pure and free of something else." Thus, for example, it would constitute *tanzīh* when one says: "God has knowledge unlike any other knowledge" or that "God is Light unlike any other light." Indeed, it is quite clear that an extreme application of *tashbīh* will merge God into the cosmos; and at the other extreme, God will be rendered utterly separate from the cosmic order if *tanzīh* is allowed to exercise its full logical force. Both these extremes are found in Islam, and in either case desperate attempts have been made to save the conception of God nonetheless from these drastic consequences.

4.5 The Theological Problem of Attributes

The *Kalām* problem of divine attributes, arising as it did in direct response to the Christian doctrine of multiple gods, has three aspects.[27] In connection with the question of God's attribute of knowledge we have already seen an illustration of the (a) logical aspect of the problem.[28] But in addition to (a), there are two more aspects of this problem: (b) ontological and (c) semantic. Note that none of these aspects has any basis in the Qur'ān.

To illustrate (b), the ontological aspect of the problem, let us return to the example of God's knowledge. The Qur'ān calls God the "Knower." Does this imply the existence in God of *knowledge* as a real and eternal incorporeal being, which, though inseparable from God's essence, is distinct from it? Similarly, God is called the "Living" and "Powerful": Are, then, God's *life* and *power* eternal incorporeal beings, inseparable but nevertheless distinct from God in Himself? If the answer is in the affirmative, then God's attributes too are gods—and this constitutes an ontological leakage from the heavily guarded principle of God's unity, a leakage that would drown the very core of Islam!

Thus, God's attributes were mere names, and names were simply utterances or words; they had no ontological significance. The reality of divine attributes was thereby denied altogether. Ash'arī reports: "The Mu'tazilite say that names and qualities are words (*aqwāl*) and that they are our words 'God is knowing', 'God is able', etc."[29] To be sure, the Mu'tazilite 'Abd al-Jabbār (d. 1024) says categorically that "the quality (*ṣifa*)—or attribute—is a word (*qawl*), just as the qualification (*waṣf*)."[30] For him, then, quality is identical with qualification, being ontologically empty of content.[31] On the other hand, there are those Mu'tazilite who in denying God's attributes say that these attributes, or qualities, are God Himself. So we have Abu'l-Hudhayl (d. 840): "In his conception, the divine unity is more compact; God's self (*nafs*) is He as His eternity (*qidam*) is He, as He is one and identical with Himself, and also His knowledge, power, grandeur, etc., are likewise God Himself."[32]

There seem to be two underlying metaphysical assumptions in the Mu'tazilite doctrine: (1) It assumes that anything eternal (*qadīm*) must be a god—an assumption that embodies quite ironically an established Christian principle, which, in its turn, was inherited by the Church from Philo Judaeus;[33] and (2) It assumes, further, that the principle of the unity of God, *tauḥīd*, excludes any internal plurality in Godhead, even if these plural parts are inseparably united from eternity. John of Damascus, trying to beat Islamic theology at its own ironic game, fabricated a debate between a Christian and a Muslim. Putting the Muslim on the spot, the Greek theologian made him admit that the Word of God is uncreated—that is, it is eternal, *qadīm*; the rest followed deductively and necessarily. Cast formally, the logical proof would look like this: Everything eternal is a god (major premise). The Word of God is eternal (minor premise). Therefore, the Word of God is a god (conclusion).[34] The heresiographer and theologian al-Shahrastānī (d. 1153) makes this very clear:

> God is *qadīm* and [the Mu'tazilites claim that] eternity (*qidam*) is the most peculiar description of His essence and consequently they deny eternal attributes altogether . . . for [they believe that] if the attributes shared with God in eternity . . . they would also have a share in divinity (*al-ilāhiyya*).[35]

Thus, in their refutation of the Mu'tazilites, the opposing group of Muslim theologians who believed in the reality of attributes, a characteristically Ash'arite position, attacked the Mu'tazilite Philonic conception of the meaning of *qidam* (eternity) and *tauḥīd* (God's unity). So we see that in his theological work *Nihāyat al-Iqdām*, al-Shahrastānī bitterly dismisses the claim that eternity means deity: "Your argument that if an attribute is eternal it must be God is a bare assertion and is subject to dispute, and your assertion that eternity is a description most peculiar to God is an assertion for which there is no demonstration."[36]

The second Muʿtazilite assumption comes under attack by Ghazālī who argues typically that the conception of the unity of God does not exclude its being internally composed of real attributes or qualities that existed inseparably from eternity. Ghazālī begins by stating his view that the description of God as *wājib al-wujūd* (the necessary of existence) means only a denial of the dependence of God upon some cause of His existence: "For a necessary being means one which subsists by itself, as independent of other beings." He then proceeds:

> If the expression "the necessary of existence" is, as it should be, taken by you to mean that which has no efficient cause, then what reason have you to derive therefrom that God has no attributes? Why should it be impossible to say that, just as the essence of Him who is necessary of existence is eternal and has no efficient cause, so also His attribute exists with Him from eternity and has no efficient cause?[37]
>
> Just as the mind is capable of the conception of an eternal Being who has no cause for His existence, so it is capable of the conception of an eternal Being endowed with attributes who has no cause for the existence of both His essence and His attributes.[38]

Let us now turn to (c) the semantic aspect of the problem of attributes. It can be formulated thus: Given that the Qurʾān teaches that nothing is to be likened to God, how are we to understand His Qurʾānic attributes? In fact we have already witnessed most of the standard approaches to this question. There is the group of traditionalists who would refrain from rational inquiry into this matter and take the Qurʾān literally to mean what it says "without asking how and without comparison." Then we have briefly looked at those rigid traditionalists who believe in the reality of divine attributes but hold that every attribute predicated of God is unlike the same attribute predicated of any other being. These uncompromising traditionalists, however, do not give new unlike meaning to the terms denoting God's attributes, unlike the Muʿtazilites who deny the reality of attributes altogether and say that new non-literal meanings are to be given to these terms of divine attribution. But there were also a small subgroup of traditionalist Muslims who took the Qurʾānic terms predicated of God in their extreme literalness, admitting into their system all the dreaded anthropomorphism. These Muslims were known by the pejorative appellation "the Likeners."[39]

Wolfson tells us that the semantic aspect of the problem of attributes takes another form: The search for a formula on the part of various groups, a formula that would express their conception of attributes. Thus, we have the formula, *bilā kayf wa lā tashbīh*; and the formula, "God's attributes are unlike any other attributes"; then there is Jarīr al-Zaydī's (fl. c. 785) "God's attributes are neither God nor other than God"—a formula espoused by another Shīʿī thinker Hishām ibn al-Ḥakam (d. 814), and also by the Sunni theologian Ibn Kullāb (d. 854).[40] As for the Ashʿarites, Ibn Ḥazm tells us that the "greatest" of them, Baqillānī (d. 1013), declared that: "God has fifteen attributes, all of them coeternal with God, *a parte ante* and *a parte post*, and all of them other than God and different from God . . . and God is other than they and different from them."[41] And Shahrastānī reports that the Ashʿarites used to say: "The Creator is knowing in virtue of knowledge, powerful in virtue of power . . . and these attributes are superadded to God's essence and they are attributes eternally existent and things subsisting in His essence."[42] It should be noted that the Ashʿarite position is a mediating one, attempting a balance between *tashbīh* and *tanzīh*, and this is the position that was later developed in the synthesis of Ghazālī.

4.6 *Tashbīh* and *Tanzīh* as Questions of Ultimate Reality

This whole problem of attributes can legitimately be cast in terms of *tashbīh* and *tanzīh*. Does the cosmos "resemble" God? Is the world of phenomena "like" God? Does God manifest Himself in the cosmic order? Is the cosmic order real? Is God the ultimate reality of all existents? Is God identical with His manifestations? And, daringly, is the cosmos identical with God? Or, indeed, are God's Qurʾānic attributes ontologically real? These are all questions of *tashbīh*, "resemblance."

On the other hand: Is God utterly "removed" from the cosmic order? Is God the only reality, and nothing else besides Him is real? Does the world share nothing with God? Is there no language to talk about God? Is ultimate reality simply the reality of the only Real? Or, again: Are God's attributes mere words, words that are ontologically empty? Questions of this kind constitute an inquiry into *tanzīh*, "removal."

It is precisely this formulation of *tashbīh* and *tanzīh* given recently by two contemporary scholars, Murata and Chittick. Explicating *tashbīh*, they say:

> It is to assert that God must *have some sort of similarity with his creatures* . . . God's signs within the cosmos and scripture designate his attributes such as life, knowledge . . . [etc.]. These attributes belong to God, but they are also found in created things. . . . [In contrast,] the perspective of *tanzīh* affirms God's oneness by declaring that God is one and *God alone is Real*.

Hence everything other than God [including his attributes] is unreal . . . *God's single reality excludes all unreality*. . . . [But] the perspective of *tashbīh* declares that God's oneness is such that *his one reality embraces all creatures*. The world which appears as unreality and illusion is in fact *nothing but the One Real* showing his signs. Rather than excluding all things, God's unity includes them. [*Tashbīh*] sees God as *immediately present in* the *soul or in the cosmos*.

The principle of *tauḥīd*, Murata and Chittick say, comprehends both *tashbīh* and *tanzīh* and balances them.[43]

4.7 *al-Ḥaqīqa* in Sufism

We have spoken above of the four tendencies in Islamic religious thinking with regard to the question of divine attributes. So far we have looked at three of them: the traditionalist tendency; the tendency to deny the reality of attributes; and the mediating tendency, about which I will have more below. We also noted that this whole issue can be cast in terms of the twin concepts of *tashbīh* and *tanzīh*—that is, in terms of a question that reduces itself to a question of ultimate reality. Let us now turn to the fourth tendency.

As has already been remarked, it is in sufi doctrines that the denotation *al-ḥaqīqa* becomes a technical term, a term that can, and in some cases ought to be, translated as "ultimate reality." In connection with the question of ultimate reality, we have already examined Ibn 'Arabī briefly and we now return to him. Indeed, the theosophical system of this Spanish sufi is so powerful and daring that it constitutes a unique phenomenon in the history of Islamic thought, a phenomenon that has indelibly influenced all later religious thinkers, one way or another. One of the most fundamental features of Ibn 'Arabī's thinking is his doctrine of the relationship of God and the cosmic order. In his system, expressed in a prose that burns like white fire, God is related to the cosmos not as the Lord is to the slave, and not as the Maker is to the made; rather God is related to the world as the Object in the mirror is related to its infinitely numerous images, as the Sun is to its multiple rays, as the Ocean is related to its countless water drops.

Ibn 'Arabī has a doctrine of divine cosmogony. God created the world because of His desire to reveal Himself and to know Himself in beings through being known by them. "I was a hidden Treasure, God said," thus begins a famous *ḥadīth qudsī* known to Ibn 'Arabī, "and I yearned to be known. Then I created creatures in order to become in them the object of my knowledge." Corbin explicates this: "This cosmogony is neither an Emanation in the Neoplatonic sense . . . nor, still less, a *creatio ex nihilo*. It is rather a succession of manifestations of being, brought about by an increasing light, within the originally undifferentiated God; it is a succession of *tajalliyāt*, theophanies. This is the context of one of the most characteristic themes of Ibn 'Arabī's thinking, the doctrine of *divine Names*."[44]

The basic maxim of Ibn 'Arabī is that we know divine Names *only by our knowledge of ourselves*. God describes Himself to us through ourselves. "The divine Names have meaning and full reality only *through* and for beings [that is, the cosmos with its variegated multiplicity, including human beings] who are their epiphanic forms (*mazāhir*), that is to say, the forms in which they are manifested. Likewise from all eternity, these forms, substrate of the divine Names [that is, *inter alia*, we human beings], have existed in the divine Essence."[45] As I cautioned above, these Names were not considered by Ibn 'Arabī to be identical with the divine Essence as such—but they did designate divine attributes, and these attributes were not different from the Essence, and, like the Essence, they too were eternal.

In the background of the declaration that after fashioning Adam, God breathed His own breath into him (15:29; 38:72; 32:9), let us hear Ibn 'Arabī himself:

> God describes Himself by the Compassionate Breath (*Nafas Raḥmānī*). But that which is qualified by a quality necessarily embodies all the implications of that quality. . . . Accordingly the Divine Breath received all the forms of the world. It is their material substance (*jawhar hayūlānī*); it is nothing other than Nature itself.[46]

And again:

> Let him who wishes to know the Divine Breath know the world, for whoever knows himself knows his Lord who is manifested in it; in other words, the world is made manifest in the Breath of Compassion by which God appeased the sadness of the divine Names. . . .[47]

And what is nature?

> Nature is in reality nothing other than the Breath of Compassion. . . . The relation of nature to the Breath of Compassion is analogous to the relation of specific forms to the things in which they are manifested . . . *Nafas Raḥmānī* is the substance in which flower the forms of material and spiritual being.[48]

What does all this mean? To begin with, it is clear that in the system of Ibn ʿArabī, Being is One. This One Being manifests itself in the multiplicity that exists in the cosmos; and we too are its manifestations. We are epiphanies of God's Names, and, thus, we too have existed in God eternally as Possibles. To know ourselves, then, is to know the Lord. Nature *is* God's Compassionate Breath: As Corbin explains, God is the object of His own Compassion because since the name is identical to the thing named, the multiple divine Names are Himself, and He is One: "That is why the concept of *creatio ex nihilo* vanishes, giving way to the notion of liberation."[49]

For Ibn ʿArabī, then: God is the only reality (*al-ḥaqīqa*), and the cosmos is this very reality manifested in its attributes. This is the famous *waḥdat al-wujūd* (ontological monism) doctrine of Ibn ʿArabī. Is it pantheism? The sufi will still say, no, for once again: The divine Names are the divine Essence itself, but they are *not* identical with divine Essence as such.

4.8 The Synthesis of Ghazālī

The famous scholar Gardet once wrote: "Ghazālī stands on the hinge between the two vocabularies of *falsafa* [Islamic philosophy] and *taṣawwuf* [Sufism].[50] This is a perfectly accurate metaphor, for like a door on the hinge Ghazālī can move this way and that way, and sometimes he is just in the middle. But it seems that in the end, ultimate reality (*al-ḥaqīqa*) for him is a deeply felt experience: an experience that flashes itself upon the heart and leads ordinary faith to absolute certainty. In his *Book of the Wonders of the Heart*, Ghazālī speaks of the revelation of the ultimate reality of the truth in all beings, and the readiness of the mind to receive it, but for the veils that need to be removed.[51]

Ghazālī used both reason and tradition. The former to demonstrate its own limitations; and the latter to control the creative imagination of the mystic in him. For him, we were both Allah's kin and separate from Allah—and here is a profound act to balance *tashbīh* and *tanzīh*. Allah was will; everywhere we see the workings of Allah; human beings too have a will and thus they were similar to Allah. Also, since Allah breathed his own breath (or spirit) in Adam, there existed a likeness between the human spirit and divine spirit in essence, quality, and action. Just as we ruled our bodies, Allah ruled the world.[52]

In his *Risāla Qudsiyya*, Ghazālī attacks the Muʿtazilites for their denial of the reality of divine attributes, and considers the question whether the difference between God and the human beings is obliterated by the idea of the latter carrying Allah's spirit. For does it not constitute *tashbīh*? Ghazālī's answer is that there will always be a fundamental duality between humanity and God because God's most peculiar quality is his self-subsistence: He subsists in Himself while everything else subsists in Him, not through its own essence. Indeed, things through their own essence have nothing but non-existence; but the existence of Allah is essential.[53] As Macdonald says, "This rules out the material *tashbīh* of the anthropomorphists, but practically leaves free scope on the mystical and spiritualizing side."[54]

Like Ghazālī, so too in the thinking of the sufi Hujwīrī (d. c. 1071) ultimate reality is gnostic experience: "By *ḥaqīqa* is meant a man's dwelling in the place of union with God, and the fixing of his heart upon this by a purIfication of his idea of the divine attributes (*tanzīh*)."[55] Sounding very similar to Ghazālī, Hujwīrī contrasts *Ḥaqīqa* and *Sharīʿa*: *Ḥaqīqa*, he says, "signifies a reality which does not admit of abrogation and remains in equal force from the time of Adam to the end of the world, like the knowledge of God and like religious practice, which only the inner purpose renders perfect."[56] Here ultimate reality is knowledge and practice of a certain kind.

Notes

1. See chapter 1 in this volume.

2. Orientalists generally called *ʿIlm al-Kalām* (literally, "Science of Speech") "Muslim Scholastic Theology"; subsequently, Islamicists referred to the discipline simply as Islamic theology; among contemporary scholars the trend (a welcome one) now is to leave untranslated the words *Kalām* and *mutakallim(ūn)* (practitioner(s) of *Kalām*).

3. Chapter 1.3.

4. In the sense of *bidʿa*.

5. Chapter 1.1.2.

6. See below.

7. A profound explication of Ibn ʿArabi's ideas are in Corbin, *Creative Imagination in the Sufism of Ibn ʿArabī* (Princeton: Princeton University Press, 1969). See below.

8. Ibid., 114–17. Also see below.

9. Ibn Sīnā, *al-Shifaʾ*, *al-Ilāhiyyāt* (Cairo: 1380 h./1960), 31.

10. Ibn Sīnā, *al-Najat* (Cairo: 1357 h./1938), 299.

11. Gardet, "Ḥaqiqa," *Encyclopaedia of Islam, New Edition*, vol. III (Leiden: E. J. Brill, 1971), 75.

12. Goichon, *Lexique de la langue philosophique d'Ibn Sīnā* (Paris, 1938), 84.

13. Cf. Haq, "Taxonomy of Truth" in *Religious Truth,* chap. 6.

14. Massignon, *La Passion d'al-Ḥallaj,* 2 vols. (Paris: 1922), 568.

15. Ibid., 801, n. 1.

16. Massignon, *Lexique technique de la mystique musalmane* (Paris, 1954), 310.

17. Rahman, *Major Themes of the Qur'ān* (Minneapolis: Biblioteca Islamica, 1989), 1.

18. Ibn Ḥazm, *Kitāb al-Fiṣal fī al-Milal wa'l-Aḥwā' wa'l-Niḥal* (Cairo: 1317–1327 h./1897–1907), v, 59–60. Cf. Haq, "Ṭabī'a," *Encyclopedia of Islam.*

19. Rahman, op. cit., 4.

20. Ibid., 5.

21. As for the first of these three classes, Allah in and by Himself, the descriptions "are at first sight a strange combination of anthropomorphics and metaphysics," but they ought to be regarded as "the still plastic metaphor of a poet." Thus the Qur'ān speaks of God's Two Hands (5:69; 38:75); His Grasp (39:67); His Eyes (54:14); His Face (2:109, 274; 6:52; and often); God on His Throne (20:4; and often); the First, and the Last, the Manifest and the Latent (56:3); the Self-Subsisting (2:256; 3:1); the One (often); the Living (2:256; etc.); the Exalted in and through Himself (13:10); the Comprehensive (2:248; etc.); the Powerful (2:19; etc.); the Self-Sufficing (2:265; etc.); the Absolute Originator (2:3; 6:101); the Enduring (verbal form occurs frequently); the Eternal (112:2); the Grand (often); the Dominant (12:39; etc.); the Haughty (59:23); the Great (often); the Laudable (often); the Glorious (11:76; 85:15); the Generous (often); He of Majesty and Generosity (55:78); the Strong (often); the Firm (51:58); the Knower (often); the Subtle (6:103; etc.); the Aware (often); the Wise (often); the Hearer (often); the Seer (often); the Holy King (59:23; 62:1); the Peace (59:23); the Best of Judges (7:85; etc.); the Benefactor (52:28); the Light of the Heavens and the Earth (24:35); and the Real (see above).

    As for Allah's epithets in relation to cosmos, the Qur'ān calls Him the Creator (often); the Shaper (53:24); the Beginner, and the Restorer (not the epithets but the idea occurs frequently, e.g., 29:18); the Giver of Life (41:39); the Giver of Death (not the epithet but the idea occurs frequently, e.g., 15:23); the Heir (15:3); the Reckoner (not the epithet but the idea frequently, e.g., 36:11); the Sender of the Dead from the Graves (not the epithets but the idea frequently); the Assembler (3:7; 4:139); the Strengthener (4:87); the Guardian (86:4); the King (often); the Governor (13:12); the Lord of Kingship (3:25); the Prevailer (18:43); and the Tyrant (59:23).

    There exist a number of other words and phrases descriptive of Allah in relation to the world that do not occur as epithets in the Qur'ān, but their roots are common as used of Allah. Thus, He is the Exalter, the Honorer, the Abaser, the Withholder, the Advantager, the Deferrer, the Advancer, the Contracter, the Spreader, and the Distresser.

Finally, in relation to humankind Allah is Compassionate and Merciful (abundantly); the Forgiver (7:154; 40:2); the Much Forgiver (often); the Forgiver *par métier* 20:84; etc.); the Pardoner (4:46); the Clement (often); the Repenter (2:35; etc.); the Grateful (35:27); the Very Patient (not the epithet but idea frequently); the Kind (2:138; etc.); the Loving (11:92; 85:14); the Watcher (4:1); the Reckoner (4:88; 33:39); the Witness (often); the Faithful, the Protector (59:23); the Guide (often); the Guardian (often); the Patron (often); the Opener (34:25); Giver (3:6); the Provider (51:58); the Bestower, and the Sufficer (not the epithets but the idea is fundamental).

Note that what we have here is still not an exhaustive list.

22. I have here paraphrased Macdonald, "Allah," *Encyclopaedia of Islam*, 304.

23. Wolfson, *Philosophy of the Kalām* (Cambridge: Harvard University Press, 1976), 112–31; Macdonald, "Allah," *Encyclopaedia of Islam*, 306. Wolfson has compared the *Kalām* terminology with that of the Christian theology and has argued that parallels exist.

24. Cf. Macdonald, op. cit., 306.

25. One of the literal meanings of the word *"islām"* is integrity.

26. Recall that the Qur'ān and Sunna are the two material sources of Islamic jurisprudence; *ijma'* being one of the procedural sources, another being *qiyas*, analogy.

27. I have here followed Wolfson's analysis that I have sometimes directly quoted.

28. See above, 81–82.

29. Ash'arī, *Kitāb maqālāt al-Islāmīyīn wa-Iḫtilāf al-muṣallīn*, 2 vols., ed. Hellmut Ritter (Istanbul: 1929–1930), 172.

30. Mughnī, VII, 117. Cf. Peters, *God's Created Speech: A Study in the Speculative Theology of the Mu'tazilī Qaḍī l-Quḍāt Abū l-Ḥasan 'Abd al-Jabbār bn Aḥmad al-Hamadānī* (Leiden: E. J. Brill, 1976), 250–55.

31. Here we have the historical context of Ghazālī's fascinating ontological problem of the relationship between (i) the name (*al-ism*; this is a Qur'ānic word) (ii) the named (*al-musamma*), and (iii) the naming (*tasmiya*). See Ghazālī, *al-Maqṣad al-Asna*.

32. Richard M. Frank, "The Divine Attributes According to the Teaching of Abū l-Hudhayl al-'Allaf," *Le Muséon* 82 (1969): 472.

33. Cf. Wolfson, op. cit., 133–37.

34. Ibid.

35. al-Shahrastāni, *Milal*, 30, II. 6–9.

36. Quoted in Wolfson, op. cit., 137.

37. Ghazālī, *Tahāfut al-Falāsifah (The Incoherence of the Philosophers)*, trans. Sabih Ahmad Kamali (Lahore: Pakistan Philosophical Congress, 1963), V. 7, 166, II. 6–8.

38. Ibid., VI, 12.

39. See Wolfson, op. cit., 206.

40. Ibid., 206–11.

41. Ibn Ḥazm, *Fisal*, IV, 207, quoted in Wolfson, op. cit., 214.

42. al-Shahrastani, *Nihayat*, 181, II. 1–4, quoted in Wolfson, op. cit.

43. Sachiko Murata and William C. Chittick, *The Vision of Islam* (New York: Paragon House, 1994), 70. All emphases added.

44. Corbin, op. cit., 114.

45. Ibid., 115.

46. Ibn 'Arabi, *Fuṣuṣ al-Ḥikam,* 2 vols., ed. A. E. Afifi (Cairo: 1365 h./1946), vol I, 143–44.

47. Ibid., I, 145.

48. Ibid., II, 334–35.

49. Corbin, op. cit., 299.

50. Gardet, "Ḥaqiqa," *Encyclopaedia of Islam,* 75.

51. Ghazali, *Iḥya' 'Ulūm al-Dīn*, 4 vols. (Cairo: 1377 h./1957), 3, 18.

52. Cf. Macdonald, op. cit.

53. Ghazali, *Iḥya',* 1.

54. Macdonald, op. cit., 310.

55. Hujwiri, *The Kashf al-Mahjūb: The Oldest Persian Treatise on Sufiism,* trans. Reynold A Nicholson (Gibb Memorial Series No. 17, 1911; Revised ed., 1936, reprinted in Karachi: Darul Ishaat, 1990), 384.

56. Ibid., 383.

5

Vedānta Deśika's *Īśvarapariccheda* ("Definition of the Lord") and the Hindu Argument about Ultimate Reality

Francis X. Clooney, S.J.
with Hugh Nicholson

❧

It is not easy to state in brief terms what the Indian religious traditions, even within particular schools of thought, have meant by "Ultimate Reality," especially if one does not retreat to an abstract position that prescinds from the specific formulations in which traditions articulate their views of reality. Nevertheless, certain characteristics can be stated. In the "Hindu brāhmaṇical context," with which this chapter is concerned,[1] *Ultimate* Reality might be described as follows: that which cannot be surpassed; that from which all realities, persons, and things come, that on which they depend, and that into which they return upon dissolution; that by knowledge of which one knows everything else and reaches liberation. This Ultimate Reality can, in certain privileged circumstances, be known by direct perception, but is best known by those who engage in faithful recourse to revealed scriptures; some features of Ultimate Reality can be affirmed by careful reasoning. In the theistic traditions that most distinctively characterize Hindu thinking, this Ultimate Reality is personal, can be invoked by one or more proper names, and can choose to become accessible in perceptible form.

Such general features become much more complex in nuance and implication, and accordingly become contentious, subject to argument over many centuries. When intellectuals asserted that a right understanding of Ultimate Reality defines the significance of the universe, alternative versions of Ultimate Reality are compelled to vie for this central place, so that efforts to define Ultimate Reality are inevitably contested. Most considerations of Ultimate Reality opened into explicit debates over the existence and nature of God; while this eventuality is not necessary, its frequency is a point of great significance in comparative study. In the pages that follow, one of our goals is to indicate how one particular discourse about Ultimate Reality is perhaps essentially argumentative, and how a complete particular discourse, such as the example considered here, inevitably draws contemporary comparativists into the debate over the nature of that Reality.

In this chapter we examine just one example of an argumentative discourse about Ultimate Reality, the *Īśvarapariccheda* ("Definition of the Lord") section of Vedānta Deśika's *Nyāyasiddhāñjana*. We have chosen this text because it offers a systematic claim about "Ultimate Reality" that stands in conscious and explicit tension with a variety of competing positions; on its own grounds but also by contestation and contrast with those other positions, it demarcates a Hindu view of Ultimate Reality that is singular and yet very amply interconnected with other Hindu and Indian views of that Reality. Insofar as our positions as modern scholars and outsiders to the Hindu traditions allow us, we have attempted to understand the topic of Ultimate Reality through the eyes of Vedānta Deśika, a very wise Hindu theologian. Understanding the purpose, methods, and arguments of his text illumines a wide range of Indian positions in a way that is more vivid and primary than an account of the "Hindu position" or a survey of the "Hindu positions" could possibly be.

5.1 Introduction: Vedānta Deśika and His *Īśvarapariccheda* ("Definition of the Lord")

5.1.1 Vedānta Deśika

Vedānta Deśika (1268–1369) was an important proponent of (Viśiṣṭādvaita) Vedānta[2] and a key theologian of the Śrīvaiṣṇava community of south India, a community deeply rooted in both the Sanskrit and Tamil

intellectual traditions. He was born in the town of Tuppil, near Conjee-
varam (today's Kanchipuram), which was a great center of learning for
several religious traditions. Writing in Sanskrit, Tamil, and a mixture of
both (a *maṇipravāḷa*, ["jewel and coral" linguistic combination]), and
composing independent treatises, commentaries, and songs, Deśika expounded the faith of the ārāvaiṣṇavas: there is one Ultimate Reality, who
is the Lord Nārāyaṇa (Viṣṇu)[3] with the Goddess Śrī, and who at the same
time is Brahman, the Ultimate Reality described in the ancient Upaniṣads.
Deśika defended these positions in exegesis, by careful reasoning, and
with persuasive rhetoric.

In two of his treatises, the *Nyāyapariśuddhi* (*The Purifying of Reasoning*, 1324) and *Nyāyasiddhāñjana* (*The Healing of Reasoning*, 1334–
35), he opted for a rigorously logical exposition and defense of his
Vaiṣṇava beliefs. Together, the two works offer a thorough defense of the
Viśiṣṭādvaita system of Vedānta according to the norms of a rational discourse he shared with the practitioners of Logic (Nyāya), the Naiyāyikas.[4] In the *Nyāyapariśuddhi*, Vedānta Deśika discusses four primary
means of correct knowledge (*pramāṇa*): perception (*pratyakṣa*), inference
(*anumāna*), verbal knowledge (*śabda*), and tradition (*smṛti*). More
briefly, he considers the proper objects (*prameya*) of these ways of knowing, according to the Nyāya logic and the naturalistic categories of the
Vaiśeṣika school. Throughout, his aim is to review and clarify problematic and unclear aspects of the system of logic set forth in the *Nyāya
Sūtras* of Gautama. Throughout his approach is critical but positive since
he values Nyāya as a useful tool and does not consider it fundamentally
inimical to Vedānta. The corrective work of the *Nyāyapariśuddhi* is complemented in the *Nyāyasiddhāñjana*, which focuses on the objects of
knowledge, considering in sequence seven topics: (1) inert material reality (*jaḍa dravya*); (2) the individual, dependent self (*jāva*); (3) the supreme
lord (*Īśvara*); (4) the eternal spiritual/material abode of the lord (*vai-
kuṇṭha*); (5) understanding (*buddhi*); (6) constitutive knowledge (*dharmabhūtajñāna*);[5] (7) qualities, which are real but not material (*a-dravya*).[6]
Both works are composed of Sanskrit verses accompanied by Vedānta
Deśika's own prose exposition of his own verses.[7]

5.1.2 The Īśvarapariccheda

The third section of the *Nyāyasiddhāñjana* is entitled the *Īśvarapariccheda* (which might be translated as "The Proper Definition of 'Lord'").
This title indicates that Deśika is entering upon the standard discourse
about God (*Īśvaravāda*) that was well known in various brāhmaṇical
contexts, and in Buddhist and Jaina contexts, long before Deśika. Indians

had by his time developed certain ways of thinking about Ultimate Reality, terms and standards that at least seemed similar enough that arguments could occur, probing whether "Ultimate Reality" meant the same as "Lord," or something else, such as "Brahman." In the *Īśvaraparic-cheda* Deśika sets forth his understanding that there is a single Ultimate Reality, which is Nārāyaṇa, the God of his particular tradition (and some allied traditions); he defends this view against a series of opposing positions introduced by way of various objections.[8] Deśika defends his understanding of "Lord" mostly on rational grounds; even his arguments with those who accept the scriptures have to do with whether they are interpreting the texts intelligently or not. Since his arguments take into account a wide range of opposing viewpoints, attention to the *Īśvaraparic-cheda* offers a reliable, manageable initial point of entry into a variety of Hindu and related ways of thinking about Ultimate Reality.

5.1.3 *Eight Aspects of the Meaning of "Lord"*

Deśika begins the *Īśvaraparriccheda* by stipulating the following meaning for "Lord": (1) The lord is ruler over all; (2) he is conscious and all-pervasive in knowing; (3) he has everything totally dependent on himself; (4) he is propitiated by all religious actions and gives all results; (5) he is the foundation for all else; (6) he is the generator of all effects; (7) he has all things as his body, his own and others, and also his own knowledge;[9] (8) all that he wishes comes true, due simply to himself.[10] Near the end of the *Īśvaraparriccheda* he adds, as will be seen below, that this personal Ultimate Reality is named "Nārāyaṇa," and his spouse is Śrī. This definition is the accepted account of Deśika's (and his great predecessor Rāmānuja's) Vedānta tradition. As in a creed, each component of the definition has scriptural roots, has been argued and refined for generations, and is judged to have strong reasons in support of it and thus to be true even on solely rational grounds. Thus, the "Lord" must be conscious, because only if the Ultimate Reality is conscious can the order and seeming purposefulness of non-conscious or variably conscious beings be explained. All things are the Lord's body, because the body and soul relationship is the best metaphor or analogy available to understand the mysterious interconnection between the Maker, who is both the efficient and material cause of the world, and the world itself; to say that all his wishes come true is to affirm that the lord is capable of volition, and also to ward off the implication that the Lord is subject to desire, or experiences need, or suffers from only partial fulfillment of his wishes, and so on. The goal of the *Īśvaraparriccheda* is not to elaborate on this list of characteristics, but rather to use the definition of Lord as

the starting point for showing the virtues of his tradition's way of thinking about Ultimate Reality, and at the same time the deficiencies in other
views of Ultimate Reality.

Study of the *Īśvarapariccheda* offers progress toward two important
goals. First, this classic of Śrīvaiṣṇava (Viśiṣṭādvaita) Vedānta theology
in Rāmānuja's tradition[11] provides a great deal of precise information
about one important and well-articulated Hindu view of Ultimate Reality. Second, because the *Īśvarapariccheda* is engaged in a wide debate and
is an argumentative text, it also offers a comprehensive though contentious introduction to other major Indian and Hindu positions on Ultimate Reality, as understood from a traditional Indian perspective. In the
following sections, we offer first an overview of the whole *Īśvarapariccheda* (section 5.2), second a closer look at several sections from it (section 5.3), and finally some observations about how attention to the *Īśvarapariccheda* contributes to the project of understanding Ultimate Reality
in a comparative context (section 5.4).

5.2 Deśika's Fourteen Points
Regarding the Lord (Īśvara) as Ultimate Reality

The following summary of the *Īśvarapariccheda* is descriptive and, in
parts, a kind of summary translation of parts of the original (which has
not been translated into any language). As a summary, it is not meant to
preclude a fuller and detailed study of the *Īśvarapariccheda* that remains
to be done. In section 5.3 we examine three of Deśika's positions more
closely, but here we simply report his views without evaluating them, and
without attempting to spell out how the same questions would appear
from the adversarial perspectives.

5.2.1 *There Is an Adequate Definition of "Lord"*

Thesis 1: There is an adequate definition of "Lord." The definition of
"Lord" stated earlier in this chapter is the opening thesis in the *Īśvarapariccheda*: the lord is ruler over all, conscious and all-pervasive in knowing, possessed of everything as totally dependent upon himself, propitiated by all religious actions and the giver all results, the foundation for
everything, the generator of all effects, the one who has everything of his
own and others as his body, even his own knowledge, the one whose
wishes always come true due simply to himself. Naturally, this definition
anticipates and puts in place positive claims and arguments that will be
useful in the arguments that appear in the course of the *Īśvarapariccheda*.

5.2.2 *Nārāyaṇa Alone Is Ultimate Reality*

Thesis 2: Nārāyaṇa alone is Ultimate Reality. One interpretation of scripture suggests that there is a threefold lord—the creator Brahmā, the preserver Nārāyaṇa, and the destroyer Śiva—but according to Deśika this is a false view, incompatible with the idea of "Lord," who can be one only, who is Nārāyaṇa. Whatever is said of the lord must be understood as true without limits such as the supposed division of labor among three gods or three forms of the divine. (This will be considered in more detail in section 5.3.)

5.2.3 *Ultimate Reality Is Everywhere Perfect and Complete*

Thesis 3: Ultimate Reality is everywhere perfect and complete and not subject to restrictions. Here Deśika responds to the objection that if the lord is everywhere, he cannot be fully present anywhere. Seeking to defend the idea that the lord is fully present everywhere, Deśika considers and rejects four alternative positions:

1. The lord is fully present in only one place, not all places; or,
2. "full presence" means only that he is capable of becoming the object of perfect apprehension, from any reference point; or,
3. he is the cause of everything, everywhere, and in that sense perfectly present, as cause; or,
4. he is possessed of all perfections and in that sense "perfect," wherever he happens to be.

Deśika argues that each of these four views is deficient when examined in view of what Ultimate Reality can reasonably mean. If one uses the word "lord," one must also stipulate that this lord is perfectly present in each and every place. (This position too will be considered in section 5.3.)

5.2.4 *Brahman Not Devoid of Qualities Positively Expressed*

Thesis 4: Brahman, the lord, is not devoid of qualities that can be expressed in positive language. Some upaniṣadic texts speak of the lord as devoid of all qualities; others attribute qualities to him. Contrary to the view of Advaita (nondualist) Vedānta, however, readers of the Upaniṣads cannot simply ignore one set of texts and prefer the other; nor do such texts cancel each other in a testimony to the futility of language. Preference for statements which say Brahman has no qualities might well lead to the more extreme (Mādhyamika) Buddhist view that nothing at all can really be said about Ultimate Reality, in which case neither set of upaniṣadic statements could be ultimately valid. If scripture is to have any authority, both sets of scriptural texts must be respected and applied to the lord, who can be spoken about in properly chastened and refined human words. Ultimate Reality is not merely an object of ordinary reference, but within the constraints of a continuing awareness of this fact, language can make useful and true claims about Reality's nature.

5.2.5 Material Evolute Is Not Merely Superimposed on Brahman

Thesis 5: The material evolute is not merely superimposed on Brahman. Despite what the nondualist Vedāntins say, it is not true that "creation" is merely a result of ignorance superimposed upon Brahman. The lord is possessed of omniscience and other good qualities, is permanently conscious, and cannot be subjected to ignorance in any way. There are upaniṣadic statements that claim that the lord is pure being and nothing else, but they intend simply to exclude rival causes of the world, not to deny consciousness. Here Deśika is refuting nondualist Vedānta and also the views of the Sāṃkhya school (which argues for separate material and spiritual causes), the Cārvākas (who argue for a solely material cause), and Buddhists (who deny significance to "causality" itself). Notice, of course, that while Deśika and the nondualists assent to the authority of the Upaniṣads while the others do not, Deśika has no problem criticizing all these positions as subject to the same rational criticisms.

5.2.6 Nondualism Is Not Compatible with Brahman as Material Source

Thesis 6: The nondualist position held by Śaṅkara and others is not compatible with the position that Brahman is the material source of the world. In the counterpositions mentioned thus far the idea of Brahman's material and spiritual causality is said to be untenable. Consequently, the quest for a coherent explanation of the world is declared doomed. But Deśika insists that it is rationally improbable to settle for less than some really adequate explanation. "Being the cause" cannot be part of the proper nature of a being without qualities, nor can it be taken merely as a power of the lord, as Yādavaprakāśa suggests.[12] Rather, the lord cannot be subject to even one internal distinction, such as "being-cause" if at the same time this lord is "really" devoid of all distinctions. Earlier Vedāntins such as Śaṅkara, Yādavaprakāśa, and Bhāskara all try to reduce difference within Brahman to a merely linguistic feature, but their efforts are self-contradictory, since it is not possible to state in words that Ultimate

Reality is not qualified in any way whatsoever. A real world requires the possibilities of real distinctions, even in the Ultimate Reality that is the cause.

5.2.7 *Brahman and the World Are Not Both Different and Non-different*

Thesis 7: It is not tenable to say that Brahman and the world are both different and non-different. Nor is it tenable to describe the relationship between Brahman and the world by saying that they are different but also not different from one another. If there is difference, there cannot be non-difference, and vice versa. Deśika puts it nicely: such thinkers—for example, Bhāskara—preserve the text's multiple meanings, but sacrifice logic by positing both difference and non-difference in God; the logicians (considered under thesis 11), by contrast, sacrifice the text in order to keep their logic straight.

5.2.8 *The Jainas' Position Is Not Decisive about Language or Ultimate Reality*

Thesis 8: The sevenfold position[13] of the Jainas does not offer any decisive information about language or Ultimate Reality. The Jainas emphasize the fluidity and ambiguity of language, and on this basis go on to assert that reality itself must be fluid and ambiguous. In doing so, the Jainas misunderstand what the very fact that language communicates must imply. (We will return to this too in section 5.3.)

5.2.9 *Brahman Is Not Limited by Space, Time, and Things*

Thesis 9: Brahman is not limited by space, time, and things. Brahman (i.e., Ultimate Reality) cannot be limited by time and space, for Brahman pervades all time and all space. Even if Brahman were shown to be spatially limited, this would not be compatible with the non-dualists' contrary theses, that is, that Brahman is the soul of all, or that Brahman is the substrate of all (mere) superimpositions, or that positive statements about Brahman must always be on a deeper level mistaken. Nor can time limit Brahman. Although it is true that every thing is the body of Brahman, even this is not a limitation of Brahman. Things truly exist and are in a true relationship to Brahman, which, however, cannot be limited by any thing in particular.

5.2.10 *Brahman Cannot Be Inferred To Be the Efficient But Not Material Cause*

Thesis 10: It cannot be proven by inference that Brahman is the efficient cause of the world but not its material cause. The Śaiva theologians, along with the teachers of the Yoga and Vaiśeṣika systems, are incorrect when they say that the lord is only the efficient cause of the world; they cannot prove this, and their argument that Brahman cannot be both the efficient and material cause is not convincing.

5.2.11 The Existence of the Lord Cannot Be Proved by Inference

Thesis 11: It cannot be proven by inference that the lord exists. Against the logicians (Naiyāyikas) Deśika argues that Ultimate Reality cannot be known with certitude through inference. Their cosmological argument does not work, since one cannot infer from the finite world that it has a perfect maker. (We will return to this in section 5.3)

5.2.12 Why It Is Important That Inference Cannot Prove This

Thesis 12: Inference cannot prove the lord's existence, and the foundations of faith rest on revelation. Here Deśika explains why it is important even for a convinced theist to deny thesis 11, that Ultimate Reality is known through an inference about the source of the world. Inference can never be totally reliable, and those who depend on it will have stronger or weaker faith depending on the quality of their inferences and the force of the rebuttals of them. Inference can support faith, but it should not precede it nor be a cause for it; faith and the proper operation of reasoning about God must be based on revelation (*śruti*).

5.2.13 The Lord Is the Undivided Efficient and Material Cause of the World

Thesis 13: Therefore, the lord is the undivided efficient and material cause of the world. To say that Brahman is both the material and efficient cause of the world is not a mere analogy; it is a claim that is plausible, compatible with both kinds of causality as properly understood. The lord is not differentiated by name and form, but has as his body all conscious and unconscious beings. By a general inherent relation, he is their material cause; as agent, he is their efficient cause.

5.2.14 The Lord Is Eternally One with His Consort, Śrī, and Together, They Are Single Ultimate Reality

Thesis 14: The lord is eternally one with his consort, Śrī, who is equal to him; together, they are single Ultimate Reality. The world is dependent on both Śrī and Nārāyaṇa, together. The lord eternally shares lordship with the Goddess Śrī, and together they form Ultimate Reality. They are equal in knowledge, bliss, and other qualities, equally the originators of the

world that depends entirely on them, equally the refuge and goal of all beings, together the sole and single recipient of all worship. Thus, while the
Īśvaraparicchedạ does not speak of the Ultimate Reality in a mythological
fashion, the ideas of a divine consort and divine male-female relationship
are preserved in the highest discourse about Reality. Deśika's concluding
words at the end of the *Īśvaraparicchedạ* are brief and to the point:
"Therefore, it is proven that Brahman, of whom everything conscious
and lacking in consciousness is a mode, is one—Nārāyaṇa with Śrī."

Before moving to a closer examination of three of these fourteen theses, let us reflect for a moment on the preceding list. In its argumentative
outreach, Deśika's learned and informed position brings into explicit
consideration many other traditional Indian views on the nature of Ultimate Reality:

1. Devotees of Brahmā, Śiva, and other gods
2. Śaṅkara, the nondualist Vedāntin who posited a non-dual Ultimate Reality
   beyond all qualifications (except being, consciousness, bliss, infinity)
3. Sāmkhya philosophers, who posit separate material and spiritual sources
4. Buddhists (of the Śūnyavāda and Mādhyamika schools), who deny substantial reality and causality
5. Carvākas, said to be total materialists
6. Jaina teachers, who reduce the problem of understanding Ultimate Reality to
   an issue of logic and language
7. Yādavaprakāśa, a Vedāntin who posits real modification within Nārāyaṇa
8. Bhāskara, a Vedāntin who says that the world is some kind of modification
   of Ultimate Reality, which is both different and non-different from the world
9. The Yoga and Vaiśeṣika schools, which posit a lord who is only the efficient
   cause of the world
10. The Naiyāyikas, who believe that the existence of a lord can be known by a
    valid inference
11. Adherents of a Vaiṣṇava tradition that regarded Nārāyaṇa as Ultimate Real-
    ity but who denied equal status to the Goddess Śrī

None of Deśika's counterarguments is extraordinary if taken alone,
and it is likely that all of them appear in other contexts, even before him.
But their combination in one place is forceful and significant, marking a
particularly persuasive Hindu position about Ultimate Reality. That
Deśika begins and ends with more sectarian issues—Nārāyaṇa alone is
the Lord, not Śiva and Brahmā, and Śrī is his Consort—suggests that he
is indeed writing a kind of "communal theology" aimed at fellow believers. That he includes arguments against the non-dualist Vedāntins sug-

gests that he wants to establish his positions as the true Vedānta; that he critiques Jainas and logicians suggests that he is seeking to affirm a public place for his positions as rationally defensible before all. Understanding Deśika's position on Ultimate Reality in the *Īśvarapariccheda* is therefore to begin to understand much of what Indians have meant when they formed ideas about Ultimate Reality, God, Lord.[14]

5.3 Three Examples of the Argument

The preceding outline will give an impression of the complexity of Deśika's discourse on Ultimate Reality. He is surely defending standard Vedānta positions found in the theology of his great predecessor, Rāmānuja (and even prior to Rāmānuja) and is probably not breaking new ground doctrinally. Nevertheless, the concise lineup of this impressive range of arguments in one place signals the remarkable richness of the *Īśvarapariccheda* as a synthetic document. Within a few pages Deśika weaves together several ways of understanding and defending Ultimate Reality, engaging a wide variety of opposing positions, each engaged differently and (to some extent) on its own grounds.

To illustrate how Deśika argues and adapts his positions, let us examine a bit more closely three of the arguments: (1) how he debates with theists of other sects, such as Śaivas, worshippers of Brahmā, and "ecumenical Hindus" who believe that Nārāyaṇa, Śiva, and Brahmā are all one Ultimate Reality; (2) atheists, such as Jainas, who would reject the idea of an Ultimate Reality; (3) theists such as logicians, with whom he disagrees not on the rational idea of Ultimate Reality, but on how far reason can go in discovering the existence of this "God." The *Īśvarapariccheda* lays a claim on the idea that these diverse audiences—sectarian believers, atheists, rationalists—can talk to one another about Ultimate Reality sufficiently well as to make worthwhile argument possible. Let us consider these three examples and identify the rules of a common conversation about God that they imply.

5.3.1 Whether It Can Be Proven that Nārāyaṇa, and Not Other Gods, Is Ultimate Reality

(Combining thesis 2, "Nārāyaṇa alone is Ultimate Reality," and thesis 3, "Ultimate Reality is everywhere perfect and complete, and not subject to restrictions.")

It is not surprising that Deśika should argue (as in thesis 3) that Nārāyaṇa alone is the Ultimate Reality, but it is interesting that he is intent on showing this to be the most reasonable philosophical position: Ultimate Reality is of this particular sort, not any other sort; Ultimate Reality is such that this specific claim should be made about it. The bulk of his argument has to do with the proper interpretation of scripture, the upaniṣads. He and these particular opponents agree both that Upaniṣads give information about the nature of reality, and that the correct meaning of the upaniṣads can be determined. Careful readers should be able to agree on which are the key upaniṣadic texts, how these texts are to be ranked in relation to one another, and how, in the end, they show Nārāyaṇa to be the One God. Texts that mention three (or more) gods, such as Brahmā, Nārāyaṇa, and Śiva, seemingly as equals, do not prove threefoldness, but rather specify the One in three ways. Although one could make a threefold distinction in Ultimate Reality, identifying different personal divinities as creator, preserver, and destroyer, there is no scriptural basis for doing so. Brahmā and Śiva cannot be Ultimate Reality, since it can be proven from the Upaniṣads that they are individual, dependent selves; texts show them to be created and destroyed, subject to karma, and so on.

The follow-up discussion (thesis 4) asks more philosophically whether it is possible to combine the idea of "Lord" with the idea of "God in three forms." Here Deśika does not rely on scripture, but argues that the very idea of "divine fullness" precludes imagining this Reality to subsist in three modes, whether the threefoldness is understood as actual limitation or, more subtly, as a question of modes of perceptibility (localized) efficaciousness, or (limited) expressibility in language. Neither experience nor reflection on what "Lord" and "fullness" mean can allow for such distinctions.

This example assumes that Deśika and his adversaries have a great deal in common. There is a shared ritual and exegetical vocabulary with the Śaivas, a shared commitment to the Upaniṣads,[15] a shared set of exegetical rules that can be applied in determining who the true lord is; notions such as "divine plenitude" can be thought through in common, with at least the possibility of a shared conclusion regarding the divine nature.

5.3.2 *The Jaina Way of Thinking Is Self-Contradictory*

(According to thesis 8, "The sevenfold position of the Jainas does not offer any decisive information about language or Ultimate Reality.")

The argument becomes more difficult with the Jainas, since they do not share neither scriptures nor theism with Deśika. According to Rangarāmānuja, who comments on the *Īśvarapariccheda*, the Jainas try to hold seven positions at once since, in their view, when an object is talked about, there are always seven ways of speaking about it: (1) it is something that exists (by nature), or (2) it is something that can be spoken about but cannot be said to exist until existence is predicated of it, or (3) it is something that is both existent-and-non-existent, or (4) it is something that is neither-existent-nor-non-existent, or (5) it is something that is existent without being either existent or non-existent, or (6) it is something that is non-existent without being either existent nor nonexistent, or (7) it is something that is existent-and-nonexistent, neither existent nor non-existent. Nothing, neither the most limited nor the ultimate reality, can be asserted unequivocally in a definitive form. It is certainly not possible to label anything "Ultimate Reality."

Since there can be no common arguments based on scripture or a shared theistic outlook, Deśika argues simply that the Jaina theory is incoherent. If all these seven possibilities are inevitable, then the general Jaina position, which identifies and asserts them so univocally, becomes itself a startling exception to its own rule. It is the only statement not subject to "sevenfoldness."

If one looks deeper, one sees that the Jainas contradict their own view of language: even the initial apprehension of the object that is to be subjected to these seven possible expressions requires that one be able to begin by saying that the object—however described—exists. Every true statement about some thing must begin with a definite apprehension of its existence. "Some object" is being affirmed in all seven statements, if the statements are to mean anything at all. Although the seven statements seem linguistically possible, any real object to which they might refer cannot be so fluidly described. From the very start, the Jainas have no sound basis upon which to argue against Ultimate Reality.

5.3.3 Whether It Can Be Proven That There Is a Personal Ultimate Reality

(Thesis 11, "It cannot be proven by inference that the lord exists.")

Deśika shares a common theistic worldview with the logicians (Naiyāyikas), including the view that there is one lord who has made the world. Deśika and the logicians share a common understanding of the lord as a perfect, omniscient being who is the cause of the world, author of the Vedas, giver of liberation. In practice and probably in theory, however, they did not share a commitment to the idea that the Vedic scriptures are the primary source of knowledge about the lord. Deśika thought this, but the logicians did not. Nor did they share a commitment to the adequacy of reason in inquiries about Ultimate Reality; the logicians thought that the lord's existence could be known by inference, while Deśika did not.

The logicians' argument for the existence of the lord is found in brief form at the beginning of the fifth book of Udayana's great defense of God's existence, the *Nyāyakusumāñjali*: "earth, etc., have a maker as their cause because they have the nature of effects." George Chemparathy explains:

> With the term "maker" is meant an agent that employs or directs the class of causes that are known to be able to produce the effect. The "maker" that is postulated here as the cause of "earth etc." is not just any agent, but one that can adequately account for the existence of the effect in question. Although this maker is not explicitly said to be the Īśvara, Udayana shows in the long exposition of the proof that the "maker" in question cannot but be eternal and omniscient and hence is none other than Īśvara.[16]

The logicians are generally not concerned with giving a full account of God's nature and powers. Instead, they were content to show that there is a personal Ultimate Reality; other issues, regarding the nature of God, and so on, were taken up only insofar as they impinged on the project of establishing the inference about God's existence. Udayana was no exception.

For the purposes of summary, Deśika's critique of the project of establishing God's existence by inference can be divided into ten parts:

1. This world, which is limited and ever-changing, cannot have an omniscient and omnipotent maker as its efficient cause. There would be no brakes on his efficacy, no reason for the gradual evolution of the world: it would have to be made all at once.

2. The logicians argue for a maker who does not have a body, but the only maker they succeed in proving could be an embodied maker, since a physical world is most easily explained as made by a physical maker. But argument about the nature of this maker is not a concession that the maker actually exists.

3. It is not possible to prove that this hypothetical maker has the perfect knowledge supposed to belong to the lord, since even a non-omniscient person or groups of persons could have made this world.

4. There is no satisfactory way to prove both that this physical universe has a maker and that this maker does not have a body.

5. But the fact it is not possible to prove a bodiless maker is not a problem; to explain the world as we find it, there is no need to stipulate that kind of maker—bodiless, perfect—anyway.

6. Indeed, since there are plausible alternative explanations for the evolution of non-conscious realities, it is not necessary to conclude that they depend on a conscious maker at all.

7. Nor is it possible to describe the act by which this perfect creator might be supposed to have created the world; he cannot be shown to have the balance of specific knowledge, specific desire, and specific effort that are required to create a specific world.

8. The fact of material limitation leads only to a recognition that what is perceived must have some cause—not that it must have a creator.

9. A created world and its creator would have to be in a continuing relationship, but it is not possible to explain this relationship (as either necessary or constructed, etc.).

10. If one merely postulates the general principle that effects have not only causes but also makers, this generalization leaves one without any specific conclusions to draw about this particular world and its particular creator.

In Deśika's eyes the logicians are naïve; they imagine a very effective world-maker and find the image plausible, but in the course of their sophisticated logic they are doing no more than adjusting their mental image, adorning it with further desired features. These adornments are confused with what is logically necessary: a perfect maker, a personal maker, a maker without a body, and so on. Despite their enormous investment in logic, they are not actually thinking their way clearly to a single, simple, adequate *idea* of Ultimate Reality. A perfect idea of Ultimate Reality simply cannot be attained by reason; that is why believers rely on scripture.

The issues Deśika raises in response to the logicians pertain even more widely in thinking about Ultimate Reality. Some criticisms pertain to the impossibility of imagining a bodiless creator, and the defective nature of the transition from such imagining to what can actually be proved about it; some criticisms pertain to the idea of an omnipotent creator, subject to no constraints, who nevertheless is supposed to create a finite world gradually, within limits; some pertain to the difference between a "cause" and a "maker"; and some pertain to the difference between a *plausible* account for the world and a *necessary* account that excludes other plausible accounts of the world. It should be clear that Deśika does not believe that one can ever determine Ultimate Reality to have precisely and only the qualities one wishes that Reality to have; it is reasonable then not to depend entirely on reasoning.

5.3.4 *Two Concluding Comments*

Two comments conclude this section. First, Deśika obviously believes it proper to argue against this wide variety of opponents in one treatise: against devotees of other Hindu Gods, against atheistic Jainas, against logicians seeking to prove that there is a God. Deśika brings together diverse elements, proving (a) by a correct reading of scripture, that Nārāyaṇa alone is God; (b) by an analysis of language, that there is no good proof that God does not exist; (c) by analyzing the nature of proof, that there can be no inference that shows that God does exist. Ultimate Reality is an intelligible reality accessible in discussion, yet it cannot be discussed in the same way all the time with all discussion partners. The discourse on Ultimate Reality is therefore a necessarily complex one that cannot be adequately treated solely by one kind of analysis.

Second, it is not certain that the *Īśvarapariccheda* reflects actual arguments with proponents of the positions attacked. Our current knowledge of the classical Hindu texts and their transmission is still inadequate, and it is not possible to assume regarding texts such as this that the mention of various opponents indicates actual debate with them. But two points seem fairly certain. First, Deśika is writing primarily for his own Śrīvaiṣṇava community, whose members' faith is presumably supported and edified by this vigorous defense of their beliefs in light of alternative systems. Second, though, in order to achieve this first, intra-community goal, the arguments must be sufficiently credible that a member of an opposing school could at least understand them. The prerequisites for a conversation about Ultimate Reality must be in place even if one does depend heavily on such conversations.

5.4 Extending the Conversation

Let us now engage the broader topic of the idea of Ultimate Reality in a comparative context.

5.4.1 Sufficient Shared Presuppositions

Deśika's ordered, rational exposition of varying Indian views of Ultimate Reality suggests that it is possible for people of different religious, cultural, and linguistic traditions to converse with one another on the topic of Ultimate Reality. Words like "Ultimate Reality," "Lord" (*Īśvara*), "perfect/full" (*pūrṇa*), and even "omniscient agent" (*sarvajña kartṛ*) seem sufficiently intelligible that even those not willing to concede the existence of "a perfect and omniscient lord who made the world and who is the Ultimate Reality" can agree that the claim is intelligible. The fact of a shared language is a necessary presupposition for argument; conversely, though, it is argument that makes the fashioning of a shared language a worthwhile and even urgent task, a task likely to be carried out. To argue and persuade, people of varying positions fashion a common language, often by compromising (and possibly misunderstanding) differences in what they intended to say. In this way they create a new, shared vocabulary that reaches beyond familiar and already available common ground and that, though imperfect, makes argument possible.

Here lies a constructive value for apologetics, polemics, and other modes of discourse that create rather than merely represent common meanings. Arguments about Ultimate Reality and defenses of particular versions of it require the construction of a common ground where these disagreements can be sorted out, alleviated, or even sharpened. To assert that there is an Ultimate Reality, or to deny this, or to opt instead for a language of experience and spiritual realization that seemingly avoids such controversies—even these imply, or can quickly be systematized so as to assert some central explanatory claims about the world as a whole.

For instance, Deśika agrees with many other traditional Hindu thinkers—in the Nyāya and Vaiśeṣika schools, and even in Vedānta[17]—that the perceptible world is not self-explanatory and cannot be its own cause. Reflection on its nature and origins poses a problem and requires some account of its origins and the more enduring realities underlying it. While it is possible to argue about precisely what is lacking, and what kind of further explanation might be sufficient, the terms of debate are nevertheless sufficiently broad and intelligible as to draw into the argument a wide array of participants from within traditional Hinduism, from other schools of thought in India, and even from other cultures and religious traditions. In the course of deliberation about whether the world has a maker and whether that maker might be termed "Ultimate Reality," inference becomes a plausible (though not universally accepted) means of knowledge and argument a viable means of moving forward the analysis.

In a comparative context too reasoned inferences can become a key resource for shared ideas. Thinking about the commonly experienced world can lead to the question of whether or not there is an omniscient, all-powerful maker for it. Broad claims about Ultimate Reality need to be made coherent and sufficiently compelling if they are to invite either assent or denial. Even when there is disagreement, as among Deśika and his various opponents, it is nevertheless possible to get quite far in a discussion of Ultimate Reality just by analyzing the world and the claims one can make about it.

5.4.2 *Arguing the Definition*

It is also necessary to go beyond shared presuppositions and vocabulary to enter into conversation with Deśika about which elements of his stated definition really need to be included in a definition of Ultimate Reality that would be defensible outside his Śrīvaiṣṇava world, and even in our contemporary intellectual context. Although his definition and its details are rooted in his own sectarian Hindu tradition, it seems plausible to suggest that Deśika would still argue that even now an integral account of Ultimate Reality should include the same features as were stated earlier in this chapter:

1. Ultimate Reality is the single source for the finite yet ordered world we perceive.
2. Ultimate Reality must be entirely conscious and all-knowing.
3. Everything depends on Ultimate Reality, but Ultimate Reality is not dependent on anything.
4. Ultimate Reality is the single referent for all the various religious ideas and practices of the human race.
5. Ultimate Reality is the ontological basis for the continuing existence of everything.
6. Ultimate Reality is at work in the entire causal chain, not just at its beginning.
7. Ultimate Reality is related to everything else, as a soul is related to a body.
8. Ultimate Reality achieves whatever it wants, without obstacle.

In introducing these claims earlier on, we gave some indication of the importance with which Deśika invests them as a set. All are important, and while they are of quite different sorts, Deśika's tradition and his mode of systematic reasoning warn us against simply picking and choosing among these features as if they come separately. At least initially one needs to engage Deśika in a discussion of the complete, integral position that he presents. Inquiry into Ultimate Reality and its representations in various traditions is enhanced by taking Deśika's complete position seriously, even if this will entail argument about whether all the features he proposes are necessary, and necessary in the same way. A serious consideration of Ultimate Reality is therefore an argumentative venture; various proposed features of Ultimate Reality need to be compared and contrasted on rational grounds, with an at least theoretical willingness to highlight or rule out some of the features proposed in one or another religious and cultural setting.[18]

5.4.3 *Getting Very Particular*

It is possible to take a further step and note a series of interlocking terms for Ultimate Reality that Deśika uses and that seem more widely available as well. In arguing about Ultimate Reality, he skillfully uses and on occasion interchanges a variety of terms for Ultimate Reality: (1) Ultimate Reality is the highest (*param*); (2) Ultimate Reality is the all-pervasive source and foundation (*brahman*); (3) Ultimate Reality is the cause (*kāraṇa*); (4) Ultimate Reality is the personal agent (*kartṛ*);[19] (5) Ultimate Reality is the lord (*Īśvara*); (6) Ultimate Reality is Nārāyaṇa, and not other deities; (7) Ultimate Reality is Nārāyaṇa as described in the statements of scripture, particularly the Upaniṣads; (8) Ultimate Reality is Nārāyaṇa along with his consort Śrī. Given the integral nature of Deśika's project, it is not legitimate to exclude the more particular claims (Nārāyaṇa; consort of Śrī, etc.) and to settle for the less particular claims (the highest, the cause, etc.), nor to admire negative claims about Ultimate Reality while hesitating about the positive claims he makes. Serious conversation about Ultimate Reality entails a comprehensive analysis of any particular position that is put forward. Partial agreements are quite possible, and differences regarding one or more points do not signify entirely different conversations, as if to talk with a non-dualist about Reality is entirely different from talking to a logician, and as if these were entirely different from talking to a devotee of Śiva or a worshipper of Śrī as the consort of Nārāyaṇa. Although Deśika disagrees with the non-dualist Vedāntins on certain important points, on most issues he and they agree. Agreements and disagreements provide foreground and background for one another.

If so, content and conclusions alone cannot be the determining factors in organizing various positions on Ultimate Reality. Attention to ongoing conversations and an appreciation of a diversified, flexible vocabulary are required, since these help us to account for the conversation that occurs not only among theists or monists or comparativists, but also with a more comprehensive set of conversation partners engaged in yet broader and more varied discourses about Ultimate Reality, modern as well as ancient, cool and detached as well as passionately committed. Reason does not easily settle for conversations that exclude too many potential participants.

5.4.4 *Further Comparisons*

The *Īśvarapariccheda* deserves serious attention not only on its own merits but also because it is typical of a certain kind of comprehensive rational and religious reasoning about Ultimate Reality that has force and relevance more broadly in the Hindu context, and even beyond India. Understanding Deśika's project makes possible a wider range of treatises on Ultimate Reality, and therefore enables further insights into how people reason about Ultimate Reality, and indeed, into what "Ultimate Reality" means. Here we introduce two examples, one contemporary to Deśika (i.e., Śaivism), and one contemporary to ourselves (i.e., British rational theology). Thereafter we will note a less favorable candidate for comparison (i.e., Chinese (non)constructions of Ultimate Reality.

5.4.4.1 *Śaiva Siddhānta: Another Hindu Exposition of Ultimate Reality*

Deśika's exposition of Ultimate Reality and his critique of competing positions are reasonable and accessible. But the *Īśvaraparticcheda* is of course still rooted in the particularities of the Vedānta and Vaiṣṇava traditions. Other texts, even from his own era, expound coherent Hindu views of Ultimate Reality with quite different points of focus. For instance, within the south Indian Śaiva religious tradition—devoted not to Nārāyaṇa but to Śiva as the supreme Lord—there is a systematic school of thought known as Śaiva Siddhānta. This tradition seems much closer to the logicians than to Deśika in its logic and exposition, because it argues that God's existence can be proven by inference.

A key Śaiva Siddhānta text is the fourteenth-century *Civañāṇacittiyār* of Aruḷananti; it is divided into two parts. One part is the *Supakkam* ("Our Own Position"), which is a positive exposition of Śaiva Siddhānta theology. It is divided in this way: Book I. Means of right knowledge (*pramāṇa*): knowledge about the world and its creator, about bondage (by which we do not see reality clearly), and about the human self (who is bound); Book II. Definitions (*lakṣaṇa*): proper definitions of human, bondage, lord; Book III. The way (*sādhana*): the teacher, the path, saving knowledge; Book IV. Results (*phala*): purification, union, bliss. The first verse of *Civañāṇacittiyār* offers a simple, minimal understanding of the need for a creator, and what he is like:

> "He, she, it," altogether, the whole world comes, abides, then goes again, so there must be one who gives it all. He is the first cause, he ends it, he creates it again; he is beginningless, free, in form pure consciousness, he alone remains and abides unchanging.

The verse is programmatic, setting forth the topics and agenda for the rest of Book I of *Civañāṇacittiyār*: the finitude and dependent nature of the world, the independence of God, the activities and powers of Śiva, the divine powers, and the limitations of lesser gods.

In the other major part of the *Civañāṇacittiyār*, the Parapakkam (expounding and criticizing "other positions"), rival viewpoints are set forth and refuted. The purpose of this apologetic presentation, according to its introductory parts, is to make the faith clear for believers and for those who are wavering. Like the famous *Sarvadarśanasaṃgraha* (*Summary of All the Systems*) of Mādhavācārya, Deśika's own *Paramatabhaṅga*, and the presentation of adversaries in the *Īśvarapariccheda* itself, the Parapakkam lists competing schools in order of diminishing error: (1) materialists (Lokāyata); (2) ascetical, non-theistic schools (Buddhist, Jaina, and Ajīvaka); (3) atheistic ritual theory (Mīmāṃsā); (4) schools of language theory (Śabdabrahmavāda) that accept an Ultimate Reality (Brahman as Word); (5) nondualists who see the world as illusory (māyāvāda); (6) ambivalent monists (such as Bhāskara) who see the world as both real and unreal; (7) dualists (such as Sāmkhya thinkers) who posit both a consciousness and a material principle, but no lord; (8) devotees of Nārāyaṇa who think that Nārāyaṇa, despite his finite, bodily appearances in the world, is God (Pañcarātrins, Vaiṣṇavas).

By this ordering of opponents—each closer to the truth than the one prior to it—the *Civañāṇacittiyār* charts a diminishment of error and a movement toward the realization of a transcendent Person who is the sovereign cause of the world. Although most of the Parapakkam is philosophical, the actual attack on Vaiṣṇavism (Deśika's tradition) refers almost entirely to the Vaiṣṇava belief in the bodily presence of the divine in the world, by way of *avatāra*s (divine descents). The *Civañāṇacittiyār* considers the idea of *avatāra* to be rationally implausible; divine involvement in the world cannot occur in a way that seemingly exposes the divine to a range of human frailties. Deśika would agree that the range of possible candidates for "Ultimate Reality" can in the end be narrowed down to just one candidate, Nārāyaṇa or Śiva. He and the Śaivas both understand that their preference entails not just a sectarian attachment but also a full philosophical position with cosmological, epistemological, and logical implications. Deśika and the Śaivas can therefore be said to offer comparable Hindu ideas about Ultimate Reality—despite their disagreement about the name of this Reality and their differences on the specifics of their belief, such as whether it demeans the Lord to take human form. But the Śaivas, like the logicians, allow for reason the ability to determine conclusively that there is an Ultimate Reality endowed with particular characteristics. The Śaivas do not see this as detrimental to the importance of scripture; they argue for a conformity of scripture and reason, expecting both sources to agree on the fact of a personal Ultimate Reality who is the efficient cause of the world. Deśika's 10th point in the *Īśvarapariccheda* is aimed against the idea that one can know by reason that God is the efficient cause of the world.

5.4.4.2 *Richard Swinburne's* The Existence of God

Reflection on argument and the balancing of particular and universal arguments in the *Īśvarapariccheda* can be further extended by comparing

Deśika's arguments with those of contemporary Western theologians and philosophers who debate the nature of Ultimate Reality; indeed, it is striking that Deśika's presentation seems to fit comfortably into the mainstream of Western expositions of Ultimate Reality; whatever its roots, a reasonable discourse about God is not easily bound by time either. By way of example we introduce several points from *The Existence of God* (1979) by the Christian philosopher, Richard Swinburne, regarding the (limited) plausibility of the cosmological argument, in order to observe the common elements of the two positions.

In chapter 5, for example, Swinburne sketches "the intrinsic probability of theism," and begins with this claim:

> Theism states the following. There exists now, and always has existed and will exist, God, a spirit, that is, a non-embodied person who is omnipresent. . . . To say that God is not embodied is to deny that there is any limited volume of matter such that by his basic actions he can control only it and such that he knows of goings-on elsewhere in the universe only by their effects on it. By contrast, to say that God is an omnipresent spirit is to say that he knows about goings-on everywhere without being dependent for that knowledge on anything, and can control by basic actions all states of affairs everywhere, that is, anywhere in this or any other universe. God is the creator of all things in that for all logically contingent things which exist he himself brings about, or makes or permits other beings to bring about, their existence. He is, that is, the source of the being and the power of all other things. . . . God is omnipotent in the sense (roughly) that he can do whatever it is logically possible to do. He is omniscient, at any rate in the sense that he knows at any time whatever it is logically possible that he know at that time. . . . He is perfectly good . . . a being who does no morally bad actions, and does any morally obligatory action.[20]

Deśika, the logicians, the Śaivas, and Christian philosophers like Swinburne share a theistic view of Ultimate Reality. For example, they agree that Ultimate Reality is a person who is omniscient, omnipresent, omnipotent, and the maker of the world. Differences in technical language and specific context do not seem to be sufficiently important to dispose entirely of this striking consensus.

In chapter 7 Swinburne turns to the cosmological proof of God's existence—the sort of proof that the logicians and Śaivas offer and Deśika rejects. Swinburne situates his work in relation to earlier versions of this argument, notably those of G. W. Leibniz and Samuel Clarke, but his own moderate viewpoint can be stated in a few steps: "[T]he supposition that there is a God is an extremely simple supposition; the postulation of a God of infinite power, knowledge, and freedom is the postulation of the simplest kind of person which there could be. . . . If something has to occur unexplained, a complex physical universe is less to be expected than other things (e.g., God)."[21] With this appeal to simplicity (the virtue of *lāghava*)—it is simpler to assume God than to assume some other explanation for the world—Swinburne echoes a value common to most Indian schools, that overly complex arguments (which suffer the fault of *gaurava*) are inferior to those that are simpler.

Swinburne goes on to argue that the probability favoring such a God is not equaled by the probability that such a God, were one to exist, would in fact have actually created this world: "There are good reasons why God should make a complex physical universe. For such a physical universe can be beautiful, and that is good; and also it can be a theatre for finite agents to develop and make of it what they will. . . . But I cannot see that God has overriding reason to make such a universe. . . . Nor can I see that he has overriding reason to make or not to make any alternative world."[22] Neither the Deśika nor the logicians make arguments from beauty or goodness, but the logicians do raise the question of God's motivation. No reason that would bind God to a particular course of action can be allowed; as is characteristic of many Hindu thinkers, the logicians suggest that motiveless enjoyment or play (*līlā, krīḍā*) can be taken as the "reason" for his activity. At the end of chapter 7, Swinburne sums up his estimate of the probabilities as follows: "There is quite a chance that if there is a God he will make something of the finitude and complexity of a universe. It is very unlikely that a universe would exist uncaused, but rather more likely that God would exist uncaused. The existence of a universe is strange and puzzling. It can be made comprehensible if we suppose that it is brought about by God."[23]

It may be that Swinburne, the logicians, and the Śaivas all disagree with Deśika regarding how important it is to link the discussion of God's existence with discussions of the nature and activity of God. All three of the former positions seem to agree that a minimal inquiry into Ultimate Reality is worthwhile, because it tells us a great deal about the existence and nature of God. While accepting the conclusions drawn, Deśika also remains true to the theological and communal heritage of Vedānta and Śrīvaiṣṇavism and postpones reasonable analysis until scripture has been accepted. He keeps drawing qualitative discussions of the nature of God back into the wider rationalistic debate over God's existence and whether it can be known by means other than revelation. In his view, it cannot not. The existence of an Ultimate Reality cannot be established prior to the establishment of other features of this Reality's nature and activity; a rational consideration of Ultimate Reality is therefore tradition-specific from the start, and it must be contested on rational and sectarian grounds

from beginning to end. As a Vedāntin, Deśika insists that efficient causality cannot be discussed apart from material causality; as a Śrīvais-
ṇava, he insists that the cause of the world is not fully known until one
knows that this Cause is none other than Nārāyaṇa whose consort is Śrī.
There is very little room for a separable, prior philosophy of God in this
system.

Swinburne himself seems quite willing to refine his philosophical positions in specifically Christian ways. In *The Christian God* (1994), his re-
hearsal of the probabilities regarding the existence and nature of God as
a personal Ultimate Reality is followed by two chapters exploring the
probabilities of Christian beliefs regarding Trinity and Incarnation. Although Swinburne does not pretend to prove that God is Trinitarian and
Incarnate, he does assert that such Christian beliefs are probable once the
existence of God is accepted as probable. His argument regarding the
Trinity is typical. After discussing the place of love within the Ultimate
Reality, and the need for love to be relational, he draws this conclusion:
"Only fairly strong inductive arguments can be given for the existence of
God. Given that, arguments for there being a God and God being 'three
persons in one substance' will be of the same kind. Our claim is that the
data which suggest that there is a God suggest that the most probable
kind of God is such that inevitably he becomes tripersonal. It is for this
reason that the doctrine of the Trinity is not a more complicated hypothesis than the hypothesis of a sole divine individual."[24]

Despite the differences in their starting points and the specific characterizations of God they offer, both Swinburne and Deśika are willing to
amplify a rational reflection on reality and its ultimate cause with views
specific to their own traditions—and without acknowledging a significant gap between the two kinds of positions. Deśika concludes that Ultimate Reality has a spouse, Śrī; Swinburne, that Ultimate Reality is a Father, Son, and Spirit. In this way both contradict the tendency to assume
that a reasonable analysis of Ultimate Reality, its qualities and existence,
should remain at a safe distance from sectarian beliefs if it is to remain a
reasonable analysis. The fact that Deśika and Swinburne seem to agree
does not of itself vindicate their positions, but it does urge us to consider
more soberly the possibility and value of an alignment of positions in rational theology that cross religious and cultural boundaries.

5.4.4.3 *A More Problematic Comparison*

The two comparisons we have drawn, with Śaiva Siddhānta and Richard
Swinburne's philosophy, could be complemented by additional comparisons within India to Buddhist positions on Ultimate Reality, and outside
of India to Judaism and Islam; in different ways, each of these would

bring to the fore further similarities and differences. The expositions of these traditions elsewhere in this volume, respectively by Eckel, Saldarini, and Haq, suggest that while important differences and even disagreements would emerge in comparison with Deśika's system, such examples would further confirm the thesis that there is an identifiable and shared discourse about Ultimate Reality either original to or successfully implanted in these traditions, thus cutting across otherwise significant religious and cultural boundaries. Jews, Christians, and Muslims should be able to enter into conversation with Deśika about Ultimate Reality, and he was already in "successful" argument with Buddhist positions as well.

The situation seems more difficult if we move to the East, however. The materials given to us by Livia Kohn in her chapter on Ultimate Reality in Chinese religion suggest a more significantly different situation: "Aside from the general term 'Dao' which can mean anything from the road one walks on through the way one speaks to the ineffable power at the root of creation, there is no clear word or phrase that conveys to a Chinese exactly what we mean by ultimate reality" (2.1.2). It seems that one would have to choose between an approach to "Reality" or to "the Ultimate," but not both at the same time. To a Chinese scholar, it may be that Deśika's project would seem useless: "'But reality is not perfect!' In other words, whatever is not, is not and there is no sense at all wasting time even trying to think about it" (2.1.2). And finally, "utopian visions of the perfect state, idols of personal virtue (sincerity), and notions of the mystical dissolution of self in the Dao or immortality" will "fall short of our abstract concept of ultimate reality on two points: they are not generally applicable but limited to individual persons or specific groups, presenting a multiplicity of situationally determined 'ultimate realities' and making it necessary to redefine the notion in terms of highly specific personal or communal goals (and their related theories of world origin and development); and they are not ultimate in the sense of being unchangeable" (2.1.2).

The practicality and context-sensitivity of these Chinese understandings of the ultimate of course have important counterparts in the Hindu context, and a comparison of Chinese and Hindu thought would profitably bring such elements to the fore. Even Deśika could be shown to have a great deal to say along these lines were we to examine, for instance, his more expansive and genially spiritual *Śrīmadrahasyatrayasāra*. But the kind of endeavor taken up by Deśika in the *Īśvarapariccheda* seems more alien to the Chinese way of thinking as presented in Kohn's chapter; it may be that a more indirect comparison would have to prepare the way, that is, via a historical study of the arrival and fortunes of Buddhist notions of Ultimate Reality in China and the Chinese language, or via the various intellectual reformulations of Chinese thought in Indo-European languages that have taken place over the centuries. But inevitably there would have to be engagement in a project such as Deśika and his Indian counterparts were accustomed to undertake: a more extended argument between proponents of the Chinese and Vedānta positions, in an effort to reduce one to the features of the other, or to show why such a reduction is neither possible or necessary. In the short run, however, the question of any common ground between the representative Hindu intellectualization of Ultimate Reality presented here and Chinese thought will remain an open question. Ultimate Reality is clarified in the public intellectual sphere only when arguments about it can take place.

5.4.5 Deśika and the Possibility of a Contemporary Interreligious Reflection on Ultimate Reality

Deśika's mix of reasoning, exegesis, philosophy, and theology offers a view of Ultimate Reality that is typically Hindu and on its own merits rather compelling. His viewpoint is reasonable, systematic, sectarian, and argumentative, and he draws his readers into a complicated conversation with himself and with his direct adversaries; by extension, too, this conversation opens into a yet more complex multilevel argument with other viewpoints, such as those of Śaiva Siddhānta (contemporary to him) and Richard Swinburne (contemporary to us). Although the broader force of the *Īśvarapariccheda* is in many ways constricted by its original context and intent, it is not so seriously limited as to make it unnecessary to take it seriously as a position regarding the nature of Ultimate Reality. Read today, it stands against the temptation to frame portrayals of Ultimate Reality as either the program of just various, separate traditions, or as a single denaturalized discourse free from all such local origins. Philosophers are therefore challenged to learn much more about the specific details of different religious and philosophical systems than anyone can possibly know already. Yet the *Īśvarapariccheda* also defends the possibility of reflection on Ultimate Reality in a comparative context—reason makes it possible for proposed features of Reality to be discussed and assessed; the *Īśvarapariccheda* can even be interpreted as affirming that comparative reflection enables us to know more, more clearly, about Ultimate Reality than we would have known had we not ventured into comparative study. It may in fact be true that Ultimate Reality is a personal God, who is ruler over all, conscious and all-pervasive in knowing, owner of everything as totally dependent on himself, propitiated by all religious actions and the giver of all results, the foundation for everything else, the generator of all effects, possessed of all things as his body, and of sufficient power and wisdom that everything he wishes comes true, due simply to himself.

It is easy to disagree with this optimistic position, but even disagreement requires reasons why Ultimate Reality should be thought about in other or less public terms, or not thought about at all.

Notes

1. By "brāhmaṇical" I mean, in a strong but non-exclusive sense, the literate and sophisticated Sanskrit-language traditions of Hindu orthodoxy. By "Hindu" I refer to those majority traditions that are neither Buddhist nor Jain, that acknowledge the authority of the Vedas and also of a wider range of other sources of religious authority, and that, most importantly and for the most part, are devotional, dedicated to great deities such as Viṣṇu, Śiva, or Devī.

2. The Vedānta school of Rāmānuja (traditionally 1017–1137) is generally referred to as the Viśiṣṭādvaita or "Qualified-nondualist" school of Vedānta, since unlike the strict nondualist position of the Advaita ("Nondualist") School, it insisted on the distinct and enduring reality of sentient and insentient beings within that Ultimate Reality, which is Brahman, the Lord: one Ultimate Reality that is yet imbued with enduring specifications (*viśeṣa*). Vedānta texts are generally in the Sanskrit language, but the Viśiṣṭādvaita is also deeply influenced by the theology and devotion of the south Indian Tamil-language tradition. It flourished there, in piety and theology, as the theology of the Śrīvaiṣṇava community that was signally devoted to Nārāyaṇa (Viṣṇu) with his divine consort Śrī. On the whole, it is far more representative of Hindu thinking than is the Advaita position.

3. Though the historical sources for the cults of Nārāyaṇa and Viṣṇu would differ, the piety and theology of the Śrīvaiṣṇavas identify the two.

4. Like Mīmāmsā ritual theory, Nyāya logic is both common currency among many schools of thought and also the defining characteristic of a specific school with its own positions.

5. *Dharmabhūtajñāna*: i.e., knowledge that is constitutive of the Lord, not simply a temporary attribute.

6. The three constituents of reality, *sattva* (lucidity), *rajas* (passion), *tamas* (inertia); the five senses, *śabda* (sound), *sparāa* (touch), *rūpa* (form), *rasa* (taste), *gandha* (smell); and *saṃyoga* (relation) and *śakti* (potency). Throughout, I use the edition of the *Nyāyasiddhāñjana* that includes the *Ratnapeṭika* of Sri Kanchi Tatacharyaya and the *Saralaviśada* of Sri Raṅgarāmānuja (Madras: Ubhaya Vedānta Granthamala, 1976).

7. Other works of Deśika, such as the *Paramata Bhaṅga* (*The Shattering of Other Views*), *Śrīmadrahasyatrayasāra* (*The Essence of the Three Mysteries*), and most important the *Tattvamuktakalāpa* (*The Necklace of Complete Truth*), consider the same topics (including the nature of the Lord as Ultimate

Reality), but the focus on logical issues evident in the *Nyāyaparisuddhi* and *Nyāyasiddhāñjana* gives this pair of works a particularly clear and systematic shape.

8. In what follows I provisionally divide the *Īśvarapariccheda* into fourteen parts (thereby making the flow of the argument somewhat clearer than it is). Satyavrata Singh gives this summary: "The 3rd chapter or the Īśvara Parichheda, presents Īśvara or the Divine as the Viśiṣṭādvaitic Absolute and identifies It with Śrī Nārāyaṇa, the highest Śrīvaiṣṇava religious ideal. The concept of 'Viśiṣṭādvaita' [complex non-dualism] has been fully analyzed. The relationship between the substrate and the subsisting, the self and the organism, the controller and the controlled, the independent and the subservient, the self and the organism, the cause and the consequent and so on, is discussed as the relationship between God and the 'cidacit'—[conscious and nonconscious] principles of life. It is this conception of the Divine that is the supreme sense of the syncretization of the Vedānta with the Nyāya." (Satyavrata Singh, *Vedānta Deśika: His Life, Works and Philosophy* [Varanasi: Chowkambha Sanskrit Series Office, 1958], 80).

9. Divine knowledge is not technically in the category of things (*dravya*) owned by the lord.

10. It is taken for granted by Deśika that this "lord" is male; the last section of the *Īśvarapariccheda* introduces his eternal female consort, Śrī.

11. The basic positions taken by Deśika are drawn from Rāmānuja's writings; for a succinct summation of these positions, see Rāmānuja's *Vedārthasaṃgraha*.

12. He was the teacher of Rāmānuja, the founder of Deśika's school of thought; early on Rāmānuja broke with Yādavaprakāśa, for philosophical reasons.

13. The "saptabhaṅgī" position.

14. "Ideas" is an important word here, for no one can plausibly claim that many of the Hindus who share Deśika's beliefs readily understand his complicated position; he argues and writes within a sophisticated intellectual milieu that is inevitably far removed from ordinary piety, even if it supports and does not contradict that piety.

15. Even if neither Śaivas nor Vaiṣṇavas would accept only the Upaniṣads as their texts.

16. George Chemparathy, *An Indian Rational Theology: Introduction to Udayana's Nyāyakusumāñjali* (Vienna: De Nobili Research Library, 1972), 86. The entire *Nyāyakusumāñjali* has recently been translated by N. S. Dravid, *Nyāyakusumāñjali of Udayanācārya* (New Delhi: Indian Council of Philosophical Research, 1996).

17. On the argument about the maker of the world, see "From Truth to Religious Truth in Hindu Philosophical Theology," chap. 2, *Religious Truth*.

18. Admittedly, a certain optimism underlies this proposed openness to argumentation. Attention to linguistic, cultural, and historical differences can

serve as safeguards against the temptation merely to dispute with Deśika based on what seems obvious or certain within other systems of rational theology; these differences can be taken into account without indefinitely postponing inquiry into Deśika's *ideas* about Ultimate Reality.

19. The character of this divine agency, however, is debated in Vedānta: that causality is personal is defended, while the limitations connected with any given agent are excluded.

20. Richard Swinburne, *The Existence of God* (Oxford: Clarendon Press, 1991), 90–92.

21. Ibid., 130.

22. Ibid., 130–31.

23. Ibid., 131–32.

24. Richard Swinburne, *The Christian God* (Oxford: Clarendon Press, 1994), 191.

6

Cooking the Last Fruit of Nihilism

Buddhist Approaches to Ultimate Reality

Malcolm David Eckel
with John J. Thatamanil

᭯

The Buddhist tradition often seems to play the role of the knotty exception in comparative studies of religion.[1] In my introductory remarks at the October meeting of this seminar, I argued that the Madhyamaka tradition of Buddhist philosophy can play the same challenging role for us as well. The Mādhyamikas of ancient India and Tibet, along with their modern successors, work with categories that we recognize. They pursue "ultimate reality" (*paramārtha-sat*) with a single-minded intensity that would gladden the heart of any Nevillean philosopher. But they pursue it in a distinctive way and with distinctive ends. They are not out to uncover a secure and stable reality behind the changeable world of appearances; they want to demonstrate that there is no stable, ultimate reality. A simple way to make this point is to state it as a paradox: for the Buddhist philosophers of the Madhyamaka tradition, the ultimate identity (*svabhāva*) of things is to have no identity (*niḥsvabhāvatā*). This "ultimate identity" is not one that can be tacked up on the bulletin board with "ultimate identities" from other religious traditions. It challenges the concept of identity itself, with all of its attendant practical and procedural presuppositions.

6.1 The Myth of Reference

One dimension of the Madhyamaka challenge has to do with the meanings of words. Mādhyamikas approach words and concepts with the idea of exploding what we might call "the myth of reference": the myth that words refer to real things. If words do not refer to things, what do they mean? Indian Mādhyamikas did not spend much time sketching a formal semantic theory, but it is possible to get an impression of one by beginning with the work of the Buddhist logician Dignāga.[2] Dignāga is well known in Indian philosophy for the theory of "exclusion" (*apoha*), in which a word functions only as a way of distinguishing a so-called "object" from the things that it is not. Dignāga's standard example is the word "cow." According to the Buddhist theory of no-self, there not only is no generic category "cow," there also is no particular cow that continues from one moment to the next. So there can be no "cowness" that inheres in the different objects named by the word "cow." The word "cow" cannot designate a cow, because there is no cow (other than a particular moment in a stream of causes and conditions): the word simply excludes everything that is "non-cow." To use Dignāga's terminology, the meaning of the word lies simply in its ability to "exclude the other" (*anyāpoha*), not to designate anything that is real in its own right.[3] This is not to say, of course, that words have no practical function. There are many situations (especially in India) when it is useful to know the difference between cows and non-cows. But when the word "cow" is examined in a critical way, it designates nothing that is ultimately real.

Despite Dignāga's best efforts to avoid the suggestion that words refer to real things, the sixth-century Mādhyamika Bhāvaviveka (on whom I based much of my discussion in *The Human Condition*) felt that the concept of "exclusion" still risked attributing too much reality to words.[4] If the meaning of a word is its "exclusion of the other," Bhāvaviveka asked, what is an "exclusion"? Having already rubbed shoulders with the Madhyamaka understanding of Emptiness, we should not be surprised to hear Bhāvaviveka argue that an "exclusion" cannot be any more real than anything else. It too is empty of any real identity. Then what does Bhāvaviveka think words "mean"? He says that a word designates an "emptiness of that which is dissimilar" (*vijātīyena śūnyatvam*). Taken literally, this means that a word refers to the fact that a particular object cannot be identified with anything that is different from it. The word "dissimilar" is normally used to name something that resides in a different "stream" or "continuum."[5] One person is dissimilar to another, for example, just as a cow is dissimilar to a goat. One should be wary, however, of the temptation to interpret this formula as a proposal for another kind of reference. My suspicion is that Bhāvaviveka's intention is not to propose a full-fledged alternative to Dignāga's theory, but to replace the word "exclusion" with a word that is more explicitly self-critical. To say that a word refers to an "emptiness" rather than to an "exclusion" is not to substitute one form of reference for another but to say that the concept of reference itself is fundamentally flawed.

Bhāvaviveka's argument about reference has important implications for our comparative study of religious terminology. If our procedure is to identify "vague" concepts (concepts with broad reference) that allow further "specification" (narrow reference), the Madhyamaka approach to reference presents a serious barrier. Mādhyamikas simply do not use words this way. If our intention is to identify comparative concepts in a way that Mādhyamikas would recognize as productive, it would be better (as I argued in my chapter for volume one) to look for interpretive principles or orientations that govern the tradition's approach to ultimacy rather than for descriptive terms that name a fixed reality. One way to do this would be to pursue the Madhyamaka suggestion that the ultimate is rational, requires a distinction between ultimate and conventional, and yields no stable foundation or resting place.[6] Is it possible that other traditions follow similar dialectical procedures in moving from the conventional to the ultimate? How do other traditions recognize the ultimate when they have found it (or when it has found them)?

Another productive way to explore concepts of ultimacy across the boundaries of traditions might be to put the microscope on the "breaking" of symbols as explained in *The Truth of Broken Symbols*.[7] There is a key verse in the *Madhyamakakārikās* in which Nāgārjuna speaks of Emptiness as a "dependent designation" or metaphor: "We speak of Dependent Origination as Emptiness: it is a dependent designation, and it is the Middle Path."[8] Are all designations of ultimate reality irreducibly metaphorical? If so, how do traditions construct their words for ultimate reality so that they call attention to their metaphorical dimension? Mādhyamikas speak of their terms as "metaphors" (*upacāra*), but in a way that constantly suggests instability of reference. They would not say that there is any stable process of analysis that can determine what a metaphor definitively "means," if by "meaning" we expect to find the object or reality that the word finally names. As the Chinese seemed clearly to perceive, the force of the Mahāyāna concept of Emptiness leads toward the Daoist critique of verbal distinctions rather than toward the process of division and classification implicit in the Confucian "rectification of names."[9] Do other traditions map the movement toward ultimacy by suggesting an unstable process of reference, where all reference is intended to undermine and clear away once and for all the presumption of real reference?[10] Or is the Buddhist tradition (particularly in its Madhyamaka manifestation) the last line of resistance to a notion that religious symbols actually refer (in Robert Neville's account of Axial Age religions) "to what is on the other side of the finite"?[11]

6.2 Hypothesis and Confirmation

In the October session I built on these remarks about reference to make a suggestion about our method of investigation. We run a risk of being misled if we follow an overly literal understanding of the scientific model of "hypothesis" and "confirmation." By "overly literal" I mean one that involves the assumption that a hypothesis proposes the existence of a certain "thing" (whether it is defined vaguely or specifically) and confirmation seeks to find it in a variety of different settings. What kind of thing is this "thing," and how do we know it when we find it? In my chapter on the human condition, I mentioned Jonathan Z. Smith's criticism of the method of "systematic description and comparison." In his well-known essay, "In Comparison a Magic Dwells," Smith argued that claims of cross-cultural similarity have the same cognitive status that J. G. Frazer attributed to magic:

> If my analysis of the magician's logic is correct, its two great principles turn out to be merely two different misapplications of the association of ideas. Homeopathic magic is founded on the association of ideas by similarity; contagious magic is founded on the association of ideas by contiguity.[12]

To say that comparison is an act of homeopathic magic is only troubling, however, if we imagine that we are doing something akin to Darwin's classification of finches in the Galapagos. I take Jonathan Z. Smith's final essay in the same volume, "The Devil in Mr. Jones," to be an example of the transmutation of magic into imagination in the service not of explanation but of understanding. Smith juxtaposes radically different instances in the history of religions (the mass suicide in Jonestown, Dionysiac cults in Euripides' *Bacchae*, and cargo cults in the New Hebrides), to remove from Jonestown what he calls "the aspect of the unique."[13] The comparison works because it respects the strangeness and particularity of the individual cases while using each one to illuminate the others. Since we are a group of historians who honor the unique and particular as well as the generic and universal, we need to find ways in each tradition to let William James's recalcitrant crab say, "I am not a crustacean. I am MY-SELF, MYSELF alone," while we also expect it to reflect on its kinship not only with other crabs but with other beasts that skitter or crawl across the floor of the cosmos.[14]

6.3 What Kind of Reality Is Ultimate?

In chapter 2 of *The Truth of Broken Symbols*, Robert Neville describes finite/infinite contrasts as "realities, or structures of reality."[15] Would it be useful in our project to shift our attention deliberately from the first member of this pair of concepts to the second and focus more explicitly on "structures of reality"? The term "reality" raises many complicated problems for Buddhist philosophers, but they have interesting things to say about the structure of a quest for ultimacy (as they would about the structure of ultimacy itself). Wilfred Cantwell Smith made a move like this when he said that the Buddha elevated Dharma "to finality, to absolute transcendence" and argued that, through their faith in Dharma, Buddhist men and women have lived lives "in what the Western world has traditionally called the presence of God."[16] Smith's theistic language often strikes Buddhists as heavy-handed. But woe betide the church leader or theologian who makes too glib a claim about the negativity of Buddhist attitudes toward salvation and ultimate reality.[17] The constant challenge of Buddhist-Christian dialogue is to develop formulations of Buddhist concepts that accurately present the negative force of Buddhist thought without depicting it as sterile, unfeeling, or nihilistic. The challenge, in other words, is to find the middle—the point of balance between excessive reification and excessive denial.

How does the Buddhist quest for ultimacy structure itself? As Wilfred Cantwell Smith has suggested, the quest presupposes a certain order and predictability in the cosmos, an order that ties wrong actions to painful results but also allows the possibility of wisdom and a final release from suffering. The name for this order is Dharma. To begin from the concept of Dharma and construct lines of investigation in other traditions would lead not merely to Hindu literature like *The Laws of Manu* or the *Bhagavad Gītā* (in which the concept of Dharma plays a similarly pivotal role) but to the various representations of the Dao in Chinese philosophy and the various concepts of rational order and natural law in the Western intellectual tradition. (Wilfred Cantwell Smith used to insist that no comparative investigation of the world's religions was complete without scrutinizing the religious dimension of Western scientific rationality.)

Another useful line of investigation might be to focus less on the order of the cosmos itself than on the actualization or realization of that cosmic order in human experience. The Mādhyamikas took the word ultimate (*paramārtha*) as having a double reference: it could refer to the nature of reality (to Emptiness as the object of cognition) or to a person's awareness of the nature of reality.[18] Of these two possible meanings, the second was considered the most important. When Nāgārjuna said, "Liberation [comes] from the extinction of *karma* and defilements; *karma* and defilements [come] from concepts; [concepts come] from the complexity of language; but the complexity of language is stopped in Emptiness," the commentators explained that the word "Emptiness" in the last quarter of the verse refers to a form of understanding or vision.[19] If we made the choice in our own comparative project to consider the ultimate as a form of experience, it would suggest a number of intriguing lines of investigation. In a conversation with Bill Moyers, Tu Weiming said that "learning to be human" is the ultimate concern of the Confucian tradition.[20] In a more systematic account of the religious dimension of Confucianism, Tu Weiming adds the element of transcendence: "We can define the Confucian way of being religious as *ultimate self-transformation as a communal act and as faithful dialogical response to the transcendent*."[21] But the shorthand version of the definition is suggestive. Would it not be productive to investigate ultimacy at precisely the point at which the ultimate becomes a reality in the life of the person whose imagination it grasps?[22] If so, the possibilities are very rich. In an earlier meeting I suggested exploring a line of connection between the biblical phrase "God is love" (1 John 4:8) and the Mahāyāna understanding of the connection between wisdom (the awareness of Emptiness) and compassion. Paula Fredriksen suggested another line of investigation in her discussion of purity in early Christianity. Buddhaghosa's authoritative account of Theravāda Buddhist practice, *The Path of Purification* (*Visuddhimagga*), would make an intriguing point of comparison. All of these possibilities share the advantage of overcoming the rigid split between the traditions that affirm a doctrine of God as creator and those that do not.

6.4 The Problem of the Absolute

These remarks have been intended to clarify the points I made at the beginning of our discussion of Buddhism in the fall. To push the discussion a step further I would like to revisit an interpretive problem that has occupied the attention of Buddhist scholars since the time when Mahāyāna philosophy first became known in the West. The problem is easy to state but not easy to solve: Are the negations that surround the Mahāyāna concept of Emptiness intended to be a form of negative theology? Are they, in other words, a negative designation of an Absolute Reality that transcends all definition and all thought? This problem was raised by some of the earliest interpreters of the Madhyamaka and continues to play an important role in recent writing about Buddhist thought.[23] It still may be the best way to understand the possibilities and limits of comparison between Buddhist concepts of Emptiness and Western concepts of God.

The first serious Western encounter with Madhyamaka thought appeared in Eugène Burnouf's *Introduction à l'histoire du Buddhisme indien*, published in Paris in 1844. This work appeared several decades after the earliest British translations of the Hindu scriptures, and its date serves as a reminder of how inaccessible most Indian Mahāyāna sources have been, even in the late decades of the twentieth century. Burnouf based his comments about Madhyamaka on a rare Sanskrit manuscript of Candrakīrti's commentary on Nāgārjuna's *Madhyamakakārikās* that had been discovered in Nepal by the British scholar and colonial official Brian Houghton Hodgson. Burnouf characterized what he saw in Nāgārjuna and Candrakīrti as a "scholastic nihilism." This interpretation caught Durkheim's attention in *The Elementary Forms of the Religious Life*, where he took particular note of Burnouf's claim that Buddhism "sets itself in opposition to Brahmanism as a moral system without God and an atheism without nature."[24] Burnouf's nihilistic interpretation of Madhyamaka gained a certain currency in French and British scholarly circles. The most direct and uncompromising account of this interpretation was written by the great Belgian scholar Louis de La Vallée Poussin as a contribution to Hastings's *Encyclopaedia of Religion and Ethics*. The article, which was simply called "Nihilism (Buddhist)," ends with these words:

> This system may not bear criticism; but it is nevertheless an honest and able attempt to cook the last fruit of nihilism—negation of suffering and of liberation—evolved from the old nihilistic seed sown by Buddha himself, in the most orthodox juice (*rasa*) of the Good Law, the juice of suffering and liberation.

It is unclear where La Vallée Poussin got the metaphor of "cooking the last fruit of nihilism," but it leaves little doubt of where he stands, and it makes for relatively juicy reading, at least by comparison to the writings of some of his contemporaries.

The La Vallée Poussin interpretation of the Madhyamaka did not go unchallenged. In *The Conception of Buddhist Nirvana*, F. Th. Stcherbatsky interpreted Madhyamaka as a form of pan-Indian monism. He said: "In Mahāyāna all parts or elements are unreal (*śūnya*), and only the whole, i.e., the Whole of the wholes (*dharmatā = dharma-kāya*) is real."[25]

He also assimilated Madhyamaka to Vedānta: "Upon the Indian side we must first of all point to the almost absolute identity with Vedānta, as a probable consequence of his [Nāgārjuna's] indebtedness to Aupanishada tradition."[26] Stcherbatsky's interpretation was taken up, polished, and defended by a series of scholars, not the least of whom was T. R. V. Murti, a śāstrī and ācārya at Banaras Hindu University. Murti drew together many of the positive elements of Stcherbatsky's reading when he said: "The Mādhyamika Dialectic as negation of thought is intuition of the Absolute; as the rooting out of passions it is Freedom (Nirvāṇa); and it is perfection as union with the Perfect Being."[27]

No good deed ever goes unpunished, and no good interpretation ever goes unquestioned, least of all by the person who first came under its spell. In one of the more instructive ironies in the history of Buddhist scholarship, both Stcherbatsky and La Vallée Poussin, after years of controversy, repented of their folly and adopted the position of the other. In a series of papers published posthumously in the *Harvard Journal of Asiatic Studies*, La Vallée Poussin said: "J'ai longtemps cru . . . que le Madhyamaka était 'nihiliste', niait l'Absolu, la chose en soi. Dans un mémoire 'Madhyamaka' (*Mélanges chinois et bouddhiques* 2), je glisse vers une solution moins catégorique. Enfin, dans la présente note, je me dispose à admettre que le Madhyamaka reconnait un Absolu."[28] Stcherbatsky expressed his change of heart in less dramatic terms, but the change was no less complete. In the introduction to a translation of a Sanskrit text known as *The Distinction Between the Middle and the Extremes*, he said:

> Now the Mādhyamikas deny the ultimate reality of both these concepts. They neither admit the reality of the *paratantra* nor of the *pariniṣpanna* = *śūnyatā*. For them these two Absolutes are as relative as all the rest. They admit no exception from their principle of Universal Relativity, no *paramārtha-sat*, no Thing-in-Itself. They, of course, have a *paramārtha-satya*, or Highest Principle, of their own, but it consists just in the denial of the Thing-in-Itself, the denial of every ultimately real Element in existence. Tsoṅ-kha-pa, a good judge, says in his *Legs-bśad sñiṅ? po* that among all system [*sic*] of philosophy, Buddhist as well as non-Buddhist, there is only a single one which denies every kind of ultimately Real; and this is the system of the Mādhyamikas.[29]

Stcherbatsky did not use the word "nihilism" to characterize his new approach, but the key to his interpretation was the idea that Emptiness involved the denial of any ultimate reality, including the ultimate reality of the two Yogācāra concepts mentioned in the paragraph (*paratantra* or Dependent Nature, and *pariniṣpanna* or Purified Nature). Both of these concepts had been taken as references to a real Absolute.

Who was right? Was anyone right? La Vallée Poussin was aware that he and Stcherbatsky had exchanged positions and took the exchange as an indication of the depth and difficulty of the problem. He was right when he said that the problem was difficult, but the problem was not impossible, and Stcherbatsky had found a way solve it. He had begun to look into the Tibetan tradition of exegesis of the Madhyamaka, represented, in the passage just quoted, by the figure of Tsoṅ-kha-pa, and he had begun to use the Tibetan tradition to distinguish between the two major schools of Indian Mahāyāna thought: the Yogācāra and the Madhyamaka. The text that elicited Stcherbatsky's comments, *The Distinction Between the Middle and the Extremes*, presented a Yogācāra account of ultimate reality. By looking at the text through Tibetan eyes, Stcherbatsky realized that the Yogācāra and Madhyamaka articulated very different visions of Emptiness.

The Distinction Between the Middle and the Extremes introduces its account of reality in the following cryptic verse:

> The Imagination of what is unreal exists. Duality does not exist in it. But Emptiness does exist in it, and it exists in that [Emptiness].[30]

In the commentary on this verse, the commentator explains that *the Imagination of what is unreal* (*abhūta-parikalpa*) is equated with the act of distinguishing between subjects and objects.[31] *Duality* consists of the subjects and objects themselves. *Emptiness* is the absence of subject and object in the Imagination. The commentary ends with a scriptural quotation about Emptiness: "The right way to define Emptiness is to say: 'One perceives truly, when one thing is not present in another, that the latter is empty of the former, and one understands correctly that whatever remains there actually is present'." The quotation comes from *The Lesser Sutta on Emptiness* (*Cūḷasuññatā Sutta*) in the *Majjhima Nikāya* and describes a series of meditations in which a practitioner is told to focus on a certain location, such as the forest where he is sitting in his meditation, and develop an awareness of its emptiness. This passage treats the awareness of emptiness as having a certain logical form: to perceive emptiness a person has to be aware that one thing (the thing that remains) is empty of another (the thing that has been removed). In the example of the forest, the forest remains and is empty of the distractions of village life. The meditator moves on from his contemplation of the emptiness of the forest to contemplate the emptiness of the earth in front of him, becoming aware that the earth is empty of forest. The process continues until the practitioner realizes the emptiness of the meditative plane on which there is neither perception nor non-perception.

What should we make of this sequence of formulas? As cryptic as they may be, the verse and commentary make three key points that characterize the tradition of Yogācāra thought. The first point is that reality can be divided into three categories: the Imagination, Duality, and Emptiness. Later in the text these three categories are called Dependent Nature (*paratantra-svabhāva*), Imagined Nature (*parikalpita-svabhāva*), and Purified Nature (*pariniṣpanna-svabhāva*). Connecting the two lists of three yields the following three-part scheme:

Duality of Subject and Object	Imagined Nature
Imagination	Dependent Nature
Emptiness	Purified Nature

To understand the way this scheme represents reality, it is best to use one of the common Yogācāra examples. Verse 17 of the text compares the function of these categories to the transformations of water, gold, and space. Water, gold, and space can be polluted by different kinds of pollutants, molded into a variety of different things, or concealed by something else, but all three possess a certain inherent capacity for purification. Water can be polluted by mud, or its surface can be obscured by waves, but when polluted water is allowed to wash the pollutants away or when turbulent water is allowed to become still, the water naturally becomes clear. Gold can be covered by dirt or transformed into a variety of different objects, but when the gold has been cleaned or melted down, it is still pure gold. The open space of the sky can be obscured by smoke, but when the smoke blows away the sky is clear. The first category in the scheme (Duality) corresponds to the pollution or the waves in water, the dirt or the different shapes that seem to conceal the nature of gold, or the smoke that obscures the clarity of space. The last category (Emptiness) corresponds to the substances in their pure state. The middle category (Imagination) corresponds to the combination of the substances in their pure state with the defilements that obscure them. These examples can be incorporated into the scheme itself.

Duality	Imagined Nature	Waves or smoke
Imagination	Dependent Nature	Water disturbed by waves
		Sky obscured by smoke
Emptiness	Purified Nature	Water without waves
		Sky without smoke

The second point to make about the three-part scheme is that it involves a judgment about the reality of each of the categories. The text says that the Imagination and Emptiness both exist (or are real), while Duality does not exist (or is not real).[32] This position is reaffirmed in the next verse.

> This is why it is said that everything is non-empty and everything is not non-empty, because [the Imagination] exists, [Duality] does not exist, and [Emptiness] exists. This is the Middle Path.[33]

The Imagination is a combination of Duality, which is not real (this is why the Imagination is first called the Imagination of what is unreal) and Emptiness, which is real.

Duality	Imagined Nature	Smoke	Unreal
Imagination	Dependent Nature	Sky with smoke	Real and unreal
Emptiness	Purified Nature	Sky without smoke	Real

To say that "this" is the Middle Path is to say that the Imagination embodies the balance between reality and unreality that constitutes the Middle Path. What does the text mean by "Imagination" (*parikalpa*)? The Imagination is best thought of simply as the mind in its active and creative capacity: the verb *pari-klp* means to construct, as in the "construction" of a concept. But the Imagination also is the mind in its deluded aspect, as it is misled by all the phantoms of ordinary experience. In and of itself the mind is real. (It may be possible to doubt the reality of the contents of a dream, but it is impossible to doubt that the mind is dreaming the dream.) The dualities that are imagined by the mind, however, are nothing more than fabrications: they are not real. To experience the inherent reality of the mind in the most direct and complete way, one has to dispel the phantoms and fictions of ordinary consciousness and allow the mind to become aware of its own deep clarity and stillness. This account of the development of the mind echoes the terminology of classical yoga, where yoga is defined as the "cessation of the fluctuations of the mind."[34] Certainly that is not unexpected from a school called "Yogācāra" ("the practice of yoga").

The third point to make about the Yogācāra map of reality is that the concept of Emptiness involves what might be called a "logic of remainder." The commentary on the first verse about the Imagination quoted *The Lesser Sutta on Emptiness* as saying that "One perceives truly, when one thing is not present in another, that the latter is empty of the former, and one understands correctly that whatever remains there actually is present." To perceive Emptiness, according to this formula, takes two elements: something had to be missing, and something had to be left. If we apply this formula to the pursuit of knowledge about the nature of the mind, it suggests that we have to know the *absence* of all the dualistic fabrications that delude the mind, and we also have to know the *presence* of what remains—the reality of the mind itself. This reality is what the text calls Emptiness.

It is hard to overestimate the significance of this formulation for the "Problem of the Absolute." The basic question that confronted Stcherbatsky and La Vallée Poussin was whether any "absolute" reality remained after the negative process of Madhyamaka thought had done its work. If Madhyamaka could be assimilated to Yogācāra, the answer would be yes. A true perception of Emptiness would be a perception of "whatever remains and actually is present" when dualities are removed from the mind. The problem, as Stcherbatsky eventually came to understand, is that the Mādhyamikas themselves did not accept the Yogācāra account of the "three natures" of reality. Before I comment on the Madhyamaka criticism of the Yogācāra, however, I should say something about the historical influence of Yogācāra thought.

It seems, as well as anyone can guess, that Nāgārjuna lived and wrote sometime in the second century of the Common Era. The founders of the Yogācāra tradition, Asaṅga and Vasubandhu lived perhaps in the third or fourth century. By about the year 400, the Yogācāra tradition had become sufficiently sophisticated to spawn a school of logic and epistemology that eventually dominated the form if not the substance of Buddhist philosophical discourse in India. In the early 500s, Bhāvaviveka wrote a series of attacks on the Yogācāra vision of reality that sharply distinguished the Madhyamaka and Yogācāra traditions. It is possible, in fact, that the very idea of Yogācāra and Madhyamaka as separate and contrasting schools dates roughly from this time. Madhyamaka and Yogācāra developed side-by-side in India for another six or seven hundred years until the eventual demise of the great Indian monastic universities in the twelfth and thirteenth centuries, with the Yogācāra becoming increasingly associated with the tradition of the Buddhist logicians and the Madhyamaka becoming more and more concerned with matters of logic and epistemology. Both schools took on new life when they were transported beyond India. The Yogācāra was popularized in China in the early seventh century by the Chinese monk Hsüan-tsang, who traveled to India in the early seventh century and studied for several years in Indian monasteries before going back to China and writing his own encyclopedic summary of Yogācāra thought. In the eighth century, the Madhyamaka was introduced to Tibet where it took root and flourished.

In China the Yogācāra school in the narrow sense was soon eclipsed by other, indigenous Buddhist schools, but Chinese Buddhists seem to have felt a genuine affinity for Yogācāra patterns of thought. It is difficult to read the classics of Chinese Buddhism without being impressed by the subtle ways Yogācāra thought insinuated itself into their views of the world. In *The Platform Sutra of the Sixth Patriarch*, a Ch'an Buddhist classic from the T'ang Dynasty, the conflict between the monks Shen-hsiu and Hui-neng over the nature of enlightenment is worked out in the framework of a Yogācāra metaphor.[35] According to the story, the teacher of the two monks challenged his students to write a verse in which they expressed their understanding of "the original nature of the *prajñā* intuition." The teacher said that if one of the monks demonstrated that he had awakened to the true meaning, the teacher would give him the robe that signified the transmission of his authority. The head monk, Shen-hsiu, wrote the following verse:

> The body is the Bodhi tree,
> The mind is like a clear mirror.
> At all times we must strive to polish it,
> And not let the dust collect.[36]

Hui-neng, who is depicted in the story as an illiterate worker, asked to have the verse read to him. When he heard it, he dictated a response:

> Bodhi originally has no tree,
> The mirror also has no stand.
> Buddha nature is always clean and pure;
> Where is there room for dust?[37]

The teacher read the verses, recognized Hui-neng's verse as a deeper expression of awakening, and summoned Hui-neng to pass on the transmission of his authority. Hui-neng then left the monastery to found one of the great lineages of the Ch'an tradition.

The image of the mind as a mirror that needs to be cleansed of dust can easily be read as a variation of one of the fundamental Yogācāra images of the mind. The issue in dispute between the two monks, as expressed in their verses, was the status of the "unreal" dualities that seem to conceal the clarity of the mind. Shen-hsiu was quite right about his account of the practice of meditation: it requires long practice to remove dust from the mind and allow its clarity and purity to be revealed. But as long as a monk gets stuck on the idea that there is real dust to be removed, he does not understand the full force of the Yogācāra vision of reality. The final breakthrough comes when a person realizes that the defilements of the mind are unreal and present no barrier to full awakening.

The Ch'an and Zen traditions abound with examples of monks grappling with the basic ontological conundrums of the Yogācāra vision of the world.

Indian Mādhyamikas grappled with the Yogācāra as well and found it wanting, for reasons that became clear to Stcherbatsky as he dug more deeply into Tibetan accounts of Madhyamaka thought. In the introduction to his translation of *The Distinction Between the Middle and the Extremes*, Stcherbatsky cited Tsoṅ-kha-pa's *Legs-bśad-sñiṅ-po* (*The Essence of Eloquent Statements*) as a major reason for his change of heart. This short work (known as Tsoṅ-kha-pa's "iron bow") has had unusual influence in the history of Tibetan Madhyamaka.[38] Tsoṅ-kha-pa was the founder of the dGe-lugs-pa lineage of Tibetan Buddhism, the lineage in which the Dalai Lamas are trained and which has governed much of the secular and religious life of Tibet since the seventeenth century. Tsoṅ-kha-pa was the founder not merely in an institutional sense. He also gave intellectual form and direction to dGe-lugs-pa religious thought. For Tsoṅ-kha-pa, Madhyamaka was the central teaching, and the *Legs-bśad-sñiṅ-po* was his authoritative distillation of Madhyamaka interpretation.

The *Legs-bśad-sñiṅ-po* can be divided into three major sections. It begins with a discussion of Yogācāra, then it uses Bhāvaviveka to refute the Yogācāra and Candrakīrti to refute Bhāvaviveka. As his primary source for Bhāvaviveka's refutation of the Yogācāra, Tsoṅ-kha-pa draws on a long appendix to the commentary on the last verse of the twenty-fifth chapter of the *Madhyamakakārikās*. The verse gives Nāgārjuna's last word on the concept of nirvana.

There is no difference between saṃsāra and nirvana, and there is no difference between nirvana and saṃsāra.
The limit of nirvana is the limit of saṃsāra, and there is not the slightest difference between them.
False views about [the Buddha] after nirvana, the ending or lack of ending [of the world] and the permanence or impermanence [of the world] are based on [false views of] nirvana, an end, and a beginning.
If all *dharma*s are empty, what has an end, what has no end, what has both an end and no end, and what has neither an end nor no end?
What is one thing and what is another? What is permanent, what is impermanent, what is both permanent and impermanent, and what is neither?
The cessation of all objectification (*sarvopalambhopaśama*) is the blessed (*śiva*) cessation of conceptual diversity (*prapañcopaśama*). The Buddha taught no *dharma* anywhere to anyone.[39]

Early Western interpreters of the Madhyamaka were understandably intrigued by the final reference in this chapter to the Buddha's silence. But what was the Buddha's silence meant to say? Bhāvaviveka's critique of the Yogācāra starts with a Yogācāra answer:

> The Yogācārins say: If it is true that "The cessation of all objectification is the blessed cessation of conceptual diversity, and the Buddha taught no *dharma* anywhere to anyone," then it is impossible to deny (*apavāda*) Dependent [Nature], which is the means by which this is understood.[40]

The Yogācārins are saying that the Buddha's silence may deny the distinctions involved in Imagined Nature, but it cannot deny Dependent Nature. Dependent Nature is what "remains" when Imagined Nature is denied, and there must be something that remains for there to be any way (or "means") for nirvana to be attained (or "understood"). This argument also appears near the beginning of *The Distinction Between the Middle and the Extremes*, where it is used to prove the existence of the Imagination in its defiled or deluded form, as the consciousness (*vijñāna*) of subject and object:

> Why not take the position that [consciousness] is nonexistent? Because (Verse 5d) [We] take the position that liberation comes from the extinction of this [consciousness].

> Otherwise [if consciousness did not exist], it would be impossible to establish bondage and liberation. One would make the mistake of denying defilement and purification.[41]

This argument makes a certain kind of intuitive sense. For someone to achieve nirvana, there has to be some way to get it, and that way, somehow, has to *be*. Among the likely candidates for this important position, what better choice than the yogi's own mind? If nirvana is not an object or a place but something like a state of mind, surely the yogi has to have a mind in order to achieve it.

Bhāvaviveka was not unaware of the force of this argument, but he had a few simple questions, generated by the Madhyamaka concept of the two truths. If Imagined Nature does not exist and the Imagination does exist, are these claims of existence made from the conventional point of view or the ultimate? If the Yogācārins were saying that Imagined Nature does not exist from the ultimate point of view, he had no reason to disagree. For him, nothing exists from the ultimate point of view. But if the claim was being made from the conventional point of view, he felt that the Yogācārins were making a crucial error: they were "denying" a conventional reality. His use of the word "deny" (*apavāda*) carried particular systematic force. In the Buddhist tradition, the word "denial" is used to name the negative extreme that the Middle Path is meant to avoid. It is a "denial" to think that the no-self doctrine frees a person from all personal responsibility, including the responsibility to choose a course of action that leads the "stream" (*santāna*) of causes and conditions conventionally referred to as the "self" (*ātman*) toward the achievement of nirvana. A "denial," in other words, is a form of nihilism, a loss of personal meaning and responsibility. Bhāvaviveka saw the dangers of nihilism lurking in what he took to be the Yogācāra claim that words have no meaning even conventionally.

He saw another kind of danger in the Yogācāra claim about the existence of the Imagination. If the Yogācārins were saying that the Imagination exists conventionally, he had no quarrel. He felt that it was appropriate even to use the word "self" in a conventional sense to designate the "stream" of consciousness. But if the Yogācārins were saying that the Imagination exists ultimately, they were making another crucial mistake. This time the mistake was the mirror image of the mistake of "denial." They were engaging in a "reification" (*samāropa*) of something that is not real. To reject this possibility, he brought to bear the full weight of the Madhyamaka argument that nothing can come into being as a thing in its own right. This argument is so familiar that it does not need to be repeated, but it is worth being reminded that the argument comes not only in a negative form, but in a positive one as well.

In the twenty-fourth chapter of the Nāgārjuna's *Madhyamakakārikās*, the movement from the negative to the positive interpretation of Emptiness turns on a small rhetorical gesture, as if it were condensing, in Wittgenstein's words, a cloud of philosophy into a drop of grammar. The chapter starts with the words of an opponent who says: "If everything is empty, nothing can arise or cease, and there can be no Four Noble Truths."[42] The chapter then moves through a series of Nāgārjuna's most widely quoted verses about the two truths:

The Buddhas' teaching is based on two truths: ordinary relative truth and ultimate truth.
Those who do not understand the distinction between the two truths do not understand the profound truth in the Buddhas' teaching.
It is impossible to teach the ultimate without resorting to the conventional, and without understanding the ultimate, it is impossible to attain nirvana.
When Emptiness is viewed incorrectly, it destroys the slow-witted, like a snake wrongly grasped or magic wrongly applied.
Everything is possible for those for whom Emptiness is possible; nothing is possible for those for whom Emptiness is not possible.

We call Dependent Origination Emptiness; it is a dependent designation, and it is the Middle Path.

There is no *dharma* that originates independently, so there is no *dharma* that is not empty.[43]

Finally the text simply inverts the opponent's opening claim by inserting a negative particle (the letter "a"). Because of the euphonic combination of the negative particle with the preceding syllable, the meter of the verse is left intact: "If everything is empty" (*yadi śūnyam idaṃ sarvam*) becomes "If everything is *not* empty" (*yady aśūnyam idaṃ sarvam*) and the verse continues as before, "nothing can arise or cease, and there can be no Four Noble Truths." The Mādhyamikas were convinced that the only way to assure the possibility of change—the possibility that things can come into and go out of existence—is if nothing exists ultimately as an object, entity, or reality in its own right.

The form of the Madhyamaka argument shows that for the Mādhyamikas, at least, this conclusion was not negative. It was, as they say, a Middle Way: it balanced the negation involved in denying that anything is ultimately real with the affirmation involved in the acceptance of conventional reality. This is not the time or place to explore what it means to say that the Mādhyamikas "accept" conventional reality.[44] Much ink has been spilled and many palm leaves sacrificed in the quest for a suitable explanation of that modest claim. But it is worth noting that conventional truth is the arena that will yield the most positive answer to the question: What do Mādhyamikas think about ultimate reality? Conventionally, ultimate reality can be equated with the Buddha (just as Emptiness can be equated with the understanding of Emptiness). The Buddha can be thought of as having two, three, or (possibly) four bodies and can be understood not only as the source of a voluminous and authoritative teaching (despite his silence) but as an object of sincere worship (despite his absence).[45] Perhaps it would be more helpful simply to illustrate the tone of the Madhyamaka attitude toward conventional reality with a pair of stories.

A few years ago the Dalai Lama visited Harvard and gave a lecture on the Buddhist concept of the self. As is often true when the Dalai Lama holds forth on such a difficult subject, there was a large and curious audience. He began by speaking in English about the importance of compassion. If you want to know who you are, he said, learn to be compassionate toward your neighbor. Then he said that the problem of the self ran somewhat deeper than this, and he would have to shift to Tibetan to explain what he meant. What followed can only be described as a mind-numbing account of the reasons why all things, including oneself and one's neighbor, are empty of intrinsic identity. Just when it seemed as if the audience could not bear another word, the Dalai Lama stopped and asked, "If there is no self, then who is speaking?" He answered with the Tibetan phrase *bdag tsam*. The translator translated these words with a phrase that sounded like "mere eye." At least that was the way the translator's words were interpreted by the reporter from the Harvard *Crimson* who wrote an article for the next day's paper in which he (or she) said that the Dalai Lama thought the self resided in the eye. The translator was actually saying "mere I." It would be just as accurate to translate the same words "just me." The Dalai Lama had just finished a long argument intended to prove that the words "Dalai Lama" had no real referent, but the argument did not prevent him from speaking of himself, with a smile, as if he were "merely" himself. The force of his Madhyamaka argument showed that it would be quite wrong to take his concluding words as a reference to a reality that lies somehow beyond the limitations of language. It was a return to the world of conventionality and an acceptance of its value for the purposes of ordinary human communication. To make that "return" effective and to make it something more than a lapse into the habits of mind that turn the conventional world into an arena of suffering, the pursuit of ultimacy had to lie close at hand. From his point of view, it was precisely the absence of an ultimate reality that made it possible for him to turn with compassion to the conventional world.

Another story, this time from the Zen tradition, illustrates how this form of thinking might be applied in the realm of ritual and devotion. An eager American student of Zen was visiting a monastery in Japan. The master of the monastery led him into a hall that held a statue of the Buddha. As they entered, the master bowed. The American student looked confused and said: "Why are you bowing? I thought you were supposed to spit on the Buddha." The master said: "If you want to spit, spit. I choose to bow." I take this to mean that there is no real reason why one should distinguish between bowing and spitting. The distinction is simply conventional. But within the conventional world, there are good reasons, having to do with matters of aesthetics, discipline, and perhaps even hygiene, that suggest bowing is a more useful and appropriate gesture than spitting. Again the situation draws forth a reflection on ultimate reality and settles the question by returning to the individual person making a moral, aesthetic, and devotional choice in a particular setting.

This is the reason why I focused so strongly, in the early stages of this chapter, on the idea that we investigate ultimacy at precisely the point at which the ultimate becomes real in the life of the person who, in Tillich's words, is grasped by it. Masao Abe has suggested that, in Buddhist-Christian dialogue, the Christian concept of God comes most clearly into focus when it is read through the image of the self-emptying of Christ in Philippians 2. Abe asks, "Is it not that the *kenosis* of Christ—that is, the self-emptying of the Son of God—has its origins in God 'the Father'—that is, the kenosis of God?"[46] By framing the question as he does, Abe is not merely examining the possibility that God might be viewed as Emptiness. He is reorienting the quest for ultimacy in a Buddhist direction, by shifting attention away from a transcendent reality that lies "out there," in contrast to the human, and redirecting it toward the realm where human beings struggle to actualize themselves in the awareness of their contingency and finitude, that is, in the awareness of their own Emptiness.

Notes

1. Emile Durkheim's choice of the concept of the sacred as a key to his definition of religion is one significant example. Durkheim based his choice on the argument that Buddhism, in the words of Auguste Barth, is "a faith without a god." See *The Elementary Forms of Religious Life*, trans. Joseph Ward Swain (New York: The Free Press, 1965), 45. Wilfred Cantwell Smith's argument that the Buddhist concept of Dharma is a functional equivalent of "God" is another. See "The Buddhist Instance: Faith as Atheistic?" *Faith and Belief* (Princeton: Princeton University Press, 1979), 20–32.

2. On Dignāga's *apoha* theory, see Dhirendra Sharma, *The Differentiation Theory of Meaning* (The Hague: Mouton, 1969); Bimal K. Matilal, *Epistemology, Logic, and Grammar in Indian Philosophical Analysis* (The Hague: Mouton, 1971), 339–49; and Richard P. Hayes, *Dignāga on the Interpretation of Signs* (Dordrecht: Kluwer Academic, 1988). There is a useful section on the *apoha* theory in Yuichi Kajiyama, *An Introduction to Buddhist Philosophy: An Annotated Translation of the Tarkabhāṣā of Mokṣākaragupta*, Memoirs of the Faculty of Letters, Kyoto University 10 (1966), 122–130.

3. The "non-cow," of course, is just as much an imaginary entity as the cow itself.

4. Bhāvaviveka's discussion of *apoha* appears in *Madhyamakahṛdayakārikā*s chap. 5, verses 60–68. Christian Lindtner has edited the Sanskrit text of the verses in the *Adyar Library Bulletin*. The text of the commentary (*Tarkajvālā*) is available in Tibetan translation.

5. In this context *jāti* is a synonym of *santāna* ("stream").

6. I made these suggestion in an essay on Frederick J. Streng's understanding of ultimate reality as "ultimate transformation." The essay was presented in the fall meeting of this seminar and will appear in the forthcoming memorial volume for Frederick Streng.

7. Robert Cummings Neville, *The Truth of Broken Symbols* (Albany: State University of New York Press, 1996). Note particularly the discussion of "boundary condition" and "finite/infinite contrast" on pages 56–58.

8. *Madhyamakakārikā* 24.18: *yaḥ pratītyasamutpādaḥ śūnyatāṃ tāṃ pracakṣmahe / sā prajñaptir upādāya pratipat saiva madhyamā.*

9. Discussion of the "rectification of names" grows from *Analects* XIII.3: "Tzu-lu said, If the Prince of Wei were waiting for you to come and administer his country for him, what would be your first measure? The Master said, It would certainly be to correct language." Quoted from *The Analects of Confucius,* trans. Arthur Waley (New York: Vintage Books, 1989). The topic is elaborated by Xunzi in his chapter on "Rectifying Names" found in *Basic Writings of Mo Tzu, Hsün Tzu, and Han Fei Tzu,* trans. Burton Watson (New York: Columbia University Press, 1967), 139–56. It has become common in Confucian scholarship to argue that Confucius's use of language is not referential in a simple or naive sense but is "performative" in the sense made popular by J. L. Austin. David L. Hall and Roger T. Ames, for example, develop an interpretation of the rectification of names that "argues against the priority of formal constructions by rejecting the suggestion that Confucius uses names reductionistically to organize the process of human experience into some preestablished pattern that is held to define the meaning, value, and purpose of life. It argues instead for the priority of aesthetic order by insisting that Confucius regarded the particular person in specific context as the source of signification." Quoted from *Thinking Through Confucius* (Albany: State University of New York Press, 1987), 274–75. See also Herbert Fingarette, *Confucius—The Secular as Sacred* (New York: Harper & Row, 1972), 11–17; and A. C. Graham, *Disputers of the Tao: Philosophical Argument in Ancient China* (La Salle, Ill.: Open Court, 1989), 22–25 and 261–67. The recognition that Confucius's words have a performative function removes the misconception that the rectification of names involves, in Fingarette's words, "an erroneous belief in word-magic or a pedantic elaboration of Confucius's concern with teaching tradition" (15), but it does not mean that Confucius is any less wedded to the notion that the distinctions embedded in language are a reflection of the normative order of things, as Benjamin I. Schwartz notes clearly in his discussion of Confucius's view of language: "[Confucius's] confidence that he belongs to a universal civilization governed by a truly normative *tao* that has already been realized in human experience leads to a further confidence that the established language used to describe the prescriptions of *li,* the institutions and the normative roles of the good society accurately reflects the normative nature of things. Language carries its own imbedded reflection of the true order." Quoted from Benjamin I. Schwartz, *The World of Thought in Ancient China* (Cambridge: Harvard University Press, 1985), 91–92.

10. One of the most important ways to pose this question to the Madhyamaka tradition is to ask whether Mādhyamikas, in the end, say anything. Do they have a position, and do they argue for that position in such a way that they produce certainty in their opponent? (This is similar to the question, discussed by Neville in relation to Duns Scotus and Paul Tillich, whether, in a system of broken symbols, there is "at least one purely positive and

non-symbolic claim." See *The Truth of Broken Symbols*, 129.) The Tibetan dGe-lugs-pa tradition, stemming from Tsoṅ-kha-pa, bases its response to this question on a passage in Candrakīrti's commentary on the *Madhyama-kakārikās*. The key section reads as follows: "Reasons and examples are impossible (*hetu-dṛṣṭānta-asambhavāt*), so one offers (*upādatta*) a proof for the point of one's assertion only in conformity to [the opponent's] assertion. Since one accepts a position that is unreasonable (*nirupapattika-pakṣa-abhyupagamāt*), one also contradicts (*visamvādayan*) oneself and is not capable of conveying conviction to opponents. This is its clearest refutation, namely, one's inability to prove the point of one's assertion. What would be the purpose here of providing (*udbhāvanā*) an inference as a refutation (*anumāna-bādhā*)?" The Sanskrit is found in Louis de La Vallée Poussin, ed., *Mūlamadhyamakakārikās (Mādhyamikasūtras) de Nāgārjuna avec la Prasannapadā Commentaire de Candrakīrti*, Bibliotheca Buddhica IV (1903–13; reprint ed. Osnabrück: Biblio Verlag, 1970), 19. The key point in this passage is that Candrakīrti does have a position, and this position is one that refutes the opponent's position, but it also is one that is self-critical and does not falsely reify either itself or the sense of certainty that it produces. Tsoṅ-kha-pa's discussion of this issue can be found in Robert A. F. Thurman, *Tsoṅ Khapa's Speech of Gold in The Essence of True Eloquence* (Princeton: Princeton University Press, 1984), 331. Both Candrakīrti and Tsoṅ-kha-pa base themselves on Nāgārjuna's *Vigrahavyāvartanī*, trans. Kamaleswar Bhattacharya, "The Dialectical Method of Nāgārjuna," *Journal of Indian Philosophy* 1 (1971), 217–61.

11. Neville, op. cit., 71. Shortly after this comment about Axial Age religions, Neville interprets a text from a fourteenth-century Tibetan rNying-ma teacher as suggesting that Buddhism in general (or is it merely this particular myth?) acknowledges a transcendent intentional reference. His argument raises an interesting question about the interpretation of this text and Buddhist texts more generally.

The text comes from a tradition where the "primary reference," as it were, of myth is the transformation of a yogi's consciousness. *The Tibetan Book of the Dead* (which comes from the same textual milieu) depicts the evolution of consciousness after death as a devolution from the fundamental unity of the mind as personified in the figure of Samantabhadra. It is not uncommon in Indian yogic literature to project the image of the inner transformation of consciousness outward into the cosmos as a whole. When Kapstein argues that the myth is not meant to be an account of creation but to describe the possibility of overcoming ignorance, he is giving primacy to the experience of the yogi rather than to the map of a cosmic narrative. In other words, the cosmos is a metaphor for the yogi's mind rather than the other way around.

The key question, then, is why Kapstein (or I) should feel justified in reading this text in a way that is contrary to what, in another tradition, would be its explicit, literal sense. The answers lie in a judgment about what the tradition is "really trying to get at" in texts like this, combined with a sense of the text's probable origin. The general Buddhist attitude toward creation narratives, for good or ill, is typified by the canonical story of "Māluṅkyaputta and the arrow" in which the Buddha warns his monks against useless speculation about whether the universe is eternal, not eternal, finite, or infinite, and advises them instead to use his Dharma as it is intended, to escape suffering and achieve nirvana. The story appears in the *Majjhima Nikāya* and is recounted widely in modern Buddhist literature, as in the chapter on "The Buddhist Attitude of Mind" in Walpola Rahula's *What the Buddha Taught*, 2nd ed. (New York: Grove Weidenfeld, 1974).

12. J. G. Frazer as quoted by Jonathan Z. Smith, *Imagining Religion from Babylon to Jonestown* (Chicago: University of Chicago Press, 1982), 21.

13. Ibid., 111.

14. William James, *The Varieties of Religious Experience*, ed. with an introduction by Martin E. Marty (Harmondsworth, Middlesex: Penguin Books, 1982), 9.

15. Neville, op. cit., 58.

16. W. C. Smith, *Faith and Belief*, 30, 32.

17. As Pope John Paul II discovered when he characterized the Buddhist tradition as having a "negative soteriology." His words touch on so many of the issues of our discussion that they are worth quoting in full: "Today we are seeing a certain *diffusion of Buddhism in the West.*

"The *Buddhist doctrine of salvation* constitutes the central point, or rather the only point, of this system. Nevertheless, both the Buddhist tradition and the methods deriving from it have an almost exclusively *negative soteriology.*

"The 'enlightenment' experienced by the Buddha comes down to the conviction that the world is bad, that it is the source of evil and of suffering for man. To liberate oneself from this evil, one must free oneself from this world, necessitating a break with the ties that join us to external reality—ties existing in our human nature, in our psyche, in our bodies. The more we are liberated from these ties, the more we become indifferent to what is in the world, and the more we are freed from suffering, from the evil that has its source in the world.

"Do we draw near to God in this way? This is not mentioned in the 'enlightenment' conveyed by Buddha. Buddhism is in large measure an *atheistic system.* We do not free ourselves from evil through the good which comes from God; we liberate ourselves only through detachment from the world, which is bad. The fullness of such detachment is not a union with God, but what is called nirvana, a state of perfect indifference with regard to the world. *To save oneself* means, above all, to free oneself from evil by becoming *indifferent to the world, which is the source of evil.* This is the culmination of the spiritual process." Quoted from *Crossing the Threshold of Hope* (New York: Alfred A. Knopf, 1994), 85–86.

18. I made this point in the essay on Frederick J. Streng's view of ultimate reality as "ultimate transformation" noted above.

19. *Madhyamakakārikā* 18.5: *karmakleśakṣayān mokṣaḥ karmakleśā vikalpataḥ / te prapañcāt prapañcas tu śūnyatāyāṃ nirudhyate.* Bhāvaviveka reads *śūnyatayā* ("by Emptiness") for *śūnyatāyāṃ* ("in Emptiness") and explains that "by Emptiness" should be supplemented by the addition of the word "understanding" (Tibetan *rtog pa*). Candrakīrti explains that "all the linguistic complexity of the world is stopped in Emptiness, that is, when one sees that all things are empty of identity (*sa cāyaṃ laukikaḥ prapañco niravaśeṣaḥ śūnyatāyāṃ sarvabhāvasvabhāvaśūnyatādarśane sati nirudhyate*). (*Prasannapadā*, ed. La Vallée Poussin: 350.)

20. The conversation is reported in Bill Moyers, *A World of Ideas II* (New York: Doubleday, 1990), but this particular formulation of the Confucian ultimate concern has to be taken from the video of the original conversation or from a transcript.

21. Tu Weiming, *Centrality and Commonality: An Essay on Confucian Religiousness* (Albany: State University of New York Press, 1989), 94.

22. As Tu Weiming suggests when he responds to a question about God in the published account of his conversation Bill Moyers. "MOYERS: And the notion of God—where does that come into focus? TU: The functional equivalent of God in Confucian humanism is Heaven. In fact, we can say that the Confucian process of learning to be human involves not only being filial to one's parents, and faithful to one's friends, and loyal to one's society, it also involves one's ability to go beyond anthropocentrism. The highest ideal of Confucian self-realization is the unity of Heaven and the human" (*A World of Ideas II*: 110).

    Behind my own argument in this paragraph lies Wilfred Cantwell Smith's discussion of the relationship between the Islamic concepts of *ḥaqqa* and *ṣadaqa*, though I have given it a Buddhist emphasis. See Wilfred Cantwell Smith, "A Human View of Truth," *Truth and Dialogue in World Religions: Conflicting Truth Claims*, ed. John Hick (Philadelphia: Westminster Press, 1974), 20–44.

    Tu Weiming draws Wilfred Cantwell Smith into his account of Confucianism when he says: "When I first approached the study of Confucianism, I came to it as a historian. Then I studied it as a philosopher, analyzing the ideas and concepts. More recently, I really studied it as a religionist, not just as a form of life, but as a particular kind of faith—faith in the perfectibility of human self-transformation, and the perfectibility of human nature through self-effort" (*World of Ideas II*: 109).

23. For a summary of the literature on this problem, see J. W. de Jong, "The Problem of the Absolute in the Madhyamaka School" and "Emptiness," *Journal of Indian Philosophy* 2 (1972), 1–15. For a recent discussion of the problem, see Thurman's account of Madhyamaka "Centrism" in *Tsong Khapa's Speech of Gold in the Essence of True Eloquence: Reason and Enlightenment*

in the Central Philosophy of Tibet (Princeton: Princeton University Press, 1984): 159, 167–68. My own review of the problem will revisit some of the points I made in my introduction to "Bhāvaviveka's Critique of Yogācāra Philosophy in chapter XXV of the *Prajñāpradīpa*," in Chr. Lindtner, ed., *Miscellanea Buddhica*, Indiske Studier 5 (Copenhagen: Akademisk Forlag, 1985), 25–75.

24. Durkheim, op. cit., 45.

25. T. Stcherbatsky, *The Conception of Buddhist Nirvana* (Leningrad: Academy of Sciences of the U.S.S.R., 1927), 41 (Quoted by de Jong, "Emptiness," 7).

26. Ibid., 52.

27. T. R. V. Murti, *The Central Philosophy of Buddhism* (2nd ed. London: George Allen and Unwin, 1960), 143.

28. Louis de La Vallée Poussin, "Buddhica," *Harvard Journal of Asiatic Studies* 3 (1938): 148.

29. *Madhyānta-vibhaṅga: Discourse on Discrimination between Middle and Extremes,* trans. T. Stcherbatsky, Bibliotheca Buddhica 30 (Leningrad: Academy of Sciences of the U.S.S.R., 1936; reprint ed., Indian Studies Past and Present, Soviet Indology Series, No. 5, 1971), 6.

30. Or "The Imagination of what is Unreal is real. The Duality in it is not real. But the Emptiness in it is real, it is real in that [Emptiness]" (*abhātaparikalpo 'sti dvayaṃ tatra na vidyate / śūnyatā vidyate tv atra tasyām api sa vidyate*). Quoted from *Madhyānta-vibhāga-bhāṣya*, ed., Nathmal Tatia and Anantalal Thakur, Tibetan Sanskrit Works Series 10 (Patna: K. P. Jayaswal Research Institute, 1967).

31. The verse is attributed to Asaṅga, the commentary to Vasubandhu. I will shorten the phrase "Imagination of what is Unreal" to "Imagination."

32. There is no distinction in the Sanskrit between the words "exist" and "real." Both English words can be used to translate the roots "*as*" (cognate with the English "is") and "*bhā*" (cognate with the English "be"). My sense of these enigmatic verses is that it is best to begin as if they were simple statements about the experience of a single moment ("This exists, that does not"), and then move to the more general claim that certain categories are real or unreal in all places at all times. It would be possible, however, to speak of "reality" from the very beginning.

33. *Na śūnyaṃ nāpi cāśūnyaṃ tasmāt sarvaṃ vidhāyate / sattvād asattvāt sattvāc ca madhyamāpratipac ca sā.*

34. *Yoga Sūtra* 1.2: "yoga is the cessation of the fluctuations of the mind" (*yogaś citta-vṛttinirodhaḥ*).

35. Philip B. Yampolsky, *The Platform Sutra of the Sixth Patriarch* (New York: Columbia University Press, 1967).

36. Ibid., 130.

37. Ibid., 132.

38. See Thurman, op. cit.

39. *Madhyamakakārikās* 25.20–24.

40. The Sanskrit of this passage is no longer extant. The Tibetan version has been edited by Christian Lindtner in "Bhavya's Controversy with Yogācāra in the Appendix to *Prajñāpradīpa*, chapter XXV," in *Tibetan and Buddhist Studies Commemorating the 200th Anniversary of the Birth of Alexander Csoma de Koros*, ed. Louis Ligeti, Bibliotheca Orientalis Hungarica 29 (Budapest: Akademiai Kiado, 1984), 77–97. A translation of the entire appendix can be found in Malcolm David Eckel, "Bhāvaviveka's Critique of Yogācāra Philosophy in chapter XXV of the Prajñāpradīpa," *Miscellanea Buddhica*, ed. Christian Lindtner, Indiske Studier 5 (Copenhagen: Akademisk Forlag, 1985), 25–75. The precise meaning of the key phrase in this passage, "the means by which this is understood," is somewhat obscured by the Tibetan translation. The Tibetan, *de rtogs par bya ba'i thabs*, has two important elements: *rtogs pa* ("understand") and *thabs* ("means"). *Rtogs pa* is frequently used to translate a group of Sanskrit words that mean to "go" (such as *gam*, *pad*, or *i*) in combination with a prefix that suggests a form of cognition (such as *adhi*, *ava*, or *prati*). The meaning of *rtogs pa* is, therefore, to "arrive at" or "make progress toward" something in a cognitive sense. The word *thabs* ("means") is frequently used to translate the Sanskrit term *upāya*, which occurs in the important compound *upāya-kauśalya* ("skill-in-means"). On the relative frequency of these forms, see *Index to the Prasannapadā Madhyamaka-Vṛtti*, ed. Susumu Yamaguchi, part 2 (Kyoto: Heirakuji Shoten, 1974).

41. Tatia ed.: 3. Sthiramati, the subcommentator on *The Distinction*, explains this passage by saying: "One can infer the existence of that [consciousness] from the position that there is defilement and purification. *Otherwise* means: if that [consciousness] were completely non-existent. *There would be no bondage and no liberation* means: If it did not exist even as sheer illusion, there would be no defilement and thus no bondage. There also would be no liberation, because [liberation] is based on the assumption that one is liberated from prior bondage." Translated from Sthiramati, *Madhyāntavibhāgaṭīkā: Exposition systématique du Yogācāra-vijñaptivāda*, ed. Sylvain Lévi (Tokyo: Suzuki Research Foundation, 1966), 21.

42. *Yadi śūnyam idaṃ sarvam udayo nāsti na vyayaḥ / caturṇām āryasatyānām abhāvas te prasajyate.*

43. *Kārikās* 24.8–11, 14, 18.

44. This is the point that separated the two branches of Madhyamaka, the Svātantrika of Bhāvaviveka and the Prāsaṅgika of Candrakīrti. Some of the dimensions of this issue are discussed in Malcolm David Eckel, *Jñānagarbha's Commentary on the Two Truths* (Albany: State University of New York Press, 1987). A more extensive discussion of the Prāsaṅgika point of view can be found in Thurman's *Tsong Khapa's Speech of Gold*.

45. On the devotional aspect of the Madhyamaka vision of the Buddha, see

150 ᵔ *Buddhist Approaches*

Malcolm David Eckel, *To See the Buddha: A Philosopher's Quest for the Meaning of Emptiness* (San Francisco: HarperCollins, 1992; reprint ed. Princeton: Princeton University Press, 1994).

46. Masao Abe, "Kenotic God and Dynamic Sunyata," *The Emptying God: A Buddhist-Christian-Jewish Conversation*, ed. John B. Cobb, Jr. and Christopher Ives (Maryknoll, N.Y.: Orbis Books, 1990), 33–65.

7

Comparative Conclusions about Ultimate Realities

Robert Cummings Neville
and Wesley J. Wildman

᷍

7.1 Defining the Vague Category

We come to understand the respects in which we compare the traditions only at the end, if then. "Ultimate realities" as the vague category of comparison means something like this: *that which is most important to religious life because of the nature of reality*. Each part of this statement needs to be glossed.

First, "religious life" is a phrase intended to finesse the question of the nature of religion until our discussion in the next volume, on religious truth. For most practical purposes we can say that the ultimate is what is most important *for human life as such*, letting religion be defined in terms of those aspects of life that relate to the ultimate or to what is most important. But there might be some purposes for which it is worthwhile to contrast religion as one dimension of life with others such as the political, the cultural, the aesthetic, the moral, and so on, and for those others what is most important might not be what the religious traditions say is ultimate. The traditions themselves differ in how they relate religion to the other parts of life. And the very definition of religion as a (social? spiritual? cultural?) phenomenon is a matter of contemporary contention.

So let this remain as a finessing phrase until we have discussed how the traditions say human beings should relate to ultimate realities.

"That which is" is intended to be vague with respect to the kind of quantity or unity claimed to be ultimate. Judaism and Islam assert the singularity of the ultimate in no uncertain terms. Christianity is problematic, especially to Muslims, with its doctrine of the Trinity, although Fredriksen limits her discussion in chapter 3 to the earliest stage in Christianity when its conception of God had not been differentiated from that of Judaism. Vedānta Deśika's Nārāyaṇa is described as wholly unified—but then has a spouse!—and Clooney does not much unpack that or treat it as a problem (because Deśika does not in that text). Eckel's ultimate in Madhyamaka, emptiness, is not a thing but rather a quality of things when understood truly rather than conventionally. Ultimate reality in Chinese religion as described in chapter 1 on the one hand can be whatever various religious virtuosi take it to be, and on the other hand is a kind of ontological mother that turns out to be non-being (*wuji*), which itself might be more like a quality of drawing on the power of the rest of the world rather than one's own reserves. All of these things can be encompassed within the vague notion "that which is."

"Most important" signifies our appreciation of the approach to ultimacy embodied in Tillich's conception of ultimate concern, an approach that is willing to allow practice and soteriological issues to shape conceptions of what is taken to be ontologically ultimate.[1] What is most important can be the Holy that demands a response, as in the West and South Asian monotheisms. But it can also be whatever it is that alleviates suffering, as in Buddhism. The discussion of Chinese religion makes clear that many people do not really care much about what is most important, and leave that to the virtuosi. Importance is determined by factors from at least two sources, the ultimate realities taken to be important, and the human condition that shapes concerns. Our phrase is vague enough to allow for all our examples.

"Because of the nature of reality" means that the religious thinkers' identifications of what is most important are not functions solely of subjective whim or arbitrary preference but of what the religious cultures take to be the nature of the case. Madhyamaka Buddhism says that in the nature of things, understood ultimately, there are no things with own-being, and that reference to ultimate emptiness cannot be like conventional reference to conventional things. This is because reality is this way, which is the positive point in Eckel's account fending off nihilism. The radical monotheisms take the nature of God to be the reason why God is most important, the ultimate reality, for people and communities. Chinese religion, as represented in chapter 1, might not take the nature of reality as ultimate to be a thing or a quality, but it does take the orientations of virtuoso religiosity to be what they are because of the nature of that peculiar kind of causation in which the ultimate of non-being pervades things. Only by reason of the nature of the Dao, variously conceived, is religious virtuosity, variously structured, the way it is. Our comparative category says that the reason our traditions identify what is most important the way they do is that they take the importance to be rooted in the nature of reality. This unites the ontological and anthropological sides of our category.

"Most important to religious life" is vague with respect to how the religious traditions say people should respond. Fredriksen details the quest for purity and holiness; Kohn and Miller discuss models of the sage and the perfected. Saldarini and Haq specify various forms of worship and obedience as crucial to the response. Clooney and Eckel focus on the knowledge of ultimate realities. In concrete practice all these and other modes of response are likely to be found in all the traditions. Our category is vague enough to encompass them. Our specialists' studies have not dwelt with much specificity on the modes of response beyond the intellectual, though it was often a topic of discussion in our meetings; it is a comparative category of considerable importance needing study in its own right.

"Ultimacy" is linked to a series, or at least to approaching a boundary. It might mean first cause, last goal, final truth, most real, or that which is most wanted when people sort their wants.

"Reality" has its medieval European meaning of things being what they are so that human judgment might be right or wrong about them. This is obvious enough when things are taken to be objects over against knowers, such as a God or ultimate ontological source such as Dao or *wuji*. But even when the distinction is denied between a judging subjective consciousness and the realities judged, as it is in the Yogācāra and Madhyamaka Buddhism described in chapter 6, the emptiness of that distinction is what is real, and to make something real of that distinction is false except for conventional truth.

So our task in this comparative chapter is to say how the various traditions and texts studied specify that which they take to be most important for religious life because of what they take the nature of reality to be. The next section summarizes those specifications. Then 7.3 puts those specifications together in a complex concept of ultimate reality indicating some ways in which the traditions reinforce, contradict, or overlap one another in what their ideas affirm about ultimate realities. Section 7.4 refocuses the issues with respect to how ultimate realities are actualized in human experience.

The task of this summary and conclusion is daunting because of the diversity of approaches taken by our specialists. Chinese religion, Judaism, and Islam are presented in terms of centuries of development, with the specialists taking pains to point out the diversity within each of those traditions. Much of the discussion of Buddhism turns on a contrast between the Madhyamaka and Yogācāra schools of Mahāyāna. The presentation on Hinduism takes up a single text in the context of its author's religious culture and treats that as an exemplification of general characteristics of Hindu conceptions of ultimate realities. The presentation of Christianity focuses on a period so early that its conception of the ultimate had not diverged from its other contemporary sects of Judaism of which it was one, and picks up on early Christian concepts such as purity, ritual holiness, and blood sacrifice, the first two of which have diminished importance in subsequent Christian developments. To bring all these together is a bit like mixing apples and oranges, in terms of the claims made. Nonetheless, bearing in mind the very selective representations of our traditions, the comparisons are interesting.

They are all the more interesting, in fact, because of the tension generated by our rereading of the specialists' papers for the sake of enriching our comparative categories comparatively. As Clooney pointed out in commenting on an early draft of this chapter:

> . . . it is clearly in your interests to have stable and comprehensive claims about each of the traditions, and that's why you clearly like the Kohn/Miller piece, for instance. But since it will clearly strike the readers that some of us—e.g., Paula [Fredriksen] most noticeably and then too myself—don't research and write in that way, you might as well make some good come out of it. I.e., these volumes are interesting in part because people like you and people like me are both contributing to them, such that we are claiming that different ways of writing and thinking can come together. In all three volumes, my essays intend to "touch" upon imbedded and pervasive Hindu ways of thinking/ways of speaking—by picking up on one or several Hindu voices and tracing from there threads to a wide variety of other conversation partners. That's why I used Deśika's *Īśvaraparic-cheda*—because attention to it puts one in touch with multiple Hindu and Indian ways of thinking about ultimate reality. But I am also claiming that advances in this area are, in the Indian context, almost essentially controversial, argumentative. Description is therefore always partisan, and descriptions of Hindu thinking subverted by the arguments about which is the real Hindu viewpoint, and whether/how it can be put into words and discussed (without or with reference to privileged revelation, etc.). I suspect that Paula is demonstrating similar sensitivities, and so too others to a lesser extent.

As you have written your chapter, though, you treat the specialist essays as data bases for theorizing. But the specialist's viewpoint is, or can be, that theory and data are more intricately interwoven, so that the act of describing ultimate reality according to one or another tradition is itself a virtuoso act, and thus you can't get away with an innocent project of theorizing from "specialists' conclusions."

As I said, since readers will notice all this anyway, you would do well to add a meta-level to your conclusions, showing consciousness of your interplay with the specialists.

Done! The readers should note that Clooney's comments were made on a draft that contained just about all of the self-conscious qualifications that are expressed in the earlier pages of this chapter. Still, the tension remains. The sensibilities of some of the specialists are indeed different from ours in the matter of making claims stable enough to build upon.

Allowing differences in sensibilities, we still suggest that Clooney's falls within the scope of our overall method. Several quick points illustrate this. First, any real comparison requires saying what the comparison is, not merely tracing out what touches what; all the specialists' chapters in this volume do this. Second, we hope it is clear that our conclusions in the present chapter, even when expressed as hypotheses for further investigation, are matters that extend beyond the kind of comparisons drawn out in the specialists' papers. Third, our method has repeatedly emphasized the dialectical interplay between formulations of comparative categories, descriptions of specifications, and the summing up of the comparisons; of course, this is a kind of intellectual work with its own excellence. That we (Neville and Wildman) are virtuosi at the task remains to be seen! Fourth, we admit the difficulty of establishing authoritative voices for any of the traditions, who represents the true Hinduism, Daoism, or Christianity; most of the traditions ring with accusations of heresy and error. As mentioned, Eckel urges us to cite only individual authors; Clooney points out that the text of Vedānta Deśika he cites in this volume is very different from other texts by Deśika. The question is whether a text can be described so as to have representative force beyond itself for a strand of a tradition, or whether it speaks only for itself alone. Comparison is possible in either case, and the ideas compared might be interesting. For our purposes, however, the former is more to the point because it addresses questions brought to the comparison by people interested in the traditions, not only in the single texts. Clooney and all the other specialists note both the particularity of the texts they cite as well as a considerable representative function.

7.2 Specifying the Category

7.2.1 *Chinese Religion*

Kohn and Miller characterize ultimate reality in Chinese religion as "harmony and transcendence and their actualization in human life" (1.1.2). They call this a matter of order and thus distinguish this complex tradition both from those that would characterize ultimate reality as a being beyond the distinction of order and matter and from those (usually the same) that would place ultimate reality beyond, or at least on the boundary of, the ordered cosmos. Constructing the artificial phrase "ultimate reality" in Chinese (*jishi*), they argue that it is an oxymoron because ultimacy is a transcendent ideal for harmony, and reality connotes hard, limited, and solid stuff. The question for ultimacy in Chinese religion is precisely to transcend reality in that sense. So the best characterization of ultimate reality for the Chinese, Kohn and Miller argue, is that it is *ideal* harmony and transcendence that needs to be made real through actualization in human experience. They point out that human experience is so various that what one person finds ultimate, that is, transcendent and harmonizing, is likely not to be ultimate for another.

All of this is true of ultimate reality, they say, because of the nature of the Dao. The Dao is not a cosmos-transcending being, principle, or power, "but rather infinitesimal, the faintest, most imperceptible of breaths, the darkest shade of light, the smallest possible contrast which, in its infinite fractal-like recursions, multiplies to constitute the shocking wealth of cosmic power. This is the ultimate mystery of Dao: that subtle void and intangible formlessness should be the root of all becoming" (1.2.1). For human beings to access this infinitesimal subtlety is to gain great power (1.2.2), whether it be political, cognitive, or spiritual. The human religious project then is to surmount the limitations of ordinary bodily and sensate life and acquire sensitivities to the Dao that are transcendent and harmonizing relative to one's sphere. This is a puzzle, however, because it is not clear how what is so differently harmonizing and transcendent for various people always comes down to infinitesimal, subtle, and intangible formlessness. Could it be that in construing ultimacy as the harmonizing and transcendent Kohn and Miller are interpreting it only in respect to its very formal element of being the object of ultimate concern, as Tillich would say? Would they agree that some candidates for harmony and transcendence, for instance, getting richer than anyone else, are materially foolish? Is not the Dao the only way to transcendence and harmony?

Kohn and Miller treat the Neo-Confucian text of Zhou Dunyi, *The Explanation of the Diagram of the Great Ultimate*, as a metaphysical analysis of Dao. That text begins with the phrase, "non-being [and also] the great ultimate." Kohn and Miller do not read these as complementary, or dualistic, as do those scholars who want to deny transcendence in Chinese culture. Rather, pointing out that non-being is not a thing, they say it still has a kind of priority: "from non-being is created great ultimate" (1.2.3). Non-being is not a substance and does not act, yet positive reality arises by means of the slightest steps from it, and somehow because of it. Moreover, according to their interpretation of Zhou, the political, religious, and spiritual hierarchies of China are all characterized by this infinitesimal beginning, or beginning in vacuity. To be in touch with this vacuity, or infinitesimally fecund Dao, is thus the ideal to be realized in actual life.

Yet, contrary to their claim that the Dao as ultimate is only ideal, it would seem that accessing the Dao, regardless of how intangible it might be compared with eating spiced cabbage or pushing a cart through the mud, is the ideal precisely because the ontological figure of least-being arising from vacuity is the true ontological causal ground of affairs. Not to be in touch with this is to be relatively powerless, not merely unideal. To put the matter another way, not only is there the temporal causal process of qi alternations in nested patterns of various sorts, there is also an ontological "process" in which the organization of qi in the interchanging elements is based on yin returning from yang, which extends from Taiji, which emerges from non-being. What seems ultimate in their account of Zhou is not nonbeing by itself but rather the hierarchy of everything insofar as it is dominated by non-being and therefore in principle accessible to subtle human control from top to bottom. As Kohn and Miller say, it is not non-being or Dao by itself that is ultimate, but that as present in the hierarchy of things down to one's own body and social practices.

Medieval Daoism envisioned the situation differently. "To begin with, creation in medieval Daoism is not a smooth transition from the nameless and invisible Dao to a formed and physical world but the active involvement of a creator God" (1.4.1). Laozi is the Dao, yet is not "completely immersed in this undifferentiated cosmic soup, but 'contemplates' and 'views' it," exerting some control over it. Kohn and Miller say that "with this dual nature" Laozi "represents the bridge between the unformed cosmos and the existing world and thus stands exemplary for the ideal of the ultimate perfected who has transformed his physical and sensory being into a state of primordiality and rests at the root of the cosmos—not in its utter chaos, however, but in its pure realm of heavenly spontaneity" (1.4.1).

This is the medieval Daoist ideal of human realization. Kohn and Miller treat this expression of the ultimate as a metaphoric or symbolic personification, though they do not say that what it personifies is the ancient conception of the Dao or the Neo-Confucian conception of the hierarchical generative relations among non-being, Taiji, yang/yin, the elements, and so forth. Rather, they suggest that it is an ontological expression of the subjective conception of harmony and transcendence in "the overcoming of the sensory field and sensual modes of experience in favor of something nonsensory, something intuitive, spontaneous, immediate, an experience that goes beyond feeling and seeing and thinking into a state of no-mind, no-perception, and no self" (1.5). Although they tend to emphasize the diversity of the human ways to this harmony and transcendence, speaking sometimes as if it were nothing but a human method, they are nearly clear in the end that the human method or Dao is normative because there is in fact "the invisible and intangible cosmic realm of nonbeing and nonaction" with respect to which one can live and perceive (1.5). They are only *nearly clear* in this regard because often their hesitancy about straightforward ontological commitments to the Dao or to *wu/taiji* seems to be little more than an allergy to what they take to be substance philosophy, as if the ontological ultimate has to be a static substance. Their last sentence is: "The ultimate in Chinese religion is a process of realization and experience, part of the world yet not accessible with worldly means, and thus the opposite of the Western concept of God, which is substantial and static, entirely beyond the world, and accessible only by transcending the world completely" (1.5). Anne Birdwhistell, in comments arising from the conference discussion, points out that many would claim that the Chinese have no conception of nature or the cosmos without humans, that the Chinese view is always from an admitted human perspective. The question is whether this is because of nature, thereby defining the human in relation to the cosmos as well as vice versa, or a mere reduction of nature to the human sphere alone.

7.2.2 *Judaism*

Saldarini's presentation of ultimate reality in Judaism appears to begin from the opposite angle to Kohn and Miller's presentation of the notion in Chinese religion. That is, God is the ultimate reality in Judaism and the many divine things or appearances discussed in the tradition are metonyms for the ultimate deity. There are several meanings of ultimacy, all of which apply to God, according to Saldarini. God is the uncaused creator of everything else, the goal of existence, the ground of intelligibility or wisdom about the world, superlative excellence, and goodness. The ultimacy of God is perceived or conceptualized in contrast with the limitations of human life (2.1).

From the human perspective God as ultimate is sought to give unity and coherence to life in a context that often looks chaotic. This primary emphasis on order is like that noted in Chinese religion. The God of Judaism is strongly affirmed to be independent of the world, however much God is known in and through the various functions of ultimacy (as creator, goal, etc.). Whereas the Chinese seem to start with a solid conception of nature, transcendence beyond which is sought in the extension of nature merely to its intangible and usually unnoticed fineness, the Jews do not think of nature without the human and they think of neither without relation to God (2.2.1).

In the biblical representations, "although God is the ultimate cause and goal of the universe and in principle unlimited by human history, functionally speaking God is always limited and his actions relativized by human responses from creation to judgment at the end of history" (2.3). Sometimes God is represented metonymically as having a body, other times as manifest in different things such as burning bushes and pillars of fire. "The Hebrew Bible, like the New Testament, Qur'ān, and many Hindu devotional texts [and we might say like medieval Daoism], portrays God as a personal force in the world and human life, using a variety of poetic and narrative literary forms. However, the Bible subtly qualifies its sense of God's immanence and intimacy by emphasizing God's power, glory, wisdom and 'strangeness'" (2.3). Rabbinic representations emphasize God's transcendence by explicitly delimiting God to roles in stories or to the exercise of judgment and mercy relative to human beings. This in turn gives rise to mysticism in which God's transcendence is focused as both revealed and hidden; highly specific elements, such as a divine body or vehicle, are taken to be symbolic of something far more transcendent. Whereas Chinese religion sometimes starts with the ultimate as distant and unreal except insofar as actualized in experience, and moves in its medieval period toward metaphoric personalization, the Hebrew Bible moves oppositely from highly personified symbols to breaking those symbols through holy strangeness to mystical transcendence. (In other respects, the Chinese take the ultimate as ever-present Qi, or Dao.) In Maimonides, theoretical knowledge of God is set over metaphors and anthropomorphisms; it is "the only kind of knowledge able to give reliable knowledge of God," and that indeed is in part through the *via negativa* (2.7).

Throughout the whole of Judaism, according to Saldarini, God is understood to be ultimate not only in relation to a series or hierarchy but also by being absolutely unique. This uniqueness was expressed by Maimonides and later more explicitly by Hermann Cohen in the Western philosophical language of being, showing that God is not categorizable as a being, or in a genus *being*. Judaism's language about God is thus person-alizing and anthropomorphic, on the one hand, and also insistent on God's difference from all these ideas. "Although a rich variety of similes, metaphors and symbols are used of God, they all revolve around God as a person who participates in human society and history and especially in Israel's life. Despite the overwhelming use of anthropomorphisms, at each step of the way, in almost all expressions of God's reality, power, activity, mercy and justice, the tradition persistently insists that God is not really like humans. God is greater, more powerful, not subject to human limita-tions and in the end beyond complete human comprehension" (2.10).

7.2.3 *Christianity*

Fredriksen's sharp focus on the Christianity of the New Testament pe-riod leads her to note that those Christians' conceptions of the ultimate, God, were not different from those of most of their non-Christian Jewish contemporaries. In both cases, God was thought of as foundation and goal of everything (3.1). What was new and interesting about those Christians, she argues, is their extending to the Gentiles the promise of God to Abraham; in particular, Christianity extended to the Gentiles a kind of holiness or non-profanity required for participating in the sacri-fices before God. Thus, Paul and slightly later writers used the images of holiness and sacrifice to interpret how Jesus had transformed the situa-tion of Gentiles in reference to God. We shall return to this in 7.4 when considering in more detail what the religions say about relations to the ultimate.

7.2.4 *Islam*

Haq's presentation of Islam draws much from the comparative context of our discussions. On the one hand Islam is in "both inherent and his-torical family resemblance with certain rationalizing religious trends in Judaism," and thus for Islam ultimate reality is conceived "as something stable, fixed, and objectively 'out there'—ultimate reality was the deity itself with all its standard Abrahamic divine attributes, including eternity and transcendence" (4.1). (Saldarini does not much stress the eternal part, so important for Islam.) Moreover, God as ultimate reality is never to be confused with the created world. On the other hand, God is the creator of the world and thus must be expressed in it in some way, par-ticularly as the divine will bears upon human personal and political real-ities. Ibn ʿArabī goes so far as to diminish the importance of the Creator/created distinction in favor of understanding the world to be the manifestation of God, such that God is really and truly present in the world (4.7). Haq asks whether this is like the more imminent ultimacy in Buddhism and Chinese religion (4.1).

The Qur'ān is primarily concerned with the moral implications of God as ultimate reality, but also stresses the absolute contingency of the cosmos on God, which "establishes the absolute centrality of God in the entire system of existence" (4.2). "The cosmic order, so it appears from the Qur'ān, is a fully integrated system in which every created entity—that is, all-other-than-God—takes its assigned place in the larger whole according to its *amr* (divine command); the cosmic order had its own autonomous laws (again: *amr*, pl. *awāmir*), and, indeed, it embodied God's signs. . . . In other words, the cosmic order has *no* rational, moral, or ontological ultimacy" (4.2). It derives its reality, structure, and significance wholly from God. Moreover, God is the infinite within which every other dimension of reality is possible.

Yet the Qur'ān treats God as "an overwhelming personality" (4.3), describable or knowable by the ninety-nine names. Haq singles out four important ways of understanding this. First is the way of piety in which the names are used to orient one's thinking to God without asking about any metaphysical puzzles. "The pious simplicity of early Islam had taken God's Names as given, with all their glaring mysteries and dark veils, to be understood not analyzed, to be found not demonstrated" (4.3). The doctrine of divine names was developed in contrast to the Christian doctrine of the Trinity that Muslim thinkers understood to represent God as insufficiently unified. Does this mean that the names signify attributes that introduce diversity into God? The second position, characteristic of the Mu'tazilite position, denies the real reference of the names or attributes and says God is beyond all names, using the logic of *tanzīh* or denial of likeness. The third position reverses the second and finds God expressed throughout all creation, with the divine nature manifest in the many created things, a position stressing the logic of *tashbīh*. The fourth balances the second and third in a conception of unity, *tauḥīd*, which stresses that God's unity embraces the world as well as the transcendent divine nature. Although the cosmos has no independent existence and depends entirely on God, its coherence expresses the divine unity.

Islamic thought about ultimate reality thus has a wider range of types than is characteristic of Jewish or very early Christian thought, including not only the simple acceptance of the symbols for their personal and social value but also serious philosophical wrestling with the problem of the one and the many in God. Saldarini attributed that concern to Greek thought, of which indeed Islam was an heir.

7.2.5 *Hinduism*

Clooney's presentation of the Indian religions' views on ultimate reality is twofold: a set of general characteristics expressed at the beginning (5.1) and the analysis of a particular version of that in a part of a book by Vedānta Deśika. As to the former, his characterization of ultimate reality is identical to that given by Saldarini for Judaism and by Haq for Islam (with Fredriksen's slice of Christianity not distinguished from Judaism). In "the literate and sophisticated Sanskrit-language traditions of Hindu orthodoxy" (5, n. 1), "Ultimate Reality is that which cannot be surpassed; that from which all realities, persons and things come, that on which they depend, and that into which they return upon dissolution" (5.1). Clooney proceeds to say that for his Viśiṣṭādvaita school, knowledge of ultimate reality is the means to know everything else and to achieve liberation. "In theistic traditions, this Ultimate Reality is personal, can be invoked by one or more proper names, and can choose to become accessible in perceptible form," again a set of conditions held in common with the monotheistic traditions. Clooney says that tensions about how to make sense of all this, tensions of the sort already encountered in the religions discussed so far, sometimes lead to argumentative discourse and this is what he examines in the work of Vedānta Deśika (1268–1369), a follower of Rāmānuja who was born in the same year as Zhou Dunyi, 1017, twenty years before Avicenna died.

Vedānta Deśika's understanding of Nārāyaṇa as Lord is neatly summarized by Clooney and that need not be repeated here. Two points are worth stressing for comparison's sake. The first is that Vedānta Deśika follows the Viśiṣṭādvaita model for the relation between Brahman (Nārāyaṇa) and the world, namely, that the world is the body of Brahman, the agential, conscious self. Thus, the world is wholly dependent on Brahman for its material body and its internal agency. In many respects this body-soul analogy is close to Ibn 'Arabī's view that the world is the expressive manifestation of God, and like it is close to pantheism. Whereas Ibn 'Arabī still asserts the independence and completeness of God apart from the manifestations in creation, Deśika opts for the soul-body identification and rejects Śaṅkara's attempt to preserve the wholly simple or nondual character of Brahman in irrelevance to the multiplicity in the world. This introduces the second point to stress in Clooney's account, namely, that Deśika defines his position dialectically, by sharpening his differences with neighboring philosophies. Clooney contends that Indian religions express many variations on the general position sketched at the beginning of his chapter, each of which is subject to argumentative defense against the others, as Vedānta Deśika attempts in this text. But

Clooney carefully avoids any assessment of Deśika's arguments, or any possible counter-arguments, and so does not comment on whether the distinctions between the various schools are real alternatives or are capable of being integrated into more inclusive views. Nor does he comment explicitly on the viability of the terms used in the arguments, only on their historical significance, and so he makes no claims about whether they constitute what logicians today would call well-formed formulas to express and draw inferences about ultimate reality as affirmed or assumed in the traditions of Deśika or his opponents. An assessment of the terms of the debates and the arguments for the various positions would have to connect the thirteenth-century arguments with contemporary conceptions of intelligibility, which Clooney approaches in the comparison with Richard Swinburne. We and our contemporaries, for instance, are puzzled by Deśika's claim that the existence of the Lord is better affirmed from Scripture because logical inference is never certain enough. Does Deśika believe that the interpretation of Scripture is more certain than logic? He seems as contentious about how to interpret Scripture as he is about how to interpret efficient and material causes. We shall return to the issue about philosophy and interpretation in 7.4.

7.2.6 Buddhism

David Eckel's presentation of Madhyamaka Buddhism on ultimate reality in one respect is very like that of Kohn and Miller on Chinese religion, namely, that ultimacy is best approached through considering how it might be actualized in human experience. And the reason for this in both cases is that reality ultimately is processive, not static, stable, substantive, or fixed. Therefore the religious question is not so much "what is ultimate reality?" as it is "how we can catch something ultimate in the flux of things?"

Eckel begins with an epistemological consideration of reference and suggests that Madhyamaka Buddhism denies reference to real things. Reference, however, is construed as referring to things that have stable identity of their own, at least for a split second. He says that Madhyamaka and Yogācāra thinkers insist that the claims about emptiness refer to reality. Things *really are empty*, according to both schools. This is the working assumption as they go about debating just what the emptiness entails, for instance, whether there has to be something emptied, as the Yogācārins would say.

This leads to a strong comparative remark. In the religions of South Asia, including Buddhism but also the various schools of Hinduism, especially those of Vedānta, a candidate for ultimate reality is assumed to be eternal in the sense of being stable and unchanging, unaffected by passing things, and admitting of internal distinctions only with difficulty. In this context, Mahāyāna Buddhism is led to deny reality to the self and other objects of potential reference. In Chinese religion, by contrast, reality is assumed to be in constant flux so that what is ultimate about it needs to be the little nothings that spark the spontaneity of the changes, or the Big Nothing that lies at the heart of the Great Ultimate from which the motions of yang and yin structure the things that change. In Chinese religion the question for ultimacy is how order comes with the spontaneity. In the Western philosophic traditions, Platonists side with the East Asians in affirming the ultimacy of concrete change and abstract principles of order, whereas Aristotelians side with the South Asians in assuming concrete stable unchanging unity as the ground for change. Christianity and Islam have been affected by both the Platonic and Aristotelian traditions, and their conceptions of God have been internally various because of that.

Eckel focuses on the debate between the Yogācāra and Madhyamaka forms of Mahāyāna Buddhism to illustrate the complexity of the claim that things are ultimately empty, which he says (6.4, last sentence) amounts to the claim that they are contingent and finite. Moreover, there is nothing that is not empty—no underlying Brahman, no substantial Dao, no creator God. The contention is over whether we should say with the Yogācārins that we have learned the truth of emptiness and therefore should acknowledge the quasi-substantial reality of our previous ignorant selves and of the truth that we learned, or rather with the Madhyāmikas that we must abandon the detritus of the quest itself including its conception of the enlightened self and the dharma. Eckel sees that Madhyamaka purism in this regard is not nihilistic; it would be so only if one held to the belief that reality has to be substantial. If you abandon all substantialism, however, what is left is the changing of things and the pragmatic groupings we place on them for the interests of life, and many of these changing things are good. The rhetoric of Madhyamaka (and Yogācāra, too, on this point) is oriented to the denial of substantialist assumptions. This rhetoric of denial conditions expressions of Ultimate Truth. If one carries through the Madhyamaka project and abandons that rhetoric, however, the Conventional Truth of pragmatic life is positive; it is authentic to say that Nirvana (the Ultimate Truth) is samsāra (the conventional one now freed of substantialists assumptions).

7.3 Comparing within the Category

This section sums up our discussion so as to give some concrete expression to the category of ultimate reality and lays out some general comparisons in terms of this category with as much thoroughness as our highly selective study allows. The comparisons we make take the form of two generalized schemas, which we call "spectra" of views of ultimate realities (7.3.1 and 7.3.2), together with an attempt to explain the schemas. What is meant by "explanation" in this context is discussed in 7.3.3, and then a philosophically oriented part-explanation is offered in 7.3.4 followed by a discussion in 7.3.5 of its consequences for religious symbolization of ultimate realities.

7.3.1 Comparative Spectra

The first comparative generalization sustained by our investigations is that ultimate realities are conceived in both ontological and anthropological terms (understanding the latter to refer to human experience, not a human-oriented cosmology). That is, ontological conceptions of ultimate reality are productive of some religious symbols, other symbols express the striving after that which is of ultimate importance to human beings, and these two sources for symbolization of ultimate realities vary in their respective importance among our traditions. All of our traditions make use of both sorts of sources for symbolization; in fact, each is internally diverse with regard to how subtraditions prefer or balance the two sources. The resulting spectrum reflects the types of balance achieved. Some traditions, such as many forms of Buddhism, tend toward symbolization drawn from the anthropological conceptions of ultimate realities while others, such as many forms of Christianity, tend toward symbolization drawn from ontological conceptions of ultimate realities. Some traditions, such as Islam, seem in their mainstream varieties to be relatively even-handed in their drawing on the two sources for symbolizing ultimate realities.

Much has been said about this spectrum already in the introduction and in several of the specialists' chapters and so more comparative detail at this point serves no useful purpose. However, we return below (7.4) to the anthropological source for symbolization with some comparative detail, which serves as a complement to the mostly ontologically oriented topics that are explored next.

The second comparative generalization is that in all of our traditions, if not in all the specific texts examined, we have found a spectrum of representations of the ontological ultimate. The spectrum ranges from earthy personifications to principles and philosophic representations so transcendent as to be beyond much if any positive knowledge. As was the case for the first spectrum, in each tradition there are a few portions of the second spectrum that more or less dominate the rhetoric and metaphors for speaking of the ultimate. In each tradition there are also pressures registered within each position on the spectrum to relativize or qualify that position and to move elsewhere on the spectrum.

The religions we studied all have their origins in the Axial Age revolution (if you count Christianity and Islam's origins in Exilic and early Second Temple Judaism) in which various forms of polytheism were subordinated or made "merely symbolic" relative to some unifying principle mirroring a unifying conception of the cosmos. In the main, the Sky God won and was then reinterpreted. The process of reinterpretation took many directions, governed by different symbolic systems and internal dialectical moves. Somewhere in that process, the traditions took their primary metaphoric or rhetorical reference points and then tended to take shape around those formative decisions.

Judaism, Christianity, and Islam never abandoned the highly personalized language of God that was so apt during Yahweh's days as a Sky God who travels with his people. Their primary scriptures represent historical stages at which God was understood also to be creator of the universe, not merely a personal force within the cosmos. Nevertheless, despite the transcendent universality of a creator of everything else, central elements of the rhetoric of these traditions represent God as a personal being relative to other personal beings within a field of interaction. Both Saldarini and Haq note the references in their traditions' scriptures to God's body, for instance, though in Judaism and Islam it is only parts of the body and not whole bodies that furnish symbolic material for God. By the first centuries of the common era, Judaism (in Philo) and Christianity (in the Johannine writings, Origen, etc.) had incorporated Greek philosophical thinking into their consideration of what it means for God to create, judge, govern, and fulfill the world. They understood perfectly well that God was not a "Big Guy in the Sky," and made that point in stressing the difference of God from human persons, as Saldarini emphasizes. Yet, except for some theologians and religious philosophers, most thinkers in these traditions continued to use the personal language, knowing it to be personifying. The strong influence of philosophy on theology in the medieval period in Islam, Judaism, and Christianity created languages in each tradition with extraordinary diversity and richness. Yet in each case the intermixing of the philosophical with the personalistic ends of the spectrum was highly qualified: for instance, by the insistence on Qur'ānic language and law in Islam, by the failure of orthodoxy to embrace Maimonides in Judaism, and by the Reformation insistence on the language of scripture in Christianity.

In China, by contrast, the dominant rhetoric of what Kohn and Miller identify as Chinese religion came from a later period in which the personifying elements of Shangdi, the Sky God, had been superseded by non-personal principles such as Dao and Heaven, later Heavenly Principle. Julia Ching and others have shown the resonance of the personalizing ancestry in Daoism and Confucianism.[2] But the personal rhetoric has been dampened except in such notions as the "Mandate of Heaven" and heaven's personal power.[3] It was not until well into the common era that Chinese medieval Daoism became highly personalized.

The religions of South Asia, by contrast with West and East Asia, have managed to carry along many portions of the spectrum mixed together. Nothing is more philosophically abstract than the conceptions of Nirguṇa Brahman in Advaita Vedānta, and yet that tradition has highly personalized representations of Brahman as Lord (i.e., as Īśvara). Vedānta Deśika's text treats the Lord as the object of scholastic philosophical categories on the one hand and as married to a goddess on the other. The candidates to which Buddhists deny ultimate reality embrace both the personal and the more abstract. Mahāyāna Buddhism itself, in its distinction between the two Truths, both of which are true, illustrates the parallel between the personalism of Conventional Truth and the abstract dialectic of Ultimate Truth.

Thus, to summarize, whereas the traditions of West, East, and South Asia all have representations of the ultimate ranging from the highly personal to the abstract, transcendent, and philosophical, with denials of the literalness of finite references to the ultimate, they differ in rhetorical centers. The West Asian religions are centered in the personifying rhetoric and need to relate the more philosophical talk back to that. The East Asian religions in their intellectual moments are centered in more universalistic and philosophical rhetoric, tending to look on the personifying elements as superstitious, save in a few instances, such as the late development of medieval Daoism. Both West and East Asian traditions engage in theological or philosophical analyses that are even more abstract than their principal rhetorical symbols, and both include apophatic affirmations. The South Asian traditions have a much broader rhetorical center, or perhaps no center at all, carrying along both personifying and abstract symbols through many contexts of thought, community practice, and devotion. This can be baffling to those accustomed to the rhetorical centers of West or East Asia, who can view the South Asian rhetoric as either too superstitious or too negative and apophatic to be either personally or philosophically satisfying. Eckel's account of Western scholars struggling to distinguish Madhyamaka from nihilism illustrates this. It would be interesting to complicate this generalization with studies of crossovers, for instance, the move of Buddhism to East Asia or the transformation of Christianity implied in the Tang Dynasty translation of the Prologue to the Christian Gospel of John as "In the beginning was the Dao."

Intriguing questions arise about the differences among the religions concerning the spectrum from personifying to philosophical. There may be some truth in the obvious suggestion that the more personal end of the spectrum appeals to popular religion whereas the more philosophical appeals to sophisticated thinkers and writers. Surely the worlds of popular religion in all the traditions have been filled with spirits toward whom people comport themselves; even contemporary Jewish-Christian-secular North America is fascinated with angels, and often with devils. There are sophisticated Buddhists deeply devoted to the cult of Guanyin, however, and Christian Thomists who know that God is the Act of Esse and that Mary is his mother. An hypothesis will be presented in 7.4 to the effect that the more personalizing metaphors function in devotional contexts and the philosophical ones in contexts defined quite differently. Popular religion tends to be devotional, and hence always receptive to personifying symbols, whereas only sometimes is philosophically articulate religion devotional. Not all devotional symbols are personifying, however; witness most mystical traditions.

As we describe in *The Human Condition* (1.3), the first of our three criteria for successful comparison of religious ideas is that there be genuine commonality in the vague categories presupposed in a comparison. One of the contentions in this book is that determining whether there is genuine commonality is inevitably a philosophical task, at least in part. To show that a vague category legitimately enables a comparison of actual similarity between apparently different religious ideas, or a comparison of actual difference between superficially similar ones, involves the construction of a philosophical interpretation of those religious ideas. This interpretation must be rich enough to show how the vague category comprehends the ideas that specify it and explain why the various specifications are voiced differently. Such an interpretation could also succeed in ruling out superficial similarities as not actually genuine by showing that there is no philosophical affinity between them despite possible verbal resemblance.

To provide such a philosophical interpretation, we contend, is to furnish the beginnings of an explanation for comparative generalizations. The two spectra described above stand in need of this kind of explanation so that we can be assured that the generalizations are in fact important ones, that they offer stable insight into the character of religion and the ideas to which religions give birth, that they can reliably be used in subsequent analyses of religious ideas, and that they have been rendered as specific as possible for the sake of efficiently exposing them to correction. Indeed, explanations of this kind are an essential component of achieving the stability and vulnerability that we demand of comparative generalizations.[4]

The philosophical aspect of these explanations is but one of several. A fuller description of the structure of the explanations needed to justify comparative generalizations is as follows. First, there needs to be a delimiting of possibilities whereby plausible religious ideas of the sort relevant to the comparative generalization are identified. For example, ultimate reality is more plausibly construed as a cosmic battle between forces of good and evil than as a Volkswagen with a toothpick glued to the rear-view mirror. Other views may be even more or even less plausible than these are. The delimiting of possibilities must give an account of what ideas are most plausible and why. It is possible to explain variations in plausibility by appealing to purely conventional causes. Alternatively, as we (Neville and Wildman) prefer, an explanation might assume that our ideas are made more or less plausible by something about the world and not just by our constructions of it. However that goes, a delimiting of possibilities that includes an indication of the more plausible ideas and the reasons for their greater plausibility is the first step in explaining comparative generalizations.

Second, there needs to be an account of the dynamic logical connections among ideas, using "logical" in the broad sense as related to conceptual structure. We noted above that the metaphoric symbol systems focused at any one place along one of our spectra tend to qualify themselves and reach out toward other places on the spectrum. The personalizing symbols obviously push toward transcendent definitions to avoid making the ultimate too mundane an object. The push works the other way too. When conceptions of the ultimate are too transcendent or abstract, they are recalled to the human project by which their objects are approached, and then often to more nearly personalizing forms. These "pushes" are expressions of dynamic logical connections among the symbolizations of ultimate reality.

Hegel's logic was intended to generalize simple, *ad hoc* accounts of the conceptual relations underlying changing ideas,[5] which was a bold move in an important direction. With most subsequent interpreters, however, we think Hegel was overoptimistic about the capacity of ideas to dictate their own development on the basis of their internal structure. He was also insufficiently realistic about the contingencies of history wherein the power of circumstances can sometimes dominate the influence of logical structure in the ever-shifting flux of ideas. Explanations justifying comparative generalizations need much less than Hegel offered on the logical side and much more than he gave by way of historical analysis. With this, we move to the third and fourth phases of explanations for comparative generalizations. Both are at least partly historical in character and each is naturally connected to one of the first two phases.

Third, then, there needs to be a genetic analysis of the specificity of symbolic representations of the religious ideas in question. In many cases reliable information for analysis of origins is scarce. Nevertheless, even speculative reconstructions of formative moments early in the history of an idea can make a contribution. Such speculative reconstructions can make use of historical, social, psychological, neurophysiological, environmental, and other considerations. For example, the beginning of a genetic analysis for the second spectrum might make reference to the difference between popular and intellectual religious interests, as was suggested above.

Fourth, and finally, there needs to be analyses of the circumstances that accompany the key shifts in symbolic representation during the history of the relevant religious ideas. Again, these analyses would make use of all of the considerations relevant to the genetic analyses just mentioned. Typically, however, there would be greater emphasis on historical events such as wars, invasions, migrations, trade, and cultural exchange.

Constructing a fully developed justification for a comparative generalization is quite a daunting task—and what is said above already presupposes the complex process of comparison that gives rise to hypothetical comparative generalizations in the first place. Nevertheless, the goal of justifying comparisons can be satisfied by nothing less, especially when the importance of the comparison is a matter of concern. Is it worth the trouble? It is hard to say in advance; after all, the question is equivalent to asking about the value of the entire project of comparative religious ideas. In some cases, it might finally prove impossible to decide between competing justifications, which would be an argument in favor of not bothering so hard with justifications the next time. Now and then, however, some comparative generalizations, especially as made vulnerable by the explanatory justifications offered for them, might become generally accepted because of the power of one of those justifications to build consensus among experts. That kind of stability, though always provisional and in search of correction, is of inestimable value for both the academic field of religious studies and for understanding religion itself.

In what follows, we make no attempt to provide a comprehensive justification for the two spectra we have introduced as examples of comparative generalizations. Rather, focusing on the second spectrum, we take the first two of the four steps described above: a delimitation of possibilities and an analysis of the logic internal to the dynamism of change in symbolizations of ultimate realities. We shall depend on remarks made in passing throughout this chapter to hint at how the last two steps might be taken. Even the two steps we do take are no more than shuffles because there are equally promising lines of argument that we do not explore, such as the logic of temporal flow and the logic of spatial extension, among others. Nevertheless, what follows is a partial justification for the comparative generalizations we have articulated as a result of our group's comparative work together.

7.3.2 The Logic of Contingency

We propose the following hypothesis. All the traditions suppose that at least human life, if not the cosmos, is contingent and dependent on ultimate causes other than itself. In the fact of this contingency, all the existential questions—of life and death, despair and happiness, meaning and vanity, suffering and peace, ignorance and liberation, as well as sheer wonder at existence—get expressed in many modes and levels. There is a structural logic to contingency according to which ultimate references addressing the existential questions can be classified. This logic moves the attempt to represent ultimate reality from one place on the spectrum to another, finally across all.

There is no completely neutral way to express the logic of contingency. If the hypothesis is right, then most of the representations of ultimate reality express it, or illustrate parts and angles of it. The following is a contemporary philosophic attempt arising from the concern to be fair to the religious positions studied. It is, of course, as historically contextualized as any other philosophic argument. It also presents the logic of contingency in some detail and thus may be difficult to digest for some readers. Moreover, its abstractness is mind-numbing to those who do not delight in philosophical play. Those primarily interested in other topics may wish to skip this section and return to it below. The main point has already been outlined and the purpose of a philosophical reflection in the context of a comparative generalization was described above.

What is contingency? What makes something contingent? There are two seemingly different answers. One is that contingency is being *this* rather than *that*. The other is that contingency is being *something* rather than *nothing*. These are connected in the fact that to be something (rather than nothing) is to be this something rather than some other thing. So the originating question of contingency is what it is to be determinate, this rather than that. Our hypothesis is that to be determinate is to be a harmony with two kinds of features, conditional and essential. The conditional features are those relative to the other things with respect to which the thing is determinate. These might be causal conditions, for instance, or logical or formal conditions, spatio-temporal connections, and so forth. The notion of conditional feature is very abstract and is illustrated in any tradition's representations of relations. Essential features are those by virtue of which the thing integrates its conditional features so as to have its position or own-being and not to be reducible to the other things in relation to which it is determinate if it is itself. Essential features might be subtle spontaneous acts of self-integration, of the sort Kohn and Miller attribute to the Dao, or continuing genetic codes that integrate an organism's interactions with the environment over time, or moral norms that integrate a person's actual and ideal life. The traditions have many variants on these distinctions between conditional and essential features, including explicit denials of them.

If a thing is determinate by virtue of being what it is over against something else (doubtless many other things), the question of its contingency is the question of how it is possible for it to be together with those other things. The question of this togetherness is deeper than might be expected. On the level of cosmic or intraworldly connections, things are together by virtue of their conditional features; they condition one another. In order for any conditioning to be possible, however, the several things must be together at a deeper ontological level in which their essential features are together. This is because the things as harmonies of conditional and essential features could neither condition nor be conditioned without their respective essential features by virtue of which they integrate their conditions. And yet their respective essential features are precisely what is not constituted by the connections of conditional features. Nāgārjuna saw this point in his critique of motion and causation: if a thing is the result only of antecedent conditions (*pratītyasamutpāda*), then it has no essential features to allow it to stand apart from those conditions and no change is possible from the antecedent to a consequent. No antecedent condition can be the ownbeing of an event or temporal thing. The nihilist interpretation of this is that there is no own-being at all, hence no change or causation, hence no real temporal things. The positive Buddhist interpretation is that events do happen with the spontaneity of the moment, a kind of evanescent essential rising-and-ceasing that makes temporal flow and causation possible and in fact is the basis for speaking of particularity. Because of the South Asian assumption that being has to have permanence, the spontaneity of the moment cannot be called being, or own-being, however it functions essentially. To put the point another way, more general than temporal flow, true relation requires true otherness, and true otherness cannot be reduced to relations alone, for there would be no realities to be related. For the sake of the hypothesis, let us call this deeper togetherness the ontological context of mutual relevance.

The question of contingency then becomes, what is the ontological context of mutual relevance? Perhaps the most obvious suggestion comes from the rhetorical shape of the notion of context, namely, that it is simply a bigger context than that constituted by conditional features, a vaster context that includes the essential features of everything as well as the conditional ones. Let the Earth and its affairs be explained by the greater Heavens of which it is a part! Yet there are two difficulties with this line of thought. If the larger context is itself determinate, something specific over and above the things contained within it, then there is a problem with how its own essential features are together with the things it contains; an even larger context would be necessary and an infinite regress results. If the larger context is not determinate, however, then it reduces to the things it contains, which were the very things needing explanation in the first place concerning how their essential features could be together.

A more plausible suggestion for the ontological context of mutual relevance, in fact developed in one form or another by all our traditions, is to say that the things of the world are together because they are simply made to be that way, with all their spatial and temporal relations. The ontological context is the act that creates them as related to one another with their conditions and essential features. The metaphors of contingency itself come from this suggestion. How are we to understand this ontological creation?

What all of our religious traditions did in their ancient roots was to parse the meaning of creation in cosmogonic myths in which one of the pantheon is symbolized as the creator and organizer of the whole, like a king who brings order by force and law by command, or like a potter who creates vessels. Each tradition brings a rich array of metaphors for creators. But the same dialectic that limited the suggestion of bigger and bigger contexts pushes at these symbols. If the creator God is determinate, by analogy or otherwise, then he [sic] seems to fall within the world of things created and the *real* creator is more transcendent. Pushed to its conceptual purity, the notion of ontological creation required to account for the possible togetherness of related but different things includes three interrelated notions. One is that the creative act is an asymmetrical move from nothing to the specific determinate character of the world. Creation is a real making of something new. The second is that the creation is made out of nothing; for, if there were something determinate out of which creation is made, that would have to be determinately related to what is created, and an even larger context for mutual relevance would be needed, a creative act behind the creative act. The ultimate source cannot be anything determinate. The third is that the creative act issues in the determinate world. The world is simply the terminus of the creative act; it has no medium of its own within which to float apart from its ontological creation. The world is also specific. Although there are complicated issues about whether the world could have developed otherwise than it did, this model of creation locates the specificity of the world in the act of creation.

Act of creating, indeterminate source of the act, determinate product of the act: these are the notions making up the larger notion of ontological act by virtue of which serious contingency can be conceived. The determinate state of affairs in which there is an ontological act of creation is among the things created; in theistic language, only by creating the world does God become creator, or anything else determinate. Apart from actually creating, there is nothing, no God who is a being with inner intentions, no substance with potentialities, no secretly pregnant non-being. For if there were something back there or behind the act, it would be determinate and hence in need of ontological relation to the determinate things it creates, requiring a deeper ground, and so forth. This is the ratchet that drives the dialectic of transcendence. The creative act itself is singular, encompassing all possible diversity within its product, including its own constituent notions. It is also eternal in the sense that all temporal connections are among the things created.

7.3.3 *Religious Representations of the Logic of Contingency*

The logic of contingency is complicated, and different traditions focus variously on different parts. Spelling out some of these foci can indicate the comparative nature of the way the traditions articulate the ultimate, each with at least parts of the spectrum from the highly personified to highly abstract, transcendent, and apophatically asserted. Begin with the elements of the idea of ontological creation itself.

Consider the asymmetrical making in the act of creation. The West Asian theisms are very clear that the world depends wholly on God's creative act. God alone is real, as Haq points out for Islam, and the reality of the world is derivative from God's reality. But because of the personifying metaphors that tend to treat God as *a being* in West Asian religions, the asymmetry tends to move from a fullness of being with no internal differentiation—expressed in the unity theme in Islam as well as Judaism and Christianity—to a determinate world. But to distinguish a wholly unified and simple beginning point for creation from nothing at all is extremely difficult. Although West Asian religions have many strong variants on the notion of creation *ex nihilo*, they often are mixed with emanationist themes in which the act of creation is the diminishment of the source, or introduction of negation into a prior fullness. Emanationism is asymmetrical, but in reverse of the creation of novelty.

Chinese religion, by contrast, is resolutely asymmetrical in its notion of the advance toward novelty. The Daoist themes of infinitesimal acts of spontaneity and Zhou Dunyi's progression from non-being to the Great Ultimate, to yang, to yin, to the base elements, and thence to the ten thousand things, both illustrate the moves from nothing to something by the least complicated possible steps. In contrast to the West Asian emphasis on the unity of the source of the creative act, Chinese religion focuses on the presence of novelty-making spontaneity in each and every occurrence, all coordinated so that the unitary flow of the Dao is realized. The brahmanical religions of South Asia share the problematic of the creation of the contingent world, but focus more on the source rather than on the creative act, and this makes a major difference from the others.

Consider the focus on the source of the creative act rather than the act itself. Like the West Asian religions, the South Asian developed monotheistic rhetoric out of the polytheism of the Vedas. But whereas the West Asian religions carried on strong notions of individual subjectivity for the creator, and hence particular intentionality, the brahmanical religions transmuted subjectivity to consciousness, indeed consciousness as pure and essentially undifferentiated by objects of consciousness. This was clearly articulated in the ancient Sāmkhya texts distinguishing *puruṣa* from *prakṛti*. Clooney's text acknowledges consciousness for Nārāyaṇa.

Far more than either West or East Asian religions, however, the South Asian focus on the source of the creative act and the product rather than the act itself. Picking up on Haq's point that for the more mystical elements of Islam, only the source is really real and the world has derivative reality (or even unreality when considered by itself), the brahmanical religions and Buddhism place an overwhelming emphasis on the reality of the source. Because it is the source of all matter and change, the source apart from that derivation is beyond matter and change, and any determinate complexity. The traditions divide into the dualistic and non-dualistic responses to the overwhelming and exclusive reality of Brahman, and still seek a middle ground. The apparently dualistic Vedantins such as Vedānta Deśika, for instance, say that Brahman is not so without qualities that the finite world, its matter, motions, and thoughts cannot be the action of Brahman, who is the material cause of the world. The non-dualists, emphasizing even more the transcendence of Brahman over any determinateness marking differences, say that the world of diversity is not quite real, māyā, though it is the context of life.

On the other side, the South Asian traditions emphasize the presence of divinity in finite things, divinizing shrines and holy places, as well as holy people. Where West Asian religions get anxious about idolatry, the South Asian are generous with and tolerant of divine vitality in just about any thing one might focus on. The "I am" sayings of Kṛṣṇa in books 9 and 10 of the *Bhagavad Gītā* are classic statements. Buddhism radicalizes the focus on the immediacy of the dependent world. It emphasizes contingency in every sense just as much as any other tradition; but with its focus on the suchness of what is contingent, it finds nothing behind that. The Buddhist schools differ widely in their interpretation of temporal process and what if anything endures through that. But they agree that any specifiable thing, including the whole if they allow reference to that, is radically contingent on something other than itself. But by the logic of contingency, there is no thing on which they are dependent. Subordinating concerns for the asymmetrical act of creation, Mahāyāna Buddhists search for ways to talk about process as if it had no enduring being of its own, the recognition of this being enlightenment about the true meaning and reality of the life of change and liberation from the sufferings that come from expecting some reality to depend on. Madhyāmikas and other Buddhists would not describe the logic of contingency as the contingent nature of the creator; that is theistic talk. They would rather say that this is ultimate truth, the moral of which is that the determinate world, such as it is, is the only thing that is determinate. Having attained that ultimate insight, we should forget the logic of contingency because it only points to nothing beyond the determinate world, and attend to freedom within change. Whereas the theistic religions employ the rhetoric of a transcendent being to describe the absolutely indeterminate source as it would be apart from creation, Buddhism employs the rhetoric of denial of transcendent reality to make the same point. No less than the other religions, Buddhism has multiple scales of personifications of its angle on the creative act or, rather, its emphasis on the dependent product of that act.

Our hypothesis about determinateness also suggests comparative points, illustrated somewhat in the texts we studied.

That things are *harmonies* of features means that part of their ontological contingency consists in their order, the plan or pattern according to which their features are together through time. Harmonies are harmonies of harmonies and themselves play roles in other harmonies. Many traditions say that creation is the source of order, or that the overcoming of chaos is part of ultimate reality. Kohn and Miller say this for Chinese religion, and the first creation story in Genesis can be interpreted as an account of ordering chaos (though it also can be interpreted as an account of the arising of any determinateness whatsoever).

That things are harmonies of a plurality of *features* means that part of their ontological contingency consists in the fecundity, creativity, and diversity of their components. Many traditions represent ontological creation in the spontaneity of diversity, and suggest that orders or patterns are somewhat temporary and easily upset. This is close to the ontological picture Kohn and Miller draw about Daoism, and also to the Mahāyāna emphasis on *pratītyasamutpāda*. Most of our religions have strains of nature romanticism and mysticism. Of our specialist chapters, only Clooney's treatment of Vedānta Deśika's text lacks that; Clooney does say that Deśika's Tamil works might lead in that direction.

That things are harmonies of *essential* and conditional features means that part of their ontological contingency consists in existential particularity, position, place in space and time, and in the singularity and uniqueness of each thing. Religions testify to this in symbols for the reality of the creator or creative energy within the soul, closer to us than our jugular veins, the presence of the Dao in our own spontaneity. Some of the forms of South Asian religions that focus principally on the source of the determinate world (derivatively real or merely apparent) deny or deflect attention from the inner core of singularity in persons. But others, such as the Viśiṣṭādvaita school of Rāmānuja and Vedānta Deśika, emphasize the divine core of each individual's consciousness and action. If we are extremely scrupulous to avoid saying that one's essential features are real in the sense of enduring entities, Madhyamaka Buddhists might not be averse to admitting that the evanescent reality of our moments, seen for the empty realities they are and however framed across time and space pragmatically, are ultimate.

That things are harmonies of essential and *conditional* features means that part of their ontological contingency is their position in life, society, and the cosmos as webbed by their conditioning connections. No individual, nor place, nor event, nor job, nor community, could be what it is without its conditional features; therefore all the things with respect to which it is determinate are as much a part of it as its essential features, and its contingency is in those defining connections. Human beings always face the distinction between the actual set of connections and ideal ones, and this provides a special kind of conditional features situating people in the world. In *The Human Condition* we defined that condition in part as living under obligation. Theistic religions, insofar as they are committed to divine intentionality, interpret this in part as providence. Chinese religions represent the mandate of heaven and the sagely task of finding one's normative destiny. For the religions of South Asia we studied, the normative contrast relative to conditional features is between the ignorance that distorts those conditions and the enlightenment that reveals what is real (if anything) in them.

This hypothesis about the logic of contingency points out several focal points for the development of symbols for ontological creativity and the ontological dependence of the world. The focal points mentioned here are the creative act itself, its source, its product (namely, the world), the order of the world as consisting of harmonies, the plenitude of the world consisting of the components of harmonies, the essential features of harmonies, and the conditional features. As the religions develop symbols systems taking off from one focal point rather than another, they seem to exhibit different logics. That difference is apparent when one traces their representations' relative places on spectra running from personifications to abstract symbols testifying to the logical elements themselves, especially to the emptiness or indeterminateness of the source apart from that of which it is the source. Yet because there is a coherence to the elements in the logic of contingency, religions exhibit pressures to give expression to logical elements that do not fit easily with their dominant symbol systems. Thus, all say something (including negative things) about the asymmetrical act of making the contingent world, about the source of that on which all depends, and about the character of determinate dependency itself, including the harmony of own-nature and relation. To be sure, the religions often say different things about these elements. But they have symbols to address them all, or exhibit tensions in those symbols seeming to exclude or neglect important elements.

To give a summary expression to what the religions we studied say about ultimate reality: It is this complex of ontological contingency and creativity. Each element in this logical complex has been construed as a finite/infinite complex. It has its own determinate finite logical structure, and yet without that structure's contribution, there would be no determinate world. So the world is radically contingent upon each element, and without that element there would be nothing, complete indetermination, the infinite. Moreover, the elements hang together logically, although there are few concrete religious symbol systems that put them all together coherently. So the overall religious worldviews that are assumed in both thought and practice by representatives of the world religions are taken as complex icons for the ultimate. Constructed together into a comparative category, they present an extraordinarily rich but logically coherent collage of visions of the ultimate, that which is most important because of the nature of reality.

7.4 Relating to the Ultimate

The discussion of ultimate realities requires a dual perspective, we found, an ontological one, as the topic would seem to require on its face, and the perspective of the human religious search for the ultimate. The discussion in the previous section attempted to dwell on the first with a frankly on-tological model for making the category of ultimacy concrete. Even there, however, we referred frequently to how people find the logic of contingency in the elements of their own lives and perceptible world. Now we need to switch the perspectives and come at the problem of the ultimate as a task of religious life.

The organization of this section shall use the three categories of religious virtuosi introduced by Kohn and Miller, the philosophical, the practical, and the mythical. These are ideal types defined by the uses of symbols, not classes of persons: the same person can be a philosopher, a practical mystic, and a weaver of myths. The interest here is not in describing three kinds or dimensions of religious life. Rather it is to study three kinds of uses of religious symbols of the ultimate. In some respects is it true to say that they signify three kinds of symbols of the ultimate: philosophical, practical, and mythical. Alas, culture is not always that neat. Sometimes the philosophical virtuosi are constrained to work with highly personified symbols at the other end of the spectrum from the philosophic; Saldarini's discussion of Judaism and Haq's of Islam illustrate this abundantly. Sometimes practical self-transformers are stuck with airy philosophical terms such as "Dao" and need to supplement this with fantastical images of charcoal furnaces in their viscera. Sometimes mythic worldviews need to combine kataphatic imagery of heavenly bureaucracies, angels and spirits, and supreme creators with consorts, with apophatic denials of anything determinate whatsoever in the source of everything contingent.

The result is that we need to examine not just the different kinds of symbols but the different uses of the symbols, because the same symbol might be used philosophically, practically, and mythically. The purpose of the use in each case, as we have seen, is the actualization of the ultimate in human experience.

7.4.1 Philosophical Virtuosi

We can begin with the philosophical virtuosi because they have been discussed so much already (being most like ourselves!). The philosophical realization of the ultimate in human experience is the understanding of it, the conceptual understanding expressed in representations that can communicate the understanding to others. To this end, philosophy seeks representations that are universal and do not have to be qualified by context or perspective, and that themselves can be used to contextualize other symbols. To say with the Jewish psalmist that God is the rock of salvation is not to make a philosophic remark, even though few are likely to ask next whether God is sedimentary or igneous. To say with the Hebrew Bible that God is a person is also not to make a philosophic remark once it is realized that God's "person" is not like any other person, that God is strange and beyond all such categories. But to say that God is not in a genus and is creator of everything that is, and can also be personified as the object of prayer and the controller of history, is to speak philosophically, as Maimonides did. That Maimonides and Cohen have never been taken to heart in Judaism, always somewhat marginalized, illustrates the point that Judaism does not emphasize philosophic virtuosity.

There are at least four kinds of philosophic representation or modes of thought, all aiming to speak without the need for further contextualization and qualification. The first and most obvious is the development of categories for describing and explaining the ultimate. Vedānta Deśika is a straightforward practitioner of this kind of philosophy, operating in a context in which his conversation partners worked on developing and refining the same categories (he also wrote in other genres). Islamic concerns over whether the plurality of names of God imply diversity within God also illustrate philosophy as categoreal thinking, thinking that explains by reference to a system of categories. The second kind of philosophic thought is dialectical in which there is a process or sequence of thought such that categories at earlier stages are transformed or reinterpreted at later stages. The Buddhist debate between the Yogācāra and Madhyamaka interpretations of the move from conventional truth to ultimate truth back to conventional truth is an example of dialectical thinking. The truth value of dialectical assertions is extremely sensitive to the position in the sequence of the dialectic. What is true at one stage ("it is not a mountain") is false at another stage.

The third kind of philosophical strategy to escape further contextualization and qualification is the use of irony. With irony, switches in context and taking-back kinds of qualifications are already built in to the philosophic position. Zhuangzi was the master ironist in philosophical Daoism, though the whole of Daoism stresses ironic presentation. The Prologue and Epilogue of the Book of Job are deliberate ironies, and Kierkegaard played ironically with categoreal philosophy. The fourth strategic philosophic use of representations of the ultimate is apophatic theology, the assertion of some characterization and then the demonstration that the referent is really beyond that characterization so that it does not apply simply or completely. Apophasis requires a positive moment, usually the assertion of a system or worldview as iconic of reality. But then it shows how this does not apply to the deepest reality. Apophatic theology is sometimes just modesty about the limitations of any representations. But in the hands of mystics, it often takes the form of tracing signs of the ultimate from immediacy in the world back through the causal processes by which the ultimate is expressed and diversely manifested, to the source that is beyond any determinate characterization as it is realized that any proposed characterization is derivative, not native to the source as such.

The four kinds of philosophic approaches to incorporate a true understanding of the ultimate rarely are separated. Most thinkers exhibit several. Perhaps Vedānta Deśika in the text studied here is purely categorial and Zhuangzi purely ironic. The others are mixtures. Narrative thought can never be philosophical except in the form of irony, because it always requires a narrative perspective that can be qualified by other perspectives on the narrative (for instance, the Egyptians' or Canaanites' view of the Exodus, the Jews' view of Jesus as Messiah).

7.4.2 Practical Virtuosi

Kohn and Miller, followed by Haq, describe the practical virtuosi as those who transform themselves so as to actualize or better relate to the ultimate. They limit their discussion to individuals, associating the process with mysticism and the attainment of personal powers in spiritual or political matters. We should also note that the ultimate is approached practically by communities as well as individuals, as when Jews attempt to conform their lives to Torah, or Muslims to the Qur'ān, or Confucians to something like a good family structure in all segments of society.

The most direct analysis of the practical approach to realizing ultimate reality is Fredriksen's study of sacrifice imagery in early Christianity. In late Second Temple Judaism of which early Christianity was a branch, "realizing ultimate reality" did not mean esoteric communion with the divine but rather proper participation in the sacrificial life of the community because that is what God had said to do, with many specifications. In order to participate in the sacrifice (in many different forms and degrees of participation, usually for men only), Jews were required to be pure and holy. Although not subject to Levitical purity laws like Jews, Gentiles were taken to be profane by definition, and Paul used the images of sacrifice (and there are many) to argue that Christ had transformed the Gentiles from profane to holy.

Because the Gentiles had their own related sacrifice traditions and understood their lives to require sacrifice in order to be rightly ordered, they too could understand and be restored by appropriating Christ as the sacrifice, Paul thought. The result is that, having been made holy by Jesus Christ, those who appropriate Christ by participating symbolically in the eucharistic sacrifice, by imitating Christ, and by many other means, are brought to God and then need daily to practice living in holy ways where the sacrificial eucharistic life of the Christian community is the appropriate way to be before God. Fredriksen emphasizes the collage organization of Paul's sacrifice metaphors—they do not fit together as a consistent set of categories, but as a mutually reinforcing set of variations on the theme of sacrifice as the life before God made possible by the restoration of purity and holiness. As Fredriksen says (3.1), "We have to stop thinking theologically, and instead think sacrificially. Purity, holiness, separation, blood, flesh, eating: these orient us in the first-century understanding of the new reality wrought in Christ."

What is most striking in Fredriksen's account is that the restoration of purity and holiness is a real change in the individuals, also manifested in their community as participants in Christ. The change is not merely an alteration in God's intention about sinners, as the later *Reformationsproblematik* would debate. It is a real change in the individuals. Moreover, it is the historical life of Jesus that accomplishes the change, along with the faithful appropriation of Jesus's sacrifice. Although the senses in which Christianity, and Judaism, are "historical" religions are very complicated, the sacrifice theme in Christianity that Fredriksen develops is plainly historical: Christians "realize" God as ultimate by relating historically to the historical Jesus.

Buddhism, Islam, and certain schools of medieval Daoism are historical religions in the sense that their dharma or revelations were delivered by historical personages and the organization of their institutions has historical connections with those founding persons or events. But the practical orientation to the ultimate in all those cases is not to an historical figure such as Jesus but to patterns or powers contemporary with practitioners and universally available at any time (at least since the revelation).

Practical virtuosity is to transform individuals (and/or communities) so as to realize what is most important to religious life in those individuals and communities. Sometimes the transformation is involved in philosophical virtuosity. Some philosophically sophisticated concepts cannot be grasped thoroughly without an elaborate yoga of transforming the soul's capacity for understanding. Meditative practices often focus on this kind of intellectual transformation. All the traditions we studied have schools of mysticism in which spiritual formation means the transformation of soul so as to be able to appropriate the ultimate by means of symbols that do not work without the special formation. Mysticisms, as noted above, can focus on the ultimate in the immediacy of contingent existence, in the power of the act of creation, and in the depths of the abyss out of which the creative act emerges (i.e., nonbeing). The dominant kinds of practical transformation to realize the ultimate in our religions, however, were not the intellectual mystical type.

The Chinese religion described in practical terms by Kohn and Miller exhibited the types of the sage and the perfected. The sage might encompass philosophical understanding but was known for special powers and shrewdness of judgment. The perfected, especially in medieval Daoism, developed special powers of influencing people and things, and also of extending life. In both cases this is because adepts are able to access the spontaneous creativity of the Dao.

In the cases of Judaism and Islam, and some forms of Christianity later than Fredriksen examined, the practical transformation is to conform human individual and communal life to divinely established patterns for such life, as in the Torah, the Qur'ān, or the image of God in human beings or the ideal church community. In all these cases symbolic systems are in tension for connecting the ideal patterns for human being with the ultimate transcendent God; somehow they are identical, but without compromising the radically asymmetry of the creator and created, or the unity of God and the diversity within the patterns for human life.

In the case of Buddhism, the transformation of the self is liberation from the bondage of ignorance by realizing the emptiness of things, with emptiness interpreted variously among the schools. Madhyamaka is one of the most intellectual of schools, and Nāgārjuna is widely interpreted as writing his philosophy for soteriological purposes.[6] The practical purpose of all religious activities shaped by symbols of the ultimate—chanting, meditating, liturgies, working, wrestling with koans and angels, as well as thinking philosophically—is liberation. All are considered "expedient means" to liberation rather than descriptions of ultimate reality. Whereas philosophical virtuosity might aim at realizing the ultimate in understanding, Buddhist practical virtuosity aims at liberation regardless of the descriptive accuracy of the symbols. In fact, many Buddhist symbols are wild and fantastic, surely not descriptive even in a sense that can be explained as metaphors. Gory gods and goddesses are intended to scare the complacent, not look like Buddha-mind or emptiness.[7]

The Buddhist case illustrates very clearly the fact that in the practice of transforming persons and communities, the payoff is not in description or explanation but in actually connecting with, entering into, or conforming to the patterns of the ultimate. How that is actualized depends on the ways each tradition of practice relates to the elements in the logic of contingency—the immediacy of temporal diversity, the power of the creative act, the nothingness of the source, the order in contingent things, the diversity of their components, the existential specificity of their ownbeing, and their place in the network of the cosmos and human history.

7.4.3 *Mythical Virtuosi*

Whereas philosophical virtuosi attempt to develop ways of thinking about the ultimate that minimize contextualization and qualification, mythical virtuosi seek representations that make sense of why a tradition's practices are supposed to work. They provide both the rationales for the practices and the levers of correction and development in new circumstances. Practices and mythologies develop together. When a tradition has an important philosophical element, the mythology needs to incorporate that. Often that incorporation means that the philosophies are required to provide an interpretation of the mythic symbols. When philosophies introduce indigestible elements into the mythology, as has happened when they mediated the modern scientific worldview to all the traditional religions, the mythologies become problematical and new virtuosi are needed. What Kohn and Miller mean by mythical virtuosi overlaps with what many contemporaries mean by theologians.

Realizing the ultimate through mythology has not been an important theme of these discussions. Kohn and Miller touched on it in connection with the medieval Daoism's divinization of Laozi as a way of envisioning the cosmos so as to make sense of Daoist internal and external practices. Philosophically, that is associated with the creation theme, as they note. Saldarini discussed the uses of mythic thinking in connection with the symbols of early rabbinic and medieval mysticism. Fredriksen focused more than the others on mythology in her discussion of divine sacrifice and its relation to the practices of the early Christian community, but found Paul and the other New Testament writers to be incomplete or incoherent in the development of a consistent set of myths of atonement. Haq stressed the tensions between taking the names of God without analysis and providing those analyses, but without suggesting that either approach by itself can integrate all the symbols. Clooney's discussion of Vedānta Deśika is relentlessly philosophical except for the repeated reference to Nārāyaṇa's consort, Srī, which is not explained either mythically or philosophically. Eckel's traditions of Yogācāra and Madhyamaka Buddhism are replete with a rich mythology of gods, Buddhas, and bodhisattvas, but he did not treat that in depth.

Perhaps the reason for the sparing treatments of approaching the ultimate through mythology is that it really is a question for the next topic in this series of comparisons: religious truth. How is mythic truth different from philosophical? By being on the personifying end of representations of ultimacy rather than the philosophic end? Hardly, for the philosophic representations often bear upon practice and thus need to be represented within the mythology. Is mythology a slightly out-of-date form of thinking for our religious traditions? Are they formed fundamentally through a rejection of mythopoeic thinking, so that already their myths from the beginning are under deconstruction? These are all serious questions that need to be addressed under the general rubric of religious truth. And they need to be answered before much can be said about how mythology is a way of realizing the ultimate in religious experience.

Notes

1. Tillich's most famous discussion is in his *Systematic Theology* (Chicago: University of Chicago Press, 1951), volume 1, Introduction, section 4. In that place he defines two "formal criteria" for theology. The first is, "the object of theology is what concerns us ultimately." The second is, "our ultimate concern is that which determines our being or not-being." The content of theology, for Tillich, has to do with determining what ought to be the object of human ultimate concern, what is worth that concern rather than of only preliminary worth. His existentialist elements appear in the discussion of being determined in being or not-being. In *The Truth of Broken Symbols* (Albany: State University of New York Press, 1996), chap. 2, Neville uses something like this idea in claiming that objects of serious (ultimate) religious reference are finite/infinite contrasts that are construed as determining elements defining our world as such. The idea of ultimate concern is particularly important for our group who represent both traditions pointing to ontological realities as ultimate and traditions, especially some forms of Buddhism, that say that realities ought not be objects of ultimate or religious concern.

2. Julia Ching and Hans Küng, *Christianity and Chinese Religions* (New York: Doubleday, 1989).

3. As Anne Birdwhistell has commented in *Transition to Neo-Confucianism: Shao Yung on Knowledge and Symbols of Reality* (Stanford: Stanford University Press, 1989).

4. See *The Human Condition*, section 1.1.

5. See Georg Wilhelm Friedrich Hegel, *Lectures on the Philosophy of Religion*, 3 vols., ed. Peter C. Hodgson (Berkeley: University of California Press): vol. 1, *Introduction and the Concept of Religion* (1984); vol. 2, *Determinate Religion* (1987); vol. 3, *The Consummate Religion* (1985).

6. Frederick J. Streng, *Emptiness: A Study in Religious Meaning* (Nashville: Abingdon, 1967).

7. Neville, op. cit., chap. 5.

8

On Comparing Religious Ideas

Robert Cummings Neville
and Wesley J. Wildman

∽

8.1 Comparison of Religious Ideas as a Cognitive Enterprise

The comparisons advanced in the previous chapters are interesting on
their own and established well enough to merit serious consideration.
Part of that merit comes from the method of collaborative practice that
defined the Comparative Religious Ideas Project. That practice in turn
originated from a philosophical conception of comparison. This theory
of comparison has been sketched briefly in the preface of this volume,
and in some greater detail in the first chapter of *The Human Condition*.
The purpose of the present chapter is to lay out the theory formally. As
has been said repeatedly in this book and its companion volumes, *The
Human Condition* and *Religious Truth*, one of the purposes of this study
has been to refine and test the conception of comparison itself.

Comparing religious ideas can be a cognitive enterprise aiming to produce true and important knowledge. Whereas this ought to be obvious,
the point is necessary to stress in a social context such as ours in which
influential thinkers assert that comparison is more a matter of will, of the
exercise of power, than of cognition. For some, comparison is a blatantly
political move to conform other cultures or religions to the agenda and
categories of the comparers' own, eventually to get all the religions compared to think of themselves in the comparers' terms. This is the burden

of Colonialist Theory as it applies to comparison of religious ideas. For others, comparison is merely the premature effort to get things into the comparers' understanding, which, lacking a valid understanding of the others, results in reducing them to the intellectual agenda and categories of the comparers; this is the error signaled by Descartes of making assertions by will when we do not have sufficient understanding to do so.[1] Any approach that affirms the primacy of cognition over will in comparison needs to be able to answer these critical positions, and we shall do so.

To defend the primacy of cognition in comparing religious ideas, it is necessary to have a theory that shows how comparisons can be true and important and a method that makes comparisons vulnerable to correction. The theory presented here asserts that truth consists of well-grounded but fallible hypotheses that interpret the subject matters for comparison in respects that are important for understanding religion. The *meaning* of truth, on our theory, is the kind of correspondence that is characteristic of interpretation theory. That is, given that a claim purports to interpret its subject matter in some respect, the claim is true if it interprets the subject matter correctly in that respect. *Correctness* in this means that the claim asserts of the subject matter that it is what it is, or denies of it that it is what it is not; this is Aristotle's definition of truth.[2] Correctness of interpretation, and hence truth, is a dyadic right-or-wrong relation of the claim to its object or subject matter.

Claims are neither true nor false except when *taken to interpret* their subject matter. The dyadic structure of truth or falsity is therefore set within the triadic structure of interpretation. The three elements of interpretation are: (1) the claim that is a sign of (2) the subject matter as its object when (3) an interpretive act takes the subject matter to be interpreted by the claim in a certain respect. We commonly suppose that the claim displays on its own face the respect in which it purports to interpret the subject matter. But this often is not so, especially in religious matters. "All is suffering," "all is craving," and "all is empty" are three claims predicating of everything, characteristics that are apparently contradictory to one another but that are reconciled in Buddhism. They are reconcilable because they interpret everything in different respects, and these different respects cannot be read off from the claims themselves. Rather, elaborating the differences and connections among those respects in which "all" might be interpreted requires a theory that helps to fit those different respects together, such as the Buddhist theory of the Four Noble Truths (*The Human Condition* 3.2). Whereas it might be tempting to say that "all" in each of the claims refers to different things, the Buddhist theory makes sense only when they refer to the same thing but in different respects of interpretation. That is (in order), everything is interpreted in respect to how it is subjectively experienced, in respect to the cause of that experience, and in respect to what everything really is as removed from that cause. Because of the triadic structure of interpretation that always lays open the question of the respect in which a claim is taken to interpret its subject matter, we rightly note that claims, and hence comparisons, can be truer than others, true in some respects but not in others, or true to an extent but potentially misleading, all as fallibly subject to further interpretation. Nevertheless, in making those qualifications, the operative truth claim remains dyadic—right or wrong—which is evident once the respect of interpretation is more exactly clarified.

The *criteria* of truth, in distinction from its meaning, have to do with the processes of correcting the claims as hypotheses. An hypothesis is well-grounded, though still fallible, when it has been subjected to the tests that we have learned to respect and require: tests of consistency, coherence, applicability to the subject matter, and adequacy. Although formal logic plays some role in testing the theoretical structures of claims, most tests are pragmatic and contingent. For instance, we have learned to test comparative claims for bias arising from the comparativists' cultural agenda and categories. The fallibility of a truth claim consists in the fact that further tests might be discovered that would qualify or even disqualify the claim.

Because claims have truth value only when affirmed in interpretations, the *meaning* of truth and the *criteria* of truth cannot be separated. The intention to interpret a subject matter with a particular claim is to suppose that there is reason to believe that the claim is right, that it passes the tests of the appropriate criteria. That supposition might in fact be false, if there is no reason, or bad reasons, or if the criteria are misunderstood. But the *intention* of the interpretation involves the supposition that sufficient criteria are met for the claim to be asserted as true. An interpretation has the logical status of an hypothesis; the intention to interpret with a given hypothesis can have subjective confidence ranging from "we can take it for granted" to "it might be interesting to explore if someone gives us a grant." When an interpretation is made without that supposition of some plausibility, then indeed the interpretation is a matter of will, not cognition: the interpretation is not an act of taking the subject matter to be the way the claim says but an act of willing the subject matter to be regarded as the claim says.

The cognitive act of comparing religious ideas thus needs to be justified by a method that gives good reasons for the comparisons according to the best criteria that can be employed. *Method* is not quite the right word, for it might falsely connote some kind of procedure or algorithm that would guarantee truth; Descartes would have liked that. Rather, what is needed is a comparative procedure that puts comparative claims in the way of being corrected, that makes them vulnerable. This requires understanding what might correct them and framing them so that they engage the tests. For this we need a theory of what comparison consists in as well as pragmatic knowledge about the relevant tests for particular comparisons. This introductory section can be concluded with four truisms.

1. *Comparison requires understanding all sides to be compared in their own terms.* If this is not done, the religions to be compared will be grasped in terms of the theoretical structure that brings them into connection. Whether recognized or not, however, that would be classification, not comparison, at least in the sense that it would classify the phenomena only in the terms of the theoretical structure. Good comparison requires that the categories and theoretical structures it employs themselves be developed through a process that recognizes the proper place of understanding things in their own terms. Defending classification against the charge that it biases interpretation with the agenda and categories of the classifiers is impossible because it does not include a representation of the things compared in their own terms that can be shown to be rightly grasped by the classificatory terms.

2. *Comparison is more than assembling accurate representations of the things to be compared; like a "third term" it says how the things relate to one another, how they are similar and different.* Although much is learned by attending to the variety of religious ideas and appreciating their juxtaposition, that has not achieved comparison. A comparison is a claim about the way the religious ideas relate, a claim that itself can be true or false and that needs explication and defense. A mere assemblage or juxtaposition of religious ideas is neither true nor false.

3. *Comparisons are claims that aim to be true in what they assert about the relations among religious ideas and they need to be grounded in processes that test them according to relevant criteria.* For beginning students who do not know anything about a particular religion's ideas and are taught by comparison with religions they do know about, a comparison will seem helpful even if it is not well-grounded because it gives them a handle on the unknown, a place to start; the subsequent process of correcting really wrong ideas is sometimes a good way to learn. For adept scholars, a comparison might produce a striking Aha! experience, putting clearly a connection they had groped to express. But the Aha! might merely fulfill and confirm the scholars' wrongheaded line of inquiry, unrelated to the truth of the comparative claim. Independently of heuristic helpfulness and productivity of feelings of insight, comparisons need to be grounded in the tests appropriate to them.

4. *Claims to the truth of comparisons ought not fade in the face of critical qualifications but should amend themselves as improved.* Some people

might be tempted to abandon a valid comparison when challenged by accusations that the comparative claim comes from only one perspective among others, or takes into account only certain kinds of material and not others, or represents only one approach among others. The proper response to these accusations is to tailor the interpretation of the claim to the appropriate respects in which the claim can be asserted. Although a claim might approach the subject matter from only one of a number of possible perspectives, it can be true or false as the interpretation of the subject matter in respect of that perspective. Of course, it might turn out that the only respect in which one's claim is true is a trivial one; but that is another matter, not to be decided by the admission that the claim is made in a limited respect.

The theory of comparison of religious ideas we defend here is based on an analysis of comparative categories, categories according to which the ideas of different religions can be compared. In this volume, the categories pertain to ultimate realities. The next several sections spell this out.

8.2 The General Principle of Comparative Categories

Comparison involves first determining a respect in which things can be compared and then laying out how they compare in that respect. This innocent-looking observation is the general principle for understanding, constructing, and correcting comparative categories: a comparative category has two elements, the respect in which things are compared and the comparisons made in that respect.

That comparisons are always in some respect or other is obvious once noticed. An idea in one religion can be compared with an idea in another only if both of the ideas interpret their subject matter in the same respect; only if both purport to be "about the same thing" can we determine whether they say the same or different things about that subject matter. "About the same thing" entails not only identity of subject matter but identity of respect in which the subject matter is interpreted. Both scholars and ordinary people commonly neglect to be self-conscious about the respect in which the comparison is being made. This is understandable because the respect of comparison has already been assumed by the time we are aware that comparison is occurring. Only when we begin to suspect some confusion, some mixing of categories, do we reflect critically on the respect in which the comparison is being made. Superficial comparisons are sometimes unmasked by the fact that the ideas compared interpret their objects in different respects; for instance, the Buddhist idea of emptiness and the Christian idea of kenosis are really different even though they seem alike.[3] In general, theological debates are often frustrating because, despite verbal similarities, the different positions interpret their objects in different respects. People are conscious of the need to agree on the same object, which can be hard enough when different symbolic histories, cosmologies, and ontologies are involved. But to be conscious of interpreting the same object in the same respect is very hard indeed.

The importance of identifying the respect of comparison was hinted at in the discussion of truth in the previous section. In an act of interpretation, a sign is taken as standing for its object in a certain respect. "The barn is red" answers the question "What color is the barn?"; the object *barn* is interpreted by *red* in respect of its color. If the question had been, "Is the barn full or empty?," the answer in terms of color would have been irrelevant and confusing, albeit true in its own way. Of course, interpretation is far more complex than can be modeled by a simple proposition such as "the barn is red." Interpretation is an act by an interpreter or community of interpreters that engages a subject matter using the proper portion of the operative linguistic or cultural semiotic system. This presupposes an entire semiotic world from signs and syntax to interpretive contexts and purposes, as well as dynamic interaction between these elements. This complexity suggests that shifts of respects of interpretation will frequently pass unnoticed. How many debates lapse into confusion because the respect of interpretation is shifted subtly in just this way! Being aware of respects of interpretations is difficult but vital for any serious discussion.

Interpretation in religious matters is still more complex than has been indicated so far. Consider assertions made about religious ideas, for example. To be sure, sometimes simple assertion is all that is intended. Far more often, however, such assertions occur in liturgies, exhortations, or communal living and in such contexts possess complex illocutionary force. They exhort or express or enact even as they assert something about the way things are. Interpreting such assertions competently requires noticing the various ways they function. In particular, if analyzed as asserting something about the way things are in a certain respect, those assertions may be true or false; but ordinarily they are simply taken as rightly describing their objects in a general way while the intentionality of their use has other functions. There are other complexities associated with interpretation in religious matters. Religious symbols come in complex systems and so the presumption is that the symbol system as a whole, or in at least some of its connections, is right about the complex of objects to which the symbols can be referred. Symbol systems such as sacred histories, myths, even theological systems, are taken to be iconic of the way things are, and then more limited interpretations can be made within those systems. Even anti-metaphysical theological systems, for instance, some forms of Buddhism that deny "objective reality" to some interpretive objects, take that lack of objective reality to be the way things are (see chapter 6; *The Human Condition*, chapter 3, and *Religious Truth*, chapter 3). In all, religious interpretation is vastly complicated with meaning systems that are difficult to render in propositional form. But this only serves to underline the importance of determining the respect of interpretation for every assertion by suggesting how quickly discussion of religious matters can unravel when this is neglected.

Determining respects of interpretation in the context of cross-cultural comparison of religious ideas—that is, identifying feasible comparative categories—is additionally problematic for two reasons. First, ideas from different religious systems presuppose different semiotic systems, different signs and symbols, both specifically in the context of particular assertions and iconically in taking reality to be one way or another. Within a semiotic system it is possible to say "this barn is red and that one is white," and "this barn is white and empty." But where the semiotic symbol systems are different, it might be difficult to interpret what symbols interpret the barn in respect of color and what in terms of fullness, as would be the case, for instance, in a language in which a color might symbolize fullness or emptiness, as "blue" and "black" symbolize moods and "yellow" connotes a lack of courage. Prior to careful translations back and forth, and setting the translations in the different cultural and historical contexts, it is difficult in matters of religion to tell what symbols can be compared in the same respect.

Second, determining the respect of comparison of different religious symbols is difficult because different semiotic systems might genuinely interpret their objects in different respects. There simply may be no valid respect of comparison, no feasible comparative category. Each religious system embodies within its symbols judgments about the respects of reality that are important to be interpreted and the different traditions actually interpret religious realities in respects that might be different. The moral is that the respect of interpretation must be determined in order to compare the traditions and there can be no facile assumption that a suitable respect of comparison will be obvious or even possible. Each comparison needs to be approached empirically on its own terms.

The dialectical character of comparison noted in the introduction is all the more apparent now. Comparison cannot begin without some assumption about the respect of comparison and that assumption itself is problematic. Only by trying out comparisons alleged to be made in some respect can we see whether or not that respect is one in which the religious ideas compared do indeed interpret a common object or reality. This dialectical interplay modifies the conception of the respect of comparison, which in turn sharpens the comparisons. We have agreed that all of the religions we study contain insights into what is religiously important about ultimate realities. But to compare those insights requires laying out the respects in which they say what they do.

A comparison compares two or more religious ideas in the same respect in which the ideas, each in its own religious context, are taken separately to interpret their subject matter. The respect of interpretation (the comparative category), as well as the subject matter, is common to both traditions, and the comparison says how the religions interpret that subject matter in that respect differently or similarly. Within each religion separately, the respect of interpretation functions as a category and might be identified as such by a theologian or a scholar in that tradition. The category becomes comparative when comparativists identify it as the respect in which different religious traditions might be compared.

Comparison is a circular mode of thought. On the one hand, it depends on comparing ideas from two traditions that are held to interpret the same subject matter in the same respect, so it has to have made a comparison of respects before it can get to the business of comparing what the traditions say in that respect. And, to make a comparison of respects, on the other hand, it has to have identified the common respects in which the respects to be compared interpret their subject matter, and so on. This is circular but not viciously so, for the following reasons.

First, comparisons are already under way, which means that the dense continuity of semantic, syntactic, and pragmatic contexts for any interpretation are all in play, contexts for contexts for contexts on to utter vagueness and triviality. Comparisons are no different from any other mode of thought in supposing an indefinitely deep and complex semiotic medium.

Second, the question to ask of comparisons is whether they are right. If the comparison under investigation presupposes other comparisons, those others might be investigated in turn, so on and on. The issue is not to justify starting a comparison but to correct comparisons already made, or lines of comparative thought. Of course, there are novel comparisons, but they move by analogy, stretched metaphors, lucky guesses, all having a hypothetical form and all supposing dense semiotic contexts.[4]

Third, any provisional comparative judgment in this ongoing process embodies the criticism of former comparisons. This process of criticism and improvement is rendered methodical in our approach by the dialectic engendered between the vaguer and more specific levels within the categories. The process of specifying a vague category in terms of the particular religious ideas being compared corrects the vaguely presupposed putative respects of comparison, and that correction in turn enables more precise specifications, developing along the way a very complex but particularized version of the category as exhibiting the ideas compared in all their relations. The movement of the dialectic may never bring all the presupposed respects of comparison into scrutiny at once but it should at least move through them all and focus on the important and problematic ones.

The language of "categories" conjures up many associations, from "category mistakes" to previous uses of the word. These are worth discussing. The objection to comparing apples and oranges is a valid objection to a confusion of categories. But of course we *can* compare apples and oranges, which is to say that we can employ categories into which both fit (e.g., fruit). Laying out the theoretical structure of a religious system of ideas is mainly a matter of working out the connections among their categories or the respects in which they interpret reality, as illustrated in the above discussion of the Four Noble Truths. Comparisons take place on many levels: the point is that at each level there is a category or respect of interpretation in play. The language of "categories" highlights and substantializes the respects of interpretation to bring them to attention for analysis and correction. It is a safeguard against unnoticed bias.

This use of the notion of category differs from Aristotle's. Aristotle's categories were basic forms of predication. This supposes that interpretation is the same as predication in language. That supposition is false, however. The internal structure of semiotic systems, including predication and far more subtle forms of intentionality, is a code or pattern of possible signs or claims. Interpretation is not a pattern but an intentional act of engaging the subject matter with the semiotic pattern. "All is suffering" is a semiotic pattern that might be taken as a sign for interpreting reality. "'All is suffering' is true" is another semiotic pattern that might be taken as a sign for interpreting reality (in a different respect, of course). But signs or semiotic patterns are not interpretations. A well-developed theology or set of religious ideas, self-conscious and self-interpreting, will create a semiotic system of theological signs that includes representations of the categories in respect of which the religion interprets the world. These will not be limited to forms of predication, as Aristotle thought, but will express what the religion takes to be real and worthy of comment.

Our use of the language of "categories" differs also from Kant's. Kant argued that Aristotelian logical forms of predication, suitably adjusted, are more than mere patterns in the semiotic system: they are in fact the only respects according to which we can interpret reality successfully. Any alleged interpretation that does not limit itself to them will fail to ground itself in a scientifically deterministic scheme that can distinguish between subjective fantasy and objective reality. We can distinguish our objective from merely subjective representations, Kant insisted, only by showing how they empirically fill in the logical forms of predication. In his theory, therefore, the logical forms of predication are really categories to which our knowledge of reality must conform in order to be objective, regardless of what reality might be in addition. Our use of "category" differs from this by being radically empirical: the respects in which reality might be interpreted are to be discovered by attempted interpretations that pass the appropriate pragmatic tests. Hence, there might be vastly more categories than either Aristotle or Kant would suspect from their analysis of predication. Language might get at religious realities, including categories in which reality might be interpreted, through all sorts of metaphoric and other probative inquiry, not just logical forms of predication. And we think it does! Religious language is highly symbolic, which is to say that it does not conform neatly to schemes of logical classification and inference. Our religious semiotic systems have learned from and been enriched by millennia of religious interpretations, and interpretations of interpretations. They are thus far richer in categories for interpreting religiously interesting matters than could be derived from analysis of the subjective forms of logical predication.

8.3 The Logical Structure of Comparative Categories

Briefly stated, our hypothesis is that comparison is by means of categories that are internally complex with two or more levels of determinateness.[5] On the one hand, categories are determinate with respect to other categories on the same level. For instance, to refer to the previous example, the category of "how all reality subjectively is experienced ordinarily" (which Buddhism specifies as suffering) is determinately different from that of "the cause of that experience" (craving, for Buddhism), which in turn is determinately different from the category of "what reality is prescinding from that causing of ordinary subjective experience" (empty, for Buddhism), which again is determinately different from "how all reality is experienced subjectively when that cause is practically removed" (bliss, for Buddhism). On the other hand, a category can be partially indeterminate or vague with respect to what might fall under it, or specify it, or instantiate it (all equivalent expressions). For instance, to continue the example, the category of the ordinary subjective experience of all reality might be specified by the Buddhist answer, suffering; but it might also be specified by a Chinese answer such as "all reality ordinarily is experienced as a fundamentally harmonious field with problematic glitches" (see *The Human Condition* 2.1–2), or by a West Asian answer such as "all reality ordinarily is experienced as a field for exercising moral responsibility" (*The Human Condition* 5.1.1, 7.3.1). The category at this level is vague in the sense that it tolerates a whole host of specifications that might or might not be compatible with each other but that individually interpret reality in the respect expressed in the category.

Categories are made more specific by laying out the comparisons they permit, comparisons that exhibit how religious ideas are similar and different and thus serve to specify the vague category in a variety of ways. The vague category of the *human condition*, for instance, is specified typically by motifs of ignorance and enlightenment in religions originating in South Asia, by motifs of disharmony and attunement in those of East Asia, and by those of disobedient injustice and righteousness in religions originating in West Asia, as Huston Smith has argued. The vague category *ultimate realities* is specified by motifs of ultimate *ontological realities* and ultimate *goals*. The former in turn are specified further by *anthropomorphic deities* and *transcendent creative principles*. To continue the previous example, the category of how reality is subjectively experienced can be specified or filled in by the instances given, and by many more. This requires laying out just what it means to say that reality is experienced as suffering, as a harmony with problematic glitches, as a field for responsible action, and so forth, with all that is entailed in each one.

For the sake of comparison the vague and specified levels of internal determinateness within a comparative category must remain distinguished. Neither by itself is the comparative category, but only the levels functioning together in comparative inquiry. It is apparent once again why comparison is dynamic and never reducible to a comparative claim at a given time: specifications can continue indefinitely, always with further clarification of the differences and similarities. As inquirers struggle to become clear about this, they also clarify the vaguer level of the category, showing just how it can tolerate its instances and so forth. Imperfect comparisons might happen because of faults at either level: the respect of comparison is not properly understood, or the things compared are not expressed properly in relation to one another so as to make them available to interpretation in the respect of comparison. The issue is further complicated by the fact that the specifications themselves might be vague on their own level; *enlightenment*, for instance, is itself vague with respect to different specifications by Buddhism and Advaita Vedānta;

Buddhist *enlightenment* is vague with respect to sudden and gradual versions, and so forth.

The hypothesis of the two-level categories of comparison is more complicated than it seems, and the purpose of this chapter is to spell out some of the complications.

8.4 Vagueness and Specificity: The Making of Comparison

Vagueness is a logical notion, first analyzed in detail by Charles S. Peirce, and in our use of it here does not mean fuzzy-minded, perversely indefinite, or mysterious.[6] Rather, it is a characteristic of a category according to which the law of non-contradiction does not apply to what might fall under the category or specify it. The category of the subjective experience of all reality, for instance, allows of being specified by the position that "life is a blast" as well as by "life is suffering." These positions cannot both be true in every shared respect because the principle of non-contradiction does apply to the dyadic true-false relation. But they both can meaningfully specify the vague category of the ordinary experience of life. That the principle of contradiction does not apply within a vague category means that things that are contradictory to one another still can fall under the category. If things that are contradictory can specify the category, then so can things that are not apparently determinate with respect to one another, that might or might not be contradictory, that relate in ways that have not been laid out by comparison. This is the case with the alternatives to suffering as the ordinary subjective experience of life listed above, namely, life as an underlying harmony with problematic disharmonies, and life as a field for the exercise of responsibility: prior to analysis it is not clear how these relate to one another. Things can be compared only when they all can specify the same category—that they all can be shown to interpret their objects in the same respects.

Vagueness in a category allows all the potential specifications to be brought under one head with the proviso that the specific relations among them remain to be determined. All the instances of the category do not have to be contradictory to one another. They can be alike, or similar in some respects and different in others. They can even turn out upon analysis to be incommensurate with one another except in the respect in which they fall under the vague category. Candidates for falling under the category might turn out, upon analysis, not to be relevant specifications of it.

That categories are vague with respect to what falls under them does not mean they have no precision with respect to other categories on their own level, as mentioned above. It is one thing to talk about *ultimate realities* and another to talk about the *human condition*, and quite another again to talk about *religious truth* (the topics of the three years of our project). Although it has not been our concern in this project seminar, it might be possible to develop a formal *theory* of religion by defining the vague categories in terms of one another, distinguishing and relating, for instance, the categories of *rituals, mythologies and cosmologies, personal spiritual practices*, and so on, each of which is vague with respect to how different religions would specify them. We have avoided developing theories of religion because of our sense that the variety of categories such a theory ought to encompass can be determined only by making much more progress in the matter of comparison than has been made so far. More will be said about theories of religion in *Religious Truth*, chapter 9, where we explain that a theory of religion cannot be a mere compilation of subcategories.

We have said that vague categories are specified, in the instance of religions, by what thinkers within the different religions, or different strains within a given religion, have to say about the category. But merely to note the fact that a category is specified by several religious positions is not yet to exhibit a comparison. Two further steps are necessary.

First, specification is not merely cataloguing phenomena under a category but translating the phenomena so that they do indeed give greater specificity to the category. None of the religions we studied in *The Human Condition* discusses the *human condition* in just those terms. Rather, to use the above example, those of East Asia say that the human condition is religiously characterized by problems of harmony and disharmony; in South Asia it is a matter of reality, ignorance, and enlightenment; in West Asia it is a matter of responsibility and reconciliation. Specification requires translating each tradition's motifs, concepts, myths, assumptions, and so forth into the language of the *human condition*, saying how each is a specification of that category. This involves a twofold enrichment of the category's language. On the one hand, the religious positions are translated into the language of the human condition, which says more about them than they said about themselves. On the other hand, the language of the human condition is enriched by having to express specifically what it did not express at the level of unspecified vagueness, namely, the details of the positions that specify it. As specified, the category is far more concrete and detailed.

The second step, once the specifying positions are interpreted in a common language, is to analyze what they claim and deny with reference to one another. At this point it should be possible to say how they are similar and different, where they are complementary or contradictory, where attempts to translate them into a common language fail so that they remain incommensurable, and when it can be concluded that they do not really fall under the same category, because they are not really about the same thing.

In the above example, we might be inclined, irenically, to say that the human condition involves all three specifications (East Asian, South Asian, and West Asian) and possibly others besides these as complementary and overlapping aspects. So, the human condition might be described in a complex way that involves all the major motifs of all three religious regions and the comparison is one of complementarity. In other comparisons, however, the religious traditions might contradict one another clearly, and that contradiction is recognized when their ideas are translated into the comparing language of the *human condition*. To take our other example of the category of the ordinary subjective experience of life's basic characters, the Buddhist claim that all is suffering is contradicted in part by the West Asian religions' claim that life is fundamentally a field of responsibility, even though Buddhists acknowledge responsibilities and West Asian religions acknowledge suffering. Perhaps more likely is the situation in which religious traditions say overlapping things about the human condition. For instance, it might be argued that all religions, save perhaps extreme deterministic versions of them, agree that individuals can make some progress toward spiritual improvement by following appropriate prescriptions; but disagree over the definition of the goals and the best way to identify the problematic or immature beginning point.

Translating the representations of the various traditions into the language of the comparative category both enriches the comparative category and allows for commensurate comparison. An enriched vague category, consciously employed at both its vague and specific levels, fosters objectivity in approaching religious phenomena, making comparisons more a matter of self-corrective empirical inquiry than of recognition of the familiar and surprise at the unfamiliar. For instance, given the above example about East, South, and West Asian Axial Age religions on the *human condition*, comparativists asking about the human condition as understood by shamanism or traditional African religions have the tools to be very clear about not superimposing the Axial Age representations on their subject. They can ask directly about whether these traditional religions specify the vague category differently. This is different from approaching traditional religions with only the specific assumptions of the Axial Age religions and without the vague category, the fault of which earlier comparativists who approach all religions with Christian assumptions about the nature of religion rightly are accused. This is different also from approaching traditional religions with the pretence of only a vague category so that the specifics of one's own tradition are smuggled in unaware.

Translation of religious phenomena into the language of the comparative category at both levels is itself the condition for comparison.[7] Only when each tradition's views of ultimate realities are registered, for instance, is it possible to tell whether they are saying similar or different things, asserting identity, are complementary, contradictory, or whatever. Religions' metaphoric systems might use the same symbols but mean very different things, or vice versa. Only by seeing what they say about the comparative category (the respect in which they are being compared) is it possible to be precise about the comparisons.

"Translation" may not be the right word for the process of specifying a vague category in terms of religions to be compared. It misleadingly suggests that there are two languages, that of the vague category and that of the religion, and that specification is merely the translation of the latter into the former. Rather, the process is one of determining what the religion asserts or assumes about the topic expressed in the comparative category, and this process is dialectical and hermeneutical, moving back and forth between both languages and enriching the understanding of both in the process. The process of specification often is indirect and itself metaphorical, moving by juxtapositions.[8] Its goal, however, is not aesthetic "aha's" but the articulation of assertions and assumptions that can be compared.

Attention should be called to the fact that comparisons need to be sensitive to differences in importance. Religious traditions might have clearly comparable understandings of, say, the cosmos, with articulable similarities and differences, but also with a very great difference in the importance of the roles those understandings play. The motifs of Judaism (for instance, in Genesis) and Chinese religion (in the *Yijing*) about the cosmos can be compared neatly. But whereas those cosmological representations are very important throughout Chinese religion, they have far less importance in Judaism. Comparison involves assessing importance as well as representational or assertive structure.

Finally, it should be noted that sometimes comparison turns up negative results. That is, a religion might not have anything to say about the topic of a comparative category that is very helpful for comparing with other religions. Recognition of this helps guard against the illegitimate superimposition of certain properties as essential to religion. There might indeed be universal characteristics, but whether this is so needs to be determined empirically. Hypotheses about these defining elements need to be tested with alertness to the possibility of negative results. The hypothesis, for instance, that all religions have rituals, conceptual representations, and spiritual practices needs to be checked out.[9]

8.5 Vulnerability and Phenomenological Testing

The great danger with comparisons is that the theoretical structure of the comparative categories will bias the representation of phenomena to be compared. Therefore explicit effort needs to be made to test and modify the categories by phenomenologically thick representations of them. "Thick description" is the phrase coined by Clifford Geertz to describe an anthropological approach to cultures through the analysis of their symbol systems and symbolic behavior.[10] The phenomenological representations of religions need to be even thicker than the anthropological ones, if that is possible. Although any tentative comparison, such as those made in this volume, can be only partial, the process itself, however far it goes, should be guided by an ideal that leaves no stones unturned in questioning whether the representations of the religions are faithful. This ideal has been operative in our work for this volume but we have only just begun the process of testing our results. A feasible way to intensify testing is to explore in more detail some of the specific results of this volume and, indeed, some of us may undertake to do this in individual work. Our next step as a group, however, has been to look at our comparative efforts on ultimate realities from the new angles made possible by similar comparative efforts in relation to the general topics of the human condition and religious truth.

The investigation of five "sites" of phenomenological analysis can help us in questioning whether a religious idea is being represented fairly: representations of an idea as it is understood intrinsically within a tradition, the perspectival interpretations of context promoted by an idea, representations of the idea in relation to other ideas, interpretations of the idea in relation to practical matters, and representations of the idea as singular and incommensurable with other ideas.[11] For convenience, we shall call these sites of phenomenological analysis intrinsic, perspectival, theoretical, practical, and singular, respectively. The following discussions of these five terms will serve to explain them in more detail.

Intrinsic representation is thinking and expressing the religious idea in its own terms, as thought by the people who think it religiously. There are diverse forms of expressions of religious ideas, of course, including specific texts, ancient motifs, commentarial traditions of re-expressions of the ideas, intellectual systems, and so forth.

Specific texts perhaps are the easiest to understand intrinsically because they allow us to try reading them as they would have been read by their supposed authors or later groups of readers. Frank Clooney's discussion of "reading texts" in his *Theology after Vedanta* and *Seeing through Texts* is a direct expression of this form of understanding. While recognizing the limits of getting inside the mind of readers within another tradition, Clooney is clear about how to improve one's reading.

Ideas in the form of ancient motifs, such as the Chinese conception of yin and yang as constitutive of natural process, are more difficult to identify intrinsically. They are not reducible to their written expressions, say in the *Yijing* or the Taijiquan classics, but need to be discerned from popular expressions and also indirectly, as from texts not about yin and yang but structured by those ideas. Moreover, motifs are reflected differently, often contradictorily, in different historical instances. Intrinsic understanding of motifs involves getting on the inside of each of the expressions as well as of the general habits of thought mediating those expressions. There is no single author or community but rather a social habit of thought shaped by the motifs and differently expressing them. The work of Livia Kohn in the first chapter of this volume and elsewhere, such as in *The Human Condition* (chapter 2) and *Early Chinese Mysticism*, is motif analysis.

The expression of ideas in commentarial traditions is perhaps the thickest way of inhabiting the intrinsic character of ideas, seeing them though permutations given with reasons against alternatives. Paula Fredriksen's treatment of Augustine's reading of the Bible (*The Human Condition*, chapter 6), Anthony Saldarini's treatment of Midrashic commentary on the Torah (*The Human Condition*, chapter 5), David Eckel's treatment of Bhāvaviveka's Buddhist commentary in *To See the Buddha*, and Frank Clooney's reading of commentaries within the Advaita Vedānta tradition in *Theology after Vedanta* all get at the intrinsic character of ideas carried down a tradition through commentary.

Systems of ideas, such as Augustine's, Śaṇkara's, or Zhuxi's, are expressed in texts, but perhaps in several texts written over a lifetime, and have elements of commentary as well as expressions of motifs. But their intellectual character lies in their systematic nature. Nomanul Haq's discussion of Jabir's system in *Names, Natures and Things* is an intrinsic representation of a system. The point of all this is to understand the texts, the motifs and their history, ideas in commentarial traditions, and systems, all in their own terms, a feat of hermeneutics.

The *perspectival* understanding of a religious idea is not how we look at it from our perspective but how that idea configures perspectives on the context of those who use it, including us. Perhaps it is too easy to rush from an intrinsic representation of an idea to its placement in a comparative category. It is important to slow down and see how that idea shapes perspectives on the world from its standpoint. Single ideas, of course, do not evoke perspectives on things by themselves, but they participate with other ideas in shaping a perspective on things. The phenomenological importance of this is to see how the world looks from the perspective of the religions being compared. For instance, most forms of Hinduism (*The Human Condition* 4.1) affirm the importance of the self (ātman), which at bottom is Brahman, whereas most forms of Buddhism (*The Human Condition* 3.3) deny the reality of that self. Is this a disagreement about reality within a shared perspective on the world? Or do Hinduism and Buddhism, despite their intertwined histories and common languages, have different perspectives on the world as expressed in and shaped by their core ideas? Surely Judaism and Christianity have different perspectives on Messianic expectations.

The *theoretical* representation of ideas has to do with their effects on other ideas, often as involved with them in symbol systems. Ideas are to be understood by their implications, their roles in larger systems, their effects in reinforcing or undermining other ideas, and so forth. Some interpreters (some pragmatists, structuralists, and deconstructionists) believe that the whole meaning of ideas lies in their theoretical implications, although that is likely going too far. The intrinsic representation of ideas is thinking them again from the context of their original authors and communities. Thinking out their implications and other theoretical consequences might move far beyond the thought-world of the religions employing those ideas. Often it has to do with tracing historical consequences of ideas and bringing more recent conceptual models to bear in order to express the extrinsic relations. This is an entirely legitimate check on the representation of religious ideas in comparisons.

The *practical* representation of ideas is the tracing of the ways they shape communities of practice. Understanding the practical bearing of ideas and the ways they affect social and personal life is crucial for testing whether ideas are being represented fairly. If ideas are interpreted and quickly brought into a comparison with a meaning that stands at odds with the effects of those ideas in the communities shaped by them, something is wrong. However similar they look on the surface, Christian love is not just like Buddhist compassion because the former is readily mated with intolerance and bellicosity in ways the latter is not; Christian love shapes its community in ways Buddhist compassion does not. Some interpreters (other pragmatists, some anthropologists, some Wittgensteinians) think the practical consequences of ideas are their whole meaning. That too is extreme. Nevertheless, the representation of the practice-shaping powers of ideas is important for correcting the biases of formal comparative categories.

The *singularity* of an idea is a peculiar notion because ideas by definition are general, not singular. Expressions of ideas in texts might be singular, but that is not the point here. The point is that ideas can have such particularity in a religious tradition that, in some respects at least, representation of them always distorts. Even intrinsic representations that get inside texts to reproduce meanings as closely as possible to authorial intention or formal structure involve representational moves from the hermeneut's culture to the text's. The singularity of an idea or cluster of ideas resists representation and translation. We point to it by means of metaphors whose very metaphorical quality says the indexed idea is more than or different from what it is pointed out to be. The singularity of ideas obviously cannot be brought into comparisons. But that very fact is important to know: whereas the idea's intrinsic, perspectival, theoretical, and practical meanings can be compared, the singularity of a religion's idea of something, in that singularity, simply is incomparable. Some critics of comparison of religious ideas hold, in our terms, that all religious ideas are importantly singular and so incomparable. This is an exaggeration; not all religious ideas have important singularity. But some do, especially those ideas with indexical or pointing reference to the ultimate that are derived from mystical experience. Often comparison finds it important to note that certain aspects of the things compared cannot be brought into the comparison. Singularity is *not* a site for our comparisons, leaving us with only four.

The point of this complicated multiphase and multilevel phenomenology is to make comparison vulnerable to correction. A vague comparative category ought to be vulnerable to correction through the discovery that aspects of the ideas being compared by means of it do not fit within its scope. Likewise, the representation of phenomena for comparison ought to be vulnerable to learning that they are not what they formerly seemed from the vantage point of the comparative category. And the process of translating or interpreting the phenomena in terms of the category, giving the category specificity in the phenomena's terms, ought to be vulnerable to correction from what is learned on the way. No comparison is ever complete, much less proven. Vulnerability should be the hallmark of comparison, accordingly. Whereas some thinkers might want well-entrenched comparisons, so as to legitimate evaluative inferences, usually to the glory of their own religion or academic tradition, we think trenches and bulwarks stand in the way of inquiry. Because of the dual levels of vagueness and specificity we recognize in comparative categories, the process of comparing is an ongoing dialectic of correction.

Comparison is an historical activity, with a history to its concepts and moves. That history should also be under constant scrutiny, even (or especially) when it seems to have produced fruitful understanding and clarity. The idea of *method* in modern intellectual work has been insidious.

Method in the Cartesian sense is supposed to guarantee the results of inquiry if it is begun with true premises and followed faithfully. In practice that means that the bias of one's starting point is methodically elaborated into distortion in the conclusions. Good inquiry, rather, is always in the middle, never starting, never justified antecedently, and hopefully corrective of antecedent biases. Good inquiry attempts to break the chains of bias. The comparative process advocated here proceeds according to no methodological principles that might bias the outcome save the recognition of the several different parts of the task and an imperative to look at things from as many angles as possible.

8.6 The Historical Provenance and Discursive Form of Comparative Categories

Comparative categories are not innocent of particular histories. They are not neutral, abstract, empty notions, created to be fair to all sides. On the contrary, the categories come from specific traditions and have to be made neutral and fair by a process of criticism, purification, and use, such as is embodied in this project.

For instance, the category of the *human condition* has such a history. To say that the *human condition* is a category with a history is to recognize that it comes from a particular tradition of understanding. Specifically, it has been made popular by twentieth-century existentialism, especially that of Jaspers and Heidegger, and is prominent in the work of influential Christian theologians such as Karl Rahner and Paul Tillich, among many others. Original as the existentialist movement was, it was developing a movement in Western thought that had core texts in Renaissance humanism and the "turn to the subject" in the Protestant Reformation, the Catholic Counter-reformation, and the Enlightenment. That movement was powerfully fed by the development of the social and human sciences, beginning with Hobbes and flourishing in the nineteenth and twentieth centuries. Its roots are even more ancient. The human condition relative to God was a primary concern for the Talmudic thinkers as well as for Christian theologians attempting to define the nature and status of Jesus. And of course the psalmist sang:

> When I look at your heavens, the work of your fingers,
> the moon and the stars that you have established;
> what are human beings that you are mindful of them,
> mortals that you care for them?

> Yet you have made them a little lower than God,
>   and crowned them with glory and honor.
> You have given them dominion over the works of your hands;
>   you have put all things under their feet,
> all sheep and oxen,
>   and also the beasts of the field,
> the birds of the air, and the fish of the sea,
>   whatever passes along the paths of the seas.
>   (Psalm 8, New Revised Standard Version)

There are, of course, parallels in other religious traditions, even if they have not independently developed social and human sciences on the Western model. Chinese Confucianism is famous as a humanism and on that ground many claim that it is not a religion but a humanistic philosophy.[12] The *Bhagavad Gītā* can be read rightly as an essay on the human condition, as confronted problematically by Arjuna on the field of battle. If there were not detailed treatments in the major traditions of the human condition, we would be sorely remiss for giving it prominence in a study of comparative religious ideas! As a matter of fact, however, the term *human condition* comes to those working on our project especially but not exclusively through the history of its use in twentieth-century existential religious thinking.

That confession of historical particularity needs to be balanced by the fact that the term *human condition* has been purified of considerable historical particularity. To refer to the *human as such* is already to have moved beyond the worldview in which the name of one's own tribe means "human" and other people are not quite of the human sort. That only "one's own" people are human is one interpretation of the human condition among others. The term also abstracts from specific interpretations of the condition of all humanity, for instance, that people are created by God with a divine image, but fallen. Tillich and others wanted the nature of the human condition to be subject to analysis and interpretation by a variety of disciplines and approaches, including the arts and sciences, that are not specifically Christian.[13] His purpose was to provide a specifically Christian resolution to certain problems within the human condition where the term itself was understood more generally at least in some ways.

In *The Human Condition* we purified or generalized the term *human condition* even further to be tolerant of whatever the world religions take to be characteristic of human life and reality. We acknowledged that *human condition* can be construed so broadly that it might have many aspects to which any religion or all religions would be irrelevant; so we sometimes spoke of the *religious dimension of the human condition*. But in practice we have not found many characteristics of the human to which religion is wholly irrelevant, whether the material conditions for existence to intellectual, artistic, and cultural life. All this is to say that we have consciously reframed the notion of the *human condition* to be properly vague so as to allow for specification by the traditions we aim to compare.

Even as purified or made vague this way, the notion of the *human condition* still has a specific historical character. As noted, it treats the universality of *Homo sapiens* as the religiously important subject. Religions differ as to what this might mean. For the religions of hunter-gatherer societies it would mean little at all. Judaism notes the creaturely status of all human beings in the first eleven chapters of Genesis, but its religious concerns deal mainly with the descendents of Abraham through Isaac. Islam by contrast, even using the same texts, prescribes religion for all human beings. The religions of reincarnation in principle do not limit their religious concerns to human beings but rather to all sentient beings; in practice, however, we did not feel that the focus on the human condition distorted those traditions as religions. The category of *human condition* also supposes that the human condition is a state of being, or a state of being caused, or a nature and result of things. Given the vagueness of the notion of *condition*, we judged that little of importance was distorted or excluded from consideration in any of the religious traditions under study by its use. For all the careful vagueness with which we have framed the category of the human condition, it is still not too vague to be helpful. Interpreting the religious dimension of the human condition is helpfully different from interpreting ultimate realities, or the nature of religious truth, however much the positions under each category cross over with implications for the others. Analogous histories can be given for the categories of *ultimate realities* and *religious truth*.

It should be clear by now that comparative categories are not well symbolized by single words and that to speak of religious ideas falling under categories for purposes of comparison tends to understate the complexity of the process of comparison. Comparative categories are to be described by elaborate theories, surrounded by accounts of their historical development, and in terms that suggest that they are in the process of being revised even as we speak. To compare religious ideas is to give a long and discursive account, an account that is better the more vulnerable it is to revision. Hence we cannot chart out our categories or comparative conclusions except by means of a kind of shorthand for a review of the discursive comparative process. This point needs constantly to be brought to mind because of the great temptation to confuse a comparison with a chart of its intellectual representations.

Notes

1. See Descartes, *Meditations*, #4.

2. See Aristotle, *Metaphysics* 4.7, at 1011b26.

3. See Neville's *Behind the Masks of God: An Essay toward Comparative Theology* (Albany: State University of New York Press, 1991), chap. 6, for an analysis of this confusion.

4. See Neville's *Normative Cultures* (Albany: State University of New York Press, 1995), chap. 2, for a discussion of the kinds of critical analyses and tests to be made of abductions.

5. The hypothesis about vague comparative categories and their diverse alternative specifications is spelled out in philosophical detail in Neville, *Normative Cultures,* chaps. 1–4. Chap. 1 discusses the problem of theory, construed as synoptic vision, in light of recent criticisms of logocentric bias, and presents a theory of theories advancing upon certain vulnerable models. The theory is indebted to Charles Peirce who first developed the "logic of vagueness" in contrast with "generality." Chap. 2 discusses value and importance as characteristics of things in reality and as built in as biases to the forms of theory; comparison is analyzed as the synoptic display of importance. Chap. 3 discusses how comparisons bring unity to phenomena but at the price of selection and trivialization; devices are presented to make sure that the important elements in the phenomena are selected and the unimportant ones trivialized, rendering the value-biases in the formal categories in correspondence with the phenomena and, though being made explicit, vulnerable to correction. Chap. 4 discusses the formal criteria that frame comparisons so as to defer to the subject matter rather than impose alien connections.

6. See Peirce's essays, "Issues of Pragmaticism" and "Consequences of Critical Common-Sensism," which are to be found in many anthologies of his writings and are in the *Collected Papers of Charles Sanders Peirce*, ed. Charles Hartshorne and Paul Weiss (Cambridge: Harvard University Press, 1931), vol. 5, at paragraphs 447–450 and 505–506. I have discussed Peirce's theory of vagueness in *The Highroad around Modernism* (Albany: State University of New York Press, 1992), chap. 1. The discussion in the present text summarizes the more extensive analysis in *Normative Cultures*, 62–68.

"Vagueness" has also become a term of art within analytic philosophy. See, for instance, William Alston's article on "Vagueness" in the *Encyclopedia of Philosophy*, ed. Paul Edwards (New York: Macmillan, 1967); and the Proceedings of the 1994 Spindel conference on vagueness in *The Southern Journal of Philosophy*, XXXIII Supplement (Memphis University Department of Philosophy: 1995), ed. Terry Horgan. Alston mentions Peirce only in the citation of Peirce's article on vagueness in the *Dictionary of Philosophy and Psychology* (New York: 1901–1905), an article in which Peirce does not mention his philosophic use of the term. Peirce is not mentioned at all in the *Southern Journal of Philosophy* volume. Generally, analytic philosophy's concern with vagueness has to do with determining whether an item falls under a category and the favorite example seems to be how many hairs a man has to have in order not to be bald. Peirce's concern, and ours, is with the fact that a vague category tolerates instances that might be contradictory to one another.

7. This discussion summarizes the one in *Normative Cultures*, chap. 3. On the logic of making similar, complementary, overlapping, or contradictory things commensurate theoretically, see Neville's *The Highroad around Modernism*, chap. 6.

8. On metaphors, see Neville's *The Truth of Broken Symbols*, 44 and *passim*.

9. This hypothesis has been put forward and explored *tentatively* and *conceptually* by Neville in *Soldier, Sage, Saint* (New York: Fordham University Press, 1978), chap. 1, and *Behind the Masks of God*, chap. 10.

10. See Geertz's *The Interpretation of Cultures* (New York: Basic Books, 1973); and idem, "Deep Play: Notes on the Balinese Cockfight," *Interpretive Social Science: A Reader*, ed. William M. Sullivan and Paul Rabinow (Berkeley: University of California Press, 1979)

11. This is a variation, for the sake of religious ideas, on the discussion of different kinds of "importance" in Neville's *Normative Cultures*, chap. 2.

12. Roger Ames and David Hall follow Angus Graham and Wing-tsit Chan in this. See their *Thinking through Confucius* (Albany: State University of New York Press, 1987); and *Anticipating China* (Albany: State University of New York Press, 1995). Also see Graham's *Disputers of the Tao: Philosophical Argument in Ancient China* (La Salle, Ill.: Open Court, 1989); and Chan's influential introductions to Confucianism in his *Source Book in Chinese Philosophy* (Princeton: Princeton University Press, 1963).

13. In *The Religious Situation*, trans. H. Richard Neibuhr (New York: Henry Holt, 1932) Paul Tillich discussed the human condition as approached from the standpoints of science, metaphysics, art, politics, ethics, mysticism outside churches, eschatological movements, and Christianity.

9

How Our Approach to Comparison Relates to Others

Wesley J. Wildman
and Robert Cummings Neville

∾

Methodological wrangling over simple tasks is a waste of time. Few people care how many ways there are to erase a chalkboard and even fewer desire to debate which way is best—surely a good thing. If reflection on method in relation to the task of comparing religious ideas has importance at all, it is only because comparing religious ideas is an important and complex task; method subserves task. Comparison of religious ideas is indeed a complex matter, which may help to explain the proliferation of approaches to comparison and the denial in some quarters of the possibility of success. Self-conscious debate about comparative method ought to be useful when there is such confusion about the primary task. Generally we[1] opt for getting jobs done over discussing how to do them. In this case, however, pausing to chew on the methodological bone promises to be worth the trouble, even if later we feel the urge to bury the result.

This chapter systematically describes a number of attitudes and approaches to comparison in the study of religion. Our aim is to join the ongoing conversation over comparative method by showing how our approach relates to others. We shall make a threefold case for our view of comparison. First, we shall indicate how we have drawn on the strengths of other approaches. We are neither proud nor even especially creative, so we happily learn from other methods even as we seek to improve on them in the hope of moving ahead with what we think is an important task. The second part of our case consists in placing a sharp focus on a pervasive weakness in extant approaches to comparison of religious ideas, a weakness that our own approach is designed to overcome. The third part of our case is to show how our proposal answers the challenges issued by various comparativists, including Jonathan Z. Smith in a famous article analyzing approaches to comparison.[2] It follows that this chapter is not so much a survey of approaches to comparison as an argument for the comparative method that we have followed in this project. There are many useful surveys to which we refer those seeking more comprehensive coverage.[3]

The organization of the chapter expresses its argumentative character. We classify a number of attitudes and approaches to comparison according to how they would answer an increasingly detailed sequence of questions. Some reject the possibility of comparison whereas we argue for its possibility. Others reject explicit categories for comparison whereas we argue that explicitness about the inevitability of comparison in categories (or respects) is a virtue overall. Still others justify categories from existing theories whereas we argue that the categories should be more vulnerable to correction and hence likely to change in the process of comparison. And yet others justify categories directly from similarities in the data whereas we argue that this is too arbitrary a procedure.

Our view, then, is that there should be a dialectic between data and comparative categories whereby the task of understanding through comparison is able to build progressively on previous results. Categories can come from anywhere so long as a dialectical process of improvement and correction is in place. Justification of the categories is a complex process depending both on data identified, articulated, and checked by means of that dialectical process and on theories in which the categories play key roles. The penultimate section of this chapter redescribes our own approach to comparison and its significance by means of a discussion of the complex relations between data and categories that this dialectic is supposed to mediate. That section restates the ways by which categories and the comparisons they facilitate are to be justified. In the final section, we review the aforementioned article of Smith and show how our own approach to comparison, though it may have weaknesses all its own, does not fall prey to the criticisms he rightly urges against extant approaches.

9.1 Comparison as Impossible

The sequence of questions by which we shall survey the field and advocate our approach begins with the basic one reflecting the contention surrounding comparison in contemporary religious studies: Is comparison possible? If this question is taken in the narrowest sense, as asking about the sheer possibility of comparison of religious ideas, it is unproblematic. While there are attitudes (not approaches!) to comparison that deny its possibility, we take ourselves to have done comparison in this and the previous volume of this series, thereby answering the question of its sheer possibility.

The question is more interesting if understood loosely, as a question about the possibility of successful comparison. In the first chapter of *The Human Condition* (1.2–3) we discussed the meaning of successful comparison and gave our argument that success is possible, at least some of the time, on some understandings of success. There we announced our triply conditional hypothesis about what it takes to make successful comparisons and we repeat it here, slightly reworded: If the category of comparison vaguely considered is indeed a common respect for comparison, if the specifications of the category are made with pains taken to avoid imposing biases, and if the point of comparison is legitimate, then the translations of the specifications into the language of the category can allow of genuine comparisons. The views denying the possibility of successful comparison do so in three ways corresponding to the three conditions of this hypothesis.[4]

First, some are so impressed by the differences between cultures that they speak of incommensurability and deny the meaningfulness of talk about vague categories that express common respects of comparison. Even when common respects of comparison seem to be present, it is not possible to assure ourselves that real commonality exists because intricate cultural embedding makes the ideas involved incommensurable. To this our answer is twofold. The biological givenness of human life places a limit on the problem of cultural impenetrability and gives a solid basis for speaking of common features of human culture. And the phenomenon of multiple religious and personal identity (for instance, Daoistic Confucians, Jewish Christians) shows that the claim of incommensurability is strained. These considerations do not automatically assure the meaningfulness of speaking about common respects of comparison but they do check objections that would arrest an attempt to find common respects of comparison before it even begins. Once the comparative process has begun, at least on our understanding of that process, the reality of common respects of comparison is largely an empirical matter.

Second, some are so impressed by the human tendency to become attached to familiar ways of interpreting the world that they view the problem of bias as intractable. They deny that religious practices, texts, and traditions can be specified in respect of the category of comparison without bias, no matter what pains are taken to be fair. Perhaps we can imagine creatures capable of fair interpretation through being less thoroughly indebted to biologically congealed habits of understanding than human beings are. But we cannot imagine ourselves capable of overcoming the limitations of imagination and perspective that plague our attempts to be fair-minded in human affairs. Our reply to this objection turns on a difference in judgment regarding the degree to which bias is problematic. We take the existence of adaptable forms of inquiry such as the natural sciences to be evidence that people are capable of establishing social arrangements wherein vulnerability and improvement of interpretations are prized. Moreover, the measure of fairness defended so ably by Wilfred Cantwell Smith that we call the qualified-adherent-approval test, despite its complexities, is a viable way of assuring ourselves that our efforts to be fair are sometimes relatively successful. Once again, however, nothing in our reply guarantees fairness, nor even a recipe for achieving it. Fair interpretation is an art form in which success turns on skill and effort as well as a clear-headed method.

Third, some might grant the meaningfulness of respects of comparison and even the possibility of making allowance for bias, yet view the point of comparison as essentially immoral, thus making successful comparison impossible where "success" connotes worthiness. Whether the goal of comparison is to satisfy curiosity, to enhance understanding, to build theories, or something else, comparison is an exercise of cultural power for which it is hard to take full and fair responsibility. If not a blatant exertion of cultural force, then it is at the very least a form of transformative praxis: comparison changes things, both the things compared and those making the comparisons. Indeed, that is the very purpose of comparison in the social context of interreligious dialogue, to bring about cultural and personal change through mutual understanding. We already discussed this problem in 1.3 of *The Human Condition* and offered a report on our own moral compass to the effect that our purposes in making comparisons are, in our context, morally legitimate. There are no guarantees in this case either, however, for moral judgments of this kind change with time and place. We have no trouble imagining settings in which curiosity should be checked and understanding sacrificed for the sake of some relatively higher moral purpose, such as the protection from scrutiny of an exquisite and fragile cultural phenomenon.

Our replies to these objections to the possibility of successful comparison all turn heavily on the process of comparison we defend. Our resistance to non-empirical pronouncements about what is possible and what is not only makes sense in the context of a serious positive viewpoint that moves beyond mere speculation or hopeful stipulation about comparative method. That alternative is a properly empirical procedure that prizes vulnerability of comparative hypotheses and actively seeks to improve them in as many ways and with as much diligence as possible.

9.2 Comparison as Something Other than an Explicit Cognitive Process

Positions answering the question of possibility in the affirmative can be differentiated by their responses to a second question: To what extent should comparison proceed as an explicitly cognitive process with the results of comparison represented as (hypothetical) ideas? The argument that an act of comparison presupposes a respect of comparison (a category) is sound; it is simply a part of the grammar of comparison that two things are similar or different *somehow*—and the *how* is the respect or category of comparison. Nevertheless, comparisons of religious ideas sometimes avoid any explicit mention of the operative categories. This may be because of lack of interest or because of inconsistency. Another goal may be served by this silence, however: resistance to making the act of comparison an explicit cognitive process. To suppress discussion of the category of comparison while still making comparisons is effectively to leave the results of comparison implicit in the comparative act.

There are at least two reasons why this goal sometimes is deemed important. First, when knowledge is viewed as an event of illumination within an ongoing process, comparison does not much serve the end of knowledge if the results are given explicit representation in the form of hypotheses about a comparative category. Rather, proper knowledge is attained when the results involve a seeing-as with potentially transformative effects. Second, the refusal to make the results of comparison explicit in the form of ideas is a hedge against so-called logocentrism. Vigilant deconstruction of comparative conclusions as fast as they materialize keeps the mind mobile, avoids the ironic trapping of theorists by their own comparative conclusions, and most adequately respects differences among traditions. Some theorists deem these virtues so important that they willingly forsake the rather different virtues of self-consciousness of procedure, vulnerability to correction, and detection of bias that pertain to acts of comparison structured as explicit cognitive processes along the lines we defend.

There are a number of examples of this reticent approach to comparison. They vary in the degree to which they oppose representation of comparison as an explicit cognitive process and of comparative conclusions as ideas, but they uniformly insist on the value of comparison in absence of a cognitive representation of the results as a third thing. Such approaches may use respects of comparison drawn from narrative structures[5] or metaphors.[6] Alternatively, they may juxtapose points of view[7] or facilitate intellectually illuminating play across differences.[8] These approaches avoid large-scale theories about categories of comparison (such as the human condition, ultimate realities, or religious truth). Moreover, they tend to be suspicious of accounts of causal factors that purport to explain conceptual similarities between traditions or texts. Why the suspicion? Because the theories about comparative categories and the causal analyses are seriously underdetermined by the comparative data.

This is an important point with which we have some sympathy. It highlights a genuine weakness, albeit one that fades (we hope) with time, in our approach to comparison. These views hold in common that successful comparison is an act of genius in which an illuminating similarity is grasped intuitively and then expressed gracefully, avoiding the unattractive mistake of smothering the insights with an unwieldy theoretical apparatus. The problem with such theoretical framing is that it explains too much. Almost any broad theoretical framework either will be too abstract to explain anything or will quickly predict not only the insight to be explained but a horde of other comparative conclusions as well. In fact, it will predict so much on the basis of such slender data that the theory will collapse before it builds up a head of steam. A theory about a comparative category is, on these views, drastically underdetermined by the data, and so extensively stipulates what ought to be the case, invariably getting too much wrong to be attractive. Making comparison into an explicit cognitive process with a dialectical methodology of vulnerability, debate, and improvement seems too facile, too unrealistic about the complex data to be accounted for in comparisons, and too optimistic about the power of theories to explain the disparate data. What is left for comparison, then, except to be the domain of genius insight? And what is the point of rendering comparison an explicit cognitive process complete with codetermination of vague categories and their specifications except boldly to hide from the fact that we are in no position to regulate our comparative efforts in the way we claim is possible in this project?

Note how modest is the objection to our approach that we infer from these viewpoints. It does not claim that successful comparison is impossible on *a priori* grounds. Rather, it plausibly assumes that a slender base of comparative data about religious phenomena and a worrying history of distortion and arbitrariness in previous comparative efforts combine with the irreducible complexity of the task to make avoiding too formalized and aggressive an approach to it the safest bet. Leave it to those deeply initiated into several traditions. Let us be content with their moments of illumination and the comparative insights they produce. Let us avoid systematization and cognitive fretting. It's just not worth it.

The relationship between this view and our own resembles the relationship between Mahāyāna and Therāvada sensibilities in Buddhism. In Therāvada, the focused journey toward enlightenment is for the monks, for the genius experts. In Mahāyāna, enlightenment is for the masses; not being genius experts, however, they must find ways to work together. In the same way, we are urging that the process of comparison should be made more public, that many kinds of people should combine forces to search for stable comparative hypotheses, and that the key to this approach is an explicit method. This method must prize stability and vulnerability to correction in comparative hypotheses, render its provisional conclusions as ideas on the way to theories about religious matters, and demand careful justification for the comparative categories that make stable comparative hypotheses feasible. We go even further, however—and here the Buddhist analogy begins to strain, though the "egalitarian rebellion" version of the origins of Mahāyāna still works. We argue that the genius insight method of comparison was never sufficiently productive of deep insights and that such insights as were won were never made as fruitful as they might have been for the work of others. In short, there is a scientific approach to comparison that promises far better results due to the coordinated work of many in place of the rare, uncoordinated insights of the few genius comparativists.

The question becomes, therefore, whether the method works. As sympathetic as we are to the criticism we have been discussing, we do think that more can be achieved than it allows. We return to these matters below. For now, our relation to this family of critics suggests an amusing image, flattering to both sides in different ways yet gently mocking both, too. What begins as conflicting bets over what would be gained by self-consciousness about method in comparison ends with the reticent, Therāvada approach having nothing to do but watch while the enthusiastic Mahāyāna crowd uses every available resource to maximize the impact of their combined efforts. The members of the disciplined monkish group, amazed at the innocence of their non-adept friends, with some justification predict that the corporate experiment will begin in optimistic methodological stipulations and, chaotically stumbling along a host of mistake-riddled paths, end in utter failure. The large, noisy group, for its part, is unconcerned with the adepts' opinions because time is on its side. Where the adepts can only watch in amusement, already pressed hard up against their self-imposed limits for what is possible in comparison, the corporate experiment's refusal to accept any limitations *a priori* on what comparison can achieve gives it time and opportunity to learn from its many mistakes and to generate new approaches and new forms of cooperation. The outcome remains an intriguing question. We bet on the mob.

9.3 Comparison Based on Categories Justified by Existing Theories of Religion

Approaches that produce explicit cognitive representations of the process and results of comparing religious practices and beliefs constitute the largest group, though it is diverse and of uneven quality. These views can be distinguished based on the answers they provide to the question about how the categories used for comparison are justified. Section 9.4 below deals with approaches that attempt to justify categories directly from "similarities" in the data of religious ideas and practices; this is an extremely dubious procedure but it has its own special virtue, as we shall see. The current section is concerned with the large group of approaches that borrow or deduce categories for comparison from existing theories about religion and justify the use of those categories by virtue of the plausibility they gain from those theories. Such approaches can be distinguished, though with some overlap, by the nature of the theory of religion that furnishes and justifies the categories. We present them here for convenience in family groupings.

First, one family of approaches begins from a confessional religious perspective, approaching other religious traditions in terms of categories dominant within their own.[9] An important social phenomenon connected with this is interreligious dialogue, in which representatives of religious traditions join in discussion over shared issues of importance or simply to increase mutual understanding. Surely this is the most natural way, in the sense of being simplest and most direct, to approach the task of making comparisons among religious ideas. What could be more straightforward or more morally satisfying than to approach the plurality of religions from one's own perspective? We heartily affirm the moral and existential naturalness of this kind of approach to comparison. Yet it has an obvious downside in that the categories for comparison are so heavily indebted to a particular confessional perspective that they cannot be as responsive to the data as scholars and theorists of religion require. There is moral and existential satisfaction to be had in the approach to comparison from one's own confessional point of view, if it is a strong one. But an ideal form of encounter for many religious-believer comparativists may not be ideal for comparativists for whose purposes the inflexibility of categories derived from and justified by confessional commitments interferes with their scholarly task. Flexible categories are better for us because improvement of comparative categories is always needed, as is refinement of any theory that produces and justifies them.

Second, another family of approaches justifies the key categories for comparison by means of a theological-mystical-metaphysical theory. This is true in very different ways of the perennial philosophy,[10] various archetype and Jungian approaches,[11] and even certain contributions in the philosophy of religion.[12] The theory in question may be more or less complete and more or less empirical, yet it is persuasive enough to commend its principal theoretical categories to the comparativist. There are many examples that might be considered here but, for the sake of specificity, we shall discuss the perennial philosophy.

The perennial philosophy offers a way to see how the adepts from all traditions hold certain key ideas in common, albeit under sometimes radically different descriptions, while explaining why non-adepts could flatly disagree with each other about the truth of religious ideas and practices. The existence of this purported common core is the reason the perennial philosophy is sometimes called the primordial tradition. It is defended by thinkers who in some cases—and preeminently in the case of Huston Smith, its best known contemporary representative—have spent a great deal of time learning about religious practices and texts from all over the world. Its advocates would say without hesitation that its plausibility derives mainly from the fact that it can make sense of a great deal of data. Just because of this, we are told, we should not hesitate to take over the categories given prominence in the perennial philosophy for the sake of making detailed comparisons. From its ontology of the Great Chain of Being we receive the categories of Godhead (*nirguṇa Brahman*), God (*saguṇa Brahman*), discarnates and other intermediate beings, human beings, animals, plants, and inanimate objects. Its cosmology offers categories such as the human condition, ultimate and proximate religious truth, savior figures and bodhisattvas, ignorance and liberation. Its view of the religious quest leads to other comparative categories such as morality, ritual, sacred texts, and special revelations, each of which is interpreted through the lens of the ontology and cosmology of the perennial philosophy. With categories furnished by a powerful large-scale theoretical interpretation of religion, comparison can proceed untroubled by the problem of categorial justification, focusing instead on comparative details. Ultimately, the result is the further illumination and consolidation of the theory of religion that furnishes the categories themselves.

What happens when some data beg for comparison in fundamental categories other than those served up by the perennial philosophy? The existence of such data is predicted within the perennial philosophy approach and explained by means of the distinction between what is ultimately and proximately true; in this way the contraindicative force of such data is undermined. Ultimately, the contra-indicating data are really not so important even if, proximately, they are pervasive and central. Going further, what happens if, by following this procedure, most of the interesting details of religious practices and ideas are effectively eliminated from having a say in what the fundamental categories for comparison should be? For example, the majority of scholars in religious studies simply cannot accept that pervasive themes in religion such as food and purity can be marginalized in the way that the perennial philosophy does. As beautiful as the perennial philosophy is, it has few followers. This is partly because of an ontology that is opposed to the naturalist tendencies of modern Western science, but also because its handling of comparative data is felt to be arbitrary. The sense of arbitrariness derives from the fact that the theory furnishing the categories for comparison is too neat, too easily able to deflect objections, and thus too convenient, too invulnerable, too unresponsive to criticism, and too uninterested in correction and improvement.

For all that, of course, the perennial philosophy might be correct, at least in its essentials. The point here, however, is that the vulnerability of comparative categories is at least as important a virtue as the coherence and simplicity of a theological-mystical-metaphysical theory that might produce them. The same goes for other members of this family, including especially the various archetype theories of religion, regardless of whether a metaphysical or other explanation for the universality of the archetypes is furnished: vulnerability of categories is an essential hedge against our ignorance about religion and the reality in which it exists.

Third, another group of approaches justifies comparative categories by virtue of a scientific-causal theory about the origin and nature of religion. Such approaches, including many of the brightest stars in the religious studies sky, usually have begun from particular scientific or social-scientific disciplines, thereafter leading out into proposals for more or less comprehensive theories of religion. Most such theories can be organized by a leading discipline: evolutionary biology,[13] anthropology,[14] sociology,[15] neuroscience,[16] and psychology.[17]

The word "causal" in scientific-causal is helpfully vague. On the one hand, it cuts in the direction of the second family's expectation that there are naturally occurring limitations on how religious ideas fit together. Of course, in the third family these limitations are explained in terms of the sphere of interest of the leading scientific discipline (e.g., social mechanisms, brain structure and function, psychological laws) rather than in the second family's more metaphysical or mystical ways. On the other hand, causation points in the direction of historical influence whereby certain comparative categories achieve a high degree of naturalness. Very often approaches in this family make appeal to both kinds of causation to justify comparative categories. This is true of many of the representative views listed above, as well as approaches to comparison that allow the philosophy of history to play as large a role as historical details.[18] The historical influences in question might vary widely, from the effects of trade contacts or missionary zeal to planned cultural engineering. Unfortunately, sometimes these views presuppose influence where none has been shown to have any historical-causal basis. Alternatively, they presuppose an evolution of ideas in which the close-knit cultural competition needed for the natural selection of ideas cannot be demonstrated.

The third family displays a relatively lower interest in an existentially and morally natural approach to religious pluralism from one's own religious point of view. It also contrasts with the second family by virtue of the limitation to recognizably scientific theories or to historical causation, at least in intention if not always in practice. The problem with the third family of approaches, however, is the same as the problem in the first and second families: comparative categories need to be more vulnerable to correction than these approaches suggest so as to be able to take account of all that is learned about religious traditions in the process of making comparisons.

It would be churlish to be critical of the many instances of creative genius in the study of religion that abound in these three families of approaches. Let us be clear that in no case is it the source of comparative categories that troubles us. Each of these theorists has bequeathed categories for comparing religious ideas and practices and the value of these categories is incontestable. The problem is rather the rigidity from which categories suffer by virtue of receiving their justification from being key terms in large-scale theories of religion. These theorists themselves, and we daresay the bulk of those making use of their comparative categories, have not taken pains to say how these categories could be made responsive to resistant data. If the categories begin to seem contrived or otherwise inadequate, the underlying theory might profit somehow, though the mechanism for this is rarely explained, but the comparative task simply folds. It has nowhere to go. Our contention is that, regardless of the source of categories for comparison, the methodology of comparison must prize vulnerability of comparative categories and of the comparisons they permit.

9.4 Comparison Based on Categories
Justified from Similarities in Data

When categories receive their justification from an existing complete or partial theory of religion, they are even less flexible and responsive than the theories themselves. When the differences presupposed in the very concept of comparison are so significant as to cause severe dissonance within a comparative category, or when too much data is not registered well enough by an array of categories, the dependence on a background theory makes flexible correction of categories almost impossible. This has long been sensed within the study of religion and by reaction has produced a fundamentally descriptive group of approaches to comparison. In this group, the justification of comparative categories derives from how well they express the relative importance of the data and of the relations between data.

Justification of this sort is an extremely delicate question. Arguably, sometimes justification has been limited to implicit reliance merely on the self-evidence of the similarities themselves. The failure of "what just seems similar" to justify categories of "the similar" is notorious,[19] however, for two reasons. On the one hand, the role of the interpreter is so powerful in appeals to the obvious that it can swamp the ideal of descriptive impartiality. On the other hand, it continues to be difficult to figure out when phenomena are "essentially similar"; comparison seems not to advance this phenomenological task so much as codify persistent perplexity about it (but see below in section 9.5 for a brief account of how philosophical phenomenology is supposed to overcome this challenge). Despite these problems, something like an appeal to the obvious is indispensable to the justification of categories in these approaches because of the insistence on allowing data to speak for themselves. The problem is unavoidable, therefore; it must be managed rather than avoided. The views in this group can be clustered into families based on strategies for managing the challenge of impartiality in judging obvious similarities.

First, one family of approaches simply does the descriptive task really well! That is, descriptive categories are adduced on the basis of intensive grounding in multiple religious traditions, with the benefit of ongoing discussions with a wide variety of people. The result is descriptions of religious phenomena and ideas that win the grudging but secretly appreciative approval of large numbers of experts. Under this heading we list the luminaries of description in the study of religion. Some of these could be called descriptive phenomenologists of religion, as against exponents of philosophical phenomenology to which we will return presently.[20] For others the phenomenological label is less apt but they are nonetheless expert observers and describers of religious phenomena.[21] There are many others of both sorts.[22] There are also many figures from the previous groups (sections 9.2 and 9.3, above) whose projects crucially depend on expertise in description so it is as well to remember that this group is distinguished primarily by a commitment to descriptive adequacy as primary justification for comparative categories.

Second, another family of approaches to comparison manages the problem of bias in description by partially relying on the lines of justification already discussed. This has to be done in precisely the right way, however: the aim is to relieve pressure on descriptive adequacy as the sole justification for comparative categories while still avoiding reliance on large-scale theories of religion in order to maintain the close ties between categories and data. One example of such a judicious hybrid approach is the comparative strategy advocated by Rudolf Otto in *The Idea of the Holy*.[23] In that work Otto blends phenomenological description with a partial theological viewpoint. There is no fully worked out theory of religion underlying Otto's categories of *mysterium* and *tremendum*; he himself says that he only focuses on the irrational element in religion, which leaves out an enormous amount of data. Yet the categories are justified not only by observations of the recurrence of phenomena that are arguably identical in substance, but also by a partial worldview that postulates the religious potency of reality.

Another set of examples supplements justification of comparative categories by their adequacy for describing data with various kinds of higher-order classifications of the data. Examples are plentiful, including the classification systems of Watson and Dilworth and Paul Tillich's analysis of God concepts.[24] In such cases, structural similarities in the ideas of diverse religious traditions suggest a classification. This classification is then supported in at least one of three ways: by a justification of the classification through elimination based on a philosophical analysis of possible options, by the theoretical beauty and economy of the classification, and by the classification's efficacy in organizing further data. These classifications may or may not be ideal, in the sense of being defined by key features that are rarely realized purely in actual instances, and they may be partial or exhaustive.

All of the approaches to justifying categories discussed in this section prescind from reliance on well-worked out theories of religion. By contrast with the views discussed in section 9.4, they content themselves with observations formed on the basis of incomplete data, without the aid of much in the way of a theoretical superstructure to add authority to the classifications and categories that result. This is so even when a hybrid approach to justification is adopted. The attempt to stay closer to the data by resisting the potentially blinkered influence of large-scale theories is to be lauded, despite the problems of justification from the appearance of similarity. From this we learn the crucial lesson that, as difficult as it may be, justification of categories by virtue of their roles in big-deal theories is to be minimized, even though it can never be eliminated completely. That is, there must be a partial distinction—it can never be made rigid—between the task of comparison that produces and justifies comparative categories and the subsequent task of theory building that takes the categories as well-attested ways of organizing data. But the increase in the empirical sensibility of this group over the more theory-dependent approaches (section 9.4) only eases the curse of invulnerability to correction; it does not escape it. While learning from this approach, therefore, we hold out for greater responsiveness to data and more clearly defined ways of correcting hypothetical comparative categories.

9.5 Comparison Based on a Dialectic of Data and Categories

With this we come to the final group of approaches to comparison. These approaches attempt, by contrast with all approaches discussed so far, to introduce procedures by which categories, however they are produced, can be improved with time. The most feasible procedure for such improvement is a thoroughgoing dialectic between the raw data and the categories used in making comparisons of the data. These approaches tend to be unwieldy because of the number of variables involved. Not only is there a large amount of data to be managed, but this data needs to be made effective for the correction of the categories in use, and the theories guiding interpretation of the data are themselves complex and subject to correction. We are aware of only three such approaches.

The first and most famous is Edmund Husserl's philosophical phenomenology.[25] Husserl's attempt to allow phenomenological generalizations to be responsive to data is truly impressive. We take ourselves to be following in his footsteps in this respect, but in few other ways. Husserl's program is, from our point of view, so plagued by awkward philosophical overhead that his approach is not helpful for a general theory of comparison. In particular, his foundationalist epistemic project seems wrongheaded to us and productive of confusions in his method that obscure the details salient for a general theory of comparison. His elaborate method for guiding phenomenological reflection is both too little in respect of attending to too few sources of corrective wisdom, and too much in respect of being thoroughly overbearing and impossibly difficult. If ever there were a comparative method for adepts it is Husserl's. That said, we do admire his attempt to found a discipline of comparative phenomenology, his scientifically minded respect for vulnerability of categories inferred from data, and his use of a dialectic between data and categories to drive his phenomenological method.

The second example also focuses on phenomenological reports: the heterophenomenological method advocated by Daniel C. Dennett.[26] Dennett's approach can be regarded either as an attempt to correct some of Husserl's excesses or as a simplified version of Husserl's own procedures. Unfortunately, Dennett does not say enough about Husserl's method to enable a fair judgment of the relationship between the two. Suffice to say that Dennett sees clearly the philosophical problems associated with the comparison of phenomenological reports and he is as keenly aware as Husserl was of how splendid it would be to have a way to know when apparently different descriptions were really essentially about the same phenomenon. We heartily agree with both Dennett and Husserl in this regard. We are betting, however, that the vision of effective comparative phenomenology will never be realized until neurophysiology advances to the point that it can make meaningful contributions to judgments about the essential similarity and difference of the experiences giving rise to the phenomenological descriptions being compared.[27]

The third example is our own approach. It has been summarized already in this volume and elsewhere,[28] and some of our main commitments have been discussed in passing in this chapter, so we confine ourselves in the next section to some comments on the meaning and significance of the dialectic between categories and data that we advocate.

9.6 The Significance of Comparison
Conducted as Dialectic between Categories and Data

In the 1960s, Imre Lakatos proposed a fairly detailed model for the operation of the natural sciences (the so-called methodology of scientific research programs).[29] It succeeded in overcoming to a significant degree the discontinuity between scientific work within a paradigm ("normal" science) and what Thomas Kuhn had identified as "paradigm shifts."[30] The discontinuity had proved awkward because the history of science suggested on the whole that paradigm shifts fit into the flow of science more easily than Kuhn's proposal allowed. Lakatos's own proposal was also controversial, however. Although it allowed for paradigm shifts, it tended to make them more rational than the history of science suggested has been the case. The controversy between Lakatos's relatively rational account of theory change and Paul Feyerabend's insistence that changing between scientific research programs cannot finally be given exhaustively rational justification is one of the great debates of twentieth-century philosophy of science.[31] It appears that, although reasons can be given for abandoning an apparently degenerating scientific research program in favor of a more progressive alternative, the decision remains a judgment call that cannot be completely rationally decided.

This shows that the dialectic between data and the principle theoretical categories is a delicate one even in the natural sciences. Its management depends on having stylishly good judgment about one's work, akin perhaps to what John Henry Newman called "illative sense."[32] That is how one balances the virtues of switching to a promising new hypothesis that (one hopes temporarily) flies in the face of important data, on the one hand, and the virtues of staying with a trusted old hypothesis that might be more consistent with data but seems to be running out of predictive steam, on the other. Newman's illative sense is the key to efficient, potent argumentation as much as it is the key to making decisions between two competing hypotheses that each call for the investment of time and energy. This artistic dimension of human reason is a sharp reminder that any dialectic between data and categories will be as subtle as it is complex.

Perhaps the most important insight of Lakatos was his detailed spelling out of how complex is the path from data to theory and back again, in contrast with Karl Popper's more straightforward focus on falsification.[33] In the natural sciences the data is incomprehensible apart from theories of instrumentation, which themselves are justified both by the sense they make of raw data and by inference from active theories about how nature works. Additional essentially interpretative theories are also needed for guiding the relating of data and for picking out essential features of the masses of data that are gathered. Most important is the way that the data, already multiply interpreted in these ways, can have an impact on the central hypotheses that guide the research program. No good scientist would ever throw over a well-tested hypothesis because of one piece of contra-indicating evidence. Rather, attempts would be made—frantic attempts, perhaps—on the one hand to test the data by replicating the experiment or confirming the theories of instrumentation, and on the other hand to explain the data with an auxiliary hypothesis that effectively protects the central hypotheses from falsification. It is the extension of theories to new data, even to potentially threatening data, by means of auxiliary hypotheses that helps to make research programs in the natural sciences seem progressive. Another sign of a progressive research program is its ability to predict novel facts. Of course, if novel facts are no longer predicted and the explanations of threatening data come to seem contrived and merely face-saving, then the research program would be judged, sooner by its critics than by its advocates, to be degenerating.

What is true in the natural sciences is no less true in the study of religion: the relationship between data and theoretical terms, including comparative categories, is exceedingly complex, as is the relation between data and research program.[34] Most of the views we have discussed recognize this. We hold that determined recognition of complexity is the precondition for resisting the extremes of data-blind enthusiasm and theory-blind confusion. This acknowledgment also involves a discriminating appreciation of similarities and differences among the various kinds of inquiries we see around us. The subject matters of religious studies are very different from those of the natural sciences or economics or literature. Nevertheless, we hold that Lakatos's methodology of research programs, in its general outlines if not in its details, fairly describes the way effective inquiry works in any context from the natural sciences to the humanities and even to commonsense problem solving. The same characteristics are crucial: a conservative approach whereby a feasible hypothesis is relinquished reluctantly, conjoined with a sense of adventure that prizes vulnerability to correction by whatever means are available given the nature of the inquiry.

The generality of the theory of inquiry implied here was first appreciated by Charles S. Peirce and then by John Dewey.[35] Peirce actually anticipated Lakatos in many details relevant to inquiry in the natural sciences.[36] Peirce's more impressive achievements in this area, however, were his rich awareness of the complex relations between data and theory and his vision for extending a generalized theory of inquiry from the natural sciences all the way into the humanities and metaphysics. We share Peirce's basic intuition. We see no reason why the confusing data of religious ideas and practices cannot be given flexible interpretative structures that render them able not only to inspire but also to correct theories of religion and of religious topics such as the human condition, ultimate realities, and religious truth.

And what form, we ask, should such flexible interpretative structures—the analogues of theories of instrumentation and interpretation in the natural sciences—take? They should take the form of the provisional conclusions of the study of cross-cultural comparative religious ideas and practices, precisely what our project is producing. That is, we understand the comparative method we advocate as the first step toward a more effective approach to the generation and testing of theories of religion and religious topics, the analogue of theories of instrumentation and interpretation in the natural sciences. The categories within which comparisons of religious ideas and practices take place are precisely the flexible means of organizing data that constructive theoretical efforts require.

Interpretative theories by which data are made available to more constructive theoretical ventures are interwoven with those larger theoretical ventures, even as theories of instrumentation are closely connected with the physical theories they serve. In section 7.3.1, we outlined some of the dimensions of this interweaving by parsing the justification of comparative generalizations into four requirements. Each corresponds to an impulse present in one or more the approaches to comparison that we have discussed. Any requirement alone is insufficient, however; coordination of these lines of justification is essential. We list them again here. There need to be (1) a delimiting of possibilities whereby plausible religious ideas of the sort relevant to the comparative generalization are identified; (2) an account of the dynamic logical connections among ideas; (3) a genetic analysis of specific symbolic representations of the religious ideas in question; and (4) analyses of the circumstances that accompany the key shifts in symbolic representation during the history of the relevant religious ideas. To these must be added the basic phenomenological point that our sense of what is similar, when carefully conditioned by scrupulous preparation and exposure to many variations, really should count as partial justification of comparative categories. These requirements indicate our indebtedness to standard commitments within both the history of religions and the philosophy of religion, and we shall list those debts more formally below (section 9.7). They are the tests by which we determine whether the data have been well organized by our comparative categories and thus whether the categories themselves are adequate. It is perfectly clear that these tests are theoretical endeavors related to the larger theories of religion and of religious themes for which comparative categories serve as the organizers and mediators of relevant data.

In connection with this, consider the theory of contingency outlined in chapter 7. It is intended to explain a relatively simple comparative point about ultimate realities, yet it does so by describing some stable abstract facts about the world that will be encountered in any cultural setting and thus will constrain any conceptual expressions and introduce dynamics of changing ideas. It is a partial and vague theory only, in the sense that it is compatible with a number of more detailed metaphysical theories that would specify the way these stable abstract facts about the world are encountered in practice. It is a theory nonetheless and one that helps justify the category of ultimate realities and a number of subsidiary categories used in this book. Of course, there would be objections. On the one hand, some critics would charge either that the theory of contingency is too abstract to be brought to bear on explanations of any comparative hypothesis or that it produces so many predictions that it will be immediately falsified. Either of those charges seems to us *prime facie* plausible, yet as a matter of fact we think that this theory beats the odds; it is a good theory that is fairly accurate and has been set in a methodological context wherein it can be improved as necessary. Moreover, if the theory of contingency holds water, then a basic characteristic of the world has been described in such a way that we are in a better position to notice the expressions of it variously modulated in the religions and cultures of the world. This would demonstrate the fruitfulness of the categories we propose. On the other hand, other critics would urge that our explanation is unduly disconnected with historical details. It is not an historical explanation, of course. Rather, it is one of the four types of explanation that jointly justify comparative categories, the third and fourth of which deal explicitly with historical contingencies and influences. Section 7.3.3 also includes a theory of the third type as a contributor to the justification of our categories.

The theory of contingency thus helps to justify comparative categories and the comparisons they permit, and other kinds of arguments make their own, more historical contribution to the same task. With all of those lines of explanation and justification in place, our approach to comparison leads out in interesting directions: to the birth of systematic comparative metaphysics; to a strengthened, potentially progressive, multidisciplinary investigation of religious phenomena; and to a more unified approach to the study of religion that coordinates the approaches of the history of religion, the phenomenology of religion, and the philosophy of religion.

The Comparative Religious Ideas Project in which we are involved is primarily concerned with the preliminary task of organizing data by means of categories for comparison in a complex dialectical process—precisely as complex, in our experience, as the formation of a community of inquiry from differently minded scholars, including specialists and generalists. There have been forays into more adventurous theoretical efforts but that is secondary. We recognize and even celebrate that the comparative categories we use have been begged, borrowed, or stolen from multiple sources, including early translations of sacred texts, all of the various sources mentioned previously in 9.2 through 9.4, and the creative intuition of project members. Comparison always begins in the middle of data-processing. Yet we also actively seek ways of correcting comparative categories in an effort to organize the data of religious ideas in the most natural, efficacious ways. In fact, we adopt a promiscuous attitude to correction, excluding a priori no source of potential wisdom, grading sources according to their actual fruitfulness for making data relevant to the refinement of the comparative categories and the comparisons they permit. If our primary task goes well enough, then we will have created a powerful reason to think both that flexible structuring of the wild data of religious ideas is possible and that a more critical and data-aware form of theory building ought to be possible, soon if not immediately.

9.7 Learning from the Past

In closing, and by way of summary, we pause to recite our list of debts and corrections to existing comparative approaches.

First, comparativists borrowing categories from existing theories are exercising a kind of wisdom, we think. They are backing categories that are at least partially attested by the theory that articulates them and they seek in that way to extend the core theory itself to new tracts of data. That is why we can admire the perennial philosophers' dogged adherence to their interpretation of the world religions, for example. Without such fidelity to core hypotheses, even sometimes to the point of arbitrary handling of data, it is almost guaranteed that some special virtue of the core hypothesis will be overlooked. Such devotion to research programs is vital to the stability of interpretative theories. Without stability, vulnerability for the sake of progressive correction is impossible. From these laborers in our vineyards we learn to take good categories from wherever they may be found and to be unafraid of the need for persistence in testing any theory of religion against data. However, we seek a fairer and more flexible approach to the data itself.

Second, comparativists that refuse to make explicit the categories in respect of which they make comparisons could well be exercising another kind of wisdom. In this case it is the recognition that analogues of scientific theories of instrumentation do not exist in the study of religion to any great degree, at least not yet. Moving gracefully among the forest of data is thus judged to be a more effective procedure than trying to map and regulate the data's wildness for the sake of evaluating its force for or against the particular interpretations of it implied in the explicit use of comparative categories. From these fellow workers we learn not to underestimate the complexity and disarray of the data of religious studies. It may be, however, that the absence of analogues for data-handling theories of instrumentation can be overcome for the study of religion.

Third, comparativists who try to maximize the virtue of empiricism in generating comparative categories from data are wisely recognizing that there must be some degree of self-conscious distance between the comparative task and the task of larger theory building in religious studies. From them we learn that categories are a middle-level beast. They help to organize data for the sake of big-deal theory construction yet they derive their justification more from their effectiveness of the data management they facilitate than from the theories that use them. However, we remain sharply aware of the problem pointed out by Jonathan Z. Smith of justifying comparative categories on the basis of apparent similarities in data. Our solution to this problem is the fourfold set of theories discussed above (section 9.6) in conjunction with an affirmation of the usefulness of phenomenological intuition of respects of similarity and difference, though only when the phenomenological imagination is properly prepared. We reaffirm Peirce's insistence that categories derived from theory for classifying data need to be checked against independent phenomenological analyses of the data to determine their suitability.[37]

Fourth, in addition to the important critique of intuitions of similarity just mentioned, Jonathan Z. Smith also argues that, at the date of his writing, there was no approach to comparison that produces or discovers, as against constructs, comparisons,[38] and further that there was no satisfactory approach to comparison under discussion anywhere.[39] We agree on the second point but demur, slightly, with regard to the first. We point out, using Smith's language, that nobody "has presented rules for the production of" discoveries in the domains of the natural sciences either, yet they happen. Moreover, we think both that the insights of well-trained describers and comparers of religions can be novel, at times, and that those insights can transcend the level of the flimsy associative connections that Smith rightly attacks. We agree, however, that this occurs more rarely than ought to be the case; its scarcity is because it is so difficult to acquire the competence that makes novel insights also profound ones. Our proposal helps, we think, by requiring less the genius of admirable comparative adepts and more scrupulous hard work. Many of the novel ideas that can be put into the dialectic of categories and data that we have described and enacted in our project may turn out to be of little use; certainly our project disposed of a lot more categories than it kept. Similarly, some categories and comparisons may never achieve the multifaceted justification on which we insist; it surely is a demanding standard for justification, after all. Those that do, however, can fairly be described as profound and, in at least some cases, novel. After that, discovery is a matter of learning to look in new situations for what worked elsewhere, tentatively extending the reach of the data-management web that comparative categories constitute, and always seeking the kinds of dissonance that should force revisions. We also believe that we have answered

Smith's call for a comparative method that can escape the weakness of extant approaches.

Finally, we also take seriously the alternatives to explicit methodologies of comparison discussed in 9.2 by trying to incorporate their strengths into the corrective procedures of our own approach. This is present, for example, in the way that theoretical justifications for categories help to deconstruct assumptions about what seems obvious, even as simple judgments of similarity for all their dangers can also call forth theoretical efforts of justification—and all this for the sake of fidelity to the data. Nevertheless, we are explicit about the categories and the provisional results of comparisons, and here we enter our wager in favor of the loosely coordinated march of many feet, all contributing to the task of generating and improving comparative hypotheses in the way we propose. Our bet includes the gamble that the chaos will in time yield to something more like the organized frenzy of the natural and social sciences. We do see reasons to think that such a transformation will be difficult. After all, the forging of our project's community of inquiry has been a demanding, drawn-out process. And then there are the intimate existential entanglements that link comparativists to their subject matters in ways that do not occur for physical chemists. That is the nature of religion: its study is often profoundly self-referential. These difficulties notwithstanding, we see no reasons to think that our bet on the future of our approach to comparison must necessarily lose. On the contrary, especially because of its promise for aiding a more critical, data-aware era of theory-building in religious studies and comparative theology, we have every reason to be hopeful.

Notes

1. First-person pronouns usually refer to Wildman and Neville and references to other members of the project will be made explicit.

2. Jonathan Z. Smith, "In Comparison a Magic Dwells," *Imagining Religion: From Babylon to Jonestown* (Chicago: University of Chicago Press, 1982). The paper was initially presented to the History of Judaism section of the American Academy of Religion, 1979.

3. There are many other ways of summarizing approaches to the study of religion and the comparison of religious ideas. In particular, see Eric J. Sharpe, *Comparative Religion: A History*, 2nd ed. (La Salle: Open Court, 1986); Helmer Ringgren, "Comparative Mythology," *Encyclopedia of Religion*, ed. Mircea Eliade (New York: Macmillan, 1987); Ninian Smart, "Comparative-Historical Method," ibid.; David Tracy, "Theology: Comparative Theology," ibid.; Walter H. Capps, *Religious Studies: The Making of a Discipline* (Minneapolis: Fortress Press, 1995); and Frank Clooney, *Seeing through*

Texts: Doing Theology among the Śrīvaiṣṇavas of South India (Albany: State University of New York Press, 1996).

4. Donald Wiebe, *Religion and Truth: Towards an Alternative Paradigm for the Study of Religion* (The Hague; New York: Mouton, 1981); and idem, *Beyond Legitimation: Essays on the Problem of Religious Knowledge* (New York: St. Martin's Press, 1994).

5. Wendy Doniger, *Women, Androgynes, and Other Mythical Beasts* (Chicago: University of Chicago Press, 1980); and idem, *Dreams, Illusion and Other Realities* (Chicago: University of Chicago Press, 1984).

6. David Eckel, *To See the Buddha: A Philosopher's Quest for the Meaning of Emptiness* (San Francisco: HarperCollins, 1992; reprint ed., Princeton: Princeton University Press, 1994).

7. Frank Clooney, op. cit.; idem, *Theology after Vedanta: An Experiment in Comparative Theology* (Albany: State University of New York Press, 1996).

8. Jonathan Z. Smith, *Imagining Religion*; and idem, *Map Is Not Territory* (Chicago: University of Chicago Press, 1978).

9. For example, Karl Rahner, "Christianity and the Non-Christian Religions," *Theological Investigations* 5 (Baltimore: Helicon Press, 1966), 115–134; Wolfhart Pannenberg, "Toward a Theology of the History of Religions," *Basic Questions in Theology*, vol. 2, trans. George H. Kehm (Philadelphia: Westminster, 1971), 65–118; and numerous others.

10. For example, Aldus Huxley, *The Perrenial Philosophy* (New York and London: Harper & Brothers, 1945); Frithjof Schuon, *The Transcendent Unity of Religions* (Wheaton, Ill.: The Theosophical Publishing House, 1984); and Huston Smith, *Forgotten Truth: The Common Vision of the World's Religions*, 2nd ed. (San Francisco: HarperSanFrancisco, 1992, first ed., 1965).

11. For example, Joseph Campbell, *The Masks of God*, 4 vols.: *Primitive Mythology, Oriental Mythology, Occidental Mythology, Creative Mythology* (New York: Viking Press, 1959–68); Mircea Eliade, *Cosmos and History: The Myth of the Eternal Return* (New York: Harper, 1959; first English ed., 1954); idem, *Myths, Dreams, and Mysteries* (New York: Harper, 1960); idem, *Images and Symbols* (New York: Sheed & Ward, 1961); idem, *The Sacred and the Profane: The Nature of Religion*, trans. Willard R. Trask (New York: Harcourt, Brace, 1959; Harper edition, 1961); idem, *Patterns in Comparative Religion: A Study of the Element of the Sacred in the History of Religious Phenomena*, trans. Rosemary Sheed (New York: Sheed and Ward, 1958); and idem, *A History of Religious Ideas*, 3 vols. (Chicago: University of Chicago Press, 1978–1985).

12. For example, John Hick, *An Interpretation of Religion: Human Responses to the Transcendent* (New Haven: Yale University Press, 1989).

13. James Frazer, *The Golden Bough* (New York: Macmillan, 1985); and idem, *Creation and Evolution in Primitive Cosmogonies and Other Pieces* (New York: Ayer, 1935); Herbert Spencer and Frederick Harrison, *The Nature*

and Reality of Religion: A Controversy Between Frederick Harrison and Herbert Spencer (New York: D. Appleton, 1885); and Edward Burnett Tylor, *Primitive Cultures: Researches into the Development of Mythology, Philosophy, Religion, Art, and Custom*, 2 vols. (London: Murray, 1873–74).

14. Emile Durkheim, *The Elementary Forms of the Religious Life*, trans. Joseph Ward Swain (New York: The Free Press; London: Collier Macmillan Publishers, 1965); Claude Lévi-Straus, *Totemism*, trans. Rodney Needham (Boston: Beacon Press, 1963); and idem, *Structural Anthropology* (Chicago: University of Chicago Press, 1976); Mary Douglas, *Natural Symbols: Explorations in Cosmology* (New York: Random House, 1972); and idem, *Implicit Meanings: Essays in Anthropology* (New York: Methuen, 1978).

15. Max Weber, *The Protestant Ethic and the Spirit of Capitalism*, trans. Talcott Parsons, 2nd ed. (New York: Charles Scribner's Sons, 1958; first English ed., 1930; first German ed., 1904–5); idem, *From Max Weber: Essays in Sociology*, ed. and trans. H. H. Gerth and C. Wright Mills (New York: Oxford University Press, 1946); idem, *The Religion of China*, trans. and ed. Hans H. Gerth (New York: Free Press, 1951); Clifford Geertz, *The Interpretation of Cultures* (New York: Basic Books, 1973); and idem, "Deep Play: Notes on the Balinese Cockfight," *Interpretive Social Science: A Reader*, ed. William M. Sullivan and Paul Rabinow (Berkeley: University of California Press, 1979); Peter Berger, *The Sacred Canopy: Elements of a Sociological Theory of Religion* (Garden City, N.Y.: Doubleday & Co., 1969); idem, ed., *The Other Side of God: A Polarity in World Religions* (Garden City, N.Y.: Doubleday & Co., 1981); and idem and Thomas Luckman, *Social Construction of Reality: A Treatise in the Sociology of Knowledge* (Garden City, N.Y.: Doubleday & Co., 1966).

16. Julian Jaynes, *The Origin of Consciousness in the Breakdown of the Bicameral Mind* (Boston: Houghton Mifflin Co., 1976); James B. Ashbrook, *The Human Mind and the Mind of God: Theological Promise in Brain Research* (Lanham: University Press of America, 1984); Eugene d'Aquili, Charles D. Laughlin, and J. McManus, *The Spectrum of Ritual: A Biogenetic Structural Analysis* (New York: Columbia University Press, 1979); Eugene d'Aquili and Andrew B. Newberg, "Religious and Mystical States: A Neuropsychological Model," *Zygon* 28.2 (1993): 177–99; and idem, "The Neuropsychological Basis of Religions, or Why God Won't Go Away," *Zygon* 33.2 (1998): 190–91.

17. Sigmund Freud, *The Future of an Illusion* (New York: W. W. Norton, 1975); idem, *Civilization and Its Discontents* (New York: W. W. Norton, 1984); Erik H. Erikson, *Young Man Luther: A Study in Psychoanalysis and History* (New York: W. W. Norton, 1958); and Ana-Maria Rizzuto, *The Birth of the Living God: A Psychoanalytic Study* (Chicago: University of Chicago Press, 1979).

18. Georg Wilhelm Friedrich Hegel, *Lectures on the Philosophy of Religion*, 3 vols., ed. Peter C. Hodgson (Berkeley: University of California Press, 1987); and Arnold Toynbee, *An Historian's Approach to Religion*, 2nd ed. (New York: Oxford University Press, 1979).

19. This criticism is made forcefully in Jonathan Z. Smith's, *Imagining Religion*.

20. E.g., Gerardus van der Leeuw, *Religion in Essence and Manifestation*, 2nd ed. with a foreword by Ninian Smart (Princeton: Princeton University Press, 1964); W. Bede Kristensen, *The Meaning of Religion: Lectures on the Phenomenology of Religion*, trans. John B. Carman (The Hague: Martinus Nijhoff, 1968); and Morris Jastrow, *The Study of Religion* (Atlanta: Scholars Press, 1981).

21. Sharpe, *Comparative Religion;* Ninian Smart, *The Phenomenon of Religion* (London: Macmillan, 1973); W. C. Smith, *Faith and Belief* (Princeton: Princeton University Press, 1979); and idem, *Towards a World Theology: Faith and the Comparative History of Religion* (Philadelphia: Westminster, 1981).

22. One of the most pervasive suppliers and reinforcers of comparative categories should be mentioned under this heading, though it is less systematic than any of the examples so far mentioned: the almost universally used classification system of the United States Library of Congress (see Library of Congress, *Library of Congress Classification Schedules: Class B, Subclasses BL, BM, BP, BQ. Religion: Religions, Hinduism, Judaism, Islam, Buddhism*, ed. Rita Runchock and Kathleen Droste [Washington, D.C.: Library of Congress, Processing Services, Subject Cataloguing Division, 1992]).

23. Rudolf Otto, *The Idea of the Holy: An Inquiry into the Non-Rational Factor in the Idea of the Divine and its Relation to the Rational*, 3rd ed. (London: Oxford University Press, 1925); and Paul Ricoeur, *The Symbolism of Evil*, trans. Emerson Buchanan (Boston: Beacon Press, 1969).

24. See Walter Watson, *The Architectonics of Meaning: Foundations of the New Pluralism* (Albany: State University of New York Press, 1985); David A. Dilworth, *Philosophy in World Perspective: A Comparative Hermeneutic of the Major Theories* (New Haven: Yale University Press, 1989); and Paul Tillich, *Systematic Theology*, Vol. 1 (Chicago: University of Chicago Press, 1951).

25. See Edmund Husserl, *Ideas: A General Introduction to Pure Phenomenology*, trans. W. R. Boyce Gibson (New York: Macmillan, 1962); and idem., *The Crisis of European Sciences and Transcendental Phenomenology: An Introduction to Phenomenological Philosophy* (Evanston: Northwestern University Press, 1970).

26. D. C. Dennett, "A Method for Phenomenology," *Consciousness Explained* (Boston: Little, Brown and Company, 1991), 66–98.

27. For one account of how neurophysiology might make such a contribution, see Wesley Wildman and Leslie A. Brothers, "A Neuropsychological-Semiotic Model of Religious Experiences," *Neuroscience and the Person: Scientific Perspectives on Divine Action*, ed. Robert John Russell, Nancey Murphy, Theo Meyering, and Michael Arbib (Vatican City State and Berkeley, Cal.: Vatican Observatory and Center for Theology and the Natural Sciences, 2000).

28. Important elements are mentioned in chapter 8, a summary and fuller account is furnished in several parts of *The Human Condition*, and a detailed

presentation may be found in Robert Cummings Neville, *Normative Cultures* (Albany: State University of New York Press, 1995), and idem, *The Truth of Broken Symbols* (Albany: State University of New York Press, 1996).

29. See Imre Lakatos, "Falsification and the Methodology of Scientific Research Programmes," *Criticism and the Growth of Knowledge*, ed. Imre Lakatos and Alan Musgrave (Cambridge and New York: Cambridge University Press, 1970).

30. Thomas S. Kuhn, *The Structure of Scientific Revolutions*, 2nd ed. (Chicago: University of Chicago Press, 1962).

31. See Paul K. Feyerabend, *Against Method*, 3rd ed. (London, New York: Verso, 1993).

32. See John Henry Newman, *An Essay in Aid of a Grammar of Assent* (Notre Dame, Ind.: University of Notre Dame, 1979).

33. See Karl Popper, *The Logic of Scientific Discovery,* 3rd ed. (New York: Basic Books, 1968).

34. Lakatosian research programs have been proposed as models for the study of religion in Philip Clayton, *Explanation from Physics to Theology: An Essay in Rationality and Religion* (New Haven: Yale University Press, 1989); and Nancey Murphy, *Theology in the Age of Scientific Reasoning* (Ithaca and London: Cornell University Press, 1989). They are used in Wesley Wildman, *Fidelity with Plausibility: Modest Christologies in the Twentieth Century* (Albany: State University of New York Press, 1998).

35. See Charles S. Peirce, "The Fixation of Belief," *Strands of a System: The Philosophy of Charles Peirce*, ed. Douglas R. Anderson (West Lafayette, Ind.: Purdue University Press, 1995); and John Dewey, *Logic: The Theory of Inquiry* (New York: Henry Holt, 1938).

36. See Charles S. Peirce, *Essays in the Philosophy of Science*, ed. with an introduction by Vincent Tomas (Indianapolis: Bobbs-Merrill, 1957).

37. On this matter, see the discussion in *The Human Condition*, chap. 8, and Robert Neville, *Normative Cultures*, 74–84.

38. Huston Smith, *Forgottten Truth*, 21.

39. Ibid., 25.

10

The Idea of Categories in Historical Comparative Perspective

John H. Berthrong

❦

10.1 Introduction

The history of the development of categories and theories about catego-real (*categoreal* pertains to categories per se; *categorical* pertains to a quality of a category, such as Kant's *categorical imperative*) thinking is a vast topic, yet each history has a beginning as a product of human judgment about the world. Notwithstanding the vastness of the topic in space, ideas, and time, the notes included here with the volume on ultimate realities are not quite as random as they might appear at first glance. They were actually generated as part of the seminars on the six specific religious traditions. While the main topic under consideration was how adherents in the six cumulative religious traditions thought about ultimate realities, a subtheme for all the discussions was the role categories played in these traditions. How did each tradition deal with the second-order nature of categoreal thinking? How did their theories of categories affect their reflections on the human predicament?

One of the most perplexing questions for anyone who considers the form of inquiry designated as the comparative study of religion is: What is to be compared? One of the things that became clear to our seminar was that we were, quite self-consciously, committed to the comparison of religious ideas. The practice of the seminar was to traffic in the domain of concepts as second-order reflections on primary religious complexes. Because concepts are themselves material of a comparative nature from within a specific religious tradition, we were actually producing a third-order comparison between and among the traditions we choose to compare. As always, one of the pressing questions was, how do we translate from one cross-cultural and cross-temporal categoreal domain to another? At least one condition that made such comparison and translation possible is the fact that the concepts we extracted from the various traditions were themselves already comparative, having been generated by the interactions of people, texts, rituals, cultural sensibilities, and the vagaries of history and local custom.

The first obvious way in which the topic was circumscribed was to focus on the cultural regions of West, South, and East Asia and their great historic religious movements. From West Asia were Judaism, Christianity, and Islam. From South Asia were Buddhism and Hinduism, and from East Asia, the various Chinese religious traditions. The reason for not differentiating the historic patrimonies of Daoism and Confucianism should have been made clear by Kohn's comments about the general nature of Chinese religion as a unified set of cultural sensibilities. Kohn argues, and this is generally accepted by most students of the history of religion in China, that there is a prototypical from of basic Chinese religion and that traditions such as Daoism and Confucianism are specialized variations on a common thematic base. Because of this regional organizational scheme, the essay on the history of categories reviews material from West Asia, South Asia, East Asia, and then, for the modern period, the peninsular world of Western Europe and North America. The inclusion of the example of category formation theory based on modern linguistic and cognitive science was included because it represents the modern Western Enlightenment viewpoint. Wilfred Cantwell Smith has argued at length that in any discussion of the religions of the world we must include the rational project of the Enlightenment as a distinct form of religious sensibility and not merely assume that it is part of the Christian tradition. It represents a different set of assumptions and is probably the dominant modern mode of intellectual discourse, even when subjected to the harshest forms of criticism. It is the reigning paradigm for what constitutes categoreal reality.

Each member of the seminar provided information he or she deemed appropriate about their specific tradition. As a member without a specific religious portfolio, I became intrigued about how concepts had come to be proposed historically within each of the three major regional areas. My contribution to the flow of the conversation at the meetings was, from time to time, to present the nuggets of my researches into the history of category formation as it pertained to the ebb and flow of the life of the seminar.

One of the stated aims of the seminar was to coax students of religious studies to explore the pleasures of cooperative research. It has been commonly observed that our colleagues in the social and physical sciences routinely work together in groups. Those of us laboring in the humanities tend to work alone in the isolation of our studies and only share our research through formal papers and publications. We also included graduate students attached to each specialist in order to demonstrate that humanists could work collectively. I believe that we were successful; others will have to judge my conviction by reading the results of our collective labors.

10.2 Categories as Intellectual Constructs

The idea of a category is a highly abstract intellectual form celebrated in many philosophic cultures as a highly venerable conceptual achievement. Categories appeared within the philosophic traditions of Eurasia after the initial phases of philosophic and religious thought had developed into mature forms, and then only as a true child of abstraction. Along with being a highly self-reflexive beast, a category is almost always a hermeneutical one, at least, when hermeneutics is understood as interpretation theory. Categories are hermeneutical signs that point in all kinds of directions, as we shall see.

Categories, like the hero of myth, are creatures with thousands of faces. Each of the great philosophic cultures of Europe and West, South, and East Asian have contributed to the grand storehouse of global categoreal thinking. As with so many other aspects of human reflection on second-order or hermeneutic thought, that is, forms of thought about thought, categories reflect their points of origin. Nonetheless, the paradigmatic thinkers of these four cultural regions believed that their categories qua conceptual structures for dealing with the world were natural and helped to define how the world really is and how it can be understood through experience, meditation, and inquiry. Neville and Wildman will try to convince any reader of these chapters of this fact about the use of categories.

When Zhu Xi (1130–1200) assumed that everything is composed of *qi* (*ch'i*) or matter-energy as structured by *li* or form and that both *qi* and *li* were integrated by the mind-heart or *xin* into the full object-event of his mature cosmology, he truly believed that this was as much the case for the barbarians beyond the Middle Kingdom as it was for any cultivated Song dynasty literatus. A philosopher's or theologian's favorite categories often expressed their most deeply held cultural sensibilities about the order and structure of the world and how this ought to be expressed in an appropriate form of discourse. In Zhu's terms, categories are fully historical and cultural object-events. The categories also exhibited internally their possibilities of being intelligible as objects of cognition. For instance, some of the perennial favorites for universality were always categories dealing with being, non-being, actuality, reality, nothingness, and emptiness.

Nonetheless, it is not entirely clear that the notion of a category is a happy idea for many philosophers to contemplate because of its range and inescapable sensibility of secondhandness. Bertrand Russell, surely writing for many exasperated thinkers over the centuries, notes

> What, exactly, is meant by the word "category," whether in Aristotle or in Kant and Hegel, I confess that I have never been able to understand. I do not myself believe that the term "category" is any way useful in philosophy, as representing any clear idea. There are, in Aristotle, ten categories: substance, quantity, quality, relation, place, time, position, state, action, and affection. The only definition offered of the term "category" is "expressions which are in no way composite signify"—and then follows the above list. This seems to mean that every word of which the meaning is not compounded of the meanings of other words signifies a substance or quantity or etc. There is no suggestion of any principle on which the list of ten categories has been compiled.[1]

Wang Yangming, the great Ming Neo-Confucian, often made the same kind of comments about Zhu Xi's desire to have an appropriate category or principle for every situation when Wang was convinced that such categoreal obsession kept Zhu from really dealing with the realization of the ultimate goodness of the mind-heart. Nonetheless, as Kohn's chapter demonstrates, all of these Confucian reflections are variations on a general Chinese sensibility about categories.

Such observations about the abstract, lifeless nature of categories can be interpreted in a number of ways. First, it could simply be that we make use of categories as we find them and that there is no ultimate or ontological reason for our list of categories. This kind of conventional view of categories fits neatly with many reflective Confucian interpretations of categoreal thinking beginning with Xunzi at the end of the Warring States period in classical China. Second, it could also be the case that we simply have not thought clearly enough about what we mean by category. For instance, the great Korean Neo-Confucian Yi T'oegye mounted a spirited and sophisticated defense of Zhu Xi's concept of *li*/principle as a living idea rather than a dead abstraction and therefore demonstrated that Zhu's category was correct though in need of further elaboration. In either case, when the discussion of categories and their comparisons is carried out in a global perspective, the difficulties multiply nonetheless. Perhaps the best that can be done is to try to be as critically self-conscious about the categories we use for cross-cultural comparison as possible because there is more art than science involved in the beginning of any new intellectual discipline such as comparative philosophy or theology.

Ernest Gellner, without sharing Russell's intense distaste for categories, maintains that categories are social creations generated by a powerful human compulsions that make them highly ambiguous intellectual property.[2] "Mankind lives and thinks conceptually. Concepts are communally shared inner compulsions. They are linked to external tokens, and to external conditions of deployment."[3] For instance, Gellner tries to show how the very idea of reason itself is a social concept, an intellectual compulsion of a particular sort though one with a universal range once any society learns to embrace both Durkheim's idea of ritual as the font of all our categories and Weber's expansion of this Durkheimian insight into the very origin of order qua reason in the modern West. As well as being reflective concepts are completely social creatures.

Raimon Panikkar, speaking for the perennialist tradition, also agrees that categories are a second-order creation of the human mind. In fact, Panikkar argues that concepts are creations of culture, or "the substitution of things by objects."[4]

For Panikkar, objects or concepts are a reflection of states of consciousness or fields of awareness; they are human social creations. "Since Socrates in the western world and Sāmkhya in the Indic scene, the *concept* has taken an upper hand over all other states of consciousness. Now, concepts are a special kind of objects. They are the rational distillate, as it were, of those states of consciousness which allow themselves to be classified as intelligible units."[5] For Panikkar, the reign of the concept is not always a success, although in his case there is no way for humankind to avoid the use of categories because they are the intellectual bricks of the historical cathedrals of human interaction with the divine reality. The best we can have, according to Panikkar, is a kind of fully rational second innocence about the world as a manifestation of divine love. The trick will be to make the best use possible of these irreplaceable social objects.

Moreover, the reflective study of the comparison of categories is yet another stage removed from the creation of the categories themselves between and among world cultures. It is a third-order hermeneutic moment. Walter Watson and David Dilworth, having developed an architectonics of meanings based on their own comparative philosophy of interpretation, suggest that such theorizing is appropriate because we now live in a globally hermeneutic age.[6] Watson argues that philosophy, or at least Western philosophy, goes through three regular if not predictable stages of conceptual reflection. The first is what Watson calls the ontic stage. This is the period wherein philosophers ask about what it means to be and invent fundamental ontologies to represent being as ultimate reality. Of course, the answer to the question of being is diverse, ranging from the Sophists' definition of man [sic] as the measure of all things to Plato's dream of the idea of the good.

The next stage is what Watson calls the epistemic. The interest of the philosophers changes from asking about the fundamental nature of being to questions concerning how we can know being at all. And finally, in the third phase, philosophers begin to ask semantic or hermeneutical questions of meaning. For instance, in reviewing the work of the first two phases, semantic or hermeneutically minded philosophers try to figure out what is being said about being and knowledge and to find ways to coordinate the teachings of the various schools under interpretation. Watson notes that post-Enlightenment Western philosophy follows much the same pattern, moving from an ontological inquiry concerning the true nature of nature, to reflections by Kant about how we can know any of this, only to end with the wonderfully hermeneutic twists and turns of linguistic or analytic philosophy. Watson quotes a delightful passage from G. E. Moore that makes the point about the semantic nature of linguistic philosophy. Moore is recounting how he became interested in philosophy and suggests he came to philosophy not by any scientific interest in the nature of things but rather through a curiosity about what philosophers said about these things.[7]

David Dilworth expands Watson's range of texts to include many more Asian classics in order to illustrate how all global philosophic texts can be addressed by the comparative methodology embodied in the architectonics of meaning. For instance, a case could be made in the Confucian tradition for an analogous movement from ontic, epistemic, and semantic or hermeneutical modes of discourse. In the unfolding of Confucianism, we have first the world of Confucius and Mencius and their definition of the really real as ethical human conduct rather than to the elaboration of being as the abstract definition of the ten thousand things (only the Mohists wanted to even think about such a venture in classical China). The Confucian case proves that some ontological commitments can be other than abstract things-in-themselves or atoms in the void. Later classical Confucians, such as Xunzi, add an epistemic element to Confucian social ethics or fundamental axiology even though he was nervous about doing so because the great epistemologists of classical China, upon whom he built his own theories, were Mohists and Daoists like Zhuangzi, hardly good philosophic company for Confucian gentlemen. The classical period ends with the refined and complicated hermeneutical arts of Dung Zhongshu in the Western Han dynasty. One could further argue that the Neo-Daoists and then the Buddhists began the cycle all over by again returning to the fundamental questions of ontology, cosmology, and metaphysics.

Of course, Watson's and Dilworth's architectonics of meaning depends upon one of the classic semantic sequencing of the Western intellectual tradition, namely, Aristotle's attempt to comprehend his previous Greek philosophic heritage. Watson and Dilworth make the point, and it is a good one, that one can do much worse than Aristotle when thinking about comparative hermeneutic methodologies. Their argument hinges on the fact that Aristotle was self-reflexive in his awareness of the rich diversity of the Greek philosophic tradition. Along with all his other interests, Aristotle provided a semantic or hermeneutical reading of the tradition that ordered its parts according to his own understanding of reality. One must start somewhere in the task of making comparisons and, if we are honest, we will confess that we start from where we ourselves are. In this regard we begin as Aristotle did, with the history of philosophy and theology; the great difference is that our world of comparison is now the whole history of world discourse and not just the history of Greek, Greco-Roman, Christian, Jewish, Muslim, and modern Western thought. As the chapters by Fredriksen and Haq illustrate, the influence of Aristotle's mode of category generation lives on in the Christian and Islamic worlds.

When Aristotle began to wonder about his ten categories of substance, quantity, quality, relative, place, time, position, having, doing or being affected, when Rabbis worry about whether it is lawful to cat catfish or shark in Toronto, when ancient Chinese sophists tried to evade paying import taxes on horses at border crossings by explaining that a white horse is really not a horse at all, when Indian rishis worried about the relationship of ritual action to being and non-being, and when modern analytic philosophers worry about the fact that most of these ideas are category mistakes, they are all taking part in the cherished pastime of the construction and deconstruction of categories.

In Aristotle's case the generation of the categories came from the flow his general philosophic project and most specifically from his question concerning "what being is." Aristotle called this a form of first philosophy and it later became known as ontology or the science of being qua being. According to Aristotle we can discuss the question of being by means of ten modes of predication or what we now designate as the ten categories. In fact, one of the chief functions of categories in all the Eurasian cultural regions is to provide a means of talking about or defining that which is or the things that specific that which is even if we cannot precisely define the ultimate characteristics of being qua being (or nothingness or emptiness if you are a Daoist or a Buddhist). As we shall see, other enduring cultural families of categories arise out of similar philosophic projects, such as the Chinese desire to classify the entities found in the natural world and the Indic inclination to discover how speech and thought are correlated.

While it has been common, as we noted above, to conjoin a theory of being with a theory of categories, this perhaps oversimplifies Aristotle's approach to categories. The problem that Aristotle was dealing with was the need to discover a way to correlate the ultimate genera of being with the most basic forms of predication. It was fairly easy to see how one could then interpret that categories as ultimate predicates that served as ultimate markers for being. As with so many other terms pressed into philosophic service, John P. Anton notes that the original Greek word for category was taken from the legal lexicon and meant to accuse someone. What Aristotle did was to take the legal term and give it a philosophic meaning to predicate or "assert something of something."[8]

If Aristotle's list of ten categories seems overly large, it is important to remember that Aristotle was more worried about the fact that many of his predecessors had too few categories than that his own list might be too long. What Aristotle was trying to do was to develop both logic and philosophy in order to describe and understand reality. Anton takes Aristotle to be about the formation of a theory of categories such that "the rules of correct and ultimate types of assertions" demonstrate a correspondence between these assertions and what truly and really is.[9] "The logical function of a theory of categories is to specify the schemata and rules of correct attribution and predication. The task calls for the careful identification of the genera of being in order to exhibit their legitimate function as predicates."[10] Ultimately Anton argues that Aristotle took categories to mean "well formed statements made according to canons and, to be more precise, to fundamental types of predication conforming to rules sustained by the ways of beings."[11] Hence the classification of things in the world could then belong to the other forms of inquiry into the world that were part of Aristotle's complex mode of philosophic discovery. Asking questions is always connected to our favorite lists of categories.

One of the things that follows from Aristotle's theory of categories is that the proper use of categories will obviously help us organize our thought and that well-formed categories cannot be substituted for other kinds of integrations of the world of second-order reflections. Whatever else categories do for Aristotle, they do not indicate simple things but point to a very complex form of human activity. If we move our focus to India, we also see that while categories point to some fundamental ways to seeing the world, there is really nothing simple about their formation. As we shall see in the Indian case, the generation of theories of categories also arises out of ontology.

Before looking at Indian and specifically Hindu notions of categories, there is the further complication concerning the relationship of classical Hindu theories of categories when compared with Buddhist thinkers. It is always good to remember that a great deal of orthodox Hindu thought was developed in a constant dialogue with Buddhism. The problem for historical analysis is the notorious lack of independent historical material for figuring who influenced whom in early Indian thought. However, it is fairly clear that early Buddhist Abhidharma theorists were interested in establishing schemes of enumeration and classification as complicated as any proposed by their Hindu opponents. The interaction of Buddhist and Hindu categoreal worldviews became more and move evident during the discussions of the papers by Clooney and Eckel. In terms of their religious significance, no other cultural region places more emphasis on the worth of categoreal reflection than the traditions deriving from the South Asian matrix.

A considerable case could be made for the coterminous genesis of Buddhist philosophy and the careful articulation of a theory of categories. The Buddhist Four Noble Truths are an excellent example of how a tradition with analytic inclinations goes about diagnosing the human condition in terms of suffering, the reason for suffering, that suffering can be overcome and the way to free oneself from suffering through the Eightfold Path. Of course, the Buddhists were asking very different kinds of questions about the nature of categories. As Paul Williams writes, "The main concern of the Abhidharma, at least as it was systematized by Buddhist scholars, is the analysis of the totality, of all that is, into the building blocks which, through different combinations, we construct into our world."[12] The name given to this ultimate set of building blocks was dharmas. According to the Theravāda tradition there are eighty-one conditioned dharmas and one unconditioned dharma.[13]

David J. Kalupahana is quick to point out that the early Buddhist thinkers did not think of these dharmas as things in themselves, but rather more like the various relations that make up the world. The nexus out of which the Abhidharma developed its categories was its theory of relations. "The enumeration and classification of concepts in order to determine their relative meanings and applications without accommodating any form of absolutism, thereby establishing their non-substantiality (*anattā*), is followed by an exhaustive description of the Buddha's positive teaching, namely, dependent arising (*pratītyasamutpāda*)."[14] The Abhidharmikas were driven by a penchant to analyze and discriminate various states of consciousness, to organize and classify these events and states. As Kalupahana and Alfonso Verdu note, if they had not carried out this classification, then they would have been left with a huge jumble of disconnected events. What drives the Abhidharma search for an analysis of the dharmic relationships is the desire to show how all the various elements do relate to each other. In order to do so they linked the major sets of categories found in the early texts such as aggregates, the faculties, the elements of consciousness, and the Four Noble Truths.

Juniro Takakusu provides us with charts of all the various elements and categories of the Abhidharma and Yogācāra schools.[15] The Yogācāra expand the earlier Theravāda lists and end up with one hundred dharmas or elements of existence. In their case, the final, non-created dharma is true suchness itself. According to the Yogācāra there are five major classifications of the dharmas, namely, mind, mental functions, form-elements, things not associated with the mind (such as impermanence, becoming, distinction, union, speed, etc.), and the non-created elements (along with true suchness, this includes space, extinction, etc.).

The earlier Abhidharma School also had five major classifications for the dharmas, namely forms, mind, concomitant mental faculties, elements neither substantial forms nor mental functions (such as acquisition, annihilation, life, birth, death, stability, decay, etc.) and non-created elements (such as space, etc.). This particular list is taken from Vasubandhu's formulation of the theory of dharmas. According to this school, as Takakusu interprets it, the early Buddhist scholiasts were basically refuting certain pan-Indian ideas about the existence of enduring entities by means of their dharmic analysis of sensation. This was a quasi-atomic theory of reality such that "All elements or *dharmas* which constitute momentary sense-data and thought-data were enumerated by the Realistic School, perhaps for the first time in the history of Indian philosophy."[16] But as with so many other forms of Indian Buddhist thought, the entire complicated dharmic world is connected by the various causal relations that obtain between the dharmas.

On the orthodox Hindu side, a characteristic classical Indian theory of categories was developed by the Vaiśeṣika School, perhaps the most category sensitive of the early orthodox Indian philosophic schools. As Wilhelm Halbfass argues, in the Vaiśeṣika system the notion of a category and what really is are always linked.[17] "The basic claim is that all entities can be listed and classified under certain fundamental 'titles' or 'categories' (*padārtha*)."[18] If the Buddhists are always concerned with finding causal relationships, what is crucial for the Vaiśeṣika thinkers is to find a proper place for everything that is within their categoreal schema as expressions of what is. In the case of the Vaiśeṣika there are six rather than ten basic Aristotelian categories. The six are substance, quality, motion, universal, particularity, and inherence. And each of the six fundamental categories can be then broken down into lists of various subcategories. However, in some variant Vaiśeṣika thinkers the six categories are augmented with four more, making for ten categories just like in Aristotle. The additional proposed categories are universality per se as existence, potentiality, non-potentiality, and non-being.

According to Halbfass, the Vaiśeṣika thinkers argued that their list of categories "are the most comprehensive units of enumeration, the ultimate divisions of reality, and the most basic correlates of thought and speech."[19] What strikes an outsider to classical Indian philosophy and religion is the persistent theme of trying to find a way to link speech and thought as a fundamental motif of all Indian systems. Of course, this makes sense because one of the continuous tasks of the various orthodox Hindu systematicians was to reflect on the correlation of language with the sacred texts. If, as was often the case, these sacred texts were taken to present reality, then there was a great need to uncover the relationship of text as revealed speech to the other structures of reality.

Just as with their Buddhist compatriots in the Abhidharma School, the Vaiśeṣika had complicated lists of subcategories for classification. For example, the category of quality or *guṇa* is subdivided into twenty-four different traits. These are "color, taste, and touch; number, dimension, separateness (*pṛthaktva*), conjunction, and disjunction; proximity (i.e., priority in space or time) and distance (posteriority); cognition, pleasure, pain, desire, aversion, and effort; gravity, liquidity, disposition (*saṁkāra*); merit and demerit (i.e., good and bad karma); and sound."[20] According to Halbfass, some of these qualities are primordial whereas some are merely momentary; some are individual and some are always found in conjunction with other qualities.

In some ways both the Buddhist and Vaiśeṣika category lists remind one of perhaps the most famous of Asian classification systems, the Chinese *Yijing* or *Book of Changes*. Joseph Needham, the great historian of Chinese science, once likened the *Yijing* to a grand Victorian roll-top desk with many drawers and small storage boxes. There was a space for everything and everything in its proper place in the capriciousness of the huge oak or teak desk. The *Yijing* functioned as a huge and orderly desk for many Chinese intellectuals in providing a way to organize what the Chinese call the ten thousand things of the world.

However, the *Book of Changes*, or at least in those parts expressing the fundamental categories of Chinese thought, are considered by the scholarly community to be rather late additions to the earliest layers of the text, sometimes perhaps even creations of the Western Han dynasty cosmologists. However, there are a number of ways to approaching Chinese categoreal thinking prior to the formation of the *Yijing*. As with so many things Eurasian, the Chinese do not always share the patterns of thought found in early Greek and Indian thought. For instance, the whole question of being qua fundamental ontology that so dominates both Greek and Indian thought is largely absent from early Chinese speculation about the world. Nonetheless, the Chinese were as eager and able to think in terms of categories as second-order patterns of thought as anyone else was.

Without a doubt the notions of yin and yang and the five phases emerge as the most important set of categories by the end of the classical period and with the rise of the Han dynasty. One of the problems with giving an account of the rise of Chinese categoreal thinking is that no one person or school comes to dominate the scene as Aristotle did for Western thought. There were a plethora of names associated with Chinese category formation. In fact, many Chinese revered Confucius himself as the author and editor of much of the Confucian canon itself (at least after the early Han where Confucius's authorship is first recorded in *The Records of the Grand Historian*), including the late Chou or early Han texts known as the ten wings or commentaries of the *Yijing*.

Yet there is something coherent or at least persistent that lies behind almost all the classic formulations of yin-yang and the five phases cosmologies. The five phases are fire, metal, wood, soil, and water.[21] The noted American philosopher Stephen Pepper argued that every philosopher has a guiding root metaphor that describes the way she or her organizes their philosophic vision. For instance, someone like Newton might see the world as a vast machine whereas Aristotle might have a more organic, vitalistic idea of how things work, more along the famous example of the acorn that finally grows into the might oak tree. In this case the Chinese cosmological root metaphor has been called correlative thinking or an arise/respond interaction model of how things behave. It has also been called a relational view of reality in that each and every item of the cosmos is linked to every other item and in fact helps to co-constitute all that is. The responsive metaphor of vital connection or *ganying* is often traced to the *Lüshi chunqiu* (c. 240 BCE) and even more definitively in the *Xunzi* of a generation later. Kohn makes the strong argument that all forms of Chinese thought represent one grand cosmological schema organized around a number of familiar categories such as yin and yang.

A. C. Graham, who taught us more about early Chinese logic and categoreal thinking than anyone else, suggested that we can learn a great deal about Chinese category formation from looking a how the early

Chinese made use of their language.[22] Of course, in this regard Graham, following Beneveniste, noticed that Aristotle linked his categories to Greek grammatical forms, especially forms for the first six categories and the various classical Greek voices and tenses. The classical Chinese thinkers were prone to do the same sort of thing, but in their cases they asked a different set of questions, the kind, Graham argues, that were allowed for when reflecting on how the classical Chinese language works. Hence, "Aristotle is guided by grammatical voice to the categories of action and passion. In Chinese philosophy the great categoreal distinction among processes is between *gan* 'arousal' and *ying* 'response', the activating and activated processes distinguished by the syntax of the ergative verb."[23] Of course, Graham never argues that a philosophic culture is strictly determined by its deep grammar and syntax. But Graham does submit that archaic Chinese language forms, just as with Aristotle, did help classical Chinese philosophers frame their categoreal schemes when they began reflecting on the relationship of language and reality.

For instance, the grand question of being is handled differently in Chinese because there is simply nothing in archaic or classical Chinese grammar that resembles the particularities of the pan-Indo-European verb 'to be'. The Chinese employ different sets of verbs to deal with the copulative functions of 'to be' and the existential verb of being. Hence Graham argues that it is pointless to search for Being in Chinese thought but more fruitful to ask how the Chinese thinkers talk about the various verbs that can stand in a nominal position. So we find the three pairs of *ran* or 'is-so' and *fou* 'is-not-so', *shi* 'is-this' and *fei* 'is-not' and *you* 'have' and *wu* 'have not'. In one of his delightful essays, Graham shows us how hard it was for the early Chinese translators to deal with Hamlet's famous question "to be or not to be" in all its literary richness and ambiguity simply because Chinese verb structure forced them to make certain specific choices about how to express the Danish prince's existential anguish.

As with so many other traditions of categoreal formation, the concepts that come to dominate the rest of Chinese philosophic history only stabilize fairly late. One of the reasons for this, which Graham and other scholars of the period note, is that cosmological speculation only enters the mainstream of Confucian philosophy at the end of the classical period or early in the Han period. If we count the beginning of the classical period with Confucius, then it would be fair to say that the main issues, at least as they are preserved in the surviving Confucian texts, deal with question of personal and social life; these are the grand questions of how to be a human being among other human beings and how to organize society so that civilization will flourish—or to escape from the dangerous and warlike Chinese world entirely and retreat into a dream of a simpler,

250 ⌒ *Categories in Perspective*

more spontaneous time if one is a Daoist rather than a Confucian, Mohist, or Legalist. Only later do we see material from works like the *Lüshi chunqiu* and the *Guanzi* that reflect other, cosmological concerns. It is from these schools of thought, often connected with medical lore, that the persistent vocabulary of the classical Chinese categories arose. As we have already seen, the most famous of these are yin-yang and the five phases.

The correlative metaphors and the theme of responsiveness/reciprocity pervade all later Chinese categoreal thinking, albeit in less vague and more specific senses tailored to the needs of the particular schools. For instance, the ideas of correlation and responsiveness become the Confucian ideal of reciprocity. The most primordial of Confucian virtues, *ren* or humaneness, is given a folk etymology that shows how this works. It is commonly understood that the graph for humaneness derives from two component, one indicating the graph for a human being and the other being the graph for the numeral two. The folk interpretation is that humaneness expresses the simple yet infinitely complex set of relationships that people have with each other. In terms of ultimate correlative relationality the *Doctrine of the Mean* states that heaven, earth, and humanity form a triad that is only complete if and only if all three elements are properly related. In terms of the pan-Chinese categoreal system, these relationships are then charted by means of the balance of yin and yang and the movement and interaction of the five phases.

One of the most characteristic technical forms of classical Chinese thinking about categories comes from the later Mohist School, probably the only school of thought in ancient China given to intense speculation about concepts and disputation. In the terms of Mohist logic, which was incorporated by Xunzi for Confucian use, when we give a name to something we often then extend the name of the known object to another object we judge to be the same. "By the Mohist theory of naming, you call an object 'horse' and extend the name to another which is like it, the same in kind (*lei*)."[24] The means by which this analogical extension or matching is conducted is described by the later Mohists as one of 'extending from kind to kind' or *tuilei*. As A. C. Graham put it,

> The West, after seeking necessary truths by logic for some 2,000 years, becomes aware of questionable assimilations and differentiations behind the formulation of the questions themselves, and discovers that instead of refuting a proposition you can undermine it by uncovering implicit paradigms and unnoticed distinctions.[25]

In terms of the study of comparative ideas, this is a good description of vague and then specific categories. We move from collecting the charac-

teristics of something and then push on to something else. If we are successful in our collecting and pushing on, then we are successful, from the
Mohist viewpoint, in our procedures for correlative cosmologies.

As with so many other comparative enterprises, the Chinese case is instructive because it was developed independently of any significant interaction with the rest of Eurasia till after the arrival of Buddhism in the
later stages of the Han dynasty. Yet the Chinese do what the other cultures have done as well. The Mohists and Confucians, in particular,
begin by classifying things by means of their characteristic features and
give them a name, such as horse, white, good, wrong, appropriate, useful, lawful, and so on. Categories serve as means of classification and
naming and then are used to extend from the already classified and
named to what has not been given a name or only shares part of a name
with something else. Jonathan Z. Smith was correct in noting that a certain form of magic resides in the art of comparison.[26] But magic can be
good or evil; good comparisons move from the vague to the specific and
are wonderful examples of what the Mohists and Xunzi would call extending from kind to kind.

10.3 Fast Forward to the Modern World

The examples of theories of category formation we have reviewed were
all taken from characteristic religious and philosophic traditions of the
great axial age cultures of Eurasia.[27] By reviewing the history of Eurasian
philosophy and theology it is manifest that the rise of these great systems
did not mark the end of the development of categories or thinking about
how categories are fashioned and how they function in intellectual discourse. Time marched on. Furthermore, with the rise and expansion of
European modernity and the spread of the Enlightenment project around
the world, there has been a concomitant increase of exchange between
and among cultures previously only indirectly influenced by developments in each regional area. North Atlantic, South Asian, and East Asian
philosophers, theologians, anthropologists, sociologists, historians, psy-
chologists, cognitive scientists, and linguists are busy studying each other
as never before in the history of the world. What began as a trickle of
orientalism in the mid-nineteenth century has become a torrent of intercultural studies at the end of the twentieth century.

It is clearly impossible to review even a modicum of the vast amount of
material generated about categories and their systems. Many of the other
chapters show how this is the case in terms of the study of specific terms
of their thematic and historical presentations. For instance, in a number

252 ⌐ Categories in Perspective

of cases the authors employ Robert C. Neville's notion of vague and specific categorization as a method to explore their specific comparisons of
the theme of the human condition in the world religions. Neville's work
represents, among other things, a modern reconstruction and extension
of Platonic sensibilities that connects these classical speculative concerns
via the semiotics of Charles S. Peirce, with contemporary theories about
categorization and cultures.[28] Neville's theory of vague categories provides space for a post-Enlightenment view of the role of reason as well as
interest in cross-cultural comparison as a means for giving more concrete
shape to the categories we use to describe religious phenomena.[29] Neville
provides the readers with a review of his theory of categories in the various introductory and concluding chapters he wrote in collaboration with
Wesley Wildman for the seminar.

However, rather than repeating Neville's own arguments about reason, categories, and comparison, we will sample the collaborative work
of a linguist and philosopher, George Lakoff and Mark Johnson, in
order to compare and contrast classical category formation theory with
a decidedly modernist approach.[30] While not embracing the notion of
postmodernism, neo-pragmatism, or any of the other host of contemporary North Atlantic attempts to restore or deconstruct the modern Enlightenment program, Lakoff and Johnson have employed contemporary
empirical studies in linguistics and cognitive science to construct an alternative model to what they characterize as the classical Western view
of categories. It is here, in theories about narratives, metaphors, and prototypes, that the voice of the classical Rabbinic traditions of Judaism
comes through in their demand for concrete specifics of time, place, and
people. Saldarini and Fredriksen reminded the seminar of these kinds of
categoreal thinking qua metaphors and textual exegesis in Judaism and
Christianity.

Lakoff and Johnson, following philosophers such as Richard Bernstein and Richard Rorty, call this dominant model of Western reflection
on categories the objectivist model. In constructing their alternative to
objectivism, the root metaphor of Lakoff and Johnson is the metaphor itself as a fundamental key to the reasoning process of human beings as
embodied, linguistic, historical, and social creatures.[31] They assert that
our lives and the worlds we live in are shaped by metaphorical, imaginative, and embodied thinking that is much richer than mere technical rationalism. But we need to be clear that Lakoff and Johnson are not anti-
rationalist; they merely want to radically expand the range of what we
take to be reason. Therefore, metaphors guide not only our imaginative
use of language but point to how we form categories and interpret these
categories within our cosmologies and ontologies based on the distinctive

logic of metaphorical reasoning. In contradistinction to objectivist and classical viewpoints on categories, Lakoff and Johnson state that we must learn to see our reasoning following "categories as experiential gestalts defined via prototype instead of viewing them as rigidly fixed and defined via set theory."[32]

There are two parts to Johnson's and Lakoff's argument as it pertains to the objectivist theory of categories; the first has to do with their description of the objectivist view of reality and, second, how this viewpoint defines the nature and generation of categories. According to their theory, the definition of categories is embedded within the grander domain of the general objectivist view of reality.

> The world consists of objects that have properties and stand in various relationships independent of human understanding. The world is as it is, no matter what any person happens to believe about it, and there is one correct "God's-Eye-View" about what the world really is like. In other words, there is a rational structure to reality, independent of the beliefs of any particular people, and correct reason mirrors this rational structure.[33]

Of course, Johnson admits that this is ideal type, itself defined by a series of metaphors. For instance, the dominant objectivist metaphor for reason is seeing or vision as defining one perfect viewpoint on all of reality. However, the metaphorical nature of objectivist reason itself is actually a virtue for Johnson and Lakoff because they also hold, as we shall see, that categories are best understood not as perfect sets as defined by reason but as idealized cognitive prototypes better understood as metaphors applied from domain to domain regulating the logic of imaginative reasoning. Johnson then defines categories within the objectivist worldview as "The classical (Objectivist) view holds that categories are defined by necessary and sufficient conditions which specify the properties shared by all and only members of the category."[34] However, the world is never that neat and we really do lack, according to Johnson and Lakoff, any recourse to God's view of reality. They are adamant about the last point. This is not just a pragmatic nor empirical claim. Following Hilary Putnam's lead, they argue that no creatures using finite logics and languages will ever be able to achieve a God's eye view of reality.

According to Johnson and Lakoff, that we cannot have a God's eye view of reality that will guarantee our rationality should not bother us inordinately. If we give up such a vain hope for cognitive perfection, then we will not feel any anxiety about not being able to define perfectly what we mean when we employ categories. "It doesn't really matter that we can't see the world through God's Eyes; for we can see the world through shared, pubic eyes that are given to us by our embodiment, our history, our culture, our language, our institutions, etc."[35] The public eyes are significant because it is the public nature of our metaphors that sustains commonality and does not lead us immediately into skepticism and radical relativism. One of the main reasons why philosophers traditionally have been loath to give up on objectivism is that they feared that the next step would be utter cognitive and moral chaos. But this need not happen in Johnson's and Lakoff's view if we develop a more ambitious, robust, and inclusive understanding of reason as metaphors we live and think by.

The classical Western (North Atlantic) philosophic tradition bears the brunt of the attack. However, the objectivist prototype can be found in other Eurasian philosophic cultures as well, and sometimes in unsuspected corners of unlikely traditions. For instance, one of the clearest expressions of this viewpoint is found in Lu Xiangshan's (1139–1193) defense of the correct interpretation of the Confucian Way against Zhu Xi. If the Song Neo-Confucians did not have a God, they certainly had a Dao that could not be compromised.[36] Lu stated that "there can exist only one most adequate truth; never can two profound meanings hold at the same time."[37] It should be noted that Zhu Xi reciprocated and often was tempted to categorize Lu as a Ch'an Buddhist, which was not a very charitable thing for one Confucian to call another. It would be fascinating to solicit Zhuangzi's opinion of this Neo-Confucian debate, but one suspects that Zhuangzi would have been much too clever to be forced to declare that there is anything like a God's eye view of reality.

According to Lakoff, categories are basically metaphors that we extend from prototypes outward to new cognitive domains by means of basic human bodily dispositions and imagination. But it is important to remember that there is nothing necessarily simple or atomistic about metaphors; metaphors can be nested within metaphors in ever increasing levels of complexification. Making use of the careful linguistic research of Eleanor Rosch, Lakoff expands Rosch's theory of prototypes to try to explain how we generate our categories on the basis of metaphoric imagination. Lakoff begins by noting that most categorizing takes place at a preconceptual level. The theory of categories as a set of things with common characteristics does not, according to Lakoff, help us very much to deal with the whole range of things that we do when we categorize the world. Lakoff tries to prove that a prototype model works much, much better. "The approach to prototype theory that we will be presenting here suggests that human categorization is essentially a matter of human experience and imagination—of perception, motor activity, and culture on the one hand, and of metaphor, metonymy, and metal imagery on the other."[38]

This is a highly suggestive way of view categorization, and certainly a contentious one based on cognitive and linguistic research. It also suggests why cross-cultural comparison is so difficult. Religions are such imaginative and complicated conceptual constructs that the metaphors used in depicting them are equally complicated, and perhaps very culture specific. This does not mean that comparison is impossible. It simply may be the case that we must find a great number of different metaphors governing the religious process. For instance, if the metaphor is THE WAY IS A PATH, one would expect a different set of themes and practices from THE WAY IS SUBMISSION, THE WAY IS NO WAY, or THE WAY IS LIBERATION.

Actually, Lakoff and Johnson define religious activity as a series of gestalts or Idealized Cognitive Models. These idealized cognitive models are built up out of more basic metaphorical images. They are needed to frame experience, especially unexpected experience. "An idealized cognitive model is a simplified cognitive gestalt that organizes selected aspects of our knowledge, understanding, or experience of a given domain."[39] While Lakoff and Johnson have not applied their method to the study of religion, they have employed it to look at ethics. Their argument is that ethics, as a complicated pattern of human activity, demands the use of idealized cognitive models in order to deal with the many domains embraced by morality. This certainly holds true for the religious dimension of human life as well.

The notion of gestalt, metaphor, and imaginative cognitive models fits the real world of religion. One of the key features of any religion is that of change and transformation, however that is parsed in the individual community of faith.[40] Transformation can be liberation, surrender, correct ritual or salvation—or many other forms as well. But, as David Tracy and others have noted, whatever else religion is about, it is about difference and change. In its most profound moments religion is definitely not about more of the same; religion is about something else happening, something that never happened before to the faithful. Because of this refreshing newness, human beings are driven to find new metaphors for the religious dimension shaped by their unique personalities and their embeddedness in community and social history. Even when we borrow old stories, such as the story of the Exodus as an icon for liberation, we apply them to new situations of injustice and liberation as has been done in North and South American and Korean theologies.

One reason that contemporary theories of categorization, such as Neville's and Lakoff's and Johnson's, are so complicated is that they recognize that we live in time when cultures and their categories are in constant dialogue. While it was hard enough to frame a theory of categories and their comparison within one homogenous cultural area, the task becomes even more difficult when the comparison is opened up to include a whole range of human religious activity. It is for this reason that theorists have resorted to theories of vague categories and metaphorical imagination. Anything less that this radical revisioning of the comparison of religious categories simply would be trivial in light of the mass of data demanding to be addressed. There is an old and ironic Chinese curse that states, may you live in interesting times. For the comparative philosopher or theologian this can be transposed into: may you live in culturally and conceptually rich times.

Notes

1. Bertrand Russell, *A History of Western Philosophy and Its Connection with Political and Social Circumstances from the Earliest Times to the Present Day* (New York: Simon and Schuster, 1945), 199–200.

2. See Ernest Gellner, *Reason and Culture: The Historic Role of Rationality and Rationalism* (Oxford: Blackwell, 1992). In his discussion of social theory, Gellner also adds language to the mix as well in order to support Durkheim's basic insight. "All our concepts, and not just the fundamental *Ordners* or organizers, are compulsively disciplined. Language itself is a kind of diffused ritual" (126).

3. Ibid., 37.

4. By objects Panikkar means that concepts are social creations of human culture and human ingenuity. See *The Intercultural Challenge of Raimon Panikkar*, ed. Joseph Prabhu (Maryknoll, N.Y.: Orbis Books, 1996), 251.

5. Ibid.

6. See Walter Watson, *The Architectonics of Meaning: Foundations for the New Pluralism* (Chicago: The University of Chicago Press, 1993), and David A. Dilworth, *Philosophy in World Perspective: A Comparative Hermeneutic of the Major Theories* (New Haven: Yale University Press, 1989).

7. Watson, *Architectonics*, 7.

8. I am here relying on the work of John P. Anton, *Categories and Experience: Essays in Aristotelian Themes* (Oakdale, N.Y.: Dowling College Press, 1996), 154–55.

9. Ibid., 161.

10. Ibid., 165.

11. Ibid., 175.

12. See Paul Williams, *Mahāyāna Buddhism: The Doctrinal Foundations* (London and New York: Routledge, 1989), 14.

13. For another study of dharma theory see Alfonso Verdu, *Early Buddhist Philosophy in Light of the Four Noble Truths* (Delhi: Motilal Banarsidass Publishers, 1985).

14. See David J. Kalupahana, *A History of Buddhist Philosophy: Continuities and Discontinuities* (Honolulu: University of Hawaii Press, 1992), 148.

15. See Juniro Takakusu, *The Essentials of Buddhist Philosophy* (Honolulu: Office Appliance Co., Ltd., 3rd Edition, 1956; ed. Wing-tsit Chan and Charles A. Moore).

16. Ibid., 64.

17. The discussion of Vaiśeṣika theories of categories relies on the work of Wilhelm Halbfass, *On Being and What There Is* (Albany: State University of New York Press, 1992). Along with a general discussion of the Vaiśeṣika theory of categories, Halbfass provides an overview of the history of Indian ontology.

18. Ibid., 70.

19. Ibid., 77.

20. Ibid., 71.

21. These five terms were often translated as the five elements, but such a rendition does not do justice to the phasic or processive nature of the Chinese concepts. It is better to think of the *wuxing* as five characteristic manifestations of the primordial *qi* or matter-energy than as eternal elements. The early Chinese cosmologists were quite clear that each phase was related to the other phases and that they would move from one state to anther in some kind of cycle. The most heated arguments were about just what kind of transformative cycle would obtain for each phase.

22. See A. C. Graham, *Disputers of the Tao: Philosophical Argument in Ancient China* (La Salle, Ill.: Open Court Publishing Company, 1989), 389–428. For another of Graham's provocative analysis of Chinese categoreal thinking, see A. C. Graham, *Yin-Yang and the Nature of Correlative Thinking* (Singapore: The Institute for East Asian Philosophies, 1986).

23. Graham, *Disputers*, 422.

24. Ibid., 149. Yet Graham is careful to point out that the Mohists are not really interested in setting up the kind of logical forms that so intrigued Aristotle. The Mohist's world is one of discourse where what is needed is an art for "testing description" as Graham notes (155).

25. Ibid., 155.

26. See Jonathan Z. Smith, *Imagining Religion: From Babylon to Jonestown* (Chicago: University of Chicago Press, 1982), 19–35. One of the points that Smith makes is that the practice of comparison in the history of religion and comparative philosophy often resembles a kind of sympathetic magic. The connections or comparisons are found more in the mind of the person making the comparison than in the material itself. However, as we shall see next in the next section, Smith neglects the power of the logics and structures of metaphor and imagination in his attempt to define religion. Perhaps there is more logic and structure to magic than we often realize.

27. For a review of Karl Jaspers' seminal idea see *The Origins and Diversity of Axial Age Civilizations*, ed. S. N. Eisenstadt (Albany: State University of New York Press, 1986).

28. See Robert Cummings Neville, *Normative Cultures* (Albany: State University of New York Press, 1995). This is the third volume in Neville's trilogy on the axiology of thinking. While Neville has always been interested in category formation, this book focuses attention on the project of how to carry out cross-cultural comparative philosophy and theology.

29. If anyone doubts that grand categoreal thinking no longer exists, we only need review the work of Charles Hartshorne. Hartshorne, who may well be the first philosopher to have lived through three centuries, has seen numerous philosophical currents ebb and flow. For one version of how he, following Peirce, would construct a list of metaphysical categories, see Charles Hartshorne, *The Zero Fallacy and other Essays in Neoclassical Philosophy*, ed. Mohammad Valday (Chicago and La Salle, Ill.: Open Court, 1997), 109–32.

30. Lakoff has worried about this problem for decades. His first review of the field was co-authored with Mark Johnson. See George Lakoff and Mark Johnson, *Metaphors We Live By* (Chicago: University of Chicago Press, 1980). For an enlarged discussion, see George Lakoff, *Women, Fire, and Dangerous Things: What Categories Reveal about the Mind* (Chicago: University of Chicago Press, 1987). What makes Lakoff useful is that he is critical of the classical view of categories, is widely influential, and (frankly) writes with humor about a topic that is not always full of mirth. From a philosophic perspective, Mark Johnson has written *The Body in the Mind: The Bodily Basis of Meaning, Imagination, and Reason* (Chicago: University of Chicago Press, 1987); and *Moral Imagination: Implications of Cognitive Science for Ethics* (Chicago: University of Chicago Press, 1993).

31. Another comparative theory has been developed by David L. Hall and Roger T. Ames, *Anticipating China: Thinking Through the Narratives of Chinese and Western Culture* (Albany: State University of New York Press, 1995). They argue that the particular genius of classical Chinese thought is correlative or interpretive pluralism. Hall and Ames are, like Neville, indebted to Peirce for framing the notion of vague concepts. Like Lakoff and Johnson, Hall and Ames notice that Chinese discourse makes use of metaphor and pays a great deal of attention to exemplars (prototypes).

32. Lakoff and Johnson, *Metaphors*, 210.

33. Johnson, *Moral Imagination*, x.

34. Ibid., xi.

35. Ibid., 211.

36. See Huang Chin-shing, *Philosophy, Philology, and Politics in Eighteenth-Century China: Li Fu and the Lu-Wang School Under the Ch'ing* (Cambridge: Cambridge University Press, 1995).

37. Ibid., 25.

38. Lakoff, *Women, Fire, and Dangerous Things*, 8.

39. Johnson, *Moral Imagination*, 93.

40. Of course, not all religions see the goal of religion this way at all. Some would argue that what religion ought to do is return us to unchanging beginnings. Perhaps a better way to put it is that all religions believe that something is wrong with the human condition. Our mundane situation needs reformation, liberation or return, and this is some kind of change. The Daoists might say that it is an unchanging change.

Appendix A

On the Process of the Project During the Second Year

Wesley J. Wildman

∽

The chapters describing the method of the Comparative Religious Ideas Project (CRIP) in this volume and elsewhere in the series stress the importance of a group of scholarly inquirers. This group makes comparisons properly vulnerable to correction and improves comparisons as efficiently as possible. The behind-the-scenes story of the project is how the CRIP scholars came together to forge an effective working group—despite profound disagreements that were introduced by design in order to strengthen the group's ability to make persuasive comparisons through juxtaposing points of view and types of expertise. The recounting of this story began in appendix A of the first volume (*The Human Condition*) and continues here, in this instance focusing on the way the group and its work developed during the second year of collaboration. The third volume has a similar appendix dealing with the third and fourth years of the Project but each of the three appendices can be read as stand-alone documents. At times in what follows I quote from the unpublished meeting reports. The personnel are listed at the end of this volume and I shall refer to participants by their first names.

At the Beginning of a Second Year

When we gathered for the first meeting of the second year the smiles were broad, the greetings were loud, and laughter filled the room. Everyone seemed genuinely glad to be together again. The first year had catalyzed serious cooperation and the result was an identity built around working together, each relying on everyone else to do their jobs to keep the project on track. For my part, while I shared everyone's concerns about the first volume, I liked this group and rated our venture's chances of solid success higher at the beginning of this second year than during the first meeting of the first year. Seeing the first volume gradually take shape helped build confidence, I think, and we diagnosed its limitations as an appropriate expression of the fact that our research depended on habits of collaboration that were still forming. Discussion about the first volume is recounted in the appendix to that volume and also in the introduction to this volume, so I shall say no more about it here, even though it was prominent in everyone's mind throughout the second year.

We met for eight days during the second year of CRIP, four times in the fall of 1996 and four more in the spring of 1997. The meetings followed the pattern established during the previous year: the first meeting introduced the theme of ultimate realities (and also discussed chapter drafts for the human condition volume); the next three focused on expositional papers from the six specialists; the subsequent three shifted to discussion of synthetic and comparative papers from the specialists; and the final meeting was a review and analysis. With regard to the meeting process, there were several differences between the first and second years. There had been a change of personnel among the graduate students with Chris replacing Tina; Hugh, John, Celeste, James, and Joseph continued throughout the project—long enough for the celebration of many life events, such as John's job and Joe's baby. Sabbaticals meant that we were without some research scholars on a few occasions, though we chose meeting dates to minimize absences. One of our advisors, Tu Weiming, was an active participant in a number of meetings. And there was time for formal discussion of the first volume's ongoing editing during several of the second year's meetings. By far the most significant difference, however, was the simple fact that we already knew something about what we were doing thanks to a year's work together.

The Delicate Balance between Specialists and Generalists

By the beginning of the second year, we had enough experience with the challenges of integrating the perspectives of the tradition specialists with those of the comparative generalists to have reached a fateful conclusion: we probably could not achieve consensus conclusions. A few of the tradition specialists, especially Frank and Paula, had so resisted characterizations of their traditions as a whole, or even large chunks of their traditions, that the comparative generalists' determination to press ahead with making such generalizations anyway was felt to make total consensus on conclusions impossible. Frank generously moved in the second and third years from the *Vivekacūḍāmaṇi*, a text about learning applicable only to a subset of male brāhmins, to the study of texts that enjoyed broader representation in India. This allowed him to present larger-scale generalizations about his tradition precisely through the viewpoint of the selected text, which was an approach he could adopt in good conscience. Paula was especially intransigent on this issue, however, urging the group to recognize that any large-scale characterization across historical periods and cultures masks more than it illumines and inevitably falls prey to the anachronistic tendency to interpret the far past and the culturally remote through the distorting and often irrelevant terms of our contemporary experience. This can be seen in the present volume: her chapter on ultimate realities in Christianity is silent about the classic Christian idea of the Trinity, precisely in order to remain faithful to the earlier period of Christian origins that she focuses on. Admirable but problematic. For their part, the comparative generalists urged the equally appealing but diametrically opposed point that the very purpose of the project was to collaborate in such a way as to create comparisons (which are always generalizations) in the sort of environment in which the ever-present dangers of bias and anachronism could be kept in check and even perhaps overcome to some extent.

Under these circumstances—a quite realistic model of the conflicted state of affairs in religious studies, I think—achieving consensus conclusions was probably out of the question. The comparative generalists would have to draw conclusions as they saw fit, thoroughly informed and subject to constant critique by the tradition specialists, while the specialists would approach their traditions from the intriguing new lens ground into shape by the empirical derivation of categories during the course of our discussions. While the abandonment of consensus conclusions was disappointing to some, and a limited failure for the project, it is important to note how much further we were going in collaborative work than is customary in religious studies. Consensus remained the goal for the process of determining which comparative categories would prove most helpful for interpreting the six traditions. And conclusions still had to pass muster for accuracy and fairness with the large group. This was a lot to ask in itself. Therefore, the decision to allow the comparative generalists (especially Bob) to draw their own conclusions about the human condition, ultimate realities, and religious truth did not dissociate generalists from the specialists but rather freed both to stay closer to their native modes of thinking and writing while keeping in place the tight constraints of serious collaboration.

My reading of this decision is that the specialists wanted it more than the generalists did. In the first volume, Bob showed his willingness and ability to confine his conclusions almost exclusively to what the specialists had said in their papers in an attempt to wring consensus from the group as a whole. But most and perhaps all of the tradition specialists were too uncomfortable with the end product and could not in good conscience sign on to the results as their own conclusions. They were unwilling, or perhaps like me intellectually and constitutionally unable, to carry off the work of synthesis that Bob had attempted in the first volume's conclusions, with its disciplined refusal to clog the already long chapters with hordes of usually obvious caveats. They were also unwilling to move into the more philosophical territory of constructing the larger-scale interpretations of the human condition or ultimate realities that full self-consciousness about vague comparative categories requires. At the beginning of the second year, this was a disappointment to Bob. The project designers had chosen several of the specialists with an eye to their interest in philosophical modes of thought within their own traditions; Nomanul, Frank, and David especially had important publications to their credit demonstrating this interest. The project designers had envisaged that the specialists would be interested in mastering the unfamiliar modes of thinking associated with philosophical balancing of interpretative generalizations, much as the generalists would try in good faith to move in the opposite direction by allowing vast mounds of historical and textual details to trip up any and every generalization they might have been inclined to make.

Bob's disappointment was somewhat ameliorated during the second year, without ever disappearing completely, because most of the specialists did indeed strive to lay out in their papers what they thought could be inferred about the human condition generally from the masses of details processed in the course of their own research and in group conversations. This shift relative to the specialist papers for the first volume indicates a serious effort on the part of the specialists to make the method work, and it would get even better in the third volume on religious truth. Despite the decision to give up the goal of thoroughgoing consensus, therefore, the method was working better during the second year. The general category of ultimate realities was being specified by the comparisons permitted by means of it, which is the easy part, and the category of ultimate realities was being infused with content by means of the comparisons and inferences made by the specialists, which is the difficult part. That made possible a much more interpretative approach to drawing conclusions than was possible in the first volume; they could be drawn from the comparisons and the inferences about ultimate realities already present in the specialist papers. This was a welcome improvement over the first year, though in my view the conclusions to the first volume have their own advantages, as the appendix to that volume indicates.

Enter Philosophy

The many factors described above led to an important development in the minds of the comparative generalists. (1) If conclusions no longer needed to win unanimous agreement from the group but needed only to meet the (admittedly severe) constraints of consensus around comparative categories and demands for accuracy and fairness; (2) if the method was working well so that specialists were making vital contributions to the elaboration of the vague category of ultimate realities and its subcategories; and (3) if everyone trying to interpret religious ideas was always inevitably involved in philosophical reflection in one form or another; then (4) it was reasonable to aim at conclusions that would present a working philosophical theory of ultimate realities rather than merely a coordination of comparisons made during the year's work. This theory could not extend very far from the data processed and the comparisons made by the group, so it could never be a highly speculative or systematic philosophical theory of ultimate realities. But it would be a generalized theory of ultimate realities nonetheless and it would lead to a relatively philosophical way of packaging the conclusions for the second volume.

This entry of philosophy into the project at the beginning of the second year might have been merely a making explicit of its presence all along. Early in the second year, for instance, Tony was memorably insistent that the philosophical moment in our work should be explicit. Moreover, he argued that its presence was inevitable and actually a good idea because it was implied already in the method's goal of constructing interpretations of the vague comparative categories sufficiently rich to take account of the mass of details organized and related by the vague categories. However that goes, envisaging this kind of conclusion for the second volume promised to solve several pressing problems for the comparative generalists, especially Bob and myself.

First, we were unwilling to produce conclusions of the sort in the first volume on the human condition. We regretted the loss associated with abandoning the phenomenological sites of importance and the systematic presentation of numerous facets of religious ideas. That was a strength of the first volume's conclusions that could not be preserved in a more philosophical, interpretative approach. Moreover, just as a childhood boating trauma keeps a grown adult away from deep water, Bob's experience of writing the first volume's conclusions made him eager to do something else!

Second, Bob and I were having extended discussions over the question of how, precisely, vague comparative categories such as ultimate realities were supposed to be specified. Of course, a host of comparisons in which the vague category or one of its subcategories is used as the respect of comparison constitutes a vital kind of specification. But that sort of specifying multiplies details without really synthesizing the sort of interpretation we have in mind when we speak of specifying something vague, such as love or democracy or modernity. To us, at least, theory seemed inevitable, albeit fragmentary and somewhat unsystematic theory, owing to the need for fidelity to the available data. Only an inevitably somewhat philosophical theory could wring from the mass of details the synthetic interpretation of the vague category of ultimate realities that the method demands.

Third, and related to the second, there was the problem of the lurking arbitrariness of the vague comparative categories, which could only be resolved if a fuller answer to the question of what it means to justify a comparative category were forthcoming. A more openly philosophical approach to drawing conclusions would help properly to frame and answer this question, which is discussed in detail below.

Among the group more generally, reactions to this limited entry of philosophy into proceedings were difficult to read. Apart from Tony's enthusiastic interpretation of this decision, and more muted approving remarks from Noman, the specialists seemed relatively unconcerned, if not indifferent. This was a consequence, I think, of the loosening of the constraints mutually binding generalists to specialists described above. This new situation demanded a respectful modicum of distance between the two, at least with regard to allowing the generalists to proceed with drawing conclusions in whatever way they saw fit.

Ultimate Reality/ies

We began the second year using the grant proposal's language of "ultimate reality," a term chosen specifically to avoid theistic connotations. While interested in the idea of God, it was not our exclusive interest and we did not want our investigations to be limited by that idea. We needed to register Buddhist ideas of ultimate reality that relate more to paths or ways of life than to an ontological ultimate, for example. This vagueness about ultimates has been noted in the comparative study of religious ideas for over a century beginning with Emile Durkheim's self-conscious use of the vague category "sacred" and continuing through Paul Tillich's deliberate adoption of the crucially vague term "ultimate concern." The project grant used the term "ultimate" in the category "ultimate reality" with this history in mind. But two problems with this terminology arose quickly. First, the singular "ultimate reality" was felt to prejudge onto-logical issues of unity and epistemological issues of intelligibility that we wanted to leave open. Everyone readily agreed to use the plural "ultimate realities" in response to these concerns. Second, some were concerned about the appearance of the term "real" in the name for the category be-cause it seemed to bias the category in the direction of ontology. My pro-posal to use the awkward terms "ultimacy" or "ultimates" never gar-nered support but everyone was conscious of the point.

These two issues were discussed periodically through the second year. The following comment from the meeting reports illustrates the group's awareness of the need to register both theistic and non-theistic religious perspectives within the category of ultimate realities. In this case, David's comment is prompted by Livia's discussion early in the year of Chinese creation stories and bears on the possibility of fair treatment of non-theistic, non-ontologically oriented ideas of ultimates when ultimate re-alities is the ruling category:

DAVID: Tillich is a shadow for this discussion; he would have found this slicing of the conceptual and terminological pies quite congenial. He used the category of ultimate concern in part to find a way to bring Buddhism into the picture in a helpful fashion. Have we not skewed the discussion by speaking too much of ultimate *realities*, though? And does this not lead to too strong an emphasis on fascinating creation myths? From a Buddhist point of view, this is all very much beside the point. The Buddhist understanding of ultimate concern bears less on ultimate realities than on the ultimate norm under which reality as it affects society and people is to be understood. That approach yields very dif-ferent insights.

At one level, this problem is merely a terminological one, and so is ad-dressed easily with periodic consciousness-raising remarks such as David's. The deeper issue raised here, however, is whether the category of ultimate realities can be given a coherent interpretation when treated so vaguely as to include both ultimate paths and ultimate realities. If no such coherent interpretation is forthcoming, then the method calls for the dis-posal of the category as overly vague and thus arbitrary. Yet any coherent interpretation would have to unite the "path" and "reality" sides of the category in a natural way. At stake in the shift to the plural "realities," therefore, was the greater permissiveness of the plural, perhaps suggesting the presence of a mindset among the group that would be content merely to catalogue conceptions of ultimate realities. This would be a return to the first year's procedure in which the first and easier half of the method was emphasized to the neglect of the second half in which the vague category is interpreted through the detailed mass of observations and comparisons made by means of it. The meeting notes record Bob's early statement of this concern, in which he makes reference both to Peter Berger's sociology-of-knowledge concept of "world-making" and to the philosophical and apologetic system of Vedānta Deśika, the figure studied by Frank during the second year:

BOB: It is useful, under certain circumstances, to call "ultimate" many of the things that are decisive for the task of what Peter calls "world-making," such as ultimate origin, ultimate grounds of meaning, ultimate destiny, ultimate place, ultimate home. However, this does not lead to a systematic interpretation of ultimate reality. I contend that it is the business of a systematic philosopher (such as Vedānta Deśika) to try to put together a lot of "ultimate" things that in popular religion might be thought of as separate, and so to seek a unified conception of the ultimate. I further contend that this systematic philosophical activity is sensible and without any knock-down arguments against its possibility, though it is peculiarly difficult, and so its possibility must be determined through assiduous efforts to do it.

As it turned out, expressions of concern such as David's and Bob's were sufficient. Most of the specialists did in fact try to draw inferences about ultimate realities based on the descriptions and comparisons they laid out in their essays (as I noted earlier) and all of them remained keenly aware of the tension between ultimate paths and ultimate realities.

Facing the Specter of Incommensurability

In one way, the entire project is about solving the problem of comparison in face of the specter of cross-cultural incommensurability of religious ideas and practices. Right from the beginning, we all knew from our own experience that everyone in religious studies makes comparisons and so presumes categories that are the respects of comparison, whether or not they admit to doing this. Even describing a single religious tradition or text involves comparative categories such as "ritual" or "God" or "purity." We also knew that plenty of scholars had raised the question of the arbitrariness of comparison, the most telling evidence in support of the incommensurability thesis. And we knew both that Bob's method was supposed to solve the problem somehow and that CRIP was supposed to test this methodological solution and refine it if possible even as it made a bunch of interesting and important comparisons.

At this beginning of the second year, however, all we had to go on was the theoretical talk of a "dialectic of vagueness and specificity" or, to put it more concretely, a dialectic between the vague descriptive categories used throughout the study of religions and the detailed descriptions usually found in the phenomenology of religion. This is the theme that received the most play in Bob's prior publications and in our group's methodological discussions, though there were rich subtleties in both that pointed further and in other directions. In practice, this meant the following for our group. The vague categories would make possible specific comparisons and descriptions and all those specifics would infuse the vague category with positive content. The adequacy of a comparative category would be determined by the ability of an interpretation of it to make coherent sense of the detailed comparisons and descriptions that the category facilitated. If a coherent interpretation was not forthcoming it would be for one of two reasons: (1) the category was too vague, arbitrarily lumping together too much data for which no compelling rationale could be given; or (2) the category was too specific (probably owing too much to one particular tradition), constantly running up against indigestible data. In both cases the absence of a coherent interpretation would demand the rejection of the category—and we rejected plenty of them along the way. To make all this work, the specialists had promised to try to make comparisons, even though they were reluctant at times, and the generalists had promised to theorize with reference to the manifold details presented by the specialists, even though the details greatly complicated their attempts to construct generalized interpretations of the comparative categories.

The end result of following these procedures was supposed to be the overcoming of arbitrariness in the comparison of religious ideas, at least with respect to the ideas and traditions we were examining. It would be simultaneously a realistic acceptance of the complexities invoked by the term "incommensurability" and a serious demonstration that the dangers of arbitrariness, distortion, bias, and anachronism could be kept in check. Such a grand plan! As Peter put it, "The outrageousness of the project should be made clear at the outset. Also, a profoundly modern form of consciousness is structuring the project, which focuses on six traditions that have very different forms of consciousness; this is one point that should be registered carefully." Or in Paula's characteristically colorful language, "The first sentence should be 'This work is the result of intellectual obsession and chutzpah'. Not only is comparison difficult, but we are working with materials hostile to comparison."

During the second year it seemed clear to most of us that the method we were using was capable of living up to most of its advance billing. We really were able to exclude many categories as too vague (arbitrary) or too specific (distorting). And we were also able to pull many details together into richly coherent interpretations of the vague categories, such as the human condition and ultimate realities. As I previously mentioned, however, there remained a lurking arbitrariness in the categories we were using. Bending ourselves out of shape to learn new styles of thinking in order to work through the dialectic of vagueness and specificity seemed to take us only so far. The limited distance traveled and the corresponding lurking arbitrariness can be discerned from two points of view.

First, when all was said and done, how could we decide whether the set of categories we adopted were better than alternative sets? For instance, could it be shown that the set of categories we used for the human condition was superior to the alternative and more narrative set proposed by David (see appendix A in *The Human Condition* for details)? Or could we demonstrate that the categories adopted for parsing ultimate realities were superior to the rather different sets of categories used within the perennial philosophy or within one of the many versions of religious naturalism?

At one level, our group was content to discover that our method had the capacity to force the rejection of inadequate categories and to generate at least one schema of categories that was adequate to the stringent tests imposed by the dialectic of vagueness and specificity just described. It was not obvious that we needed or even wanted to become entangled in questions about the relative merits of sets of categories. For instance, the meeting notes record the following question about assessing the adequacy of a scheme of categories versus just trying to say something relevant about the religious ideas under discussion, together with a telling reply. The context is a discussion of the first volume:

WESLEY: Do the categories we choose matter for the purposes of detecting the religiously important? Or is the religiously important detected with any arbitrarily chosen categories by means of the hard work required to apply those categories to each individual tradition or text? That is, are we concerned with the superiority of the schema of categories we use in this book over competitive schemas? I think that *is* one of our concerns, but I don't think this point is clearly made in any of the chapters at present.

BOB: This is one of our concerns, but we also need to preserve the possibility that we must use whatever categories we come up with to detect the religiously important as best we can, delaying assessment of the adequacy of the categorial scheme until later.

In his reply we see Bob indicating his priorities: first we just try to get *any* scheme of categories that can meet the demands of the dialectic of vagueness and specificity. That would be a difficult and important achievement in itself. After that, energy and time permitting, we can worry about the relative merits of schemes of categories.

At another level, however, the specter of incommensurability and the problems it poses for comparison of religious ideas (or anything else with a cross-cultural aspect) demands more. Not all of us were interested in the philosophical and methodological adventures of evaluating the relative merits of categorial schemes. In periodic discussions of this topic a number of voices typically dropped out, patiently awaiting the conversation's eventual return to details more directly relevant to the topic for the year. Nobody ever complained about having to suffer through the ongoing methodological debates, however, presumably because the project called for evaluating and improving the method as well as producing interesting comparisons and coherent interpretations of vague comparative categories. For those interested, a great deal seemed to hinge on the question of evaluating the relative merits of categorial schemas, including the very concept of a scientific theory of religion. If our scientific approach could only rule out certain categories and sets of categories but not produce a putative "best" schema for and interpretation of ultimate realities, then it seems to follow that a theory of religion could never be sufficiently analogous to other theories in the social or natural sciences to be fairly called "scientific." At root the reason for this would be the incapacity of the subject matter to correct hypotheses about it so as to be able to determine the most adequate from among the set of worthwhile alternatives. By itself this is not a problem because there are many areas of life in which we do not demand "best" interpretations and cannot hope to get them. But the possibility and nature of theories of religion are important topics to which our project has a direct contribution to make. I will return to these issues in the appendix to the volume on religious truth because it is in that volume that we take up the question of theories of religion most formally.

Second, the lurking arbitrariness can also be detected by reflecting on the relation between our principal way of justifying comparative categories (as of the middle of the second year) and ways adopted elsewhere within the study of religion. This volume treats the issue in some detail and I will not summarize those discussions here. It appeared to those concerned with the question of categorial justification (mostly the generalists) that we were relying too exclusively on the dialectic of vagueness and specificity, to the neglect of more conventional methods of evaluating interpretations of comparative categories. This overemphasis is not surprising, in retrospect, because making sure that interpretations of comparative categories make coherent sense of masses of details is the part of comparative method most often neglected in other approaches. But interpretations of comparative categories also need to make historical and philosophical sense. These are the perspectives from which the study of religion has usually assessed comparative categories, though rarely are both applied together. That is, while correcting the deficit of existing approaches that neglect the adequacy of comparative categories to the details those categories comprehend, we also needed to continue paying attention to the historical and philosophical analyses that formed the backbone of the two dominant approaches to the justification of comparative categories—respectively, and broadly construed, the history of religion and the philosophy of religion.

We could see no reason for keeping apart historical and philosophical considerations bearing on the adequacy of interpretations of comparative categories, a traditional division perpetuated by the professionalization and complexification of religious studies and the resulting sharp distinctions oftentimes drawn between historians and philosophers of religion. Nor did we detect any tension between the use of an empirical method for evaluating the adequacy of comparative categories (the dialectic of vagueness and specificity) and these other lines of justification for comparative categories. As Bob suggests at a few places in *Normative Cultures* and elsewhere, all available resources should be brought to bear on the correction of interpretations. The traditional separation of resources and the consequent neglect of their combined power need not inhibit us from insisting that the dialectic of vagueness and specificity (roughly, the phenomenology of religion understood in a particular way) should work in concert with the history of religion and the philosophy of religion.

By the end of the second year, therefore, our procedures had forced an enrichment of the method we were following. We still emphasized the adequacy of the category "ultimate realities" to the phenomena it is supposed to comprehend and we kept in place the complex collaborative procedures needed to ensure that this assessment could be made. But the justification of categories was also understood to include providing sophisticated interpretations of them that accounted for both (1) the philosophy of religion's concerns to identify (1a) the range of *possible* ideas of ultimate realities and (1b) the range of possible dynamic variations in symbolic representation of the idea of ultimate realities over time, and

(2) the history of religion's concerns to identify (2a) the historical influences on the original emergence of particular ideas of ultimate realities and (2b) the historical circumstances conditioning the dynamic changes of symbolic representations of ultimate realities over time. The chapter setting out the conclusions for this volume, profiting from the limited entry of philosophy into the project, is self-conscious about this multifaceted sort of justification and even offers a few philosophical arguments and historical suggestions, despite the obvious enormity of the task. In our view, this represents a great advance on the problem of lurking arbitrariness and so in turn on the specter of incommensurability.

At the End of a Second Year

Overall, year two was a great year for CRIP. We had decided on a sliver of space between specialists and generalists by rejecting the goal of consensus conclusions. Yet the collaborative method worked smoothly and, as I have just explained, it was enhanced under the impact of our use of it, though those enhancements impacted primarily the work of the generalists. The party at the end of the final meeting of the year was, as I recall, a most enjoyable event.

At the final meeting we asked the graduate students about their reactions to the collaborative process of which they had been a part, some more active than others, most for two years. Trying to capture their responses in my notes was difficult but here is how the meeting reports express the gist of their comments. Even in written form, it is not hard to detect the wry smiles we sometimes saw as these mini-reports were given.

HUGH (Hinduism): I have learned especially that comparison is difficult and risky. I have also learned that there are some topics and some approaches that are best avoided.

CELESTE (Islam): I have found it helpful to see scholars hard at work—we don't see that very often—and the more so because the topics are complicated.

CHRIS (Christianity): This has been of real practical value for me in terms of my goal of Christian ministry because it will help me help others come to terms with the religiously plural settings of contemporary churches. It will also prove helpful in communicating with clergy colleagues for whom religious pluralism might be intimidating and confusing.

JAMES (Chinese Religion): Being taught by more than one person at a time is very useful, in part because it draws attention to what is debatable and how to broach those debates.

JOHN JT (Buddhism): I am fortunate to have all three of my dissertation advisors in this group and so I am enjoying learning with my professors all at once. It is also informative to watch professors write and rewrite.

JOE (Judaism): Graduate students are not much trained or encouraged to enjoy themselves, but I am having fun and learning a lot at the same time. Being involved makes my thinking more fluid and malleable, and helps my writing and my teaching.

The experience of the graduate students is not the most prominent topic within these appendices, but reporting on it in closing this appendix is most apt. After all, the project from the beginning was designed to train these young scholars in collaborative modes of research and its success is to be measured in part through its impact on a new generation of comparativists, beginning with these six.

Appendix B

Suggestions for Further Reading

❦

The Comparative Religious Ideas Project was designed to involve students both as participants in the seminar meetings and in background tasks. One of the more adventurous student projects has been the development of a set of twelve annotated bibliographies on a number of topics relevant to the project. These bibliographies are suggestions for further reading in each topic covered. I am grateful to the students involved in the annotation project: Marylu Bunting, John Darling, Greg Farr, Andrew Irvine, He Xiang, Mark Mann, Matt McLaughlin, David McMahon, Glen Messer, James Miller, and Kirk Wulf. I am also grateful for the suggestions of books to annotate that we received from Profs. Jensine Andresen, John Berthrong, Frank Clooney, Jonathan Klawans, and Frank Korom. The first bibliography in this volume contains suggestions for further reading on the topic of the volume, ultimate realities. Subsequently there are tradition-specific bibliographies on Chinese Religion, Buddhism, and Hinduism. Each contains annotations on reference works, primary texts in English translation, and secondary sources that discuss various aspects of the tradition. The final bibliography contains annotated suggestions for further reading in the area of comparative method, which is intended to help those wanting to evaluate the method used in this project against other approaches to the comparison of religious ideas.

—Wesley J. Wildman

Annotated Bibliography: Ultimate Realities

Abe, Masao. *Divine Emptiness and Historical Fullness: A Buddhist-Jewish-Christian Conversation with Masao Abe*. Valley Forge, PA: Trinity Press International, 1995. Ed. by Christopher Ives.

Abe has been a leader in Buddhist-Christian dialogue since the 1960s. This book reprints Abe's major theological statement, "Kenotic God and Dynamic Sunyata," which has previously appeared in *The Emptying God*, edited by Cobb and Ives (cf. *Human Condition* bibliography). The respondents in the present volume press Abe on a number of metaphysical and dialogical issues, especially whether similarities in metaphysical expression constitute genuine agreement, and whether disagreements effect real transformation of the participants' positions.

Berger, Peter L. *The Other Side of God: A Polarity in World Religions*. Garden City, NY: Anchor Press/Doubleday, 1981.

The polarity invoked in the sub-title refers all experience of religious ultimacy either to a reality external to the self or to a reality resident in the depth of (self-)consciousness. It was proposed as a heuristic device for a 1978–80 seminar, "Monotheism and the World Religions." Part I considers the polarity in monotheistic traditions; Part II, Hinduism and Buddhism. The polarity in question is critically addressed as the participants think through the implications of global religious encounter for, especially, Western monotheistic assumptions.

Brück, Michael von. *The Unity of Reality: God, God-Experience and Meditation in the Hindu-Christian Dialogue*. New York: Paulist Press, 1991. Trans. by James V. Zeitz from *Einheit der Wirklichkeit*.

Brück's project is Christian theology in dialogue with Advaita ("nondualist") Vedānta. Working with mainly twentieth-century "neo-Advaita" thought in Part I, and the German mystical tradition of Trinitarian thought in Part II, Brück proposes a Christian-Advaitic theology of the Trinity. God's unity and the unity of all reality are realized in nondual experience; an experience which liberates the experiencer for the world. The author acknowledges substantial differences in Advaitin and Christian metaphysical and epistemological assessments of unity and duality. Nevertheless, he makes abundant evidence for the creative possibilities in dialogue between the two tradition.

Carter, Robert Edgar, ed. *God, the Self, and Nothingness: Reflections Eastern and Western*. God, the Contemporary Discussion Series. A New ERA Book. New York: International Religious Foundation, 1990.

Nineteen essays drawn from a series of conferences (1986–1988) focus on convergences and divergences between Hindu, Buddhist, Jewish and Christian conceptions of ultimacy. The sources for reflection range from Jewish Kabbalah to Kierkegaard, Advaita Vedānta to Nishitani. The writers reconsider religious traditions from within and from comparative perspectives as they elucidate their understanding of God, nothingness, and the individual's relationship to either one or both of them.

Copleston, Frederick Charles. *Religion and the One: Philosophies East and West*. Gifford Lectures. London: Search Press, 1982.

This much lauded book parallels Father Copleston's Gifford Lectures of 1979 and 1980. The first half of this work carefully surveys the subject of 'the One', the alleged ultimate and transcendent reality grounding the world, as it is dealt with in Taoist, Buddhist, Vedāntin, Islamic, Judaic, and Christian sources. The second half of this text discusses particular aspects of the structures and logics of the many metaphysical theories surveyed: for example, the role of 'mystical experience', and the conclusion to monism or theism. The final chapter discusses the hypothetical nature of such theories, criteria for assessing their truth, and historical development. Copleston argues that, within such limits, Christian theism seems to be a more adequate theory.

Deutsch, Eliot. *Humanity and Divinity: An Essay in Comparative Metaphysics*. Honolulu: University of Hawaii Press, 1970.

The author is a pioneer in cross-cultural religious and philosophical studies, as this book shows. Deutsch defines metaphysics as "the articulation of a path to spiritual experience and a disciplined reflection upon that experience." Starting from the discovery of the absolute in the self, Deutsch develops an analysis of the absolute as Being, which in turn leads to a theory of humanity as "diverted being" for whom, then, the absolute stands as divine ground and pattern. This book forges a distinctive metaphysics drawing widely and deeply on the philosophies of the Christian West and India.

Duerlinger, James, ed. *Ultimate Reality and Spiritual Discipline*. God, the Contemporary Discussion Series. A New ERA Book. New York: Paragon House Publishers, 1984.

The editor claims that "spiritual discipline is any activity in which one conscientiously engages for the sake of ultimate reality." The many contributors to this volume, working from a great many religious traditions, take up four topics: the nature of spiritual discipline, efficacy of spiritual discipline, spiritual discipline in a secular world, and spiritual disciplines in pursuit of ultimate reality. In view of these topics, each contributor attempts to define (or resists defining) ultimate reality from his or her own situation at the outset.

Eckel, Malcolm David. *To See the Buddha: A Philosopher's Quest for the Meaning of Emptiness*. Princeton, NJ: Princeton University Press, 1994 [1992]. Originally published by San Francisco: HarperSanFrancisco, 1992.

It is difficult to underestimate the richness of the sense of vision, and the word, "vision," in Indian religious thought and practice. Eckel takes the sixth century Madhyamaka philosopher, Bhāvaviveka, as his focus in creating his own vision of Mahāyāna Buddhist philosophy and devotion as symbiotic activities set within a lush and living culture. The logic of seeing the Buddha (who, having achieved Nirvana, is not visible in any conventional way) is explored through Eckel's translation of a portion of Bhāvaviveka's *Verses on the Essence of the Middle Way* and its autocommentary. Through this logic the meaning of emptiness, the lack of self-existence that is ultimately real, can be realized.

Eno, Robert. *The Confucian Creation of Heaven: Philosophy and the Defense of Ritual Mastery*. SUNY Series in Chinese Philosophy and Culture. Albany: State University of New York Press, 1990.

Eno examines the meaning and role of *T'ien* as a clue to the core interests of early Confucianism. He approaches early Confucianism as a movement of men concerned more with ritual cultivation than with either doctrinal expression or political leadership. Eno proceeds on two fronts: a careful study of the character, *T'ien*, in early texts, and a more speculative reconstruction of the Confucian project. He argues that Confucianism is a philosophy, but that its roots are not in logical analysis as it centrally is the case in Western philosophy. Furthermore, Eno argues that no distinction between theory and practice is fundamentally entertained in Confucian thought. *Li*, or ritual, is the ultimate concern for which *T'ien* is a highly mutable legitimating motif.

Gregory, Peter N. *Inquiry into the Origin of Humanity: An Annotated Translation of Tsung-Mi's Yüan Jen Lun with a Modern Commentary*. Classics in East Asian Buddhism. Honolulu: University of Hawaii Press, 1995.

Tsung-mi was a Buddhist master in ninth-century China. His *Inquiry* is a systematic overview and classification of major teachings within early Chinese Buddhism and, as such, offers insight into contemporary Confucian, Daoist, and Buddhist dialogue. Tsung-mi's process of classification leads to a narrative concerning the origin of the world as the consequence of a fall from primordial unity of Buddha-nature into a bifurcated consciousness. Such consciousness is said to account for attachment and bondage to the cycle of karma. Gregory provides a valuable introduction and running commentary as well as a glossary and a guide to supplemental readings.

Griffiths, Paul J. *On Being Buddha: The Classical Doctrine of Buddhahood.* SUNY Series, Toward a Comparative Philosophy of Religions. Albany: State University of New York Press, 1994.

The bulk of this book is a study of the doctrine of the Buddha's three bodies, as developed in a number of third- to ninth-century scholastic texts produced in Medieval India. The approach is described as a "doctrinal study of doctrine," primarily concerned with "transhistorical systematic" issues. Griffiths focuses especially on metaphysical problems inherent in the attempt to reconcile the changeless, self-sufficient dharma body with the relational and experiential situations of the transformation ("earthly") and enjoyment ("celestial") bodies, relating them to similar problems in Christian theology. Griffiths concludes that doctrine concerning the Buddha is beset with intractable metaphysical problems, which force Buddhists back upon a sheerly soteriological interpretation of reality.

King, Sallie B. *Buddha Nature.* SUNY Series in Buddhist Studies. Albany: State University of New York Press, 1991.

The author gives a detailed exposition of 'Buddha-nature' according to the mid-sixth-century Chinese *Fo Xing Lun* ("Buddha Nature Treatise") and interprets it in light of Western thinking about the being and existence of persons and the development of Buddhist tradition in the West. Chapter One provides a thorough introduction to the history and traditional importance of the motif of Buddha-nature and of the *Fo Xing Lun.* Succeeding chapters present the Chinese text's theory of Buddha-nature, with respect to soteriology, selfhood, ontology, spiritual cultivation, and implications for Western religious thought. The ultimate identity and universality of Buddha-nature is explicated in terms of its being a metaphor for religious cultivation of enlightenment, a "skilful means."

Lott, Eric J. *Vedantic Approaches to God.* Totowa, NJ: Barnes & Noble, 1980. Originally presented as the author's thesis, Liverpool, 1977.

Lott provides a comparative and detailed description of three major schools of Vedānta represented by Śaṅkara, Rāmānuja and Madhva. A brief orientation to Vedānta and common features among the schools is followed by studies of distinctions in their treatment of Brahman's transcendence, the appropriateness of personal categories to describe Brahman, Brahman as supreme cause, cognitive, soteriological, and other relations between the individual self and Brahman, and means of approach to the transcendent end. Lott effectively argues for understanding the schools of Vedānta as theological disciplines akin to Western theology.

Muhammad, A. *The Theology of Unity*. London: Allen & Unwin, 1980 [1966]. Trans. by Ishaq Musa'ad and Kenneth Cragg from *Risalat al-Tauhid*.

In the esteem of co-translator, Kenneth Cragg, 'Abduh (1849–1905) was the most decisive single factor in the twentieth-century development of Arab Muslim thought and renewal. 'Abduh describes the theology of unity (*tauḥīd*) as "the science that studies the being and attributes of God, the essential and the possible affirmations about Him, as well as the negations that are necessary to make relating to Him. It deals also with the apostles and the authenticity of their message." In addition, 'Abduh discusses Islam as the culmination of religion.

Netton, Ian Richard. *Allah Transcendent: Studies in the Structure and Semiotics of Islamic Philosophy, Theology, and Cosmology*. London: Curzon Press, 1993 [1989].

A somewhat controversial book, in which Netton advances the thesis that Islamic philosophy and theology develop in ever more trenchant estrangement from the Qur'ānic paradigm of Allah's absolute transcendence of the world. Netton applies semiotics and structural analysis, first to develop a model of the "Qur'ānic Creator Paradigm," and then to study an array of important classical and sectarian Muslim thinkers in support of his thesis. The book offers detailed, if sometimes tendentious, introductions to Islamic metaphysical speculation.

Neusner, Jacob, ed. *God*. Pilgrim Library of World Religions, vol. 1. Cleveland, OH: Pilgrim Press, 1997.

Five scholars approach five traditions as cultural systems to address such questions as: How do Hindus, Buddhists, Jews, Christians, and Muslims understand God, or gods?; Do these gods all fit a common category, or fill a similar role?; How do religious participants interact with the divine?; and, How does religious practice relate to ideas expressed in the literature of each tradition? A useful introductory-level text.

Neusner, Jacob. *The Theology of the Oral Torah: Revealing the Justice of God*. McGill-Queen's Studies in the History of Religion. Montreal: McGill-Queen's University Press, 1999.

Neusner's claim in this massive book (670 pages from prologue to epilogue), which surveys the whole of rabbinic literature, is to have established four principles that define Rabbinic Judaism. First, God created the world according to a plan revealed in Torah. Second, the perfection of creation, realized in the rule of exact justice, is signified by the conformity of human affairs to but a few, changeless paradigms. Third, perfection is marred by the sole power capable of standing on its own against God, namely, human will; Israel's fortunes are the benchmark for assessing this situation. Fourth, God will restore the perfection of Torah.

Neville, Robert C. *Behind the Masks of God: An Essay Toward Comparative Theology*. Albany: State University of New York Press, 1991.

In this volume, Neville again takes up his argument for God the Creator but in the context of the search for "vague categories" that would provide the metaphysical backdrop for comparison between world religions. His aim is to provide not only a methodology of comparison that focuses on truth, but also to show how this methodology works when applied. First, Neville deploys his metaphysics developed in his earlier work, *God the Creator*, arguing that while such thought originates in a Christian context, it has the potential to be a metaphysical foundation of comparison. Second, he explores how his conception of creation *ex nihilo* (including the tripartite distinction between the created, the source of the created, and the act of creation) can not only be found in certain forms of Confucianism, Taoism, and Buddhism, but also how the expressed form of this conception in these religions can help to further clarify the Christian notion of creation *ex nihilo* so as to provide a more adequate and truthful understanding of this notion overall.

Neville, Robert C. *God the Creator: on the Transcendence and Presence of God*. 2nd ed. with a new introduction. Albany: State University of New York Press, 1992 [1968].

Here, Neville makes the argument that most cosmologies are insufficient to account for the world because they amount to a unified set of principles concerning determinate things without accounting for the existence of those determinate principles themselves. He contends that the determination of such first principles depends on an indeterminate source (which he takes to be being-itself or God) for any determinate source would again demand an account of its determinateness. He thus proposes the theory of God being the Creator of all determinate things. This theory maintains that God (being-itself) is wholly indeterminate apart from the act of creation, which gives determination not only to all beings created, including the principles of determination, but also to God, now with the determinate attribution of Creator. Ultimate reality is thus finally construed as indeterminate and a mystery, but also as metaphysically intelligible and gaining determinate second-order attributes via the effects and character of its act of determinate creation.

Nishitani, Keiji. *Religion and Nothingness*. Nanzan Studies in Religion and Culture. Berkeley: University of California Press, 1982. Trans. by Jan Van Bragt.

   Nishitani is among the leading representatives of the Kyoto School of Japanese philosophers of religion. The original Japanese title of this book is *What is Religion?* Nishitani's command of Western philosophy and theology infuses a rich discussion of the meaning of religion in light of the Zen ultimate—Emptiness. Nishitani advances a mutual reinterpretation and reevaluation of Zen and Christian metaphysical thinking and religious imagination. Especially important to this work is its emphasis on distinguishing Emptiness from relative nothingness.

Olson, Alan M. and Leroy S. Rouner, eds. *Transcendence and the Sacred*. Boston University Studies in Philosophy and Religion, vol. 2. Notre Dame, IN: University of Notre Dame Press, 1981.

   These essays are compressed treatments of big themes, carried out with strong cross-cultural interests. Contributors include J. N. Findlay, Hans-Georg Gadamer, Huston Smith, and Robert Thurman. Part I, "Reflections on method in comparative studies," raises questions such as: Is transcendence a genuine philosophical topic?; Is transcendence a quality of an object, or a process?; In either case, can transcendence be made an object for study? Part II contains four scholarly studies of Vedānta, the philosophy of Nāgārjuna and Mahāyāna Buddhism, Japanese Kamakura Buddhism, and Nag Hammadi Gnosticism. Four essays in Part III, "Modes of transcending," focus on human ways of engaging and/or being engaged by transcendence.

Robinson, Timothy A., ed. *God*. Hackett Readings in Philosophy. Indianapolis, IN: Hackett Publishing, 1996.

   This reader in Western, predominantly Christian philosophical theology is useful in two main ways. First, it provides brief selections from important figures, beginning with Augustine and ending with a diverse range of twentieth-century thinkers. The selections are arranged not chronologically but topically; examples of topics include the ontological argument, cosmological argument, and theodicy. Second, it displays major options taken in modern philosophy of religion: critical explanation, phenomenology, constructive atheism, and reconstructive theism.

Schuon, Frithjof. *Logic and Transcendence*. Rev. ed. New York: Harper & Row, 1975. Trans. by Peter Townsend from *Logique et Transcendance*.

   Schuon revives the theory of degrees of being in support of his thesis that religions are to be discriminated according to an esoteric/exoteric distinction. "Exoterically," religions differ, presenting ultimate reality in various forms, as is necessary in the human world of space and time. "Esoterically," they converge upon the Absolute Unity that is the source of everything. However, esoteric knowledge can be had only by a minority of religious adepts who suprarationally intuit their unity with the absolute. A classic post-Kantian theory of religions.

Sontag, Frederick and M. Darrol Bryant, eds. *God, the Contemporary Discussion*. Conference Series (Unification Theological Seminary), vol. 12. New York: Rose of Sharon Press, 1982.

Twenty-two essays are collected here. They were presented at the first of a series of ecumenical conferences sponsored by the Unification Church, and this perhaps accounts for the heterogeneous character of the collection. The first essay, by Heinrich Ott, investigates "Mystery" as an alternative name for God and therefore as a basis for interreligious dialogue. Other essays present a traditional view of God from the perspectives of Eastern Orthodoxy, the Unification Church, and the Anlo people of West Africa. Christian philosophical theology is an approach of many of the papers, but approaches from Jewish, Buddhist, and Indian thought are also included.

Summerell, Orrin F., ed. *The Otherness of God*. Studies in Religion and Culture. Charlottesville: University Press of Virginia, 1998.

Summerell introduces the fifteen essays in this volume as falling into three groups. The first set of essays addresses a single figure in Western philosophical theological tradition and tends to approach the title-phrase as referring to the divine nature as wholly other. The second group, more broadly influenced by deconstruction and continental philosophy, attempts to conceive the otherness *per se* as somehow definitive of religious experience. The third group applies the title to what is other than God, addressing the being of profanity/secularity in theological perspective.

Tessier, Linda J., ed. *Concepts of the Ultimate*. New York: St. Martin's Press, 1989.

A strong point of this book is the inclusion of numerous responses to, and replies from, the authors of the major papers. This allows significant differences to emerge more clearly. Stephen T. Davis argues for, "Why God must be unlimited" (presenting his "classical Christian theism"). John Cobb defends his theology against Davis in "A process concept of God." June O'Connor discusses "Feminism and the Christ." Sushanta Sen recommends "The Vedic-Upaniṣadic concept of Brahman." Christopher Ives considers "Emptiness: Soteriology and ethics in Mahāyāna

Buddhism." And John Hick maintains and defends his philosophical position in "The Real and its personae and impersonae."

Tillich, Paul. *Biblical Religion and the Search for Ultimate Reality*. Chicago: University of Chicago Press, 1955.
    This short book defends the relevance of philosophical, especially ontological, thought for a proper understanding of biblical religion. By this latter, Tillich means the human reception of divine revelation documented in the language and diverse symbols of the Bible, and handed on in church tradition. The root of anti-philosophical stances in Christian theology is the personal character of the experience of the holy. This character is experienced wherever the holy is encountered, but personhood emerges as the key to relationship with the divine in biblical religion. Nonetheless, the religious life lived in response to revelation—that is, faith (defined as "the state of being grasped by an ultimate concern")—is concern for, not mere certainty about, that which *is* really ultimate. Thus, biblical faith precedes but also implies questions about ultimate reality. In this way, ontological questioning and personal faith are not contradictory attitudes.

Tu, Weiming. *Centrality and Commonality: An Essay on Confucian Religiousness*. Rev. ed. SUNY Series in Chinese Philosophy and Culture. Albany: State University of New York Press, 1989. Originally published as *Centrality and Commonality: An Essay on Chung-yung*.
    Taking an interpretive rather than exegetical approach to *Zhong yong* (commonly known as the *Doctrine of the Mean*), Tu Weiming endeavors to show how there is an inner logic running through the seemingly unconnected statements in this classic Confucian text. After an initial chapter on the text itself, Tu Weiming spends the next three chapters analyzing the three key notions of *junzi* (the profound person), *zheng* (politics), and *cheng* (sincerity), endeavoring to demonstrate that through the interrelated issues of the profound person, the fiduciary community, and moral metaphysics, one can discern a holistic, humanist vision in *Zhong yong*.

Zizioulas, Jean. *Being as Communion: Studies in Personhood and the Church*. Contemporary Greek Theologians, vol. 4. Crestwood, NY: St. Vladimir's Seminary Press, 1985.
    Zizioulas explicates his notion of being as communion, which he sees as Christianity's fundamental contribution to metaphysics. With the concept of the Trinity, Christianity asserts that to be at all is to be in relation, for even God can be said to become Father, Son, and Spirit only in the begetting of the Son and the procession of the Spirit. All creation thus finds its

true nature in relation, but it is fallen by virtue of its assertion of autonomous existence. Christ is the perfect savior because as a wholly personal savior (that is, wholly relational, receiving his nature only in relation to the Father and the Spirit) he reveals the ultimately relational character of reality. By union with and in Christ, humankind and the cosmos thus receive not only true relationality, but also true life by virtue of this relationality.

Annotated Bibliography: Chinese Religion

Reference Works

Bibliographies

Thompson, Laurence G. *Chinese Religion in Western Languages: A Comprehensive and Classified Bibliography of Publications in English, French, and German Through 1980.* 2nd. ed. Monographs of the Association for Asian Studies, vol. 41. Tucson, AZ: University of Arizona Press, 1985. Originally published as *Studies of Chinese Religion*, 1976.

Thompson, Laurence G. and Gary Seaman. *Chinese Religion: Publications in Western Languages, 1981 Through 1990.* Monographs of the Association for Asian Studies, vol. 47. Ann Arbor, MI: Association for Asian Studies, 1993.
  These two bibliographic volumes document publications in English, French and German.

Yu, David C. and Laurence G. Thompson. *Guide to Chinese Religion.* Asian Philosophies and Religions Resource Guides. Boston: G. K. Hall, 1985.

Yu, David C. *Religion in Postwar China: A Critical Analysis and Annotated Bibliography.* Bibliographies and Indexes in Religious Studies, vol. 28. Westport, CT: Greenwood Press, 1994.
  This is a comprehensive volume of annotations of selected Chinese- and Western-language works published between 1945 and 1990. It begins with an overview of religion in modern China as viewed by both Chinese and Western scholars. The volume is then divided into two main parts, the first covering works by Chinese scholars, the second by Western scholars.

Dictionaries, Encyclopedias, and Overviews

Boltz, Judith M. *A Survey of Taoist Literature: Tenth to Seventeenth Centuries.* Chinese Research Monographs, vol. 32. Berkeley: Institute of East

Asian Studies and Center for Chinese Studies, University of California, Berkeley, 1987.

This invaluable reference work for scholars of Daoism surveys texts from the vast corpus of the Daoist canon (*Daozang*). The texts are described in considerable detail and classified thematically. A useful epilogue describes helpful reference and bibliographic material in Asian and western languages.

Ching, Julia. *Chinese Religions*. Maryknoll, NY: Orbis Books, 1993.

This is a clear and comprehensive introduction to Chinese religions. Having alerted the reader to the problematical concept of "Chinese religions," the book divides into three roughly chronological sections. Part 1 deals with origins and the indigenous traditions of Confucianism and Daoism. Part 2 considers the influence of foreign religions (Buddhism, Christianity, and Islam) and the response of Neo-Confucian orthodoxy. Part 3 concludes with the issues of syncretism, popular religion, and the contemporary influence of Marxism and Christianity.

Jochim, Christian. *Chinese Religions: A Cultural Perspective*. Englewood Cliffs, NJ: Prentice-Hall, 1986.

This book presents a general picture of Chinese religions from a cultural perspective, outlining the basic features of their theories, practices, and social organizations. It focuses on the interactive relationship between religion and other aspects of Chinese culture, such as arts, literature, politics, and philosophy. A glossary of Chinese terms is also provided.

Kohn, Livia, ed. *A Handbook of Daoism*. Leiden: E. J. Brill, 2000.

Differing from the traditional encyclopedia format, the work consists of twenty-eight comprehensive essays on the major traditions and themes of Daoism from ancient times to the present day, and also essays on Daoism in Japan and Korea and Daoist and music. The essays generally follow a standard format consisting of an introductory description, history, texts, and worldview.

Overmyer, Daniel L. *Religions of China: The World as a Living System*. Religious Traditions of the World. San Francisco: Harper & Row, 1986.

This popular introduction to Chinese religions takes a broadly anthropological approach and emphasizes popular festivals and rituals. After a survey of the history of Chinese religion and an exploration of its general worldview, the author presents a series of short studies describing actual practice of particular festivals and cults.

Pregadio, Fabrizio, ed. *Encyclopedia of Taoism*. London: Curzon Press, 2000.

This encyclopedia promises to be a vital reference work as it has enlisted the services of scholars from around the world. In a traditional encyclopedia format, the work contains short articles on the major texts, traditions, divinities, and personages of Daoist history.

Schipper, Kristofer Marinus and Franciscus Verellen. *Handbook of the Daoist Canon*. Chicago: Chicago University Press, 2000.

Primary Sources

Bokenkamp, Stephen R. and Peter S. Nickerson, eds. *Early Daoist Scriptures*. Taoist Classics, vol. 1. Berkeley: University of California Press, 1997. Translation of several Chinese religious texts with extensive analysis, commentary, and notes. A Philip E. Lilienthal book.

Six substantial early Daoist texts are translated here, beginning with the Xiang'er commentary on the *Daode jing*, and including texts from the three major Daoist movements, the Celestial Masters, Shangqing (Highest Clarity) and Lingbao (Numinous Treasure). Each translation is preceded by a detailed introduction, and the book also contains a general introduction to the worldview of Daoist religion.

Chan, Wing-tsit, ed. *Instructions for Practical Living, and Other Neo-Confucian Writings by Wang Yang-Ming*. Records of Civilization, Sources and Studies, vol. 68. New York: Columbia University Press, 1963.

This is a translation of the *Chuanxi lu*, a collection of Wang Yangming's conversations and letters in three parts compiled by his disciples. Containing all of Wang's fundamental doctrines, it represents the major work of what Chan refers to as the "idealistic" wing of Neo-Confucianism. Also included, among other short supplementary works, is Wang's *Inquiry on the Great Learning*, a fairly systematic embodiment of the essential ideas of the *Instructions for Practical Living*.

Chan, Wing-tsit, ed. *Neo-Confucian Terms Explained: The Pei-Hsi Tzu-i*. Neo-Confucian Studies. New York: Columbia University Press, 1986.

This is a translation of the *Beixi ziyi*, a work explaining Neo-Confucian philosophical terms written by Chen Chun (1159–1223), one of Zhu Xi's students. There are altogether 26 categories in two chapters, starting with *ming* (mandate, destiny) and ending with treatments of Buddhism and Daoism. Chan's translation also includes three supplements, one being Chen Chun's well-known lectures at Yanling, and fourteen appendices.

Chan, Wing-tsit, ed. *Reflections on Things at Hand: The Neo-Confucian Anthology Compiled by Chu Hsi and Lü Tsu-Ch'ien*. Records of Civilization, Sources and Studies, vol. 75. New York: Columbia University Press, 1967.

The first English translation of the *Jinsi lu*, *Reflections on Things at Hand* is an anthology of the "rationalistic" wing of Neo-Confucianism. It comprises 622 passages selected by the compilers from the works of four Northern Song masters, Zhou Dunyi, the Cheng brothers, and Zhang Zai, and offers a comprehensive survey of Neo-Confucian philosophy. Beginning with a chapter on the substance of the way, it proceeds to such topics as self-cultivation, the regulation of the family, national order, heterodox systems, and the dispositions of Confucian sages and worthies, all of which are governed by the fundamental idea of principle (*li*).

Chan, Wing-tsit, ed. *A Source Book in Chinese Philosophy*. Princeton, NJ: Princeton University Press, 1963.

The first anthology to cover the entire historical development of Chinese philosophy, this source book provides substantial selections from the works of all the major thinkers and schools in the ancient, medieval, and modern periods. Chan not only translates the whole material himself so as to achieve consistency, but also offers helpful introductions before each translation with extensive comments and notes throughout the texts.

De Bary, William Theodore et al., eds. *Sources of Chinese Tradition*. 2nd ed. Introduction to Asian Civilizations, vol. 1. New York: Columbia University Press, 1999.

This is a revised and expanded edition of the two-volume *Sources of the Chinese Tradition* published close to forty years ago. Volume One is an anthology of primary texts covering the three thousand year period from the late Shang dynasty to the end of the Ming dynasty (1644 CE). This updated volume includes not only new translations of most of the materials in the first edition, thus doing justice to recent progress in scholarship, but also many new selections. The readings are arranged chronologically in four groups: the Chinese tradition in antiquity, the making of a classical culture, later Daoism and Mahāyāna Buddhism, and the Confucian revival and Neo-Confucianism. Volume Two is not yet published at the time of writing.

Graham, A. C., ed. *Chuang-Tzu: The Seven Inner Chapters and Other Writings from the Book Chuang-Tzu*. London: Allen & Unwin, 1981. Selected translations from *Nan-hua Ching*.

Graham's critique of the previous translators of the *Zhuangzi* is that they for the most part follow the traditional commentators without coming to grips with the textual, linguistic, and philosophical problems. He argues that one should not treat *Zhuangzi* as if it was a whole-length book written in prose and divided into chapters. As reflected in his own translation, Graham does not intend to offer integral renderings except of certain homogeneous blocks such as the *Inner chapters*, and he specifically attributes different chapters to different "authors" such as the Primitivist, the Yangists, and the Syncretists.

Henricks, Robert G., ed. *Lao-Tzu Te-Tao Ching: A New Translation Based on the Recently Discovered Ma-Wang-Tui Texts.* Classics of Ancient China. New York: Ballantine Books, 1989.

This translation is based on the two texts of the *Dedao jing* found in the Mawangdui excavations in 1973. These ancient texts reverse the traditional order of the *Daode jing*, beginning with Chapters 38–81 (the *Dejing*) and continuing with Chapters 1–37 (the *Daojing*). Part 1 of Henricks's book offers a straightforward translation. Part 2 repeats the translation but adds a textual commentary and reproduces the two Chinese texts on which the translation is based.

Knoblock, John, ed. *Xunzi: A Translation and Study of the Complete Works*, 3 vols. Stanford, CA: Stanford University Press, 1988.

Comparing Xunzi's (c. 298–238 BCE) domain of knowledge to Aristotle's, John Knoblock aims to produce a literate English translation that conveys the full meaning of Xunzi's philosophical arguments. Volume I contains a general introduction and the first six books of Xunzi's works, which discuss self-cultivation, learning, and education. Published in Volume II are Books 7–16, discussing political theory, ethics, the ideal person, and the lessons to be drawn from history. Volume III has two parts: Books 17–24 discuss problems of knowledge, language and logic, nature of the world and human beings, and the significance of music and ritual; Books 25–32 are Xunzi's poetry, short passages, and historical anecdotes.

Kohn, Livia, ed. *The Taoist Experience: An Anthology.* SUNY Series in Chinese Philosophy and Culture. Albany: State University of New York Press, 1993.

Kohn's anthology of translations encompasses a wide range of Daoist texts, with an emphasis on the major religious movements of the medieval period. Each translation is briefly introduced by the author, who has arranged the texts thematically under the four major headings of "The Tao," "Long Life," "Eternal Vision," and "Immortality." The book contains a useful bibliography and index.

LaFargue, Michael, ed. *The Tao of the Tao Te Ching: A Translation and Commentary*. SUNY Series in Chinese Philosophy and Culture. Albany: State University of New York Press, 1992.

LaFargue, a scholar of hermeneutics, takes care to explain each element of his translation, and offers a useful commentary. The text does not follow the usual arrangement, but is arranged thematically, and an index dispels potential confusion. His psychological interpretation shows that the Dao of the *Daode jing* is best understood as an ideal mode of existence rather than as a cosmological or metaphysical entity.

Lau, D. C., ed. *The Analects of Confucius*. 2nd ed. Hong Kong: Chinese University Press, 1992 [1979]. Originally published without the accompanying Chinese text by Penguin Books, 1979.

The text of the translation is preceded by an introduction in which Lau offers a detailed analysis of Confucius's philosophy. In the three appendixes, Lau provides more information concerning the events in the life of Confucius, the disciples as they appear in the *Analects*, and the history of the *Lun Yu*.

Lau, D. C., ed. *Mencius*, 2 vols. Bilingual ed. Chinese Classics, Chinese-English Series. Hong Kong: Chinese University Press, 1984.

The book of Meng Ke (Mencius, c. fourth century BCE) is a profound but accessible work of Confucian moral philosophy. This classic translation contains an introduction and five appendices illuminating the text, its author, and his historical background.

Lopez, Donald S., ed. *Religions of China in Practice*. Princeton Readings in Religions. Princeton, NJ: Princeton University Press, 1996.

This anthology of translations by a variety of China scholars avoids undue emphasis on philosophical texts and instead attempts to represent the diversity of Chinese religious history, covering texts from Buddhism, Confucianism, Daoism, popular religion, minority religions, and state cults from ancient times to the present day. The book is arranged thematically, though there is a chronological index, and an index by tradition. Each text is introduced by the translator.

Rickett, W. Allyn, ed. *Guanzi: Political, Economic, and Philosophical Essays from Early China: A Study and Translation*, 2 vols. Princeton Library of Asian Translations. Princeton, NJ: Princeton University Press, 1985.

The *Guanzi*, an "amorphous and vast repository of ancient literature," is one of the largest politico-philosophical documents of the pre-Han or early Han period. Rickett's work—a project of three volumes—is the first full translation and study of the *Guanzi* in a Western language.

The present two volumes are devoted to the full translation of the text with notes and bibliography, and the third will be devoted to separate studies by various scholars.

Rosemont, Henry and Roger T. Ames, eds. *The Analects of Confucius: A Philosophical Translation.* Classics of Ancient China. New York: Ballantine Publishing Group, 1998.

This book opens with an introduction in two parts, offering the historical and textual as well as the philosophical and linguistic backgrounds of the *Analects of Confucius (Lunyu).* The purpose of the philosophical introduction is to enable the reader to take the Confucian way on its own terms without overwriting it with cultural interests and importances that are not its own. The English translation is juxtaposed with the original Chinese text, and the book ends with a discussion on the recently discovered *Dingzhou Analects* and some further remarks on language, translation, and interpretation.

Wilhelm, Richard, ed. *The I Ching or Book of Changes.* 3rd ed. Bollingen Series, vol. 19. Princeton, NJ: Princeton University Press, 1967 [1950]. Trans. into English by Cary F. Baynes.

This English translation of Wilhelm's classic German translation of the *Yijing* (Book of Changes) remains popular not least because it contains a substantial foreword by Carl Jung on the subject of divination, causality, and chance.

Secondary Sources

Texts, Figures, and Traditions

Ames, Roger T. *The Art of Rulership: A Study in Ancient Chinese Political Thought.* Honolulu: University of Hawaii Press, 1983. Includes an English trans. of *Huai-nan Tzu.* 9 by Chu shu hsün and Huai-nan tzu.

The *Zhu shu (Art of Rulership)* is Book 9 of the *Huainanzi.* Before offering a translation of the text, Ames first presents a study of the philosophy of history in ancient China and then traces the evolution of five key concepts, namely, *wuwei* (nonassertive action), *shi* (strategic advantage), *fa* (penal law), *yongzhong* (utilizing the people), and *limin* (benefiting the people), in early Chinese political philosophy up to the time of the *Art of Rulership,* showing that the *Art of Rulership* contains a systematic political theory with precepts of Daoist and Confucian origin.

Berling, Judith A. *A Pilgrim in Chinese Culture: Negotiating Religious Diversity.* Faith Meets Faith. Maryknoll, NY: Orbis Books, 1997.

Berling, a scholar of Chinese religions, and Dean of the Graduate Theological Union at Berkeley, presents a personal exploration of the themes of religious diversity and cross-cultural dialogue. Her aim is to relate contemporary questions of religious diversity to the way the Chinese religious scene has traditionally encompassed an extraordinary breadth of religious cultures.

Berthrong, John H. *Transformations of the Confucian Way.* Explorations. Boulder, CO: Westview Press, 1998.

In this historical survey of the Confucian tradition throughout East Asia, Berthrong covers each of Confucianism's major transformations and also the less talked about periods of the Han, T'ang, and the modern era. The spread of Confucianism to Korea and Japan is taken into consideration as well, and Berthrong ends the book with a report of its recent spread to the West.

Ching, Julia. *Mysticism and Kingship in China: The Heart of Chinese Wisdom.* Cambridge Studies in Religious Traditions, vol. 11. Cambridge: Cambridge University Press, 1997.

Julia Ching offers a survey of Chinese religious culture using the paradigm of the sage-king. Her argument is basically twofold: that the institutions of kingship were bound up with communication with the spirits, and that this concept of the sage-king was appropriated as a private religious ideal. The sage-king thus lies at the heart of the political and spiritual worlds.

De Bary, William Theodore. *Neo-Confucian Orthodoxy and the Learning of the Mind-and-Heart.* Neo-Confucian Studies. New York: Columbia University Press, 1981.

This is an intellectual history of what De Bary terms "Neo-Confucian orthodoxy," i.e., the "Cheng-Zhu" lineage of teaching that, in its various forms, claims descent from Zhu Xi and his "learning of the mind-and-heart." The book has three parts: Part I deals with the rise of Neo-Confucian orthodoxy in Yuan China, Part II with the Neo-Confucian learning of the mind-and-heart, and Part III with Neo-Confucian orthodoxies and the learning of the mind-and-heart in early Tokugawa Japan.

Feng, Yu-lan. *A History of Chinese Philosophy,* 2 vols. 2nd ed. Princeton: Princeton University Press, 1952. Trans. by Derk Bodde.

On the subject of the history of Chinese philosophy, Feng's distinctive work remains one of the most complete and learned. Volume I, "The Period of the Philosophers," covers the history from the beginnings to about 100 B.C. when Confucianism became the state ideology. Volume II, "The Period of Classical Learning," continues the story from the second century B.C. to the end of Qing dynasty.

Fingarette, Herbert. *Confucius: The Secular as Sacred*. New York: Harper & Row, 1972.

Fingarette, a noted philosopher, attempts to discover the true teaching of Confucius through an investigation of the first fifteen books of the *Analects*. Emphasizing the ritual performance of moral codes, Fingarette starts with the thesis of human community as holy rite and ends with a Confucian metaphor, namely, the noble person is a holy vessel. This was one of the first modern Western studies to suggest that the Confucian way can make great contributions to our contemporary understanding of the world and society.

Graham, A. C. *Disputers of the Tao: Philosophical Argument in Ancient China*. La Salle, IL: Open Court, 1989.

This book offers a general picture of Chinese philosophy in the classical age (500–200 BCE) with the focus on debate between rival schools, hence its title. Graham organizes the discussion of Confucius, Mencius, Mozi, Zhuangzi, Laozi, Xunzi, and other thinkers, following a dramatic line: from the breakdown of the world order decreed by heaven to the social and metaphysical crises when heaven parts from humankind; and from this separation to the reunification of the empire, heaven, and humankind. Graham adds two appendixes, one on the classification of Chinese moral philosophies in terms of the quasi-syllogism, one on the relation of Chinese thought to Chinese language.

Hall, David L. and Roger T. Ames. *Anticipating China: Thinking Through the Narratives of Chinese and Western Culture*. Albany: State University of New York Press, 1995.

In this sequel to *Thinking through Confucius*, the two authors clarify and develop many ideas they have been discussing in the previous book. To illumine the contrasting assumptions shaping classical Western and Chinese cultures, Hall and Ames provide two parallel accounts of cultural development, one culminating with the work of Augustine and the other represented by the thinking of the Han dynasty. In doing this, they aim to offer a better way of understanding Chinese culture with less bias and distortion.

Hall, David L. and Roger T. Ames. *Thinking from the Han: Self, Truth, and Transcendence in Chinese and Western Culture*. Albany: State University of New York Press, 1998.

This volume completes Hall and Ames's trilogy on comparative studies of Chinese and Western culture. Here they choose to focus their comparative discussions on the subjects of self, truth, and transcendence, as they believe that these subjects lie at the heart of human issues causing mutual misunderstanding between the two cultures.

Hall, David L. and Roger T. Ames. *Thinking Through Confucius.* SUNY Series in Systematic Philosophy. Albany: State University of New York Press, 1987.

Using a method termed by the authors themselves as "cross-cultural anachronism," Hall and Ames seek to understand Confucius's ideas as expressed in the *Analects* by recourse to contemporary Western philosophical and cultural issues. They believe that in comparative philosophy difference is more important than similarity, and that the recognition of this difference can provide mutual enrichment by suggesting alternative responses to problems that resist resolution within a single culture.

Hansen, Chad. *A Daoist Theory of Chinese Thought: A Philosophical Interpretation.* New York: Oxford University Press, 1992.

Attributing a theory of language and mind to ancient Chinese thinkers that differs fundamentally from the popular Western view, Hansen identifies and examines four progressive stages in Classical doctrines about language and mind: the positive *dao* period, the antilanguage period, the analytic period, and the authoritarian period.

Henderson, John B. *The Development and Decline of Chinese Cosmology.* Neo-Confucian Studies. New York: Columbia University Press, 1984.

This work is a history of Chinese cosmology. Chapters 1 and 2 examine correlative thought and geometrical cosmography in Early China, with the next two chapters devoted to medieval criticisms and extensions of correlative cosmology and its status in the Neo-Confucian tradition. Chapters 5 and 6 discuss the intellectual transition in Early Qing, and Chapters 7 and 8 discuss criticisms of correlative cosmology and geometrical cosmography in late-traditional China. Henderson ends the book with a chapter on Qing scholars' anticosmological worldview.

Ivanhoe, P. J. *Confucian Moral Self Cultivation.* The Rockwell Lecture Series, vol. 3. New York: Peter Lang, 1993.

Based on three lectures, this work focuses on the concept of moral self-cultivation in the Confucian tradition. After an initial introduction of related ideas in the Shang and Zhou dynasties, Ivanhoe turns to the philosophy of Confucius, Mencius, Xunzi, Zhu Xi, Wang Yangming, and Dai Zhen for the specific treatment of the notion of self-cultivation.

Kohn, Livia. *Early Chinese Mysticism: Philosophy and Soteriology in the Taoist Tradition.* Princeton, NJ: Princeton University Press, 1992.

This work is a scholarly survey of mysticism in Daoist thought and practice from the fourth century BCE through to the T'ang dynasty (618–960 CE). It dwells equally on the earlier writings of Laozi and Zhuangzi as well as the later Daoist movements. The book begins with a theoretical exposition of mysticism in human experience and demonstrates the continuous development of Daoism as a form of mystical philosophy well before and during the impact of Buddhism.

Kohn, Livia. *God of the Dao: Lord Lao in History and Myth*. Michigan Monographs in Chinese Studies, vol. 84. Ann Arbor: Center for Chinese Studies, University of Michigan, 1998.

This is a comprehensive study of Laozi as the divine persona of the Dao and is divided into two roughly equal sections. The first surveys the historical evidence in hagiographies, inscriptions, and art, while the second aims to uncover the mythological significance of the data. The work thus combines the methods of the sinologist and the scholar of comparative religion in an attempt to paint a more complete picture of Lord Lao.

Kohn, Livia and Michael LaFargue, eds. *Lao-Tzu and the Tao-Te-Ching*. Albany: State University of New York Press, 1998.

This collection of essays by leading Daoist scholars presents the person and the text together. Scholarly essays on the textual interpretation of the *Daode jing* are complemented by historical studies of Laozi, the legendary author of the text, and his incorporation into the Daoist pantheon.

Lagerwey, John. *Taoist Ritual in Chinese Society and History*. New York: Macmillan, 1987.

This rich and detailed study aims to answer the question "What is Daoism?" by examining its religious practices. Part I examines the cosmological context of Chinese religion. Part II analyses specific Daoist liturgies for the living and for the dead. Part III is concerned with the relationship between liturgical Daoism and Chinese society.

Lewis, Mark Edward. *Writing and Authority in Early China*. SUNY Series in Chinese Philosophy and Culture. Albany: State University of New York Press, 1999.

This book studies the evolution of writing in early China, examining all sorts of materials from divinatory records, written communications with the dead, and official documents, to philosophical texts, chronicles, and scholastic commentaries. In so doing, the book demonstrates the various functions of these writings, such as governing people, controlling officials, and forming communities. Lewis argues that this culture of writing ultimately produced a body of literature upon which imperial authority was built.

Liu, Shu hsien. *Understanding Confucian Philosophy: Classical and Sung-Ming.* Contributions in Philosophy, vol. 61. Westport, CT: Greenwood Press, 1998.

Widely recognized as a representative of contemporary Confucianism, Liu complains that little work has been done in the West to study the tradition from a contemporary, rather than a historical, perspective. This book, of which two-thirds are previously written articles and one-third new materials, is just such an attempt on the part of Liu to fill this gap.

Machle, Edward J. *Nature and Heaven in the Xunzi: A Study of the Tian Lun.* SUNY Series in Chinese Philosophy and Culture. Albany: State University of New York Press, 1993.

Arguing against naturalistic interpretations of Xunzi's concept of *Tian* (Heaven), Machle here offers a close reading of the *Tian Lun*, which is usually referred to in English as the *Essay on Nature* or the *Discussion of Heaven*. The core of the work is a translation of the *Tian Lun*, with extensive commentary, and it is both preceded and followed by other chapters dealing with interpretive problems and other issues.

Mair, Victor H., ed. *Experimental Essays on Chuang-Tzu.* Asian Studies at Hawaii, vol. 29. Honolulu: Center for Asian and Pacific Studies, University of Hawaii, 1983.

This book is a collection of eight essays plus a bibliographical appendix, the experimental nature of which lies in its contributors not being all sinologists. The stated aim of this collection is to view Zhuangzi from "many different vantage points while using diverse methodological approaches." The contributors include A. C. Graham, Chad Hansen, Victor Mair, Michael Saso, and Hideki Yukawa, the 1949 Nobel Prize winner in physics.

Major, John S. *Heaven and Earth in Early Han Thought: Chapters Three, Four and Five of the Huainanzi.* SUNY Series in Chinese Philosophy and Culture. Albany: State University of New York Press, 1993.

Written over the course of more than twenty-five years, this work offers for the first time full English translations of the three key chapters on cosmology in the *Huainanzi*, which are *Tianwen xun* (The Treatise on the Patterns of Heaven), *Dixing xun* (The Treatise on Topography), and *Shici xun* (The Treatise on the Seasonal Rules). Additionally, there is an appendix of related material by Christopher Cullen

Porkert, Manfred. *The Theoretical Foundations of Chinese Medicine: Systems of Correspondence.* MIT East Asian Science Series, vol. 3. Cambridge: MIT Press, 1974. Trans. of the author's Habilitationsschrift published under the title *Die Theoretischen Grundlagen der Chinesischen Medizin*, Munich.

This work is a technical, comprehensive, and detailed guide not only to the theoretical basis of Chinese medicine but also to the traditional Chinese way of correlative thinking. The correlation of yin-yang and the five phases with the seasons, physiological systems, and the heavens is presupposed by many Chinese religious ideas and practices.

Raphals, Lisa Ann. *Sharing the Light: Representations of Women and Virtue in Early China*. SUNY Series in Chinese Philosophy and Culture. Albany: State University of New York Press, 1998.

This book examines historical and philosophical changes in the representation of women and virtue in Early China. It is organized into two parts. The first deals with two divergent views of women in early texts, for example, either as agents of virtue or as causes of chaos, with particular attention given to the textual analysis of the *Lienü zhuan* (Collected Life Stories of Women). The second part focuses on the discussion of two pairs of concepts, yin-yang and nei-wai (inner-outer), both of which have been used to justify the inferior status of women. Lisa Raphals ends the book with remarks concerning the role of contemporary "Neo-Confucian" ideologies and their appropriations of Chinese views of gender.

Robinet, Isabelle and Phyllis Brooks. *Taoism: Growth of a Religion*. Stanford, CA: Stanford University Press, 1997. Trans. by Phyllis Brooks.

This historical survey is a vital introduction to Daoism from the Warring States period (403–222 BCE) through to the Yuan dynasty (1279–1367 CE). Eschewing the division of Daoism into "philosophy" and "religion" the work presents the development of Daoist thought and practice hand in hand, emphasizing the medieval period, which saw the rapid flourishing of the major Daoist movements. The work is intended for a general educated audience and thus does not include an extensive academic apparatus.

Robinet, Isabelle. *Taoist Meditation: The Mao-Shan Tradition of Great Purity*. SUNY Series in Chinese Philosophy and Culture. Albany: State University of New York Press, 1993. Trans. by Julian Pas and Norman Girardot.

This book is an expanded edition of the French original published in 1979, and presents a detailed, systematic survey of the Shangqing (Highest Clarity or Great Purity) movement that began around 365 CE with a series of revelations to a religious visionary, Yang Xi. The movement became one of the three major schools of medieval Daoism, emphasizing the inner vision of gods in the body.

Schipper, Kristofer Marinus. *The Taoist Body*. Berkeley: University of California Press, 1993. Trans. by Karen C. Duval from *Le Corps Taoïste*.
Schipper trained as a sinologist in Paris before moving to Taiwan where he became the first Westerner to be ordained as a Daoist priest. This combination of scholarly training and first hand experience has resulted in a remarkable book. It is perhaps the only general guide in English to the actual practice of Daoism, its social significance, and its theoretical and historical foundations.

Schwartz, Benjamin Isadore. *The World of Thought in Ancient China*. Cambridge, MA: Belknap Press of Harvard University Press, 1985.
In dealing with the world of thought in ancient China, Schwartz intentionally avoids comprehensive coverage and instead chooses to concentrate on issues and themes that he deems of particular significance. By focusing on modes of thought reflected in the texts of the so-called "high culture," such as Confucianism, Daoism, and Legalism, Schwartz suggests that the elite culture of China, while sharing a possible common Neolithic background with the popular culture, later diverges in crucial ways from it.

Shaughnessy, Edward L. *Before Confucius: Studies in the Creation of the Chinese Classics*. SUNY Series in Chinese Philosophy and Culture. Albany: State University of New York Press, 1997.
Convinced that ancient China was already a highly literate culture hundreds of years before Confucius, Shaughnessy devotes the eight essays collected in this volume to the study of the works allegedly produced by the Zhou people. By examining China's oldest classics, which include the *Zhouyi* (*Changes of Zhou*), the *Shangshu* (*Venerated Documents*), and the *Shijing* (*Classic of Poetry*), Shaughnessy tries to determine the original meaning and context of the text. In some cases he is also able to show how this original meaning may have been changed or obscured by later traditions.

Taylor, Rodney Leon. *The Religious Dimensions of Confucianism*. SUNY Series in Religious Studies. Albany: State University of New York Press, 1990.
Nine previously published or presented papers form the nine chapters of this volume, with such topics as Confucianism and the political order, scripture and the sage, the sage as saint, Christian and Confucian dimen-

sions of the problem of suffering, and a contemporary Confucian phenomenon in Japan. To the question of whether Confucianism is a religion or not, Taylor's answer is a positive Yes.

Tsukamoto, Zenryu. *A History of Early Chinese Buddhism: From Its Introduction to the Death of Hui-Yüan*, 2 vols. Tokyo: Kodansha International, 1985. Trans. by Leon Hurvitz from *Chugoku Bukkyo Tsushi*.

This monumental, detailed history covers the introduction of Buddhism to China in the Latter Han dynasty up to the death of Hui-Yüan (433 CE).

Tu, Weiming. *Centrality and Commonality: An Essay on Confucian Religiousness.* 2nd ed. SUNY Series in Chinese Philosophy and Culture. Albany: State University of New York Press, 1989. Originally published as *Centrality and Commonality: An Essay on Chung-yung.*

Taking an interpretive rather than exegetical approach to *Zhong yong* (commonly known as the *Doctrine of the Mean*), Tu Weiming endeavors to show how there is an inner logic running through the seemingly unconnected statements in this Confucian classic. After an initial chapter on the text, Tu spends the next three in analyzing the three key notions of *junzi* (the profound person), *zheng* (politics), and *cheng* (sincerity), seeking to demonstrate that through the inter-related issues of the profound person, the fiduciary community, and moral metaphysics, one can discern a holistic humanist vision in *Zhong yong.*

Tu, Weiming. *Confucian Thought: Selfhood as Creative Transformation.* SUNY Series in Philosophy. Albany: State University of New York Press, 1985.

Through the nine essays collected in this book, Tu Weiming attempts to answer the question posed to him by Robert Bellah: "What is the Confucian self?" Taking seriously the centrality of self-cultivation in the Confucian tradition, Tu explores the many subtle dimensions of Confucian thought by trying to understand Confucius in the light of Mencius and Mencius in the light of Wang Yangming.

Tu, Weiming. *Way, Learning, and Politics: Essays on the Confucian Intellectual.* SUNY Series in Chinese Philosophy and Culture. Albany: State University of New York Press, 1993.

This collection of articles offers historical and comparative cultural perspectives on the Confucian intellectual, the underlying thesis being that the Confucian literati exemplify the intellectual spirit when they conscientiously repossess the way, transmit culture, and rectify politics. The nine essays are grouped in three interrelated parts: the first four deals with the classical period, the next three with the Neo-Confucian era, and the last two with modern times.

Weber, Max. *The Religion of China: Confucianism and Taoism.* New York: Free Press, 1968. Trans. and ed. by Hans H. Gerth from *Konfuzianismus und Taoismus,* published in 1922 in vol. 1 of Weber's *Gesammelte Aufsätze zur Religionssoziologie.*

Based on his celebrated analysis of the affinity between Protestantism and capitalism, Weber aims to investigate the relationship of capital and religion in Chinese society. Part One draws a picture of the sociological foundations of China, including discussions on Chinese money, city and guild, central and local governments, and feudal and fiscal as well as army organizations. Part Two examines the literati and the Confucian life orientation. Part Three considers Daoism, and then discusses the relationship between Confucianism and Puritanism.

Weinstein, Stanley. *Buddhism Under the T'ang.* Cambridge Studies in Chinese History, Literature, and Institutions. Cambridge: Cambridge University Press, 1987.

The penetration of Buddhism in Chinese society reached its zenith in the T'ang dynasty (618–960 CE). This historical survey emphasizes the relations of the Buddhist church with the central government rather than Buddhist thought or liturgy.

Contemporary Philosophy and Religion

Ch'eng, Chung ying. *New Dimensions of Confucian and Neo-Confucian Philosophy.* SUNY Series in Philosophy. Albany: State University of New York Press, 1991.

This book represents over twenty years of scholarly work on the part of Ch'eng, a leading contemporary Confucian philosopher. Grouped into three parts, "Chinese Philosophical Orientations," "Confucian Dimensions," and "Neo-Confucian Dimensions," these articles, while individually self-contained studies of specific topics, collectively present a thorough and detailed image of Confucianism for the philosophically literate reader.

Ching, Julia. *Probing China's Soul: Religion, Politics, and Protest in the People's Republic.* San Francisco: Harper & Row, 1990.

This powerful and provocative book is a meditation on China's intellectual and religious situation in the light of the Tian'anmen massacre on June 4th, 1989. Julia Ching's focuses her analysis on the question:

"Which is more important: to be human or to be Chinese?" The book contains an appendix of documents.

De Bary, William Theodore and Tu Weiming, eds. *Confucianism and Human Rights*. New York: Columbia University Press, 1998.

This book contains papers from a conference on "Confucianism and Human Rights" held at the East-West Center in Honolulu in 1995, with a variety of topics ranging from the Yellow Emperor tradition to rites and rights in Ming China. W. Theodore de Bary offers in the introduction a general survey of the basic thesis and argument of each essay as well as seven statements in the form of a rough consensus for future dialogue between China and the West. The book ends the discussion of "Confucianism and Human Rights" with two epilogues written by Tu Weiming and Louis Henkin.

Feuchtwang, Stephan. *The Imperial Metaphor: Popular Religion in China*. London: Routledge, 1992.

This anthropological study of popular Chinese religion covers the major Chinese festivals, local and official cults in Taiwan and China, and contemporary Daoist practices. Based on the author's fieldwork, as well as, that of other anthropologists and scholars of religion, the text describes numerous rituals and offers a systematic explanation of the functioning of Chinese religion.

MacInnis, Donald E. *Religion in China Today: Policy and Practice*. Maryknoll, NY: Orbis Books, 1989.

This is an anthology of documents relating to the Chinese religious situation since the cultural revolution. It is divided into two sections: documents of religious policy by government and religious leaders, and documents dealing with religious practice, including Chinese Buddhism, Tibetan Buddhism, Daoism, Islam, Christianity, atheism, and Marxism.

Tu Weiming, Milan Hejtmanek, and Alan Wachman, eds. *The Confucian World Observed: A Contemporary Discussion of Confucian Humanism in East Asia*. Honolulu: Institute of Culture and Communication, The East-West Center, 1992.

This book comes out of a workshop on Confucian humanism sponsored by the American Academy of Arts and Sciences in 1989. The purpose of the workshop was "to explore Confucian ethics as a common intellectual discourse in East Asia from a multidisciplinary and cross-cultural perspective," with special attention given to its role in the shaping of such perceptions as selfhood, family relations, gender, social organization and political authority, popular beliefs, and economic culture in East Asia.

Weller, Robert P. *Unities and Diversities in Chinese Religion*. Seattle: University of Washington Press, 1987.

Based on his fieldwork in the town of Sanxia in Taiwan from 1976 to 1979, Weller takes in this study the ghost-feeding ritual as the starting point for a more general analysis of religious unity and diversity in China. By examining the viewpoints of three major kinds of participants in the ceremony—ordinary worshippers, religious specialists and the secular elite—he tries to demonstrate how the same ritual can be differently experienced and interpreted by different people.

Annotated Bibliography: Buddhism

Reference Works

Bibliographies

Inada, Kenneth K. *Guide to Buddhist Philosophy*. Asian Philosophies and Religions Resource Guides. Boston: G. K. Hall, 1985.

Reynolds, Frank E., John Strong, and John Holt. *Guide to Buddhist Religion*. Asian Philosophies and Religions Resource Guides. Boston: Hall, 1981.

Dictionaries and Encyclopedias

Humphreys, Christmas. *A Popular Dictionary of Buddhism*. 2nd ed. 1976 [1962]. Previous ed. published by London: Arco, 1962.

A concise "glossary" of Buddhist peoples, places, texts, and terms. Entries provide very little beyond basic definitions, making this work useful primarily as a quick reference for those lacking familiarity with Buddhist tradition.

Prebish, Charles S. *Historical Dictionary of Buddhism*. Historical Dictionaries of Religions, Philosophies, and Movements, vol. 1. Metuchen, NJ: Scarecrow Press, 1993.

A single volume encyclopedia covering "significant persons, places, events, texts, doctrines, practices, institutions, and movements." An outline of Buddhist scriptures, a chronology, and a brief introductory section providing historical perspective and descriptions of fundamental Buddhist concepts make the text more accessible to beginning students of Buddhism. The historical framework of the text limits its value with respect to contemporary aspects of Buddhist culture.

Primary Sources

Conze, Edward, ed. *Buddhist Scriptures*. Penguin Classics, vol. L88. Harmondsworth, Middlesex: Penguin Books, 1959.

This brief and highly accessible collection of texts was designed with the lay reader in mind. Included are excerpts from the Jataka tales, Ashvaghosha's *Buddhacarita*, and works dealing with central doctrines of Buddhism, including the *Dharmapada* and *Dhammapada*, and "The Questions of King Milinda." Conze's compendium concludes with a treatment of the "other worlds" of Buddhism as depicted in Tibetan and Pure Land sources.

Conze, Edward, ed. *Buddhist Texts Through the Ages: Translated from Pali, Sanskrit, Chinese, Tibetan, Japanese, and Apabhramsa*. Harper Torchbooks, vol. TB 113. New York: Harper & Row, 1964.

Surveying the broad linguistic, geographic and philosophical expanse of the tradition, this collection offers selections from the Hīnayāna/Tradition of the Elders, Mahāyāna, Tantric, and Sino-Japanese branches of Buddhism. Translations are presented without commentary or explanatory notations.

Conze, Edward, ed. *The Perfection of Wisdom in Eight Thousand Lines and Its Verse Summary*. Wheel Series, vol. 1. Bolinas: Four Seasons Foundation, 1973. Translated from the Sanskrit.

Accessibility and intelligibility outweigh literal precision in Conze's translation of the verse and prose texts of the *Prajñāparamita*. The *Ratnaguṇa* (verse sūtra) presents a lively and direct encapsulation of early Mahāyāna thought, employing similes throughout to illuminate key concepts. The *Ashta* (prose text) presents a dialogue among the Buddha, his leading student, and various other interlocutors which rationally and more systematically presents Buddhist doctrine and ethics.

Cowell, Edward B. et al., eds. *The Jataka: Stories of the Buddha's Former Births*, 6 vols. Delhi: Cosmos Publications, 1973. Reprint of the ed. published by Cambridge University Press, 1895–1907.

A comprehensive and entertaining collection of myths and folklore surrounding the lives of the Buddha. The *Jataka* are translated together with their presumably apocryphal introductions, which ostensibly locate their narration within the course of the Buddha's teaching. These stories colorfully capture central Buddhist concepts concerning the human condition and ethics as well as encapsulating early popular beliefs.

Lopez, Donald S., ed. *Buddhism in Practice*. Princeton Readings in Religions. Princeton, NJ: Princeton University Press, 1995.

This collection of texts, together with Lopez's supplementary materials, emphasize the practical and experiential dimensions of Buddhism, rather than the philosophical-theoretical. Lopez seeks to represent texts, voices, and traditions often excluded from academic anthologies. Selections include prayers, songs, autobiographies, and ritual manuals, many appearing for the first time in translation. Detailed introductions and notations provide readers with necessary background and make available the innovative insights of recent scholarship.

Lopez, Donald S., ed. *Religions of Tibet in Practice*. Princeton Readings in Religions. Princeton, NJ: Princeton University Press, 1997.

This collection of diverse texts introduces readers to the complexity and richness of Tibetan religious culture. Entries reflect both Buddhist and Bn perspectives on a variety of topics, including hagiography, demonology, prayer, death, and ultimate reality. Ample preparatory materials furnish historical and theoretical background and trace the connections and cross-fertilization among traditions.

Secondary Sources

Abe, Masao and Steven Heine. *A Study of Dogen: His Philosophy and Religion*. Albany: State University of New York Press, 1992.

Marrying the comparative philosophical approach of the Kyoto School with rigorous textual scholarship, Abe introduces readers to the thought of Dogen Kigen, founder of the Japanese Soto Zen sect. Featured discussions include Dogen's views of the Buddha-nature, time/space, and death and rebirth. The author offers a helpful glossary of Sino-Japanese terms.

Abe, Masao. *Buddhism and Interfaith Dialogue*. Honolulu: University of Hawaii Press, 1995. Ed. by Steven Heine. Part One of a two-volume sequel to *Zen and Western Thought*.

This work continues the comparative and critical elaboration of Buddhist philosophical engagements with Western philosophical and theological issues. The goals are to clarify Abe's interpretation of the Zen philosophy of the Kyoto school and the articulation of a common spiritual basis for human exchange and fulfillment. Particular attention is paid to the thought of leading twentieth-century Christian theologians, including Tillich, Altizer, and Knitter.

Abe, Masao. *Zen and Comparative Studies*. Honolulu: University of Hawaií Press, 1997. Ed. by Steven Heine. Part Two of a two-volume sequel to *Zen and Western Thought*.

The second companion volume to Abe's *Buddhism and Interfaith Dialogue*, which continues the comparative and critical elaboration of Buddhist philosophical engagements with Western philosophical and theological issues. Abe's interpretation of the Zen philosophy of the Kyoto school is made explicit, as is the articulation of a common spiritual basis for human exchange and fulfillment. Particular attention is paid to the thought of leading twentieth-century Christian theologians, including Tillich, Altizer, and Knitter.

Abe, Masao. *Zen and Western Thought*. Honolulu: University of Hawaii Press, 1985. Ed. by William R. LaFleur.

These essays by a leading scholar seek to clarify the authentic spirit of Mahāyāna Buddhism and reveal the profound philosophy undergirding the often unphilosophical practice of Zen. Steeped in the tradition of the Kyoto School and arguing from the position that philosophy is necessarily a comparative discipline, Abe engages perennial Western philosophical questions and categories, while also elaborating the Buddhist perspective. He also asserts a peronalistic cosmology, rooted in the ultimate of Emptiness/Suchness, which may provide the spiritual foundation for humanity in a global age.

Batchelor, Stephen. *The Awakening of the West: The Encounter of Buddhism and Western Culture, 543 BCE–1992*. Berkeley: Parallax Press, 1994.

A historical review of the relationship between Buddhist Asia and the European West, emphasizing the evolution of Western attitudes toward Buddhism. The text focuses on developments in the nineteenth and twentieth centuries, and does not consider the influence of Buddhism in North America. The anecdotal style of the text makes it especially accessible to non-academics seeking understanding of the dialogue between Buddhist and Western thought.

Batchelor, Stephen, ed. *The Jewel in the Lotus: A Guide to the Buddhist Traditions of Tibet*. A Wisdom Basic Book. London: Wisdom Publications, 1987.

A generally accessible overview of Tibetan Buddhism focusing on selected representative primary sources. An introductory section examines the historical context for the development of Tibetan Buddhism and provides an outline of the fundamental doctrines common to the various schools. Subsequent sections individually address the textual sources and specific doctrines of the early Kadam and extant Nyingma, Kagyu, Sakya, and Geluk traditions.

Beyer, Stephan. *The Cult of Tara: Magic and Ritual in Tibet.* Hermeneutics, Studies in the History of Religions, vol. 1. Berkeley: University of California Press, 1973.
Beyer furnishes a detailed introduction to the ritual, indeed, the performance art, of Tibetan Buddhism. Rituals of the cult of the goddess Tara are presented in their entirety and exhaustively explained, offering counterpoint to more theoretical, historical, and literary treatments of living Tibetan traditions.

Bstan-'dzin, rgya mtsho. *Freedom in Exile: The Autobiography of the Dalai Lama.* New York: HarperCollins, 1990.
In addition to telling the extraordinary life story of the fourteenth Dalai Lama, this volume provides firsthand historical perspective on the plight of Tibetan Buddhism under Chinese rule, and occasional insight into Buddhist ritual and doctrine from one of the most acclaimed modern thinkers in the Tibetan scholastic tradition.

Bstan-'dzin, rgya mtsho. *The World of Tibetan Buddhism: An Overview of Its Philosophy and Practice.* Boston: Wisdom Publications, 1995. Translated and annotated by Geshe Thupten Jinpa.
This collection of lectures, originally delivered to the Tibet Foundation, London, articulate an altruistic orientation toward life in the world and introduce readers to the Vajrayāna Buddhism practiced in Tibet. His Holiness provides an outline of the specific beliefs, practices, and organizing principles of the Tibetan Tantric tradition, while locating that tradition within the broader Buddhist movement by emphasizing the history and interpretations shared among the Three Vehicles (Theravāda, Mahāyāna, and Vajrayāna).

Buswell, Robert E. *The Zen Monastic Experience: Buddhist Practice in Contemporary Korea.* Princeton, NJ: Princeton University Press, 1992.
The author combines outstanding scholarship with five years of personal experience to offer a rare glimpse into the daily individual and institutional life and meditative practice of Korean monasticism. Buswell surveys Buddhist religion, and Zen in particular, in the Korean context, then explores topics including the early stages of a monk's career, monastic relations with laity, institutional organization of monastic life, and

the daily and annual schedule of monasteries. Through its candid portrayal, this work offers a needed balance to Western (mis)conceptions of Zen Buddhism.

Conze, Edward. *Buddhist Thought in India: Three Phases of Buddhist Philosophy*. Reprint with corrections. London: Allen & Unwin, 1983 [1962].

Conze offers a straightforward interpretation of central debates and major themes in Indian Buddhist thought. Part One examines the doctrines of early ("archaic") Buddhism as well as the scholarly difficulties that attend any such examination. Part Two explores the historic traditions of the Sthaviras (Theravādins), examining scholastic debates and soteriological theories, while Part Three surveys the Mahāyāna tradition, with some discussion of broadly held doctrinal positions, more detailed treatments of Mādhyamika and Yogācāra schools, and a review of Buddhist logic.

Conze, Edward. *A Short History of Buddhism*. London: Allen and Unwin, 1980.

This work provides a useful historical outline of the development of the Buddhist tradition, best used in combination with more detailed sources. Conze divides his survey into four periods, each characterized by different geographical and cultural contexts, philosophical orientations, and soteriological conceptions of the ideal human. The first period (500–0 BCE) occurred in India, emphasizing psychology and propounding the ideal of the Arhat; the second (0–500 CE) marks Buddhism's expansion into East Asia, and emphasizes ontological reflection with the Boddhisattva as its ideal; the third period (500–1000 CE) witnesses the establishment of Buddhism as a pan-Asian cultural and religious force, with attention directed to cosmology and the figure of the Siddha. Conze argues that the last period, spanning the past thousand years, has seen no renewal of the tradition, but has demonstrated its dogged persistence.

Eckel, Malcolm David. *To See the Buddha: A Philosopher's Quest for the Meaning of Emptiness*. San Francisco: HarperSanFrancisco, 1992.

Subverting distinctions between philosophy and religion, and between high and low traditions, Eckel reviews the concept of emptiness and the figure of the Buddha through the eyes of Bhāvaviveka, a sixth century Buddhist philosopher, monk, and devotee. Central to this quest is the identification in Mahāyāna thought of the Buddha and emptiness and prolonged reflection on the act and meaning of seeing. Relying heavily upon the travel diaries of the Chinese monk Hsuang-tsang, and drawing on artistic, philosophical, and literary sources, the author reconstructs

Bhāvaviveka's imaginative world, locating the concept of emptiness within a system of religious symbolism and practice, and offers insight into the devotional and philosophical relationship of presence and absence as experienced in confronting the image (or "no-image") of the Buddha. The book concludes with translated excerpts of Bhāvaviveka's *Madhyamakahrdayakārikā* (*Verses on the Essence of the Middle Way*) and its autocommentary *Tarkajvālā* (*Flame of Reason*).

Fields, Rick. *How the Swans Came to the Lake: A Narrative History of Buddhism in America.* 2nd ed. Boston and London: Shambhala, 1986.

A comprehensive, and at times anecdotal, record of the religious figures and schools which have contributed to the establishment of Buddhism in the West. Field begins with a survey of the life of Śākyamuni Buddha and early Buddhism, then traces the diverse currents of the tradition as they flowed into America. Special attention is paid to the role of Sir William Jones in introducing Buddhist thought to the West, and to the American Transcendentalists in particular, the significance of the first World Parliament of Religions (1893), and to representing the histories and experiences of Indian, Tibetan, Chinese, Japanese, Korean, and Vietnamese Buddhists. A final chapter reflects upon problems facing contemporary communities and movements, and the struggle over the future form of Buddhism in America.

Friedman, Lenore and Susan Ichi Su Moon, eds. *Being Bodies: Buddhist Women on the Paradox of Embodiment.* Boston: Shambhala, 1997.

Mixing Buddhism and feminism, the authors relate women's experiences with and reflections upon the spiritual journey. Essays treat critically the negative impact of body-eschewing practices and traditions, issues of body image and female identity, and affirm that the body, as the intersection of the internal and external worlds, is the locus of true spiritual struggle and fulfillment.

Gombrich, Richard Francis. *How Buddhism Began: The Conditioned Genesis of the Early Teachings.* New Delhi: Munshiram Manoharlal Publishers, 1997.

This detailed and erudite compendium of articles, drawn from lectures delivered at the School of Oriental and African Studies, University of London, clarifies the influences upon and constitutive elements of the early formation of Buddhist doctrine. Gombrich addresses themes that include the Buddha's critique of essentialist philosophy, the subtle connections between Buddhist and brahmanical thought, the role of allegory and satire in religious discourse, and historic trends toward literalist interpretations of canonical sayings.

Gombrich, Richard Francis. *Theravāda Buddhism: A Social History from Ancient Benares to Modern Colombo*. Library of Religious Beliefs and Practices. London: Routledge & Kegan Paul, 1988.

Gombrich synthesizes recent scholarship and provides a valuable introduction to one of the "three vehicles" or branches of Buddhism. The author organizes his narrative around three major points of change: Śākyamuni's founding of the tradition, the introduction of Buddhism to Sri Lanka and the resultant shift in Theravādin thought and identity, and the impact of and responses to Protestant missionary and British colonial activities. Throughout, Gombrich explains essential Theravādin interpretations of Buddhist doctrine while situating them within their sociohistorical context. Notable is his treatment of "Protestant Buddhism" in contemporary Sri Lanka.

Gross, Rita M. *Buddhism After Patriarchy: A Feminist History, Analysis, and Reconstruction of Buddhism*. Albany: State University of New York Press, 1993.

A feminist reconstruction of Buddhist theology, aimed at reasserting the central role of egalitarian and liberating symbolism in Buddhist doctrine, as opposed to patriarchal and misogynist practices of Buddhist institutions. Gross contends that a post-patriarchal Buddhism must reemphasize this-worldly spirituality, adopt an androgynous human model (one that affirms both maleness and femaleness), and recognize the particularly feminine aspects of the Buddhist sangha (community). The author also provides a broad historical overview of Buddhism and an analysis of key Buddhist concepts and they relate to her feminist critique.

Harvey, Peter. *An Introduction to Buddhism: Teachings, History, and Practices*. Cambridge: Cambridge University Press, 1990.

An introductory text aimed at conveying the living tradition of Buddhism by "relat[ing] Buddhism to modern ways of thinking." The author provides a section on formative historical events and doctrine of Buddhism in India through the emergence of the Mahāyāna school, and in Central, East, and Southeast Asia. A second section extensively surveys Buddhist practice, with emphasis on both its classical sources and its role in contemporary Buddhist life. The inclusion of figures, maps, and a topical bibliography should increase the attractiveness of the work for beginning students and general readers.

Herman, A. L. *An Introduction to Buddhist Thought: A Philosophic History of Indian Buddhism*. Lanham, MD: University Press of America, 1983.

An introduction to the central religious and philosophical concepts of early Buddhism, from the Buddha through the development of early

Hinayana and Mahāyāna schools. The text is intended for beginning students and general readers and assumes no familiarity with Buddhist tradition. Besides providing historical background and a systematic survey of Buddhist doctrine, the author also attempts to use Buddhist thought as a means to introduce important aspects of the study of philosophy, often through critical evaluation of Buddhist doctrine.

Hirakawa, Akira and Paul Groner. *A History of Indian Buddhism: From Sakyamuni to Early Mahāyāna.* Asian Studies at Hawaii, vol. 36. Honolulu: University of Hawaii Press, 1990.

A translation of a 1974 Japanese text surveying early Indian Buddhist history. The work is divided into 3 sections: early Buddhism (from pre-Buddhist Indian religion to the reign of Asoka), Hīnayāna Buddhism, and early Mahāyāna Buddhism. Each section deals with both historical development and with central doctrines and practices of the various traditions. Special emphasis is given to the emergence of the Hīnayāna and Mahāyāna schools, particularly Hiakawa's contended portrayal of the latter as an organized movement of the Indian laity.

Iida, Shotaro. *Facets of Buddhism.* Delhi: Motilal Banarsidass Publishers, 1991.

An anthology of ten essays collectively intended to provide an introduction to the Buddhist worldview. Central Buddhist concepts are illustrated through direct discussion of Buddhist doctrine (particularly the axiom of dependent co-origination), consideration of various forms of Buddhist practice (specifically Tantric visualization and female roles in Buddhist tradition), examination of classical and contemporary Japanese literature, and a comparative religion approach to Buddhist mysticism.

Jones, Ken. *The Social Face of Buddhism: An Approach to Political and Social Activism.* London: Wisdom Publications, 1989.

A work directed at a general audience on the potential contribution of Buddhist thought to understanding society and implementing political and social change. Includes discussions of the Buddhist view of the human condition, relationship of Mahāyāna tradition to the understanding of social phenomena, Buddhist training and practice and the different forms of Buddhist social activism, foundations of historical and contemporary Buddhist societies, and the application of Buddhist thought to a variety of modern social problems. Buddhist thought is contrasted with Western "egoic" dualism, and the value of Buddhism in the "transformation of contemporary Western consciousness" serves as a central theme.

Kalupahana, David J. *A History of Buddhist Philosophy: Continuities and Discontinuities.* Honolulu: University of Hawaii Press, 1992.

A survey of Buddhist thought examining both general philosophical foundations and historical development. A central current of the text is the explanation of Buddhist doctrine in terms of contemporary (typically Western) philosophical themes; the work thus requires significant philosophical background to be of great value to the reader.

Kalupahana, David J. and Indrani Kalupahana. *The Way of Siddhartha: A Life of the Buddha*. Lanham, MD: University Press of America, 1987 [1982]. Originally published by Boulder: Shambhala Publications, 1982.

A narrative retelling of the life of the Buddha as a historical figure, focusing on formative influences on Siddhārtha's philosophy and a detailed portrayal of his travels and teachings subsequent to his enlightenment. The text provides both a readable historical account and a useful introduction to Buddhist philosophy as presented primarily through narrative translations of the Buddha's later discourses. Philosophical categories touched on throughout the biography include Buddhist metaphysics, epistemology, ethics, and socio-political views.

Keown, Damien. *Buddhism: A Very Short Introduction*. Oxford: Oxford University Press, 1996.

A concise introductory work, made accessible to those with no familiarity with Buddhist tradition. With the use of simple explanatory text, Keown focuses primarily on Buddhist thought and practice, with limited mention of historical foundations (i.e., a brief section on the life of the Buddha), and some discussion of the role of Buddhism in the modern world.

Kitagawa, Joseph Mitsuo. *Religion in Japanese History*. Lectures on the History of Religions, vol. 7. New York: Columbia University Press, 1966.

A historical survey of the contributions of various aspects of Japanese religion to the economic, social, and political development of Japan. Kitagawa examines a number of themes in approaching the role of religion, including religious leadership, means of apprehending truth, the interaction of religious and feudal systems, and issues of modernity. The work addresses Japanese Confucianism, Buddhism, Shintoism, Christianity, and the "new religions."

Klein, Anne C. *Meeting the Great Bliss Queen: Buddhists, Feminists, and the Art of the Self*. Boston: Beacon Press, 1995.

Klein opens a dialogue concerning the self between Tibetan Buddhist and modern Western feminist perspectives, based in part on their mutual emphasis upon practical action and the marriage of theory with experience. Mixing theoretical analysis of Mahāyāna thought, feminist insight, and Tibetan conceptions of the self as embedded in a network of relations, with a clear emphasis upon liberating practice centered on the figure of Yeshe Tsogyal, Great Bliss Queen and protector of the Great Completeness tradition, the author seeks to open transformative avenues for both scholarship and daily living.

Murakami, Shigeyoshi. *Japanese Religion in the Modern Century.* Tokyo: University of Tokyo Press, 1980 [1968].

Originally published in 1968, this text provides a survey of Japanese religious history from the Meiji Restoration (1868) to the latter half of the twentieth century. In sections on the Difficulties of Modernization, Religious Oppression under Militarism, and the Age of Religious Freedom, Murakami explores in particular the influence of Japanese economics and politics on the development of religious movements. The author espouses a separation of religion and government, and devotes significant energy to discussions of the Shinto religion, with emphasis on critiques of modern State Shinto. The text also explores the roles of Buddhism, Christianity, and the "new religions" (sectarian organizations deemed "pseudo-religions" by the Japanese government).

Nakamura, Hajime. *Indian Buddhism: A Survey With Bibliographical Notes.* Buddhist Traditions, vol. 1. Delhi: Motilal Banarsidass, 1987 [1980]. Originally published: Hirakata, Japan: KUFS Publication, 1980, as Intercultural Research Institute monograph series, vol. 9.

A comprehensive survey of Indian Buddhist thought, exhaustively annotated throughout with both bibliographic references and the author's addenda. This volume is clearly offered as a sourcebook for advanced students of Indian Buddhism, as indicated both in its detail and the fact that over half the text consists of bibliographic footnote. The focus of the work tends to be on Japanese scholarship in the field, and may therefor be of particular value to Western students.

Nishitani, Keiji. *Religion and Nothingness.* Nanzan Studies in Religion and Culture, vol. 2. Berkeley: University of California Press, 1982.

A philosophical treatise built around the dialogue of Buddhist thought with Western religion and philosophy. Primarily through the exploration of the concept of śūnyatā (emptiness/nothingness) Nishitani offers a critique of classical Western dualistic thinking (both religious and secular) and a reinterpretation of Western philosophical and religious concepts from a Buddhist perspective. The complexity of some of the author's arguments suggests the assumption of some prior familiarity with Buddhist philosophy.

Ortner, Sherry B. *High Religion: A Cultural and Political History of*

Sherpa Buddhism. Princeton Studies in Culture/Power/History. Princeton, NJ: Princeton University Press, 1989.

Articulating a vision of practice theory which prioritizes actors' intentions and interpretations of events, Ortner examines why the Sherpas, who for centuries had practiced a form of Buddhism led by married lamas, went through great effort to found celibate monasteries in the early twentieth century. Central to her narrative is the Sherpa cultural schema of heroic rivalry, exile, and triumphant return. The author combines data from ethnography, oral, and political-economic history to reveal the interaction between internal structural contradictions and external forces that contribute to the rise of cultural crises and the articulation of innovative solutions, and offers a perceptive study of the integral role socio-economic forces play in shaping traditions.

Paul, Diana Y. and Frances Wilson. *Women in Buddhism: Images of the Feminine in Mahāyāna Tradition.* 2nd ed. Berkeley: University of California Press, 1985 [1979].

These selections, some translated into English for the first time here, together with Paul's insightful commentary, explore the impact of religious and ideological constructs upon the gender definition and women's conceptions of the self. Part One explores the traditional feminine imagery of temptress and mother; Part Two examines the figures of the nun and boddhisatva, treating the sociological paths available to women; Part Three offers the most positive images of women set forth in Pure Land texts and the story of Queen Śrīmala, a future Buddha. This work fills a significant gap in scholarship of the Mahāyāna tradition.

Prebish, Charles S. *American Buddhism.* North Scituate, MA: Duxbury Press, 1979.

An overview of Buddhism in America intended for those familiar with the basic concepts and schools of Asian Buddhism. The text considers the historical development of American Buddhism from its emergence in the late 19th century to the present (with emphasis on the interrelationship of Buddhism with the new American cultural context); the specific manifestations of American Buddhism as illustrated through eight major groups of various Asian origins; and the potential of Buddhism as an influential aspect of general American religious life and culture.

Radhakrishnan, S. *Indian Philosophy.* 2nd ed. London: Unwin Hyman, 1987 [1923].

A general survey of Indian philosophy as expressed primarily through the religious thought of Hindu, Buddhist, and Jain traditions. The author attempts to introduce fundamental characteristics of Indian thought and trace the development of these in religious text and doctrine. Comparative treatments of the philosophies of these three religions and illustrations of their influences on Indian thought in general are provided throughout.

Rahula, Walpola. *What the Buddha Taught.* 2nd ed. Bedford: Gordon Fraser Gallery, 1967 [1959].

A standard introduction to the teachings of the Buddha as translated from the classical texts of the Pali canon. Excerpts of the canon are chosen to illustrate the central concepts of Buddhism, including the Four Noble Truths, the Eightfold Path, karma, rebirth, dependent co-origination, and the doctrine of no-self. The author provides thorough and readily accessible commentary throughout, directed at general audiences seeking a basic understanding of Buddhist thought.

Reat, N. Ross. *Buddhism: A History.* Religions of the World. Berkeley: Asian Humanities Press, 1994.

An introductory text aimed at providing a straightforward narrative account of Buddhist history to the general reader and beginning student. The author presents chapters on early Buddhist development (the life and teaching of the Buddha through the emergence of Mahāyāna), and then considers individually the historical development of Buddhist tradition in its present homes throughout Asia and the West. An extensive glossary and topical bibliography serve as further aids for those unfamiliar with the tradition.

Robinson, Richard H. and Willard L. Johnson. *The Buddhist Religion: A Historical Introduction.* 3rd ed. Religious Life of Man. Belmont, CA: Wadsworth Publishing Co., 1982 [1970].

A widely accepted textbook providing a critical/historical introduction to Buddhist tradition. The text explores ritual, doctrine, and institutions as major themes throughout its primarily historical survey of Buddhism. Special emphasis is given to Indian Buddhism (roughly half the text), inasmuch as it provides the "common stock" of thought for later Buddhist traditions. Useful appendices (an overview of scriptures, glossary, and topical bibliography in particular) add to the accessibility of this work as an introductory text.

Samuel, Geoffrey. *Civilized Shamans: Buddhism in Tibetan Societies.* Washington, DC: Smithsonian Institution Press, 1993.

Samuel argues that all forms of Buddhism exist somewhere on a continuum between the shamanic (embodied by the tantric lama whose power and authority derive from inspirational and charismatic experience) and the clerical (wherein authority rests with monks who derive their power from scholarship, rationality and discipline). Tibetan Buddhism is exceptional to the degree that the shamanic element remains vital throughout the various manifestations of the tradition. Part One surveys the diversity of Tibetan Buddhist institutions and traditions in light of this shamanic-clerical scheme. Part Two catalogs the beliefs, rituals, and various practitioners of Tibetan Buddhism, and demonstrates the impact of the shamanic orientation upon ethical, pragmatic, and compassionate practice. Part Three sketches the historical introduction and development of Buddhism in Tibet, noting the subtle interactions among the several schools.

Sharma, Arvind. *The Philosophy of Religion: A Buddhist Perspective.* Delhi: Oxford University Press, 1995.
   A readily accessible introduction to Buddhist philosophy for Western audiences. Sharma presents major Buddhist concepts by exploring the response of Buddhist thought to a number of familiar Western religious and philosophical concepts, such as God and the Holy, the Problem of Evil, revelation and faith, claims of ultimate truth, and human destiny and immortality.

Skilton, Andrew. *A Concise History of Buddhism.* 2nd ed. Birmingham: Windhorse, 1997 [1994].
   A broad historical overview of Buddhism from the pre-Buddhist Indian context to the nineteenth century. The majority of the text is devoted to Indian Buddhism, with traditions in other nations receiving individual chapters of approximately five pages each. The text presents a chronological and developmental discussion of the various doctrines and schools, with consideration of the associated institutions. This volume is intended as an entry into the study of Buddhist history, and it provides a comprehensive topical bibliography to stimulate further inquiry.

Smart, Ninian. *Religions of Asia.* Englewood Cliffs, NJ: Prentice Hall, 1993.
   An accurate yet exceedingly shallow (of necessity, given its brevity and scope) survey of the major religious traditions of Asia: Hinduism, Jainism, Buddhism, Asian Islam, Sikhism, Confucianism, Taoism, and Shintoism. Smart attempts to give a balanced view by systematically exploring specific dimensions of each tradition: ritual, religious experience, myth, doctrine, ethics, and society. Intended for those seeking a broad and readily accessible introduction to any or all of the Asian religions.

Strong, John. *The Experience of Buddhism: Sources and Interpretations.* Religious Life in History Series. Belmont, CA: Wadsworth Publishing Co., 1995.

An anthology of primary texts and other writings addressing Buddhist doctrine, ritual, myth, community, and daily life. Translated texts include both canonical and non-canonical sources; various other works include anthropological observations of Buddhist ritual and practice, and essays by historians of religions and travelers in Buddhist nations. The text is broadly divided into sections, first on the foundations of Buddhism in India (focusing on the "Three Jewels" of doctrine, Dharma, and Saṃgha), and then on the development of the tradition outside of India.

Suzuki, Daisetz Teitaro. *Zen and Japanese Culture*. New York: Pantheon Books, 1988 [1959]. First published by Princeton University Press, 1959.
The author contends that "to understand the cultural life of the Japanese people . . . it is essential to delve into the secrets of Zen Buddhism." He accordingly provides a survey of Zen influences on various aspects of Japanese culture, including Samurai and the art of swordsmanship, haiku, the art of tea, the visual arts, and reverence for nature. A brief section on the nature of Zen serves as an introduction.

Suzuki, Daisetz Teitaro, William Barrett, and Ludwig Bachhofer. *Zen Buddhism: Selected Writings*. Garden City, NY: Doubleday, 1956.
A collection of translated classical writings providing a broad introduction to Zen Buddhism, directed primarily at non-academic Western readers seeking some understanding of the meaning and practice of Zen.

Swearer, Donald K. *The Buddhist World of Southeast Asia*. 2nd ed. SUNY Series in Religion. Albany: State University of New York Press, 1995.
An introductory text on the role of Theravāda Buddhism in defining the societies of Southeast Asia and Sri Lanka. The influences of the Buddhist worldview in three different societal contexts (the traditional village, the nation state, and the modern urban center) are explored. The text is divided into three sections, respectively addressing the importance of popular Buddhist thought and ritual in synthesizing religious ideal with personal and social life, the use of Buddhism to legitimate political structure, and the response of the tradition to changes associated with modernity.

Thurman, Robert A. F. *Essential Tibetan Buddhism*. San Francisco: HarperSanFrancisco, 1995.
This excellent introduction unites philosophical and historical surveys of the Tibetan Buddhism with core texts of the tradition. Throughout

Thurman emphasizes the centrality of religious and spiritual leaders in shaping belief and practice. Primary texts in the translation include treatments of mentor worship, practicing liberating wisdom, meeting the Buddha in the mentor, and the Dalai Lama's address in Oslo upon receipt of the Nobel Peace Prize.

Warder, Anthony Kennedy. *Indian Buddhism.* 2nd ed. Delhi: Motilal Banarsidass, 1980 [1970].

Warder surveys the origins and spread of Buddhism across the South Asian subcontinent up to the Muslim invasions, explaining core doctrines and major philosophical debates within their social, intellectual, and historical contexts. After treating issues of methodology, the author examines Indian civilization prior to and during the life of the Buddha, offers a brief biography of Śākyamuni, and gives an encapsulation of his teachings. The work then treats theories of causation, the popularization of Buddhism, particularly under the reign of Asoka, the rise of Sthaviravada and Mahāyāna traditions, Buddhist idealism and knowledge theory, and the rise and influence of Buddhist universities. Warder sticks close to primary texts, paying special attention to the collections of Tripitakas, and is ever attuned to issues of text formation and interpretation.

Williams, Paul. *Mahāyāna Buddhism: The Doctrinal Foundations.* Library of Religious Beliefs and Practices. London: Routledge, 1989.

An introduction to the diversity of Mahāyāna doctrine and practice intended for those having some familiarity with Buddhist tradition. The text covers historical and philosophical origins, central doctrinal ideas and textual sources for various Mahāyāna schools, and practice-oriented facets of the tradition including devotional aspects in the cults of key Boddhisattvas and Buddhas.

Yamasaki, Taiko. *Shingon: Japanese Esoteric Buddhism.* Boston: Shambhala, 1988. Trans. by Richard and Cynthia Peterson, ed. by Yasuyoshi Morimoto and David Kidd, with a forward by Carmen Blacker. Based on the author's *Mikkyo Meiso To Shinso Shinri* and *Mikkyo Meisoho.*

This valuable work traces the history of esoteric Buddhism, beginning in India through its arrival and development in Japan. Yamasaki outlines key tenets of Shingon, including its emphasis upon enlightenment in this life and an emphasis upon the possibility of marshalling desires for soteriological ends, and surveys Shingon psychological theory and the types and uses of mandalas. Most significant are the authors in depth treatments of ritual and visualization practices.

Annotated Bibliography: Hinduism

Reference Works

Bibliographies

Potter, Karl H. and American Institute of Indian Studies. *Bibliography of Indian Philosophies*. Encyclopedia of Indian Philosophies, vol. 1. Delhi: Motilal Banarsidass for American Institute of Indian Studies, 1970.

Dictionaries and Encyclopedias

Stutley, Margaret and James Stutley. *Harper's Dictionary of Hinduism: Its Mythology, Folklore, Philosophy, Literature, and History*. New York: Harper & Row, 1977.

A concise and extensive reference covering texts, persons, gods, philosophical terms, cultural artifacts, and other topics. Entries tend to focus on Vedic literature and tradition, and little is made of developments after the fifteenth to sixteenth centuries. Accessibility of this work to general readers is complicated by the usage of exclusively Sanskrit entries, although the addition of a limited selection of English equivalents, provided as an appendix, mitigates the difficulty to some extent.

Sullivan, Bruce M. *Historical Dictionary of Hinduism*. Historical Dictionaries of Religions, Philosophies, and Movements, vol. 13. Lanham, MD: Scarecrow Press, 1997.

A single volume reference with entries on significant religious, social, and political figures, textual sources, doctrines, rituals, schools and movements, and central Hindu religious and cultural concepts. A brief introductory section provides a very broad historical perspective and some overview of Hindu doctrine and community. Entries typically offer little detail but should be useful as introductions for readers lacking familiarity with Hinduism. An extensive topical bibliography provides ample suggestions for further reading.

Walker, Benjamin. *The Hindu World: An Encyclopedic Survey of Hinduism*, 2 vols. New York: Praeger, 1968.

An illustrated two volume reference touching broadly on all aspects of Hindu religion and culture. Entries on religion tend to focus on Hindu mythology rather than philosophical concepts.

Primary Sources

Dimmitt, Cornelia and J. A. B. Buitenen, eds. *Classical Hindu Mythology: A Reader in the Sanskrit Puranas*. Philadelphia: Temple University Press, 1978.

A collection from the ten million couplets traditionally ascribed to the classical Puranas, the primary sources for the study of Hindu mythology. Puranas are grouped according to specific foci of Hindu worship, most prominently the gods Viṣṇu, Kṛṣṇa, and Śiva. With the exception of introductory sections for each general grouping, the stories are presented in generally accessible translation without commentary or annotation.

Hume, Robert Ernest, ed. *The Thirteen Principal Upaniṣads*. Oxford: Oxford University Press, 1968.
  See next annotation.

Olivelle, Patrick, ed. *The Early Upaniṣads: Annotated Text and Translation*. South Asia Research. New York: Oxford University Press, 1998.
  Olivelle's volume is a recent collection of twelve of the principal Upaniṣads, presented alongside the original Sanskrit texts and offered in accessible contemporary translation. A general introduction (providing a historical and social overview of the Indian context and a survey of Vedic ritual and thought) and brief individual summaries are provided. The text is extensively annotated, and the relegation of notes to a separate appendix, while potentially frustrating to scholarly investigation of the work, should be a welcome feature for the beginning student and general reader. Hume's text represents a widely adopted collection of scholarly translations, including a comprehensive introductory section on the philosophy of the Upaniṣads. Translations are again exhaustively annotated, but presented here in a more archaic style than that of Olivelle.

Miller, Barbara Stoler and Barry Moser, eds. *The Bhagavad-Gītā: Krishna's Counsel in Time of War*. New York: Columbia University Press, 1986.
  A popular translation of the classic epic text. Intended for general readers, Miller's simple English translation attempts to preserve the literary qualities of the Sanskrit original. Includes a brief introduction aimed at providing ideological and textual perspective within the wider context of the Hindu epic literature, and an afterward on Henry David Thoreau's take on the Gītā offers a more familiar Western interpretation of the text.

O'Flaherty, Wendy Doniger, ed. *The Rig Veda: An Anthology: One Hundred and Eight Hymns, Selected, Translated and Annotated*. Penguin Classics. Harmondsworth, Middlesex: Penguin Books, 1981.
  An admittedly "eclectic" collection of hymns culled from the classic Vedic text, translated with the general reader in mind. Hymns have been selected for the insight they provide into Vedic mythology, philosophy,

and ritual, or simply on the basis of their universality and poetry. Individual hymns are provided context by the author's brief introductions, and annotations are helpful but unobtrusive.

O'Flaherty, Wendy Doniger, ed. *Textual Sources for the Study of Hinduism*. Textual Sources for the Study of Religion. Totowa, NJ: Barnes & Noble, 1988.

An anthology of primary texts from sources throughout the Hindu tradition, including the Vedas, Upaniṣads, epics, puranas, shastras, tantras, and several poetic schools. The aim of the work is to provide for the beginning student or general reader a very broad introduction to Hindu primary texts in a single concise volume. Introductory passages are brief, and notes are limited to bibliographic reference.

Radhakrishnan, S. and Charles Alexander Moore, eds. *A Source Book in Indian Philosophy*. Princeton, NJ: Princeton University Press, 1957.

An indispensable resource for beginning students, this work gathers translations of important texts of nearly all major Indian philosophical schools. Radhakrishnan and Moore offer selections from the Vedas and Upaniṣads, the Gītā and Mahābhārata, and representative works of orthodox Hindu philosophical schools, including the Nyāya, Vaiśeṣika, Pūrva Mīmāṁsā, and Vedānta traditions. The sourcebook concludes with selections from the writings of Sri Aurobindo and Radhakrishnan's own work. The editors' introductions and outlines provide necessary historical and theoretical background for students new with Indian philosophical thought, and the bibliography is an outstanding resource for further intellectual exploration.

Secondary Sources

Allchin, Bridget and F. Raymond Allchin. *The Rise of Civilization in India and Pakistan*. Cambridge World Archaeology. Cambridge: Cambridge University Press, 1982.

Synthesizing recent scholarship in archaeology and paleontology, the authors present a comprehensive and detailed survey of the cultural development of the South Asian subcontinent. Part One describes the constitutional elements of Indian civilization, including prehistoric environmental factors, hunter-gatherer and nomadic pastoralist societies, and the rise of agriculture. Part Two examines the growth of an urban Indus civilization, while Part Three examines its legacy in later cultural development, including trends in subcontinental unity and diversity.

Alper, Harvey P., ed. *Understanding Mantras*. SUNY Series in Religious Studies. Albany: State University of New York Press, 1989.

This rich collection of essays explores mantras from a variety of philosophical, religious, and linguistic perspectives. Authors assess the relations and relevance of mantras to a range of subjects, including Wittgensteinian word games, comparative theology, tantric ritual, meditation, cosmology, and ancient medicinal practice.

Babb, Lawrence A. *The Divine Hierarchy: Popular Hinduism in Central India*. New York: Columbia University Press, 1975.

Babb is concerned with describing the unity of the Hindu tradition, wherein there is a seeming disjunction between the traditions philosophical and popular religious manifestations, and among the plurality of ritual and devotional systems. Through a focused study of beliefs and practices in the rice-growing region of Madhya Pradesh known as Chhattisgarh, the author discloses patterns and consistencies that underscore the systemic aspects of the broad Hindu tradition. His microcosmic analysis may prove fruitful for reflection on macrocosmic issues.

Baird, Robert D., ed. *Religion in Modern India*. 2nd ed. New Delhi: Manohar Publications, 1989 [1981].

This collection offers descriptive analysis of a number of movements and figures that have shaped Indian religious life and thought in the past century. Essays examine politicized Hinduism, S. Radhakrishnan, Gandhi, Sri Aurobindo, Svami Vivekananda, and Ramakrishnan. Note: the first edition includes a third section, "Religion and National Goals," which surveys contemporary religio-political issues.

Banerjea, Jitendra Nath. *The Development of Hindu Iconography*. 2nd ed. Calcutta: University of Calcutta, 1956.

A detailed and comprehensive study of the religious material culture of ancient and medieval India. Combining glyptic, numismatic, archaeological, and art historical research, Banerjea explores the origin and evolution of image worship, iconographic terminology, and artistic codes, while also exploring the religious import of cultic icons and introducing readers to the core tenets of the schools and traditions under consideration.

Basham, A. L. *The Wonder That Was India: A Survey of the Culture of the Indian Sub-Continent Before the Coming of the Muslims*. 3rd ed. London: Sidgwick and Jackson, 1967 [1954].

This masterful survey introduces readers to the social, political, artistic, linguistic, agricultural, and intellectual history of Pre-Muslim India. The various religious traditions are introduced within their broader cultural context. A treasure-trove of appendices covers topics ranging from cosmology, epistemology, and logic to physiology, coinage, and weights and measures.

Bhattacharyya, Narendra Nath. *History of the Sakta Religion*. New Delhi: Munshiram Manoharlal Publishers, 1974.

The author surveys the origins of Saktism, the religion of the great goddess and personification of primordial energy and transforming power, from its roots in the prehistoric cult of the Mother Goddess through its modern manifestations. Throughout Bhattacharyya underscores the responsiveness of the tradition in adapting to new contexts and pressures, while also stressing its unifying characteristics. Throughout its long and variegated history, the cult of Sakti has remained a vital religion of the masses, ever identifying the Feminine Principle with both the plight and hope of the oppressed.

Bhattacharyya, Narendra Nath. *History of the Tantric Religion: A Historical, Ritualistic, and Philosophical Study*. New Delhi: Manohar, 1982.

Bhattacharyya introduces the intricate and polyphonic literature, art, history, and thought of Indian esoteric traditions, and sketches the evolution of Tantrism in Hindu and Buddhist traditions, noting internal structural developments and external influences. Chapters treat Tantric elements in early/pre-Vedic Indian religions, their development in medieval religious systems, the relation of Tantrism and popular piety, and the growth of sophisticated Sakta traditions.

Brockington, J. L. *The Sacred Thread: Hinduism in Its Continuity and Diversity*. Edinburgh: Edinburgh University Press, 1981.

A compact but informative overview of the development of Hindu religious thought and experience from Vedic roots through the modern era. Brockington surveys early impersonal and theistic trends in devotion and literature, and the development of orthodox, heterodox and sectarian movements. Particularly commendable are the treatments of Bhakti (devotional) movements in the North and South and the author's insights into the continued adaptability and strength of the broad Hindu tradition.

Chatterjee, Margaret. *Gandhi's Religious Thought*. Notre Dame, IN: University of Notre Dame Press, 1983.

Chatterjee clearly and succinctly traces the myriad streams of religious and philosophical thought, ranging from Hinduism, Islam, Jainism, and evangelical Christianity, which fed Gandhi's own unique perspective. She explores connections among religion, morality, and practice, Gandhi's communal understanding of *moksa* (liberation), his approach to the reality and richness of religious pluralism, and the doctrine of ahimsa and its relation to the truth.

Chatterjee, Satischandra and Dhirendra Mohan Datta. *An Introduction to Indian Philosophy*. 6th ed. Calcutta: University of Calcutta, 1960 [1939].

A straightforward and highly accessible overview of major historic traditions of Indian and Hindu thought, including Vaiśeṣika, Sāṅkhya, Yoga, Mīmāṁsā, and Vedānta schools. The introduction provides some historical framework and highlights commonalities among traditions.

Clooney, Francis Xavier. *Seeing Through Texts: Doing Theology among the Śrīvaiṣṇavas of South India*. SUNY Series, Toward a Comparative Philosophy of Religions. Albany: State University of New York Press, 1996.

Clooney invites readers to immerse themselves in the songs of the Tiruvaymoli, composed by the ninth century Hindu poet-saint for the god Viṣṇu/Kṛṣṇa, and to explore with him the religious worlds that texts unlock for their readers. Drawing on these songs and their rich commentarial tradition, Clooney examines the relations among text, reader, and context, and illumines the ways in which texts form religious experience and inform theological thought. Ever sensitive to the problems of comparative religious studies, Clooney provides the reader with an intensive examination of Hindu religious thought from within.

Clooney, Francis Xavier. *Theology after Vedānta: An Experiment in Comparative Theology*. SUNY Series, Toward a Comparative Philosophy of Religions. Albany: State University of New York Press, 1993.

Clooney explores the theological and interpretive process in the writings of Śaṅkara and other Advaita Vedānta texts, arguing that these works are best understood as part of the Mīmāṁsā tradition of Vedic interpretation. While a work of comparative theology, it is included here for its worthwhile contribution to the understanding of the Advaitin practice of theology and exegesis, not to mention its subtle and sensitive treatment of the problem of comparisons across religious traditions and of the relations which pertain between religious texts, their readers, and truth.

Dasgupta, Surendra Nath and Surama Dasgupta. *A History of Indian Philosophy*, 5 vols. Cambridge: University Press, 1969. Includes *Surendranath Dasgupta*, a memoir by Surama Dasgupta.

This massive chronological account of Indian thought represents major traditions and movements and articulates the subtle and contextual significance of Indian philosophical terminology. Major topics included are the Vedas Brāhmanas and Upaniṣads (vol.1), the Śaṅkara school of Vedānta (vol. 2), Vaiṣṇava thought and southern theism (vol.

3), the Madhva school, monist-dualist controversies, and Caitanya (vol. 4), and southern schools of Śaivism. Dasgupta relies on primary sources and commentaries in interpreting traditions.

De Bary, William Theodore, ed. *Sources of Indian Tradition*. Records of Civilization, Sources and Studies/Introduction to Oriental Civilizations, vol. 56. New York: Columbia University Press, 1958.
   Designed for a general audience, this comprehensive anthology illustrates major patterns and trends in religious life in South Asia. Volume One deals with the major traditions of Brahmanism, Jainism and Buddhism, Hinduism, Islam, and Sikhism. Special emphasis is placed upon the devotional and social aspects of Hinduism, rather than the philosophical. Volume Two charts the interaction of traditions with the West, Hindu and Muslim renaissance, and the interplay of Indian traditions within political life.

Dhruvarajan, Vanaja. *Hindu Women and the Power of Ideology*. Granby, MA: Bergin & Garvey, 1989.
   This feminist critique of the ideology of *pativrata* examines the ideal of womanhood in Hindu tradition and Indian culture. Through studies of and interviews with the village women of her birthplace and historic generalizations, Dhruvarajan explores the impact of religious standards upon social structures, identity, and the daily lives of women.

Dumont, Louis. *Homo Hierarchicus: An Essay on the Caste System*. The Nature of Human Society Series. Chicago: University of Chicago Press, 1980. Trans. by Mark Sainsbury, Louis Dumont and Basia Gulati. Original French edition published in 1966.
   This seminal and enduringly controversial work explores the caste system in India with regard to its relationship to paradigms of social organization, the categories of pure and impure, and examines the impact of caste upon the structure of daily familial, political, and religious life. Dumont also compares differing conceptions of hierarchy and caste in India and the West as well as the intellectual and prejudicial pitfalls that beset academic study of the topic.

Eck, Diana L. *Darsan: Seeing the Divine Image in India*. 3rd ed. New York: Columbia University Press, 1998 [1981].
   A sophisticated and sensitive introduction to the Hindu tradition centered around (*darśan*) the sacred. Eck's work provides needed balance to the primarily textual emphasis of other studies, and skillfully guides readers through a survey of the religious significance of the rich material culture of India.

Eck, Diana L. *Encountering God: A Spiritual Journey from Bozeman to Banaras*. Boston: Beacon Press, 1993.

This eloquent and insightful inquiry into religious pluralism and the benefits of inter-religious dialogue combines Eck's exemplary scholarship with the testimony of her personal experiences, ranging from Montana Methodism to time spent as a student of the Hindu tradition in India. Eck illustrates the intellectual and spiritual value of concepts and practices from the Hindu tradition for followers of other faiths, addresses issues surrounding exclusivist, inclusivist, and pluralist approaches to religious difference, stresses the need and inherent worth of honest, respectful conversation, and charts the history and future of religious diversity in America.

Eliade, Mircea. *Yoga: Immortality and Freedom*. 2nd ed. Bollingen Series, vol. 56. Princeton, NJ: Princeton University Press, 1970 [1954]. Trans. by Willard R. Trask from *Le Yoga, Immortalité et Liberté*.

Noting that questions concerning the human condition (and, in particular, the temporality and historicity of human existence) have been at the forefront of modern philosophical speculation, Eliade invites Western thinkers to open themselves to Indian understandings of human consciousness and techniques for its liberation. Towards this end, he offers a comprehensive exposition of Yogic history, doctrine, and technique. Topics receiving special attention include the symbolism and methodology of Yoga and Yoga's relation to tantrism, Indian folklore, and aboriginal devotion. Eliade's subtle and sensitive treatment highlights the Yogic tradition's unparalleled insight into the conditioning of human consciousness and the means by which one restores consciousness to its pure, unconditioned—and therefore free and immortal—form.

Farquhar, J. N. *Modern Religious Movements in India*. 1st Indian ed. Hartford-Lamson Lectures on the Religions of the World. Delhi: Munshiram Manoharlal, 1967 [1924].

This somewhat dated though still helpful study explores the rise of new religious movements in the nineteenth and early twentieth century. Farquhar pays close attention to the commingling of influences arising from the "old faiths" of India (Hinduism, Buddhism, Jainism, Islam, and Zoroastrianism) and modern Western missionary Christianity that contribute to the self-definition and evolution of these reform, revolutionary, and reactionary movements.

Flood, Gavin D. *An Introduction to Hinduism*. Cambridge: Cambridge University Press, 1996.

Drawing upon a wealth of primary sources, Flood offers an insightful and balanced introduction to significant devotional, philosophical, ritual, and artistic themes in the traditions that comprise Hinduism. Topics include the significance of the Vedas, the rise of classical orthodoxy, the cults of Viṣṇu, Śiva, and various goddesses, and contemporary manifestations of the ancient tradition. Flood's bibliography is comprehensive and commendable.

Fowler, Jeaneane D. *Hinduism: Beliefs and Practices*. The Sussex Library of Religious Beliefs and Practices. Brighton: Sussex Academic Press, 1997.

Designed for students new to the Hindu tradition, this concise text portrays the constituent elements of "living Hinduism" and opens avenues for discussion and dialogue. Part One, "The Hindu Way of Life," explains central beliefs, symbols, rituals, festivals, deities, and surveys the caste system. Part Two, "History and Traditions," provides a condensed introduction to the history of Indus valley civilization, the Vedic period, and the development of Vedānta and Bhakti schools.

Fuller, C. J. *The Camphor Flame: Popular Hinduism and Society in India*. Princeton, NJ: Princeton University Press, 1992.

Fuller offers a portrait of popular Hindu belief and practice that critically synthesizes recent anthropological research while remaining accessible to the general reader. Focusing upon the central themes of divine-human relations and hierarchic structures, the author examines the Hindu pantheon, worship and sacrifice, the caste system, women's devotions, and misfortune. Fuller treats the Hindu calendar in its own appendix and provides a useful glossary and bibliographic guide for further study.

Gupta, Sanjukta, Dirk Jan Hoens, and Teun Goudriaan. *Hindu Tantrism*. Handbuch Der Orientalistik, vol. 4. Leiden: Brill, 1979.

In this concise and well-documented introduction, Goudriaan offers readers a historical overview and discussion of central tenets, while Hoens surveys the constituents of Tantric practice with a heavy emphasis upon the function and role of mantras, and Gupta explores elements of worship (puja) and meditation (yoga).

Hardy, Friedhelm. *Viraha-Bhakti: The Early History of Kṛṣṇa Devotion in South India*. Oxford University South Asian Studies Series. Delhi: Oxford, 1983.

In this intense piece of literary and historical scholarship, Hardy investigates the origins of viraha-bhakti (emotional devotion) to the god Kṛṣṇa. Analysis of the Bhāgavata-Purāṇa, Cankan, and Alvar texts illumines the birth and transformation of Kṛṣṇa myths and their incorporation in devotional life.

Heesterman, J. C. *The Inner Conflict of Tradition: Essays in Indian Ritual, Kingship, and Society.* Chicago: University of Chicago Press, 1985.

A collection of essays outlining the underlying tension between unchanging and transcendent religious ideals and the imperfect and immanent realities of human society. Specifically, the Hindu ideal of Brahman and the worldly order symbolized by the king are depicted in a relationship of often problematic co-existence. Heesterman focuses primarily on the Vedic sacrificial system and the ancient Indian political order of kingship, with further commentary on the responses of Indian tradition to modernity.

Hertel, Bradley R. and Cynthia Ann Humes, eds. *Living Banaras: Hindu Religion in Cultural Context.* SUNY Series in Hindu Studies. Albany: State University of New York Press, 1993.

This collection inquires into the nature and practice of popular religion in the urban setting of Banaras. Essays, ranging in subject matter from the Ramlila (dramatizations of the epic of Ram), to contemporary Muslim-Hindu conflict, to the influence of market impulses upon devotion, combine to paint a vivid portrait of the complex vitality of this ancient pilgrimage site and of the modern manifestations of the Hindu tradition.

Hopkins, Thomas J. *The Hindu Religious Tradition.* Religious Life of Man Series. Encino, CA: Dickenson Publishing Co., 1971.

The author provides a broad and surprisingly detailed (given its brevity) historical survey of the central themes of Hinduism, from pre-Aryan societies to Hindu reform movements in the twentieth century. Aspects of Hindu tradition not strictly religious (e.g., cultural and political aspects) are largely unaddressed.

Keith, Arthur Berriedale. *The Religion and Philosophy of the Veda and Upanishads.* Delhi: Motilal Banarsidass, 1976 [1925]. Reprint of Harvard University Press edition of 1925.

A classic text on Indian thought, despite its age. Keith provides a comprehensive account of Vedic philosophy with thorough reference to primary texts. The impressive detail of this two-volume work and the absence of translations of original sources within the text itself (requiring either extensive cross referencing or intimate knowledge of the field) limits its accessibility to more advanced students of Hinduism.

Kinsley, David R. *Hindu Goddesses: Visions of the Divine Feminine in the Hindu Religious Tradition.* Berkeley: University of California Press, 1986.

A "sourcebook" providing portraits of the central Hindu goddesses. Historical perspectives are provided along with a summary of particular myths and rituals associated with each goddess. The text also explores the significance of these figures in illustrating Hindu religious concepts, with an emphasis on the influence of goddess imagery on Hindu perceptions of the feminine.

Kinsley, David R. *Hinduism: A Cultural Perspective*. 2nd ed. Englewood Cliffs, NJ: Prentice Hall, 1993.

A concise introductory overview of Hindu religious thought and tradition. Historical perspective is provided for analysis of Hindu philosophy, myth, ritual, art, and social structures. The author's portrayal of the Hindu world view as a "tension" between dharma (duty) and moksa (release) serves as an underlying theme in discussions of central Hindu beliefs and associated cultural forms. The second editions includes an expanded section on feminine imagery and participation in Hinduism.

Klostermaier, Klaus K. *A Survey of Hinduism*. 2nd ed. Albany: State University of New York Press, 1994.

The author attempts to convey "the living tradition of the Hindus" through a survey of Hindu religion as it influences contemporary thought and culture. The text provides an introduction to the development of Hinduism and its textual foundation and underlying theology; a discussion of the three marga (paths of salvation) of work, knowledge, and loving devotion as they feature in contemporary worship; an examination of Hindu philosophy, social order, and the sacralization of time and space as they provide support to the structure of Hindu tradition; and some mention of the contemporary interaction of Hinduism with the West.

Knipe, David M. *Hinduism: Experiments in the Sacred*. Religious Traditions of the World. San Francisco: HarperSanFrancisco, 1991.

A brief introduction to Hinduism presupposing no prior knowledge of the tradition. The text is divided primarily into sections on historical foundations, Hindu representations of reality, and Hindu ritual practice, with a minor section on contemporary Hindu society.

Leslie, Julia. *Roles and Rituals for Hindu Women*. Rutherford, NJ: Fairleigh Dickinson University Press, 1991.

An attempt to portray Hindu women as "active agents of their own positive constructs" through a consideration of the part played by women in a variety of religious rituals. Four categories of feminine roles and ritual are explored: the ritual wife, power in the home, the ritual of dance, and the pursuit of salvation. Through feminist interpretation of Hindu text and tradition, women are portrayed as more than passive victims of oppressive Hindu ideologies. Emphasis is placed throughout on interpretations of Hindu ritual as seen by its female practitioners, thus providing often surprising insight into the motivation behind feminine participation in Hindu religious practice.

Lingat, Robert. *The Classical Law of India.* Berkeley: University of California Press, 1973. Trans. of *Les Sources du Droit Dans le Système Traditionnel de l'Inde.* Sponsored by the Center for South and Southeast Asia Studies, University of California, Berkeley.

A discussion of the traditional Hindu understanding of law prior to the adoption in India of Western judicial concepts. Lingat explores the relationship between the religious notion of dharma (duty) and the establishment of a juridical system by first extensively examining the traditional and textual sources of dharma and subsequently systemizing the development of interpreted dharma into rule of law through the influence of custom and royal ordinance.

Lott, Eric J. *Vedāntic Approaches to God.* Library of Philosophy and Religion. Totowa, NJ: Barnes & Noble, 1980. Originally presented as the author's thesis, Liverpool, 1977.

A comprehensive comparative study of three schools of Vedānta deriving from the thought of the Hindu theologians Śaṃkara, Rāmānuja, and Madhva. The author stresses the diversity of Vedantic study in referring to distinctions between these schools in the understanding of Brahman, epistemology, and transcendence.

Majumdar, Ramesh Chandra, Hemchandra Raychaudhuri, and Kalikinkar Datta. *An Advanced History of India.* 3rd ed. London: Macmillan, 1967.

A comprehensive survey of Indian history from pre-Aryan peoples to the formation of an independent state in 1947, with the addition of several brief appendices on developments in the following two decades. Special emphasis is placed upon political, social, economic, and cultural developments, as opposed to specific personalities. As suggested by the title, the text is intended for those with some previous knowledge of Indian history.

Mandelbaum, David Goodman. *Society in India,* 2 vols. Berkeley: University of California Press, 1970.

A detailed general study (conducted in the middle third of the twentieth century) on the basic social principles guiding Indian village life. The text focuses on the primary societal groups and the interactions between them, with the aim of fostering understanding of Indian caste society. Economic, political, and religious influences on social order are generally not considered. The detail and size (two volumes, over 650 pages) of this work recommend it to those seeking more than simply an introduction to Indian social order.

Marriott, McKim, ed. *India Through Hindu Categories*. Newbury Park, CA: Sage Publications, 1990.

These essays apply ethnographic and ethnosociological approaches, employing South Asian concepts and categories, to the study of Indian religions and cultures. Entries include discussions of issues arising in the ethnosociological discipline, the question of distinctly Indian modes of thought, interpretations of misfortune, and the concept of purity.

Nelson, Lance E., ed. *Purifying the Earthly Body of God: Religion and Ecology in Hindu India*. SUNY Series in Religious Studies. Albany: State University of New York Press, 1998.

A collection of essays by various authors addressing the intersection of the Hindu religion and Indian environmentalism. Both positive and negative influences of Hindu thought are examined, with special emphasis on the symbolism and imagery that form the basis of Indian attitudes and behaviors toward nature. Specific issues explored include the potential role of the ascetic outlook in ecological ethics, the role of karma, the sacralization of Hindu time and space, concepts of purity and impurity, the influence of the orthodox emphasis on transcendence, and the relationship of Hindu worldviews to modern secular environmentalism.

Pintchman, Tracy. *The Rise of the Goddess in the Hindu Tradition*. Albany: State University of New York Press, 1994.

An examination of the understanding of the Great Goddess in Hindu Brahmanical tradition. The text traces historic origins of goddess motifs in the Vedic and Brahmanic traditions, explores the formulation of the Great Goddess through the principles of prakṛti (Nature/material existence), śakti (enery/power), and māyā (illusion), and considers the cultural implications of this formulation, especially with respect to contemporary gender issues in Hindu society.

Renard, John. *Responses to 101 Questions on Hinduism*. New York: Paulist Press, 1999.

A highly accessible introductory text aimed at providing some initial familiarity with various aspects of Hindu religion and culture. Topics covered include historic development, doctrine and practice, ethics, spirituality, philosophy, and contemporary issues such as gender and the influence of Hinduism on the West.

Rowland, Benjamin. *The Art and Architecture of India: Buddhist, Hindu,*

Jain. 3rd ed. The Pelican History of Art, vol. Z. Baltimore: Penguin Books, 1971.

A comprehensive historical and geographical survey of Indian art and architecture. Contributions of Buddhist, Hindu, and Jain traditions are examined, with consideration of the mythic and metaphysical aspects of specific forms. The text is extensively illustrated throughout, and artistic themes are developed through reference to particular works. Most likely to be of greatest interest to students of art and architecture, this work provides an excellent introduction to the art forms common to South Asia and their historical and cultural foundations.

Sivaraman, Krishna. *Hindu Spirituality: Vedas Through Vedānta*. World Spirituality, vol. 6. New York: Crossroad, 1989.

A collection of nineteen essays aimed at providing a diversity of approaches to the understanding of Indian spirituality of the "classical period." Essays range from those of general scope (e.g., "Vedānta as philosophy of spiritual life") to those with highly specified foci (e.g., an article on the use of the term boddhiyoga in the *Bhagavad Gītā*). Some articles assume prior familiarity with Hindu philosophy. The focus of the collection is on spirituality as developed in the elite intellectual tradition of classical Hinduism.

Whicher, Ian. *The Integrity of the Yoga Darsana: A Reconsideration of Classical Yoga*. SUNY Series in Religious Studies. Albany: State University of New York Press, 1998.

A textual, historical, and interpretive re-reading of the Yoga Sūtra and the thought of Patanjali aimed towards a more complete understanding of the relationship of Yogic theory to Yogic practice. The author challenges common conceptions of Yoga darśana by contending that Patañjali's Yoga promotes a "responsible engagement" of spirit and material existence toward a liberated selfhood which enables a more fulfilling worldly existence without subjection to worldly identification. The text provides a survey of early Hindu Yogic forms as well as a treatment of the theoretical issues. The complexity of Whicher's argument assumes some knowledge of Hindu philosophy.

Williams, Raymond Brady, ed. *A Sacred Thread: Modern Transmission of Hindu Traditions in India and Abroad*. Chambersburg, PA: Anima, 1992.

This fascinating collection of essays paints a vivid, incisive, and often humorous portrait of the diversity of the Hindu diaspora. Part One examines the changing faces of Hinduism in India and explores the interplay between a tradition's mode of transmission and its content. Part

Two surveys issues surrounding the transplantation of Indian religious traditions onto foreign soil, primarily focused upon the religiously and culturally diverse landscape of America. Topics include the impact of Western missionary and educational activity upon the evolution of Hindu traditions, questions surrounding translation of texts, the role of ritual in transmission of religious belief, and intellectual and spiritual cross-pollination among traditions.

Zimmer, Heinrich Robert and Joseph Campbell. *Myths and Symbols in Indian Art and Civilization.* Bollingen Series, vol. 6. Princeton, NJ: Princeton University Press, 1972. Original ed. published by New York: Pantheon Books.

A survey of some of the dominant myths and mythological symbols of the Hindu tradition, accompanied by examples of their representations in Indian art and architecture. The central focus of the text is directed to Hindu mythology, with illustrations serving primarily as supporting material. Common themes and homogeneity within the diverse world of Hindu myth are explored, with occasional treatment of issues of methodology and interpretation.

Annotated Bibliography: Theories of Comparison

Boon, James A. *Other Tribes, Other Scribes: Symbolic Anthropology in the Comparative Study of Cultures, Histories, Religions, and Texts.* Cambridge: Cambridge University Press, 1982.

This work embarks upon a complex investigation of the history, dialectics, and current practice of the symbolic analysis of cultural diversity with an aim of formulating a general comparative approach to the study of symbolic processes. Boon examines the interrelationships of cultures as they differ in time and space through the medium and critique of various sociological and philosophical methods. In addition, Boon uses an array of cross-cultural and historical discussions to integrate different secular and religious symbolic forms in order to form a model of the type of symbolic analysis Boon advocates. More specifically, Boon proceeds upon the hypothesis that both cultures and the methods of investigating them are plural, and posits, for the examination of cultures, a method of dialectical analysis that employs the interrelation of opposed yet complementary comparative theoretical approaches.

Bouquet, A. C. *Comparative Religion: A Short Outline.* 6th ed. London: Penguin Books, 1961 [1942].

This work develops a brief account of the history of comparative religious studies and a general overview of the major religious traditions of the world. The individual analyses of each of the major religious traditions in this investigation focus on the notion of deity and selfhood that is given expression by each of the major religions in their sacred texts. Of particular interest for contemporary comparative studies is the final chapter of this work, which identifies and classifies several primary categories for comparison developed by a number of European scholars.

Carpenter, J. Estlin. *Comparative Religion*. The Home University Library of Modern Knowledge, vol. 60. New York: Henry Holt and Company, 1944.

Working to draw comparisons primarily in the panoramic field of primitive religions, this investigation locates its comparative trajectory in the initial analysis of external or outward acts that fall within the sphere of religious activity, and then in the internal world of thought and feeling. Such external objects for comparison are described as including the places where religious acts are performed, the people who perform them, the means required for religious action, and the occasions to which such actions are attached. Internal acts for comparison are said to include elements of belief, conceptions of the significance of ritual, and the understanding of Powers toward which worship is directed. These later internal acts are construed to be located most explicitly for investigation in the myth, literature, and history of more highly organized religions, which externalize belief through their modes of worship. Within this larger methodological framework, comparative analysis of an array of religious traditions is pursued under the topics of sacred act, spirits and gods, sacred products, and religious morality.

Charing, Douglas et al. *Comparative Religions: A Modern Textbook*. London: Blanford Press, 1982.

Offering some preliminary explanations concerning the broader elements of the comparative study of religions and acknowledging the necessity for a kind of religious dialogue that takes into account cultural differences, this work introduces central themes evident in the religious faiths of Hinduism, Judaism, Christianity, Islam, and Sikhism. By identifying the differences evident in these faiths, chosen specifically because they are commonly practiced in every country of the English-speaking world, it is the authors' intent to illustrate a picture of the whole diverse range of religious worship. Other categories for comparison are suggested as well, including prayer, religious festival, and communal belief.

Eliade, Mircea. *Patterns in Comparative Religion.* 5th ed. New York: The World Publishing Company, 1996 [1958]. Trans. from *Traité d'Histoire des Religions* by Rosemary Sheed.

This extensive comparative study explores commonalities shared by primitive religious traditions in accordance with those exhibited in patterns manifest in cosmic heirophanies understood as sacred. Eliade analyses of divine forms, myths, religious symbols, and other natural heirophanies considered sacred in primitive religions, facilitating a more specialized comparative study of religions. A bibliography arranged according to topical study follows each chapter.

Jordan, Louis Henry. *Comparative Religion: Its Genesis and Growth.* Atlanta: Scholars Press, 1986 [1905]. Originally published by Edinburgh: T & T Clark, 1905.

This exhaustive historical account of the emergence and growth of the discipline of comparative religious studies offers a broad introduction to the major fields, schools, and central theorists in the comparative study of religions. Of primary concern is the outline of methodological strategies and the tracing of their theoretical development.

Lessa, William A. and Evon Z. Vogt, eds. *Reader in Comparative Religion: An Anthropological Approach.* 4th ed. New York: Harper & Row Publishers, 1979 [1958].

This work provides the readers with a wide array of literature concerning what anthropologists have found out about religion over the past one hundred years. The various selected essays are viewed by the editors to represent two types of 'comparative religion'. The first involves the method by which common denominator conceptual generalizations are extracted from a mass of variants and used as tools to make comparisons between similar types of phenomena. The second understands similarities in cultural form and structure as providing key typologies or categories for comparison that achieve a kind of objectivity that allows for comparative neutrality. Other essays present comparative perspectives that employ both methods or in some way fall under the broader anthropological concerns addressed in this collection.

Mugambi, J. N. K, ed. *A Comparative Study of Religions.* Nairobi, Kenya: Nairobi University Press, 1990.

This series of essays providing introductory material in all the major religious traditions as well as in African, Near East, and Eskimo traditions, is itself introduced by essays on the scope of comparative theories of religion. Later essays then draw comparisons on major religious themes including creation, models of relationships, the nature and destiny of man, good and evil, salvation, death, and immortality. Final considerations are given to central contemporary religious movements and themes relevant to the future of religion.

Neville, Robert C. *Behind the Masks of God: An Essay Toward Comparative Theology*. Albany: State University of New York Press, 1991.

Acknowledging the hypothetical character of contemporary comparative methodologies, Neville posits that the central task of comparative theology is the disclosure and understanding of the contexts in which various religious expressions of divinity are true. Necessary to this task, for Neville, is the development of a methodology for comparing religious traditions that may in fact be incommensurate. Accordingly, Neville argues that such a methodology must identify and critically assess a general conception of divinity that allows other conceptions, symbols, and images of divinity to be related and ordered, and, further, to make explicit descriptive speculative hypotheses that articulate and contextualize this conception of divinity for the purpose of generating plausible philosophical categories that might serve as a conceptual ground for comparison. Upon such premises, Neville advocates a general conception of divinity based on a specialized account of creation *ex nihilo* and dialectically explores the fundamental categories of creativity and nothingness as they relate to the intellectual traditions of Christianity, Buddhism, and Confucianism.

Paden, William E. *Religious Worlds: The Comparative Study of Religion*. Boston: Beacon Press, 1988.

Paden develops the far-reaching concept of "world," specifically in the sense of being an environment or "place," as an organizing category for the study of religion. More precisely, the concept of "world" for this study is construed as the operating environment of language and behavioral options that persons presuppose and inhabit at any given point in any particular form of human action. With such an encompassing idea of *context* and the further thesis arguing for the presence of multiple worlds, this work endeavors to investigate distinctive life-categories of the "insider" across the lines of different religious traditions while specifically examining religious myth, ritual, deity, and systems of purity. Also included is a brief synopsis and critique of traditional strategies of comparison employed in the study of religions.

Platvoet, J. G. *Comparing Religions: A Limitative Approach; An Analysis of Akan, Para-Creole, and IFO-Sananda Rites and Prayers*. Religion and Reason; Method and Theory in the Study and Interpretation of Religion. The Hague: Mouton Publishers, 1982.

Platvoet argues for the abandonment of global modes of comparison that impose no restrictions upon the number and type of religions to be compared, instead favoring the adoption of a limitative, restricted approach to the comparisons of religion. This work employs a number of analytical tools for comparison derived from a theory of religion that postulates religion as a process of communication between a human being or a group of human beings and one or more of the "meta-empirical" beings whom they believe to exist and to affect their lives. The central premises posited for a limitative comparative study of religion include the in-depth study of both the particular facets of religion selected for comparison and the subjective lives of the authors who wrote on them. The methodological tools employed for such analytical and comparative work include descriptive accounts of the communication networks ('field'), modes of communication ('process'), and the larger historical and institutional contexts ('context') considered relevant to the facet of religion selected for comparison.

Sharpe, Eric J. *Comparative Religion: A History*. London: Gerald Duckworth and Company, Ltd., 1975.
 Although not developing its own methodology for the comparative study of religion, this work reviews the conceptual development of the academic field of comparative religious studies, highlighting its major trends and the thought of its most central theorists. Following a preliminary examination of the antecedents of comparative religious studies is a detailed account of the way different thinkers and early intellectual movements in anthropological, sociological, psychological, and philosophical disciplines contributed in shaping the efforts and concerns of the contemporary comparative study of religion.

Smith, Wilfred Cantwell. *Towards a World Theology: Faith and the Comparative History of Religion*. Philadelphia: The Westminster Press, 1981.
 This work operates under the premise that there exists a coherence or unity in humankind's religious history (exemplified in certain metaphysical truths), and endeavors to reflect on how the understanding and perspectives of distinct religious traditions resemble this common history in different ways. Further, Smith considers and critiques the way conceptual categories evident in each of the major religious traditions of the world may, according to their own character, potentially function as comparative categories of universal significance in relation to all forms of religion. Central to this analysis is the belief that conceptualizing and understanding the concepts of others must be historically anchored (even in the case

of history-transcending or self-transcending concepts such as those associated with deity).

Wach, Joachim. *The Comparative Study of Religions*. Lectures on the
History of Religions, American Council of Learned Societies. New York:
Columbia University Press, 1958.

Wach develops a systematic approach for the analysis of religious experience, drawing on sociological, historical, philological, and phenomenological methodology to develop a broad philosophical account of
the nature of religious experience. Also, there is an account of the methodology developed for this study and a defense of typological categorization for the purpose of organizing the endless variety of phenomenon
provided by the history, psychology, and sociology of religion.

Contributors

JOHN BERTHRONG is Associate Dean of the Boston University School of Theology and Director of the Institute for Dialogue Among Religious Traditions. He is a founding member of the North American Interfaith Network and has specializations in comparative theology as well as Chinese religion and philosophy, especially Confucianism.

FRANCIS X. CLOONEY, S.J., Professor of Comparative Theology at Boston College, is past president of the the Society for Hindu-Christian Studies. He specializes in certain Sanskrit and Tamil traditions of Hindu thought and their implications for Christian theology.

MALCOLM DAVID ECKEL is Professor of the History of Religion at Boston University and does research and teaching in Buddhism.

PAULA FREDRIKSEN is the William Goodwin Aurelio Professor of the Appreciation of Scripture and Professor of New Testament and Early Christianity at Boston University. She has a particular research interest in Augustine of Hippo, and has also published in the areas of Hellenistic Judaism, Christian origins, and Pauline studies.

S. NOMANUL HAQ is currently on the faculty of Rutgers University and a visiting scholar at the University of Pennsylvania. He has published extensively in the general area of Islamic intellectual history, including theology, philosophy, and science.

LIVIA KOHN is Professor of Religion and East-Asian Studies at Boston University. She is a specialist of medieval Daoism.

JAMES MILLER, a graduate of Durham University and Cambridge University, is currently a Ph.D. candidate at Boston University, and an adjunct lecturer in the Department of Theology at Boston College. He is co-editor, with Norman Girardot and Liu Xiaogan, of *Daoism and Ecology,* a volume in the series on world religions and ecology published by Harvard University's Center for the Study of World Religions.

ROBERT CUMMINGS NEVILLE is Professor of Philosophy, Religion, and Theology, and Dean of the School of Theology at Boston University.

Neville is the past president of the American Academy of Religion, The International Society for Chinese Philosophy, and The Metaphysical Society of America.

HUGH NICHOLSON is a Ph.D. candidate in the Theology Department at Boston College and is currently writing his dissertation relating Indian philosophical thought to theological and philosophical questions and concerns of the Christian West.

ANTHONY J. SALDARINI has taught early Judaism and Christianity in the Department of Theology at Boston College for over twenty years and publishes in the area of early Jewish-Christian relations.

JOHN J. THATAMANIL is a member of the religious studies faculty at Millsaps College, and recently completed his dissertation comparing the thought of Paul Tillich and Śaṇkara.

TU WEIMING is a distinguished New Confucian intellectual. He is Professor of Chinese History and Philosophy in the Department of East Asian Languages and Civilizations at Harvard University. He is widely published in the area of Chinese intellectual history, Asian and comparative philosophy, East Asian religious thought, and Confucian studies. He is also director of the Harvard-Yenching Library and served as a Senior Advisor to the Comparative Religious Ideas Project.

WESLEY J. WILDMAN is Associate Professor of Theology and Ethics at Boston University. He teaches and does research in the areas of contemporary Christian theology, philosophy of religion, and religion and science.

Index of Names

Abe, Masao, 142–43
Abraham, 43, 45, 61, 160, 208
Abu'l-Hudhayl, 85
Adam, 90–91
al-Ghazālī, Abū Ḥāmid, 75, 82, 85, 87, 90–91
al-Ḥallāj, 78
al-Jabbār, 'Abd, 85
al-Shahrastānī, 85
al-Sulamī, 78
Albo, Joseph, 52
Allen, Christopher, xvii, 273
Alston, William, 209
Ames, Roger T., 144, 210, 258
Anton, John P., 244
Aristotle, 7, 49, 56, 188, 195–96, 240, 243–44, 247–49, 257
Arjuna, 207
Asaṅga, 136, 148
Asclepius, 72
Augustine (St.), Bishop of Hippo, xx, 203
Austin, J. L., 144
Avicenna, 78

Baqillani, 87
Barth, Auguste, 143
Beneveniste, 249
Berger, Peter, xvii, 268–69
Bernstein, Richard, 252
Berthrong, John H., xvii, xx
Bhāskara, 101–2, 115
Bhāvaviveka, 126–27, 136, 138–40, 143, 147, 149, 203

Birdwhistell, Anne, xv, 158, 185
Brāhma, 100, 104–6
Buddha, 2, 129, 131, 1380–42, 146
Buddhaghosa, 130
Bultmann, Rudolf, 53
Burnouf, Eugène, 131

Cabezon, Jose, xv, xxv–xxvi
Campbell, Joseph, 32
Candrakīrti, 131, 138, 145, 147, 149
Chan, Alan, 13
Chan, Wing-tsit, 210
Chemparathy, George, 108
Ching, Julia, xv, xviii, 167
Chittick, 87–88
Clarke, Samuel, 116
Clooney, Francis X., xvi–xvii, 2, 8, 152–55, 162–63, 177, 184, 203, 245, 262–64, 268
Cohen, Hermann, 42, 53–55, 159, 180
Confucius, 242, 248
Corbin, 89–90
Confucius, 15, 144, 249

Dalai, Lama, The, 141–42
Darwin, Charles, 128
Dennet, Daniel C., 225
Descartes, René, 188–89
Deśika, 96–123, 152, 154–55, 162–63, 167, 175, 177, 180, 184, 268
Devī, 121
Dewey, John, 227
Dignāga, 126–27, 143

Dilworth, 241–43
Dishkin, Rabbi Y. Y., 59
Dorff, Eliott, 40–41
Douglas, Mary, 72
Dravid, N. S., 122
Dung Zhongshu, 242–43
Duns Scotus, 144
Durkheim, Emile, 131, 143, 241, 256,
    267

Eddy, Mary Baker, xx
Eckel, Malcolm David, xvi, xx, 2, 3,
    7–9, 70, 119, 152–53, 155, 163–
    64, 184, 203, 245, 264, 267–69
Euripides, 128
Ezekiel, 45

Fei Changfang, 29
Feterabend, Paul, 225
Fingarette, Herbert, 144
Flower Maiden, 30, 35
Frazer, J. G., 128, 146
Fredriksen, Paula, xvi–xvii, 2, 8, 130,
    152–54, 160, 162, 181–84, 203,
    243, 252, 262–63, 269

Gardet, 90
Gaon, Saadia, 41
Geertz, Clifford, 202
Gellner, Ernest, 241, 256
Gikatlia, Joseph, 49
Gengsangzi, 15–16
Gimellow, Robert, 33
Graham, Angus C., 12, 210, 248–50,
    257
Guanyin, 168

Halbfass, Wilhelm, 246–47, 257
Hall, David L., 144, 210, 258
Hamar, Imre, 32
Hamlet, 249
Haq, S. Nomanul, xvi–xvii, 2, 8, 119,
    153, 160–62, 166, 174, 179, 181,
    203, 243, 264
Hardy, Julia, 13
Hartshorne, Charles, 258

Hegel, G. F. W., 169, 240
Heidegger, Martin, 32, 206
Hirsch, Rabbi Samson Raphael
    Hirsch, 55
Hishām ibn al-Ḥakam, 87
Hobbes, Thomas, 206
Hodgson, Brian Houghton, 131
Hsuan-tsang, 136
Hua Tuo, 22, 34
Hugong (the Gourd Master), 29
Hui, King of Liang, 20
Hui-neng, 137
Hujwīrī, 91
Husserl, Edmund, 224–25

Ibn 'Arabī, 77–78, 88–90, 160, 162
Ibn Ḥazm, 79, 85
Ibn Kullāb, 87
Isaac, 208
Isaiah, 45, 61

Jabir, 203
Jacob, 61
Jade Emperor, 26
James, William, 128
Jaspers, Karl, 206, 258
Jeremiah, 43
Jesus, 2, 8, 61–71, 143, 160, 181–82,
    206
Josephus, 71
Joel, 46
John of Damascus, 81, 85
John Paul II, Pope, 146
Johnson, Mark, 252–55, 258

Kalupahana, David J., 245–46
Kanaofsky, Joseph, 274
Kant, Immanuel, 195–96, 237, 240,
    242
Kapstein, 145–46
Katz, Steven, 9
Kierkegaard, Sørn, 180
Kohn, Livia, xvi–xvii, xx, 2, 7–8, 70,
    75, 119, 153–54, 156–58, 166,
    172, 176–77, 179, 181, 183–84.
    203, 238, 240, 248, 267

Kook, Rabbi Avraham Yizhak HaKo-
    hen, 55–56, 59
Kṛṣṇa, 176
Kuhn, Thomas, 225

La Vallée Poussin, Louis, 131–33, 136
Lakoff, George, 252–55, 258
Lakatos, Imre, 225–27
Laozi, 17, 26–27, 32, 157, 184
Leibniz, G. W., 116
Li Rong, 24
Lindtner, Christian, 143
Liu An, 15, 30
Lü Dongbin, 29, 35
Lu Xiangshan, 254

MacDonald, 80, 91
Maimonides, Moses, 41–42, 48–51,
    159, 166, 180
Mary (the mother of Jesus), 168
Maslow, Abraham, 13
Mencius, 20, 242
Mendelssohn, Moses, 55
Milgrom, Jacob, 72
Miller, James, xvii, 75, 153–54, 156–
    58, 166, 172, 176–77, 179, 181,
    183–84, 273
Moses, 44, 45, 49, 67
Moore, G. E., 242
Moyers, Bill, 130, 147
Murata, 87–88
Murti, T. R. V., 132

Nāgārjuna, 7, 127, 130–32, 136, 138,
    140, 145, 172, 183
Nārāyaṇa, 97–98, 100, 103–6, 110,
    113–15, 118, 121–22, 152, 162,
    175, 184
Needham, Joseph, 247
Neusner, Jacob, 72
Neville, Robert C., 4–7, 128–29,
    144, 155, 169, 185, 209, 232, 239,
    252, 255, 258, 264–66, 268–72
Newman, John Henry, 226
Newton, Isaac, 248
Nicholson, Hugh, xvii, 273

Nishitani, Kitaro, 32
Noah, 44
Nock, Darby, 71

Origen of Alexandria, xx, 166
Otto, Rudolf, 223

Panikkar, Raimon, 241, 256
Paul (St.) of Tarsus, 62–70, 73, 160,
    181–82, 184
Pearlson, Jordan, xv, xviii
Peirce, Charles S., 198, 209–10, 227,
    252, 258
Pepper, Stephen, 248
Philo (Judaeus) of Alexandria, 71, 85,
    166
Plato, 56
Popper, Karl, 226
Putnam, Hilary, 253

Qu Baiting (Lad Qu), 30

Rahner, Karl, 206
Rāmānuja, 98–99, 105, 121–22, 162,
    177
Raṅgarāmānuja, Sri, 106, 121
Rorty, Richard, 252
Rosch, Eleanor, 254
Russell, Bertrand, 240, 241

Sahara, 43
Śaiva Siddhanta, 114, 118, 120
Saldarini, Anthony J, xvi–xvii, 2, 8,
    61, 119, 153, 158–62, 166, 179,
    184, 203, 252, 265
Samantabhadra, 145
Sāṃkhya, 175, 241
Śaṅkara, 7, 101, 104, 162, 203
Schwartz, Benjamin I., 144
Sharma, Arvind, xv
Shangdi, 166
Shen-hsiu, 137
Shepardson, Tina, xvii
Sima Chengzhen, 21, 30, 35
Singh, Satyavrata, 122
Smith, Huston, 197, 219

Smith, Jonathan Z., xv, xxv, 7, 128, 212, 231–32, 251, 257
Smith, Wildred Cantwell, 7, 129, 143, 147, 214, 238
Śiva, 100, 104–6, 113–15, 121
Socrates, 241
Sonnenfeld, Rabbi Y. H., 59
Śrī, 97–98, 103–4, 113, 121–22, 184
Stackhouse, Max, xviii
Stcherbatsky, F. Th., 131–33, 136, 138
Stowers, Stanley, 65, 71–72
Streng, Frederick J., 143, 147
Sullivan, Celeste, xvii, 273
Stackhouse, Max, xv
Swinburne, Richard, 115–20, 163

Takakusa, 246
Tatacharyaya, Sri Kanchi, 121
Thurman, Robert, 147
Tillich, Paul, 2, 142, 144, 152, 156, 185, 206–7, 210, 223, 267
Titus, 63
Thatamanil, John J. xvii, 273
Tracy, David, 255
Tsoṅ-kha-pa, 132–33, 138, 145

Udayana, 108
Underhill, Evelyn, 10

Vajda, Georges (Judah Arieh), 58

Vasubandhu, 136, 148, 246
Vedānta Deśika, *see* Deśika
Verdu, Alfonso, 246
Viṣṇu, 121; *see also* Nārāyaṇa

Wang Bi, 13, 33
Wang Yangming, 240
Watson, Walter, 241–43
Weber, Max, 241
Weiming, Tu, xv, xviii, 2, 130, 147, 262
Wildman, Wesley J., xvii, xix, xxiii, 6, 155, 169, 232, 239, 252, 270
Williams, Paul, 245
Wittgenstein, Ludwig, 140
Wolfson, 81, 86

Xunzi, 144, 240, 250–51

Yadavaprakasa, 101, 104, 122
Yahweh, 166
Yearly, Lee, xv
Yellow Emperor, 30, 35
Yi T'oegye, 240

Zhou Dunyi, 20–21, 34, 156–57, 162, 175
Zhu Xi, 34, 203, 239–40, 254
Zhuangzi, 14, 180–81, 242, 254

Index of Subjects

❧

1 Corinthians, letter to, 64–66, 68, 71
1 Thessalonians, letter to, 64–65
2 Corinthians, letter to, 66

Abhidharma, 245–47
Absolute, the, 130–43; in Madhya-
    maka and Yogācāra, 136–38
Abstraction, and category formation,
    239–40; in justifying categories,
    228–29
Abyss, 182
Act, of ontological creation, 173–74,
    178; of Esse, 168
Actuality, 240; versus the ideal, 17
Actualization, of cosmic order in ex-
    perience, 129–30
Adam, in Islam, 89, 91
Adepts, in rabbinic mysticism, 47; see
    also Perfected, the
Advaita Vedānta, 100, 104, 113, 197,
    203
Aesthetics, in conventional truth, 142
African Independent Churches, xxi
African religions, 200
Ahl al-Ḥadīth, 82–84
Ajīvaka, 115
All things as the Lord's body, 98
Allah, 8, 76–77, 79–80, 90–93; per-
    sonal and namable, 161; see also
    God
Al-Muḥīṭ, 80
Alphabet, Jewish, in mysticism, 52–53
Amr, 79, 161
Anachronism, 263
Analogy, in Chinese category making,
    250–51
Analysis of shifts in ideas, in justifica-
    tion, 228

Angels, 57; in America, 168; in Rab-
    binic mysticism, 47
Anthropocentrism, 1
Anthropology, xxiv, 202, 220, 251; as
    approach to ultimates, 1–3, 153,
    179–85
Anthropomorphism, 43, 55, 82, 91, 159
Antiquity, Roman or Hellenistic, and
    cults of sacrifice, 62
Anumāna (inference), 97
Apocalypse, Jewish, 47
Apophasis, 18, 82–84, 130–33, 167,
    180–81; in Jewish thought, 38–39,
    49; see also Negative theology;
    Kataphasis
Appearance, the world as, 54; see also
    Māyā
Appearances, of God disguised, 44
Apples and oranges, how to compare,
    195
Arbitrariness, 220; in comparison,
    268–70; of vague categories, 266
Archetypes, theory of for deriving cat-
    egories, 219
Argument, creates shared language,
    110–11
Argumentative discourse about ulti-
    mate reality, in Hinduism, 96
Arise/respond interaction, 248–49
Aristotelianism, in categories, 195;
    categories of compared with Chi-
    nese, 248–49; in Christianity and
    Islam, 243; theory of truth in, 188
Art-and-religion studies, xxiv; in com-
    parative judgment, 226; in justify-
    ing categories, 241
Ascension, in Daoism, 28–29
Ascetic non-theism, 115

Ash'arite theology, 85–87
Asia, West, South, and East, 238
Asymmetry, in creation, 173–75, 178, 183; of non-being and being, 21; of non-being and the Great Ultimate, 157
Atheism, 105–7, 109
Atonement sacrifice, 64
Attributes, of God, 75; in himself, in relation to cosmos, and in relation to humans, 80–82, 92–93; thirteen, in Talmudic tradition, 39–46
Authority, divine, 46
Authorship, in this Project, xxiii
Axial Age, xxiv, 166, 200, 251
Āya, 79

Babylon, 43
Baptism, 66
Beautiful Names, of God in Islam, 80
Being, 240, 243; and God, 54; fullness of, 174; as stable and permanent, 172
Bezels of Wisdom, 77
Bhagavad Gītā, 129, 176, 207
Bias, 4–5, 188, 190, 195, 206, 213–14, 263;
Bible, Hebrew, 40–45, 51, 180
Biology, 220; and common humanity, 213
Blood sacrifice, Jesus as, 62–71, 154
Bodhisattvas, 219
Body, of Christ, 66; of Christians, 71; God's 43, 158, *see also* God; as ultimate, 30
Book of Creation, 49, 51–53
Boston Confucianism, xxvi
Brāhma, 100, 104–6
Brahman, 97, 101, 165, 204; efficient and material cause of world, 102–3; Nirguṇa and Saguṇa, 167, 219; with all positive qualities, 100–1; unlimited, 102; relation to world, 162; *see also* God
Brahmanical religions, 175–76; defined, 121

Brāhmins, male, 263
Bread/flesh, 69
Breath, 89
Buddha, 129, 131; Buddha, Dharma, Saṅgha, xx; for Madhyamaka, 141
Buddhas, 184
Buddhism, 2, 7, 16, 19–20, 70, 101, 104, 115, 118–19, 121, 152, 175–76, 182–85, 188, 191–92, 196–97, 200, 203–4, 238, 244, 254, 266–67, 273; as atheism, 1; versus Brahmanism in Burouf's interpretation, 131; in China, 251; and Christian dialogue, 142; difficult to fit into comparative categories of this Project, 125; and Hinduism compared on categories, 245–47; and Jainism, 97–98; ultimate realities in, 163–64; *see also* Ch'an, Huayan, Madhyamaka, Mahāyāna, Theravāda, Yogācāra, Zen

Canon, Confucian, 248
Cartesianism, 188, 206; in this Project, xxv–xxvi
Carvāka philosophy, 101, 104
Categoreal, distinguished from categorical, 237
Categories, xii; as accidental, 240; adequate but not justified, 270–71; in Aristotle, 243–44; borrowing of, 230; comparative, defined, 191–94, as respect of interpretation, 194, selection of explained, xviii–xix; as a comparative idea, 237–56; as cultural entities, 239–40; in China, 247–48; flexibility of, 218–19; fruitfulness of, 229; in Indian thought, 244–47; interpreted by Lakoff and Johnson, 253; and metaphoric reasoning, 253; natural, as believed by different cultures, 238–40; of personal life, 249–50; social construction of, 240–41; derivative from theories of religion, 218–21

Causation, 220–21; of conceptual similarities, 216; efficient and material, 118; in Indian categories, 246–47

Cause, ultimate or universal, 98, 171–74

Ch'an Buddhism, 137, 254

Change, 165, 175, 255; conditions for, 141

Chanting, 183

Chaos, 40; feared by philosophers, 254

Chariot, divine, in rabbinic mysticism, 47

Chinese religion, 2, 7–8, 152, 154, 201, 203; on asymmetry, 175; compared with Buddhism and Judaism, 11; as a category, xx; on ordinary experience, 197; relating human condition and ultimate reality, 11–12; and mandate of Heaven, 177; medieval period, 26; and order, 176; realization of the ultimate in, 14–17; ultimate realities in, 9–32, 156–58; "ultimate" no "real" and "reality" not "ultimate," 12–13; unity of, 238

Christ, *see* Jesus Christ

Christian philosophy, and Hermann Cohen, 54

Christian theology, in Islam, 81, 85

Christianity, 1–2, 4, 8, 118–19, 152, 154–55, 166–68, 181–83, 191–92, 204, 206, 238, 243, 252, 273; assumptions in concerning comparison, 200–1; on asymmetry in creation, 174; in China, 167; Jewish, 213; growth from a sect within Judaism, 71; on ultimate realities, 61–71, 160, compared to Chinese, 70

Christology, 61; Pauline, 65–66

Church (*ekklesia*), 64

Chutzpah, 270

Circumcision, 63–64

Civañāṇacittiyār, 114–15

Classification, 223; in Abhidharma, 245; in China, 251; versus comparison, 190

Cleansing, through sacrifice, 65

Cognitive science, 251–52, 255; and category formation, 238

Coherence, in ultimacy, 40

Collaboration, xxiv, 261–63; in this Project, 187, 232, 239

Commandments (*Mitzvot*), 53, 57

Commentarial traditions, 203

Comparative Religious Ideas Project, xv–xxvi, 1, 229, 262–62, 273

Comparison, approaches to as related to this Project, 211–32; as circular, 194; as cognitive, 187–88, 215–18; collaborative problems with, 4–6; constructed or discovered, 231; explicit expression of, 155, 199–200; immorality of, 214; improved but not abandoned, 190; and justification, 190; versus juxtaposition, 190; always in the middle, 229; Neville's theory of, 251; as possible, xii, 213–15; as more than specification of vague categories, 3–4; theory of, 187–208; transforms things compared, 214

Compassion, 141

Complementarity, 200

Complexity, in arguments a vice, 117; of relating data to theory, comparing Lakatos and Popper, 226–27; needs more explanation than simplicity, 116–17; and suspicion of theory, 230; or world, 40

Compulsion, as source for categories, 241

Conceivability, of God in Islam, 83

Concepts, as states of consciousness, 241

Concrete existence, 77–78

Conditional features, 171–74

Confessional theories of religion, categories from, 218–19

Confirmation, 128

Confucianism, xx, 2, 144, 167, 181,
    207, 238, 242, 254; compared to
    Buddhist quest for liberation, 130;
    Daoistic, 213; and power, 20; in this
    Project, xxvi; on reciprocity, 250
Consciousness, 40, 139, 269; in Chi-
    nese religion, 21–22; in creator,
    175; in the Lord, for Deśika, 98
Consensus, 262–63, 273
Consorts, of Gods, 167, 179; *see also*
    Śrī, Nārāyaṇa
Constitutive knowledge, in Deśika, 97
Contexts, devotional versus philo-
    sophical, 168; for global philoso-
    phy, 241–42
Contingency, 143
Contingency, 95, 143; of cosmos in
    Islam, 79; expressed across spec-
    trum from personal to abstract
    ideas, 171; logic of, 171–79, 183,
    228–29; on the Lord, 98; ontologi-
    cal in Buddhism, 176; theory of,
    228–29
Contraction (*tsimtzum*), 52–53
Contradiction, 198; in Jaina theory,
    107; between ultimacy and reality,
    31
Control, in actualization, 21–22; di-
    vine, of the universe, 46
Convention and ultimacy, 127
Conventional truth, 139–40, 165,
    180; as personalistic, 167
Core, belief systems in all religions,
    219–20; texts and motifs, xx, 21
Correction, of comparative hypothe-
    ses, xii, 189, 194–95; as promiscu-
    ous, 229–30; *see also* Vulnerability
Correlation, as Chinese root meta-
    phor, 248–50
Cosmogony, 173–74
Cosmological argument, 103, 116–18
Cosmology, 199, 219, 243; in Chinese
    categories, 250
Cosmos, place in, 183; relative to
    human beings, for Chinese religion,
    158

Counterfactuals, in Chinese thought,
    12
Counter-Reformation, 206
Cows, and non-cows, 126
Creation, 10, 52; in Chinese religion,
    267; *ex nihilo*, 174–75; in medi-
    eval Daoism, 26, 157; for God to
    be known, in Ibn 'Arabī, 89; in Ju-
    daism, 37; in Rabbinic mysticism,
    47; order in, 38; of Great Ultimate
    from Non-being, 21
Creator, 51, 78–80, 166; distinct
    from world, 160–61; *see also* God
Criteria, of truth, 189
Crucifixion, 69
Cults, in ancient Roman world, 62
Culture, as defining public, 254
Curse, Chinese, to live in interesting
    times such as now, 256

Dalai Lamas, 138, 141–42
Dao, 11–14, 24–27, 31–32, 71, 153,
    156–58, 165, 167, 172, 175, 177,
    179, 254; in *Daode jing*, 17–20; in-
    finitesimal, not infinite, 18
Daode jing, 13, 24
Daoism, xx, 12–13, 23, 30–32, 155,
    177, 180, 182–85, 238, 242, 244,
    258; on asymmetry, 175; medieval,
    157–58, 167; philosophical, 14; re-
    ligious, 14–15
Daoren (man of the Way), 31
Data, fidelity to, 232; similarities in
    for justifying categories, 222–24
Death, 246; of Christ, 65, 68; fear of
    dissolved, 25; of sacrificial animal
    not important, 65
Deconstruction, 204, 215; uses for, 232
Deep grammar, 249
Defilements, 130
Definition, 243–44
Deity versus God, 78; ultimate reality
    of in mythology, 10
Delicacy, in comparison, 216–17
Denial (*apavāda*), 140
Dependent Nature, 132, 134–36, 139

Dependent Origination (*pratītyasamutpāda*), 127, 141, 172, 245–46
Description, 222–24; of the ultimate,
180
Determinateness, defined, 171–74;
and indeterminateness in compara-
tive categories, 196–98; as ulti-
mate, 176
Deuteronomy, book of, 45–46, 67, 69
Devils, in America, 168
Devotion, in conventional truth, 142
Dharma, 38, 129, 141; not taught by
Buddha to anyone, 138
Dharmas, 245–47
Dialectic, 229; in comparison, 155,
193–96, 224–25; of conventional
and ultimate, 127; between data and
categories, 212, 224–25; Hegelian,
169; of the ultimate, 180; of vague-
ness and specificity, 197–269
Dialogue Among Civilizations, United
Nations designated year, xiii
Dialogue, interreligious, 218
Difference and non-difference between
Brahman and world, 102
Dimensions, of life, 151–52; religious,
207–8
Disagreements, through confusing re-
spects of comparison, 192
Discourse, in Jewish thought charac-
terized, 41; on ultimacy, 10
Disease, in Chinese religion, 22
*Distinction between the Middle and
the Extremes*, 132–33
Divine fullness, 106
Divine image, 207
Divine simplicity, in Islam, 84
Divinization, of Laozi, 184
Doctrine of the Mean, 250
Doxa (kavod), 63, 67
Dragon, 30; flying, 28
Drugs, medicinal, 22–23
Dualism, 175; in Islam, 91; in divine
knowledge, 82
Duality, as Yogācāra category of real-
ity, 134

Dynamism, in comparison, 197

Early Chinese Mysticism, 203
Earth, 173
East Asian religions, 199–200
Eating, 62–71; *see also* Food
Ecology, xxiv, 44
Ecstatic pervasion, 25–26
Efficient causes, 163
Ego, 25
Egyptians, 43
Eightfold Path, 245
Ein Sof, 48, 52
Emanationism, 89, 174–75
Emanations *(Sefirot)*, 52–53
Emotions, in Chinese religion, 21–24
Empiricism, in comparison, 230–31;
defended in this Project, 214–15;
in our theory of categories, 196
Emptiness, 127, 130, 152–53, 163–
64, 183, 240–44; awareness of,
133; in Bhāvaviveka, 126; Bud-
dhist, compared to ideas of God,
131–32; in Chinese culture, 127; in
Yogācāra and Madhyamaka, 133–
39
Enjoyments, heavenly, 28
Enlightenment, 1, 197; renaissance, as
a religious discourse, 238
Enthusiasm, data-blind, versus theory-
blind confusion, 227
Epistemic stage of philosophy, 242
Epistemology, 41, 267; in Confucian-
ism, 242
Erudition, through collaboration, 4
Eschatology, Christian, 70
Essence, 79; of God, 75; in Islam, 91;
of religion, xxi
Essential features, 171–74
Eternal abode of the Lord, in Deśika,
97
Eternity, of God, in Islam, Christian-
ity, and Judaism, 85
Ethics, 255; in Confucianism, 242; in
Rabbinic mysticism, 49, in Talmud,
39

Etiquette, of altar, 68
Eucharist, 67, 182
Evil, 52
Examinations, as symbols for length of spiritual discipline, 28–29
Excellence, of God, 38, 44, 158
Exclusion, Dignāga's theory of, 126–27
Exegesis, 120; in Deśika's argument, 97
Existence, 79, 107; of God, 86, 96, comparing Swinburne, logicians, Śaivas, and Deśika, 117–18; of the Lord not proved by inference, 103; and non-existence in Yogācāra, 135
Existential particularity, 177
Existentialism, 206
Exodus, 181, 255
Exodus, book of, 44–46, 67, 70
Experience, 10, 13–14, 31–32; of God, 53; as the locus of ultimacy in Buddhism and Chinese religion, 163; ordinary versus extraordinary, 10; of ultimate realities, 153
Explanation of the Diagram of the Great Ultimate, 20, 156–57
Explanation, of perceptible world, 111
Eyes, of God, 81, 83

Face, of God, 76, 81, 83
Faith, and reason, 50, 103
Fallibility, 189–90
Falsification, 226, 229
Family structure, 181
Features of harmony, essential and conditional, 171–74
Fecundity, in creation, 176–77
Fei, 249
Feminism, xiii, xxv–xxvi
Field, of responsibility, 197, 200
Finite and infinite, 40; finite/infinite contrasts, 178, 185; in Rabbinic mysticism, 47
Finitude, 143
Five phases (or agents), 248, 257
Flesh, 62–71

Flood, the, 44
Folk religion, xxiv
Food, 220; in Chinese religion, 22–23
Fou, 249
Foundation, of all things, 98
Four Noble Truths, 140–41, 188, 195, 245–46
Fragmentariness, of this Project, xxi, xxiv, 6
Framework, conceptual, for experience, 9
Freedom, 40, 132, 176; from space–time limitations, 15; see also Liberation
Fundamental Principles of Torah, 50

Galatians, letter to, 66, 71
Generalists, and specialists compared, 6; resistance of to specificity, 263; roles of in this Project, xvii–xviii, 229
Generalization, of scientific inquiry into the humanities and metaphysics, 227
Generosity, divine, 80
Genesis, book of, 67, 176, 201, 208
Genetic analysis, in justifying comparative categories, 170, 228, 273
Gentiles, 64, 181; and Jewish sacrificial rites, 63; in Paul's thought, 65–66; inherently profane (unholy) though not inherently impure, 63; redeemed from profane to holy, 65–68
Genus, 244
Glory, and transcendence of God, in Talmud, 46–49
Glossolalia, 70
Goals, of religion, 200
God, 1–2, 46, 114–15, 152, 160–61, 207; Abrahamic attributes of, 160; as a being, 174; body of, 43, 38, 58, in Vedānta, 108; body parts of, 76, 81, 83–84, 166; in Buddhist–Christian dialogue, 142; as creator, 2, 158, 165, becomes by creating, 174,

in medieval Daoism, 26–27, 157; existence of according to Swinburne, 115–18; not in genus, 180; as goal, 158; and Godhead, 75, 82, 219; as hidden, 42; in history, 43; image of, 207; immateriality of in Maimonides, 49; as ground of intelligibility, 158; intimacy with, 53; limited by relating to human beings, 44; moral implications of in Islam, 161; names of, in Islam, 184; nature of, 96; as personal 54–55, 158, in Islam, 80–81, among religions compared, 166; as different from persons, 166; as real or true (*al-Ḥaqq*), 78; as rock neither sedimentary or igneous, 179–80; how seen, 44–45; self of, 85; shape and sound of, 48; as ultimate reality, ruler, conscious, etc., 120, in Christianity, like Judaism, 61–62, in Islam, 76, in Judaism, 37, 50, 158–60; uncreated, in Judaism, 38; undifferentiated, in Ibn ʿArabī, 77; as warrior, 43; Western concept of, substantial and static, as conceived by Daoists, 32; God/world distinction, softened by Ibn ʿArabī, 160–61; the world as body of, in Viśiṣṭādvaita compared to Ibn ʿArabī, 162; *see also* Allah, Brahman, Īśvara, Lord, Nārāyaṇa, Shangdi, Tetragrammaton, Yahweh
Gods, 1–2, 184
Golden Calf, 46
Good, idea of, in Plato, 242
Goodness, of life for Chinese religion, 11
Grace, divine, 46
Graduate students, in this Project, 4, 239, 262, 273
Grand Beginning, in Daoism, 26–27
Grand Immaculate, in Daoism, 26–27
Great Chain of Being, 219
Great Ultimate (Taiji), 20, 157–58, 164, 175
Greek philosophy, 54, 243; in Islam,

81–82, 161; in Judaism and Christianity, 166
Greek theology, 85
Grid, of categories, xviii, xxvi, 5
Guanyin, cult of, 168
Guanzi, 250
Guṇa, 247
Gymnastic, in Chinese religion, 22–23

Haecceity, 7
Hamartia, 65
Hands, of God, 81, 83, 84
Ḥaqīqa, 76–79, 88–91
Ḥaqq, 78–79
Harmony, 156–58, 178, 197; bodily, 22; in Chinese religion, 13–14; of cosmic order destabilized in ancient Christianity, 71; as defining determinateness, 171–72, 176–78; through loss of self-power, 19–20
Hartshorne, Charles, 258
Hasidism, 42, 53
Heaven, 10, 17, 19, 26, 57, 77, 157, 167, 173; bureaucracy in, 179; in Chinese religion, 15; Daoist, described, 27–28; and Earth in Chinese religion, 24; as God in Confucianism, 2, 147; as physical, in Jewish thought, 48; in Rabbinic mysticism, 47
Hebrew Bible, 158
Hebrews, letter to, 62, 65, 68–70
Hegemony, in comparative discourse, xiii
Hellenism, in Avicenna, 78; in Islam, 83
Herbs of no death, 27
Heresy, 155
Hermeneutics, xxv; in category formation, 239–40; in comparison, 201; as stage of philosophy, 242; third-order, 241–42
Heterophenomenology, Dennett's, 225
Hierarchy, in Daoism, 18–19; in Neo-Confucian ontology, 157; in this Project, xxv–xxvi

Hilastērion, 65

Hinduism, xx, 7, 113, 154–55, 204, 238, 273; Brahmanical context of, 95–96; developed in dialogue with Buddhism, 245; compared to Chinese religion on ultimate reality, 119–20; devotional texts in, 158; compared with Dharma, 129; orthodoxy in, 121; theology compared to Swinburne's, 115–18; ultimate realities in, 162–63

History, 238, 251; of comparative categories, 206–8; God in, 55–56, 180; of philosophy and theology, 243; as defining public, 254; in religions compared, 181–83; of religions, 272; theories of religion based on, 221

Holiness, 62–65, 153–54, 160

Holy Spirit, 71; resident in temple, 66

Holy, the, 152

Huayan, 32–33

Human Condition, The, 4, 6, 177, 187–88, 197, 203–4, 213–14, 261

Human condition, xxv, 3–4, 197, 199–200, 206–8, 216, 227, 262–63; categories for, 270

Human, learning to be, in Confucianism and Buddhism, 130

Humanism, Renaissance, 206

Humility, in epistemology, 41

Humor, 258

Hunter-gatherers, 208

Huwa Huwa, 76

Hypothesis, 128, 271; comparative, 217, analogous to theories of instrumentation in science, 227; in comparative studies, xxii; concerning contingency and ultimate causes, 171–74; as extending beyond specific comparisons, 155; modification or replacement of, 226–28

Iconicity, 180, 192–93

Icons, of ultimate, 178

Idea of the Holy, 223

Ideal types, 253

Ideality, of ultimacy in Chinese religion, 156

Ideas, already comparative second-order reflections on religious phenomena, 237–38, 238

Identity, in Buddhism, 125; transcendence of the personal, 24–30

Idolatry, 175; in Judaism, 49

Ignorance, 197, 219

Illative sense, Newman's, 226

Image, of God, 183; *see also* God

Imagination, 133; in comparison, 128; constructive and deluding, 135; as Yogācāra category of reality, 134

Imagined Nature, 134–36, 139

Immanence, of creator in world, 175; in Islam compared to Buddhism and Chinese religion, 161; and transcendence of God in Islam, 80–82, in Talmud, 46–49

Immortality, in Chinese culture, 12, 27–28

Imperialism, in the study of religions, xv–xvi

Impermanence, in Islam (*tanzīh*), 82

Importance, differences in, 201; in definitions of the ultimate, 152

Incarnation, in Christianity, 118

Incommensurability, 198, 213–14, 268–69; in respects of comparison, 193

Incompleteness, of comparison, 205

Indeterminacy, 174

Indexical reference, 204

Indifference, to philosophy, 266

Inert material reality, in Deśika, 97

Infinity, not character of Dao, 18; as divine character, 38

Influence, social and historical, in causal analyses, 221

Inquiry, good or bad, 206; in Islam, 81

Inscription for the Holy Mother, 26

Institutions, as defining public, 254

Instrumentation, theories of, in science and religious studies, 226, 230

Intelligibility, absolute, in Islamic philosophy, 77–78

Intentionality, in creator, 175, 182; in interpretation, 189, 192–93

Interpretation, as intentional act, 195; theory of, 188–89

Intervention, divine, 38

Intrinsic representations, 5, 202–5

Intuition, in comparison, 216–17; in sageliness, 15–17

Irony, in speaking of ultimacy, 180, 215

Irrationality, in religion, 223

Islam, xxi, 2, 4, 8, 118–19, 152, 154, 166–68, 179, 181–85, 208, 238, 243, 273; on asymmetry in creation, 174; compared with Buddhism, Chinese religion, and Judaism, 76–77; and Christian theology, 81; and Greek philosophy, 81–82; as influence on Jewish theology and philosophy, 56–57; on names, 180; on ultimate realities, 75–91, 160–61

Israel, xxi, 43, 36, 55–56, 68; as holy nation, 63

Īśvara, 108, 167

Īśvarapariccheda ("Definition of the lord"), 70, 96–120, 154

Jade Emperor, 26, 28

Jainas, 104, 106–7, 115, 121; on language and ultimate reality, 102

Jeremiah, book of, 46

Jerusalem, 43, 69; temple in, 62

Jesus Christ, 143, 206; being in, for Paul, 66–67; as high priest, 69; as kosher, 70; as sacrifice, 69, 181–82; as ultimate reality in Christianity, 61–71

Jews, 181; *see also* Judaism

Job, book of, 39, 180

John, gospel of, 62, 68–70, 167

Jonah, book of, 46

Judaism, xxi, 2, 4, 8, 118–19, 152, 154, 166, 179–80, 182–83, 201, 208, 238, 243, 252, 273; on asymmetry in creation, 174; mysticism in, 51; compared with paganism, 62; ultimate realities in, 37–57, 158–60

Judea, 43

Judeo-Arabic philosophy, 49

Judgment, in balancing theory and data, 225; divine, in Islam, 79

Jugular vein, God closer than, 177

Jungian theory, 219

Justice, divine, 39, 46

Justification, of the approach to comparison in this Project, 211–32; of comparative categories, xix, 218, 272–73, and vulnerability, 170; of scheme of categories, 270–72; of classification systems, 223–24; of comparative generalizations, 169–70, 228

Juxtaposition, 201, 216

Kabbalah, 42, 48–49, 52

Kalam, 75, 91

Kantianism, in categories, 195–96; in Jewish Enlightenment thought, 53–54

Karma, 106, 130, 247

Kataphasis, 179; *see also* Apophasis

Kenosis, 143, 191–92

King, in Chinese religion, 19

Knowledge, 153; in God in Islam, 81–82, 84–86; of God through ourselves, 89; pragmatic, 189–90

Kunlun, 27

Language, 40; in creation, in Rabbinic mysticism, 48; to express Dao, 17–18; as defining public, 254; religious, 196; theory of, 115

Laozi, as God and the Dao, 26–27, 157

Law, in Judaism, 37, 40

Laws of Manu, 129

Lesser Sutta on Emptiness, 133
Leviticus, book of, 67
Li, in Zhu Xi, 239; in Yi T'oegye, 240
Liberation, 219, 255; knowledge for, 95; in Nāgārjuna, 130
Liberationism, xiii, xxv; liberation theology, 255
Library of Congress, as source of comparative categories, 235
Life, lived "in the presence of God," in Buddhism, 129
Light without end, 52
Likeness, of God in Judaism, 160
Limitations, of human relative to the divine, 38, 158; of this Project, xxiii–xxvi, 6–7
Limits, physical and sensory overcome, 15–17
Linguistics, 251–52, 255; and category formation, 238
Listening, as method, xiii
Literalness, 167
Liturgy, 183
Logic, in early China, 248–49; in justifying comparative categories, 169, 228, 272–73; of remainder in Yogācāra, 135–36; of vagueness, 198
Logicians, 116–17
Logocentrism, 215–16
Lord, the, 110; Brahman as, 167; defined by Deśika, 98–99; and his consort Śrī are one ultimate reality, 103–4
Love, 118; God as, 130; to God, 45
Lushi chunqiu, 248, 250

Madhyamaka Buddhism, 2, 7, 100, 125–27, 131–43, 152–54, 163–64, 167, 177, 180, 183–84; in Tibet, 133, 136–37; two branches of, 149; assimilated to Vedānta, 132
Madhyamakakārikās, 127, 131, 138, 140
Magic, 15; in comparison, xxv, 7, 128, 251, 257

Mahāyāna, 165, 167, 177, 217; on compassion and wisdom, 130
Mana, 19
Mandate of Heaven, 167
Manifestation, of God in the cosmos, 77
Material cause, of world, 162
Materialists, 115
Matthew, gospel of, 62, 68–70
Māyā, 175
Meaning, architectonics of, 241–44; of truth, 188–89
Meat, in Eucharist, 68
Mediating theology, in Islam, 82
Meditation, 182
Mercy, divine, 39, 46; this Project's plea for, xxv
Messiah, Jesus as, for Judaism, 181
Messianic redemption, 56
Metaphor, 216, 248, 252; in Buddhism, 127; extended from prototypes outward, 254
Metaphysics, 70, 243; in some Buddhism denied, 193; in Neo-Confucian conceptions of ultimacy, 156–57; Sufi, 76; systematic and comparative, 229
Method, 205–6; in comprison, 189–90; in this Project, 264; for stability, 217
Methodology, xii, xxii, 211
Metonymy, 254; in the divine nature, in Judaism, 158–60
Middle Path (Middle Way), 127, 135, 141
Middle Way, *see* Middle Path
Mind, 135; as mirror, in Yogācāra, 137–38
Minister, 66–67
Mirror, imagery, in Islam, 88; mind as, 137
Mishnah, 45
Mob, Mahāyāna, our crowd, 216–17
Models, idealized cognitive, 255–56
Modernity, European, 251
Mohism, 242, 250–51

Monism, 115; Madhyamaka as, 131–32

Monotheism, 1–2, 54, 152, 162; in Deśika, 98; in Islam, 77; versus polytheism, 175

Morality, 64, 219; in conventional truth, 142; in the Qur'ān, 79

Motifs, 203

Movement, in Chinese religion, 22–23

Mu'tazilite theology, 82, 84–87, 90–91, 161

Mukhālafa, 83

Multidisciplinary study of religious phenomena, 229

Mushrooms, divine, 27

Mysterium tremendum, 223

Mysticism, 9–10, 38, 40, 42, 57, 75–76, 158, 175, 177, 180–82; Rabbinic, 47–49, 184

Myth, in Islam, 76; role of in practice defined, 184; virtuosi in, 184–85

Mythology, 199

Myths, cosmogonic, 173–74

Nahum, book of, 46

Naiyāyikas, 103–4

Names, Natures and Things, 203

Names, of God, ninety-nine in Islam, 77–78, 80–81, 161

Nārāyaṇa (Viṣṇu, the Lord), 97–120, 152, 162, 175, 184

Narrative, 38, 56, 181, 216, 252; as alternative structure for this Project, xxvi; biblical, 43, 70; in Judaism, 40, 158

Native American religions, xxim xxiv

Naturalism, opposed to Perennial Philosophy, 220

Nature romanticism, 177

Nature, 38; in Islam, 89–90

Negation, 174–75

Negative results, in comparison, 201–2

Negative theology, 18, 82–84, 159; in Buddhism, 130–33; positive claim in, 144–45; *see also* Apophasis

Nehemiah, book of, 46

Neo-Confucianism, 240

Neo-Daoism, 242

Neo-Platonism, 89

Neo-pragmatism, 252

Neurophysiology, in comparative theory, 225

Neuroscience, 220

New Age religions, xxiv

New Testament, 158, 184

Nihilism, 129, 152, 165, 172; cooking the last fruit of, 131–32; scholastic, in Nāgārjuna and Candrakīrti, 131–33

Nine Chapters on the Unity of God, 49–51

Nirvana, 139, 165; not different from samsāra, 138

Nominalism, 155; and realism debated, 7

No-mind, in Chinese religion, 158

Non-being, 31, 152, 158, 164, 175, 183, 240, 243; creation out of, 173–74; and Great Ultimate, 18, 34; not a substance, 157; Ultimate of, 20–21

Non-contradiction, 198

Nondualism, 115, 175; incompatible with Brahman as material source of the world, 101

Non-literate religions, xxiv

Normativeness, in the Dao, 17–18

North Atlantic, religious cultures of, 251–56

No-self, in Chinese religion, 158

Nothingness, 183, 240, 244; in Chinese ontology, 13; and contingency, 171–72

Novelty, of insights in dialectic, 231

Numbers, book of, 46, 67

Nyāya (logical school of philosophy), 97

Nyāya Sūtras, 97

Nyāyakusumāñjali, 108

Nyāyapariśuddhi, 97

Nyāyakusumāñjana, 96–97

Obedience, 153

Objectivism, 252–53

Obligation, lying under, 177

Oblivion, entranced in the Dao, 25–26

Omnipresence, of the Lord in Deśika, 100

Omniscient agent, 110

On the Essential Meaning of the Absorption of Qi, 22–23

One and the many problem, in Jewish thought, 40

One reality, in Islam, 89–90

Ontic stage of philosophy, 241

Ontological context of mutual relevance, 172–74

Ontology, 219, 242–43, 267; of causation in Chinese ultimates, 157; of divine attributes, 84–86; in ultimacy, 1–3, 153

Order, 165; in Buddhist cosmology, 129; and creation, 176–77; cosmic, 3, 161, actualizing, 21–26; in Judaism and Chinese religion compared, 159; in ultimacy, 40

Orientalism, 251

Orientation, 2

Original substance, in Chinese ontology, 13

Origins, of creation, 13

Orthodox Indian Schools, 246–47

Orthodoxy, in Islam, 76

Otherness, ontological, 172–74

Padārtha, 246

Pagans, 61

Pantheism, 54, 76–77, 82

Paradigms, shifts in, in natural science, 225–26

Paramatabhaṅga, 115

Party, enjoyable, 273

Paschal sacrifice, 64

Passion, control of, 23–24

Passover, 69

Patriarchy, xxv

Patristic theology, 61, 70; and Islam, 81

Patterns, 157; ideal, 183

Pauline writings, 62–71

Penglai, Isles of, 27

Perception, non-bodily, 15–16; of ultimate reality, 95–96

Perennial philosophy, 230, 241, 270; as source of categories, 219–20

Perfected, the, in Chinese religion, 14–17, 153, 182; ultimate, 157

Perfection, 2, 132; in cognition, 253–54; in God, 55; in Hinduism and Chinese religion compared, 119

Person, as symbol for God, 180

Personal identity, rejected, in Daoist purification, 24

Personality, in Allah, 161; in God in theistic Hinduism, 162

Personification, 158, 169; in Buddhism, 176; in Chinese religion and Judaism compared, 158; of Dao, 17–18; of impersonal philosophical conceptions, 166; of Wisdom as divine companion, 38

Perspectival representations, 5, 202–5

Pesach, 64, 69

Pharaoh, 43

Phenomenological sites of analysis, 5, 202–3, 265–66

Phenomenology, 231, 269; in checking comparisons, 202–5; Husserlian, 224–25; of religion versus philosophical, 222

Philippians, letter to, 143

Philosophers, Nevillean, 125

Philosophy of history, 221

Philosophy of religion, 219, 272

Philosophy, 10, 57, 120, 251; analytic, 242; in category construction, 168; in comparison, 263; in Jewish thought, 40, 49–51; and methodological interest in this Project, 271; constrained to work with personal symbols, 179; stages of, 241–42; systematic, 268; in representations of ultimacy, 167; virtuosi in, 179–81

Piety, in Islam, 81, 161; in Jewish mysticism, 50
Place, in Indian categories, 246–47
Platform Sūtra of the Sixth Patriarch, 137
Platonism, 164, 252
Plausibility, in justifying comparative categories, 169, 228, 272–73
Plenitude, 178
Plurality, of things in creation, 176–77
Poetry, 38, 40, 56
Pollution, in Yogācāra, 134
Polytheism, 54
Popular religion, xxiv, 168
Porneia, 64; and impurity, 65
Post-Enlightenment, 252
Postmodernism, 252
Power, in Chinese views of ultimacy, 156; in creation, 183; creative, in Laozi, 27; (de) in Daoism, 19
Practical representations, 5, 202–5
Practice, in Chinese religion, eclectic, 11; communal virtuosity in, 181; religious, 152, in Islam; religious virtuosi in, 181–83
Pragmatism, 204; and testing hypotheses, 196; and the theory of this Project, 227
Prajñā, 137
Prakṛti, 175
Pramāṇa (correct knowledge), 97
Prameya (objects of modes of knowledge), 97
Pratyakṣa (perception), 97
Prayer, 38, 57, 180; to God, 51
Precision, in vague categories, 199
Predicament, human, 10
Predication, 195–96, 243–44; of existence, 107
Prediction, 226
Preference, 152
Presence and absence, in knowing Emptiness, 135–36
Pressures, to fill out comparative spectra, 166, 169, by logic of contingency, 178–79

Presuppositions, shared, 110–13
Priests, Jewish, 62
Primordial tradition, 219
Principle (Neo-Confucian), 167
Priordial reality, 157
Process, 31–32
Product, of creation, 178–79
Programs, of research, lingering devotion to, 230
Project, the human, 2
Prophets, 10, 43, 56, 67, 70
Propitiation, 98
Prototypes, 252; of metaphors, 254
Providence, 38
Psalms, book of, 39, 43, 36, 179
Psychology, 220, 251
Public discussion requires the possibility of argument, 120
Public, for comparative study, 4
Publicity, in Deśika's philosophy, 104–5
Purification, in Chinese religion, 21–24
Purified Nature, 132, 134–36
Purity, 62–65, 153–54, 220; in early Christianity, 130; and proximity to sacrificial altar, 63
Purposes, divine, 39; of this Project, xv
Puruṣa, 175

Qi, 20, 157, 159, 239–40
Qohelet (Ecclesiastes), 39
Qualification, of symbols by context, 179–80
Qualities, in Deśika, 97
Quest, for ultimacy, 2, 129–30
Qur'ān, xxi, 76, 78–84, 86, 158, 161, 166, 181, 183
Rabbinic thought, 252; of ultimacy, 158
Rabbis, in Toronto, 243
Radical Jewish mysticism, 56
Ran, 249
Ransom, 69
Rationalism, 252–53

Rationality, in paradigm shifts, 225
Realism, and incommensurability, 269–70; in Indian philosophy, 246; and nominalism debated, 7
Reality, 240; nature of, in definition of the ultimate, 152–53; versus ultimacy in Chinese religion, 119; as that which one can be wrong about, 153; in three categories for Yogācāra, 134
Reason, 25; in Deśika's argument, 97; in justifying hypotheses, 189–90; in Islam, 90–91; in religion, 54; versus scripture, 109; for knowing ultimate reality in Hinduism, 95–96
Reconciliation, 65
Record of the Historian, 30, 248
Record of the Ten Continents, 27
Rectification of names, 144
Redemption, of Gentiles and world, 63–71; historical, 70
Reference, 167, 188–89; in Confucianism, 144; in Madhyamaka, 163–64; myth of, 126–28; to mind or cosmos in myth of transcendence, 145–46
Reformation, Protestant, 67, 166, 206
Regions, as sources of religious movements, 238–39
Reincarnation, religions of, 208
Relationality, 177; in China, 248
Relations, theory of in Abhidharma, 245
Relativism, avoided, xii
Religion, definitions of, 151; as a dimension of life, 2, 151–52; as expanding boundaries, 255
Religions, selection of for this Project, xx
Religious studies, 227
Religious Truth, 187
Religious truth, xxv, 4, 184–85, 199, 208, 216, 227
Ren, 250
Reorganization, of body in sacrifice, 62–63

Respect, of comparison, 191–94, 215, understood only at end, 151; of interpretation as comparative category, 194
Responsibility, field of, 197, 200; in Middle Path, 140
Resurrection, 69
Revelation (Apocalypse), book of, 62, 65, 68–70
Revelation, 70, 219; in Judaism, 37
Rhetoric, in Deśika's argument, 97
Righteousness, 197
Rishis, 243
Ritual studies, xxiv
Ritual theory (Mīmāṁsā), 115
Ritual, 62, 106, 154, 199, 219, 238, 255
Romans, letter to, 63, 65–66, 71
Ruler of all, the Lord as, 98

Sabbath observance, 57
Śabda (verbal knowledge), 97
Sacred, the, as comparative category, 143, 267; and profane, in Rabbinic mysticism, 47
Sacrifice, 160; in ancient paganism, 62; as binding together a community, 70, blood, 154; a male preserve, 62; mythology of, 184; as practical transformation, 181–82
Sages, 2, 26, 153; in Chinese religion, 14–17, compared with ancient Christianity, 71, as transformative, 182; in Confucianism, 15
Saints, 10
Śaiva Siddhānta, 114–15, 120
Śaivism, 105–6, 114–15
Salvation, 1
Sāṁkhya philosophy, 101, 104, 115, 175, 241
Samsāra, 165; not different from nirvana, 138
Sanctification, 65
Sanctuary, 65
Sanskrit, and Tamil in Vedānta Deśika's works, 97

Saviors, 219

Scapegoat, 65, 69

Science, 214, 220; in interpretation, 196; Lakatosian model for, 225–27; models of, misleading for religious analysis, 128; has having a religious dimension, 129

Scripture of Laozi's Transformations, 27

Scripture, 98, 100–1, 162, 219; Hindu, 131; for knowledge of ultimate reality in Hinduism, 95–96

Second Temple, 38, 57, 64; destroyed, 63

Second Temple Judaism, 66, 166, 181

Secondhandness, in categories, 240

Second-order reflection, in Judaism, 40

Sectarianism, 117–18

Seeing through Texts, 203

Self, 204; in Buddhism, 141–42, transformation of, 183; defined for Chinese adept, 24–25; self-consciousness, 216; and denial in Madhyamaka, 140; in Deśika, 97; dissolution of, 12; self-evaluation, within this Project, 3; self-identity of God, 85; self-reference to one's religion in religious comparison, 232

Semantics, in Buddhism, 126; of divine attributes, 86–87

Semiotics, 192; Peirce's in this Project, 252

Senior advisors in this Project, xviii

Sensation, 158, 246; in Daoism, 24–28

Separation, 62–65

Septuagint, 65

Shamanism, 200

Shangdi, 166–67

Shi, 249

Shifts, analysis of, in justification of categories, 273

Shi'ite theology, 87

Siddhis, in Daoism, 15; in Rabbinic mysticism, 47

Sifre Deuteronomy, book of, 46

Signs, 192

Silence, Buddha's, 139–40

Similarity, defining, 222; and justification of categories, 231

Simplicity, in Brahman, 162

Sin, offering, 64–65, 69; punishment of, 43

Sincerity, 12

Singular representations, 202–5

Singularity, 7, 177; of ultimate, religions compared, 152

Śiva, 100, 104–6, 114–15

Sky God, 44, 166

Smṛti (tradition), 97

Social life, and practice, 204

Social sciences, xxiv

Sociology, 220, 251; of knowledge, 268

Sophism, 242; in China, 243

Sophisticated religion, versus popular religion, 168

Soteriology, 152; negative papal view of Buddhist soteriology, 146

Soup, cosmic, 27

Source, of creation, 175, 178, in mysticism, 181; of comparative categories, irrelevant, 221

South Asia, emphasis on categories in, 245; religions 197, 199–200, and West Asian religions compared, 175

Space, and time, for God in Jewish thought, 41; space-time conditions, 171

Specialists, diversity among, 154; and generalists, 262–65, separated, 273; papers of, 262; roles of in this Project, xvi–xviii, 2, 229

Specificity, in categories defined, 197; *see also* Vagueness and specificity

Spectrum, of anthropological and ontological views, 165; of personifying and abstract philosophical expressions of ontological ultimacy, 165–68, 174–79

Spirit (*shen*), 23–24

Spiritual practices, 199
Spit, 142
Spontaneity, 31, 157, 164, 172, 175, 177, 183
Śrī (consort of Nārāyaṇa), 97–98, 103, 184
Śrīmadrahasyatrayasāra, 119
Śrīvaiṣṇavas, 96–97, 99, 110, 112, 117–18, faith of characterized, 97
Śruti, 103
Stability, 246
Stream, of consciousness, 140
Structuralism, 204
Structure, of the volumes of this Project, xxiii
Subject and object, 139, 153
Subjectivity, in creator, 175; of ultimate reality in Chinese religion, 13
Subsistence, in Islam, 91
Substance, philosophy, 158, 165, denied in Chinese religion, 20–21; versus process in ultimate realities, 158
Suffering, 1, 131, 152, 188, 196–97, 245; overcome by the Perfected, 16–17
Sufism, 76, 88–91
Sunna of the Prophet, 83
Sunni theology, 87
Superimposition, denied by Deśika, 101
Supplementary Immortals' Biographies, 30
Supreme Lord *(Īśvara)*, in Deśika, 97
Surrender, 255
Suspicion, hermeneutics of, xxv, 187–88
Symbols, breaking, 127–29; bridging theory and practice, 10; philosophical, practical, and mythical uses of, 179–85
Synaesthesia, in Confucianism, 15
Syntax, 192

Taiji, *see* Great Ultimate
Taijichuan classics, 203
Talmud, 39, 45, 51, 53, 56–57, 206

Tamil, works of Vedānta Deśika, 177
Tanak, 67
Tanzīh, 83–84, 87–91, 161
Tashbīh, 83–84, 87–91, 161
Tauḥīd, 77, 81, 85, 88, 161
Telos, 95
Temple, Christians as, 66; heavenly, 68–69; holiness of, 66, in Jerusalem, 67; none in New Jerusalem, 69
Temporality, 172–73, 183
Ten thousand things, 175, 247
Tests, of method in this Project, 3
Tetragrammaton, 50–51
Teva', 38
Texts, 238; authorship of: persons or traditions, 7; idiosyncrasies of, 5; studies of, xxiv; in traditions for comparison, xx, 162
That which is, in definition of the ultimate, 151–52
The Distinction Between the Middle and the Extremes, 138–39
The Path of Purification, 130
Theism, 8, 105–9, 267; and obligation, 177; probability of, 116
Theology, 120, 206, 251; and description blended, as in Otto's work, 223; rational for crossing cultural boundaries, 118
Theology after Vedānta, 203
Theoretical representations, 5, 202–5
Theories, 195; in comparison, 216, 266; theory-dependence, 224; interpretative in science, 217–18; versus phenomenology, 202; of religion, 199, 228, 232, 271, mystical, theological, and metaphysical, 219, in this Project, 3, causal-scientific, 220–21
Theosophy, in Islam, 77, 88–90
Theravāda Buddhism, 130, 217, 245–46
Thessalonians, as former idolaters, 65
Thick description, 202
Thought, related to speech, in Indian thought, 247

Throne, of God, 81, 83
To be (the verb), 249
To See the Buddha, 203
Togetherness, ontological, 172–74
Torah, xxi, 37, 47, 53, 64, 67, 181,
   183, 203; Torah-based Way of life,
   45–46; mediating knowledge of
   God, 45–46; as Wisdom in Rab-
   binic literature, 38
Totality, 245
Tradition, as Bible, Talmud, and lit-
   urgy, 41–42; in Islam, 90–91
Traditionalism, in Islam, 82, 86, 88
Traditions studied here, compared, 5
Trance, 16
Tranquility, 23
Transcendence, 39, 129, 158, 169,
   174; in Chinese religion, 13–14,
   156; in Confucianism, 130; denial
   of, 176; and immanence of God, in
   Islam, 80–82, in Judaism, 41
Transformation, 255; analyses of in
   ideas for justifying comparative
   categories, 170; from physical to
   spiritual flesh, 71; to relate to the
   ultimate, 181–83
Translation, 6–7, 205, 213, 238; in
   comparison, 199–202; in this Pro-
   ject, xxiv–xxv
Translucence to cosmic power, in
   Daoism, 19–20
Trees, as soul-returning, 27–28
Trinity, in Buddhism, xx; in Chinese
   religion of Heaven, Earth, and the
   Human, 11; in Christianity, 61,
   118, 152, 263, opposed in Islam,
   81, 84, 161; in Hinduism of
   Brāhma, Nārāyaṇa (Viṣṇu), and
   Śiva, 100
Triviality, 194
True man, in Chinese religion, *see* Per-
   fected, the
Truth, in comparison, 187–91;
   dyadic, 188; ultimate and proxi-
   mate, 219–20; a Western, not Chi-
   nese, question, 13

Two truths doctrine, in Buddhism,
   139–40, 152, 165, 167; *see also*
   Conventional Truth, Ultimate
   Truth

Ultimacy, as anthropological and ontological, 1–3; categories of: philosophical, practical, mythical, 75;
   defined in Judaism, 38; as first or
   last, 153; and social order in Islam,
   82–84; subcategories of, 3; in time,
   place, and perception in Rabbinic
   mysticism, 47; *see also* Ultimate realities, Ultimate reality
Ultimate concern, 2, 152, 156, 185,
   267
Ultimate identity (*svabhāva*), 125
Ultimate realities, 4, 199, 208, 216,
   227, 262–66, 272–73; as anthropological and ontological, 1–3, 9–
   10, 153, 165, 178–79, 267–68; in
   Buddhism, 125–43, 163–64; categories for, 197, 270; explained as
   comparative category, 1–3; in
   Christianity, 160; summarily defined, 151; in Hinduism, 95–121,
   162–63; in Islam, 160–61; in Judaism, 37, 158–60; plural, xi, 266–
   67; a theory of, 265–66
Ultimate reality, xxv, 1; abstract versus
   textual definitions of, 95–96; as
   Buddha, a conventional truth, 141;
   in Chinese religion, 156–58, defined, 11, as transcendent, versus
   reality as physical, 27–28; characters of, for Deśika, 112; as highest,
   source, cause, personal agent, Lord,
   Nārāyaṇa, as described by scripture, and as Nārāyaṇa plus Śrī,
   113; experienced concretely, xii; as
   final, 26; in Hinduism, generally
   like that in Christianity, Islam, and
   Judaism, 162, defined in brahmanical context, 95–96, as reality and
   as awareness of reality, 129–30;
   relative to human condition, 10;

Ultimate reality*(continued)*
  ineffable, xi; in Islam, as practice,
  91, stable compared with other religions, 76–77, 160–61, and Sufism,
  88–90; in Judaism, medieval mysticism, 51–53, of Torah, 67; as
  order, or beyond order, 156; as perfect and complete, 100; as personal,
  namable, and revealing, 96; as philosophical, practical, or mythical,
  10; provable as personal, 107–9; as
  single, in Nārāyaṇa, 100; as having
  spouse versus being Father, Son,
  and Spirit, 118; as stable versus
  changeable, 125, 163–64; Ultimate
  substantial realities denied in
  Daoism, 20
Ultimate truth, 138–40, 165, 180; abstract and dialectical, 167
Understanding, 40; in Deśika, 97
Unification, of approaches to the
  study of religion, 229
Uniqueness, of God in Jewish thought,
  54, compared with Chinese religion, 159
Unity, and asymmetry, in Islam, 174–
  75; of God, 51, in Islam, 161; of
  world expressing unity of God in
  Islam, 161; in ultimacy, 40
Universality, in philosophic represen-
  tations, 179–80
Unsurpassability, 95
Upaniṣads, 97, 100, 106
Utopia, 18–19

Vacuity, in Dao, 18
Vagueness, 194; in comparative categories, xii, xxiv, 3, 127–29, 168,
  196–97, 265; growing, 4–5; as defined by Peirce, 209; and specificity,
  3–4, 8, 127, 194–95, 198–201,
  213, 216, 250–52, 269, 271–72;
  in definition of the ultimate, 152
Vaiśeṣika philosophy, 97 103–4, 246–
  47
Vaiṣṇavas, 104

Vedānta, 97–98, 105, 114, 117, 175
Vedas, xx, 107, 121, 175
Vessels (*keilim*), 52–53
Virtue, 12
Virtuosi, at comparison, 155; reli-
  gious, 10–11, 75, 152–53, 179–
  85
Virtus, 19
Vision, of God, in rabbinic mysticism,
  47; as metaphor for knowing, 253
Viśiṣṭādvaita Vedānta, 96–97, 99,
  162, 177; described, 121
Vivekacūḍāmaṇi, 263
Void, in Daoism, 26–27
Volition, in the Lord, 98–99
Volkswagen, with toothpick, 169
Vulnerability, to correction, xii, xxi–
  xxii, xxiv–xxvi, 7, 168, 202–6,
  214–15, 220–21, 227, 230–32

Waḥdat al-wujūd, 77
Way, the, comparative examples of,
  255
West Asian religions, 197, 199–200
Wholes, reality of, 131–32
Will, 23–24; in Allah, 90–91
Wine/blood, 69
Wisdom literature, 43
Wisdom, and comparison, xi; as God's
  agent, 38
Word of God, eternal and therefore a
  god, 85
World, as appearance in relation to
  God, 54; as determinate, 173–74;
  world-making, 268; as real or illu-
  sory, 115
Worship, 153
Wrestling, with kōans and angels, 183
*Writings of the Master of Heavenly Se-
  clusion*, 22
Wu, 249
Wuji, 158

Xin, in Zhu Xi, 239
Xunzi, 248

Yahweh, 166
Yellow Emperor, 30
Yijing, xxi, 201, 203, 247–48
Yin-yang, xx–xxi, 21, 24, 157–58,
 175, 203, 248
Yoga, 104, 135, 182; philosophy, 103
Yogācāra, 132–39, 154, 163–64, 180,

184, 245; history of, 136; in China,
 136–37
Yom Kippur, 65, 69
You (to have), 249

Zen, 138, 142–43
Zionism, 56